Y0-BJN-953

THE LEISURE CLASS
IN AMERICA

This is a volume in the Arno Press collection

THE LEISURE CLASS IN AMERICA

Advisory Editor
Leon Stein

A Note About This Volume

At 18, Browne (1833-1902) departed from his father's banking establishment to become a reporter in Cincinnati. When the Civil War began, he went into the field as special correspondent for the *New York Tribune* and was captured by Confederate forces while trying to run the Vicksburg blockade. Thereafter, for some 18 months, he endured great suffering while being shunted from prison to prison. He finally escaped, traversed several hundreds of miles of enemy territory to regain his freedom. In the years after the war he not only worked for the *Tribune* and the *New York Times* but also produced a number of popular books of which this is a fine example. His work as a reporter had given him insights into the life of different classes in the big city. This book pictures the pastimes of the upper class of its day and contrasts them with the widespread crime and poverty of the mass of the city's population.

See last pages of this volume for a complete list of titles.

THE

GREAT METROPOLIS

A

MIRROR OF NEW YORK

BY
JUNIUS HENRI BROWNE

ARNO PRESS

A New York Times Company

New York / 1975

Fordham University
LIBRARY
AT
LINCOLN CENTER
New York, N. Y.

Reprint Edition 1975 by Arno Press Inc.

Reprinted from a copy in
 The University of Illinois Library

THE LEISURE CLASS IN AMERICA
ISBN for complete set: 0-405-06900-6
See last pages of this volume for titles.

Manufactured in the United States of America

Library of Congress Cataloging in Publication Data

Browne, Junius Henri, 1833-1902.
 The great metropolis, a mirror of New York.

 (The Leisure class in America)
 Reprint of the 1869 ed. published by American Pub.
Co., Hartford, N. J.
 1. New York (City)--Social life and customs.
2. New York (City)--Social conditions. I. Title.
II. Series.
F128.47.B88 1975   974.7'1'03   75-1833
ISBN 0-405-06902-2

THE GREAT METROPOLIS.

A Mirror of New-York.

1869.

THE
GREAT METROPOLIS;

A

MIRROR OF NEW YORK.

A COMPLETE HISTORY OF METROPOLITAN LIFE AND SOCIETY, WITH SKETCHES
OF PROMINENT PLACES, PERSONS AND THINGS IN THE CITY,
AS THEY ACTUALLY EXIST.

BY

JUNIUS HENRI BROWNE.

Issued by Subscription only and not for sale in the Book Stores. Residents of any State in the Union desiring a copy should address the Publishers, and an agent will call upon them.

HARTFORD:
AMERICAN PUBLISHING COMPANY.
R. W. BLISS & CO., TOLEDO, OHIO.   BLISS & CO., NEWARK, N. J.
H. H. BANCROFT & CO., SAN FRANCISCO, CAL.
1869.

ENTERED according to Act of Congress, in the year 1868, by
AMERICAN PUBLISHING CO.,
In the Clerk's Office of the District Court of Connecticut.

Electrotyped by
LOCKWOOD & MANDEVILLE,
HARTFORD, CONN.

TO THE

GOOD MEN AND THE GOOD WOMEN

WHO WALK WITH CHARITY,

AND SCATTER THE SUNSHINE OF THEIR PRESENCE IN THE DARK

WAYS OF THE GREAT CITY,

THIS UNASSUMING RECORD OF ITS LIFE IS

EARNESTLY INSCRIBED.

PREFACE.

THE sketches in this volume, begun more than two years ago, have been continued from time to time in the midst of journalistic duties, as personal observation and inquiry furnished new facts and illustrations of the Great City. These chapters have been written to represent the outer and inner life that makes up the beauty and deformity, the good and evil, the happiness and misery, which lie around us here so closely interwoven, that only charity can judge them wisely and well.

>   In Faith and Hope the world will disagree,
>   But all mankind's concern is Charity.
>   All must be false that thwart this one great end,
>   And all of God, that bless mankind or mend.

J. H. B.

NEW-YORK, December, 1868.

ILLUSTRATIONS.

		Page
1.	CHURCHES IN NEW YORK, . . . Frontispiece.	
2.	ILLUSTRATED TITLE PAGE, ...	
3.	ARCHITECTURAL CONTRASTS, ...	23
4.	BUSINESS CONTRASTS, ...	23
5.	STOCK EXCHANGE, BROAD STREET, ...	48
6.	BLACKWELL'S ISLAND, ...	77
7.	STREET VENDERS, ...	90
8.	"UMBRELLAS,"	92
9.	CHINESE CANDY DEALERS, ...	98
10.	FORT LAFAYETTE, ...	109
11.	THE MALL, CENTRAL PARK . . . . . , .	121
12.	UNION SQUARE, ...	128
13.	PILOT BOAT, ...	176
14.	BARNUM'S MUSEUM, 1860, ...	176
15.	THE BATTERY, ...	242
16.	PRINTING HOUSE SQUARE, ...	310
17.	PARK BANK, BROADWAY, ...	344
18.	WASHINGTON MARKET, ...	408
19.	STREET ARABS, ...	427
20.	STREET BEGGARS, ...	457
21.	MACKERELVILLE TURN-OUT, ... , .	465
22.	HOWARD MISSION, -	526
23.	ROOM IN HOWARD MISSION, ...	526
24.	CITY MISSIONARY, ...	547
25.	LOW GROGGERY, ...	659
26.	THE FIRST SNOW, ...	696

CONTENTS.

CHAPTER I.
THE RICH AND POOR.

Fashion and Famine.—Charms and Counter-Charms of the Metropolis.—Lights and Shadows Everywhere.—Life at its Best and Worst.—Marble Palaces and Squalid Tenement Houses.—What They Contain.   23

CHAPTER II.
NEW YORK SOCIETY.

Its Divisions and Characteristics.—The Old Knickerbocker Families.—The Cultivatedly Comfortable.—The New Rich.—The Mere Adventurers.—Social Shams and Snobs.—The American Gentleman and Lady.   31

CHAPTER III.
WALL STREET.

The Banking-House of the Continent.—Money-Getting and Mammon-Worship.—The Mania for Stock and Gold Operations.—The Exchange and Gold Room.—Great Wealth of the Quarter.—Its Redeeming Virtues.   40

CHAPTER IV.
THE POLICE.

The Force in the City.—Its Strength and Effectiveness.—The Best and Worst Class.—Their Habits and Operations.—The Station House and Prisoners.—Scenes and Characters.—Detectives and their Varieties.   50

CHAPTER V.
THE SHIPPING.

Sea-Ports and Sea-Thoughts.—Commerce of the Great City.—Its Trade all over the Globe.—Vessels and Sailors.—Scenes at the Dock and on Shipboard.—The People who Arrive and Depart.   .   .   59

CHAPTER VI.
THE ROUGHS.

Their Physiology and Psychology.—Haunts and Habits of the Class.—Their Education and Associations.—Defeated Justice and Dangerous Elements.—The Wild Beasts in an Unseen Lair.   .   .   67

CHAPTER VII.
BLACKWELL'S ISLAND.

The Abode of Paupers and Criminals.—The Different Buildings and their Inmates.—Mysterious Babies and Notorious Thieves.—Curious Lunatics and Peculiar Characters.—A Fancied Napoleon Bonaparte.—An Imaginary Prophet. 76

CHAPTER VIII.
THE FIRST OF MAY.

Moving in Manhattan.—Origin of the Custom.—House-Hunting and House Hunters.—Among the Rich and Poor.—May-Scenes and Experiences.—Change and Chaos from the Battery to the Park. 86

CHAPTER IX.
THE STREET-VENDERS.

The Bohemians of Trade and Bedouins of Traffic.—News and Flower Dealers.—Dog-Fanciers and Toy-Peddlers.—Retail Shams and Small Swindles.—Bowery Breakfasts and Park-Row Dinners.—Old Clothes Hawkers and Chinese Candy-Sellers. . . . 92

CHAPTER X.
THE FERRIES.

Their Number, Location and Business.—Different Classes of Passengers.—Occupation and Toil, Hope and Success on the Waters.—The Refluent Wave of Humanity.—The All-Night Boats.—Journalists and Printers on their Way Home. 100

CHAPTER XI.
GREENWOOD.

Picturesqueness of the Cemetery.—Its Extent and Range of View.—Activity of Funerals.—Sentiment and Pathos.—Burial of a Prosperous Merchant.—The Tearless Widow.—The Last of the True Wife and Mother.—The Poor Outcast at the Tomb.—Epitaphs and their Hollowness.—A Romantic Maiden who Would Not Die. . . 110

CHAPTER XII.
THE PARKS.

Decay and Abandonment of the Old Plazas.—The Central Park, its People and Prospects.—The Resort of the Wealthy and Indigent.—The Two Carriages and their Occupants.—A Pair of Nobodies.—Glittering Discontent. 121

CONTENTS.

CHAPTER XIII.
THE BOWERY.

The Quarter and its Habitués.—Tricks and Tradesmen There.—The Bowery Merchant's Manner of Dealing with Customers.—A Sailor and Land-Shark.—After Night-fall.—The Bowery Boy Extinct. 129

CHAPTER XIV.
THE FORTUNE-TELLERS.

The Mystic Tribe and its Patrons.—Dowdy Priestesses and Common-Place Oracles.—Scenes of Sorcery.—Interior of a Temple of Fate.—Revelations about Wives.—A Tawdry Witch of Mysterious Pretension.—Superstitions of Business Men.—The Calling not Profitable. 138

CHAPTER XV.
THE BOHEMIANS.

Popular Idea of the Class.—The True and False Guild.—What They are and Believe.—The Original Tribe in New York.—Sketches of the Prominent Members.—Disreputable Specimens.—The Earnest Disciples. 150

CHAPETR XVI.
THE LAGER BEER GARDENS.

Their Numbers and Variety.—Peculiarities of the Manhattan Beverage.—German Characteristics and Customs.—Teutonic Simplicity and Enjoyment.—The Atlantic Garden.—Music, Tobacco, Talk and Tippling. 159

CHAPTER XVII.
THE CHURCHES.

Their Number and Wealth—Their Liberality and Beauty.—Religion as a Form—A Fashionable Temple.—Repulsion of Humble Strangers.—An Elegant Congregation.—Characters.—Pulpit Oratory.—Genuine Christianity. 167

CHAPTER XVIII.
THE THEATERS.

Dramatic Assumptions of the Metropolis.—Character of its Audiences.—Dramatic Temples.—Their Different Patrons.—Wallack's, Niblo's Garden, the Olympic, Pike's Opera House, the Academy of Music, the New York, the Théâtre Français, the Broadway, Wood's, Booth's and the Bowery. 175

CHAPTER XIX.
THE DEAD BEATS.

The Higher and Lower Sort.—Requirements and Peculiarities of the Calling.—Variety and Contrast of the Life.—Photograph of the Creature.—Sketch of his Career.—Reclaiming a Prodigal.—Freedom from Debt the Sole Independence. 186

CHAPTER XX.
THE ADVENTURESSES.

Man's Vanity and Woman's Cunning.—Origin of the Strange Women.—Their Ample Field in the City.—Their Mental and Moral Code.—Operations at the Hotels.—War Widows.—Examples of Interesting Poverty.—Advertising Tricks.—Emigrants.—The Traveling Sisterhood.—A Remnant of the Woman Left. . . . 196

CHAPTER XXI.
THE BOARDING HOUSES.

The Fashionable Establishments and their Noticeable Features.—Mrs. Dobbs and her Patrons.—The Landlady from Life.—Weal and Woe of her Happy Family.—Comfortless Comfort of a Home.—The Salesman, Law Student and Reporter.—Dreary Dinners.—Evening Entertainments. 205

CHAPTER XXII.
HORACE GREELEY.

Prevalent Ideas of Him.—His Early Years.—Establishment of the Tribune.—His Indefatigable Industry and Great Popularity.—His Fancy Farm at Chappaqua—His Family and Charities—His Eccentricities.—The Verdict of his Countrymen. . . . 214

CHAPTER XXIII.
THE FIFTH AVENUE.

Architecture of the Street.—Its Exclusiveness and Wealth.—Inner Life and Outward Show.—Pretension and Refinement.—Oppressive Monotony.—Gorgeous Interiors.—The Queen of the Drawing Room.—The Devotee of Fashion.—Blazing Hearths and Ashen Hearts.—Fate of the Unrecognized.—Untold Histories. . . . 219

CHAPTER XXIV.
HENRY J. RAYMOND.

The Beginning of his Career.—Entry into Journalism and Politics.—The Times Office.—The Elbows-of-the Mincio Article.—Personal Appearance and Private Affairs.—Temperamental Peculiarity. . 230

CHAPTER XXV.
THE BATTERY.

What it was and is.—Its Historic Associations.—Its Lingering Attractions.—The Emigrant Dêpot at Castle Garden.—Idiosyncrasies of Foreigners.—How They are Fleeced.—Germans, Scotch, Irish, French and Italians. 236

CHAPTER XXVI.
THE GAMBLING HOUSES.

Twenty-Five Hundred in the City.—The Fashionable Faro Banks.—Description of their Habitués.—Vulgar Haunts and Common Blacklegs.—Princely Proprietors and Plebeian Plunderers.—Phenomena of Faro.—Varieties of Gaming. 243

CHAPTER XXVII.
HENRY WARD BEECHER.

School Days and Theological Training.—Eccentricities of Character.—His Power and Influence in his Pulpit.—Journalistic, Political and Literary Career.—"Norwood" and the Forthcoming "Life of Jesus."—Popularity as a Lecturer.—His Domestic Affairs. . . 252

CHAPTER XXVIII.
THE RESTAURANTS.

Up-Town and Down-Town.—Eating-Houses.—Their Great Variety.—Over Five Thousand in Town.—The Guerilla System of Dining.—People You Have Met.—Lunching Makes Strange Companions.—Late Suppers.—Elegant Dissipation. 260

CHAPTER XXIX.
MANTON MARBLE.

The "Man of the World."—His Early Love of Journalism.—His Experience in Boston.—The Great Democratic Organ.—Its Antecedents and Progress.—Shrewd Management of the Editor-in-Chief.—The Manhattan Club. 267

CHAPTER XXX.
THE FIVE POINTS.

The Notorious Locality.—Poverty, Misery and Vice.—Baxter Street Life and Morals.—The Swarm of Children.—Etchings from Nature.—Representative Races.—The Callings of the Place.—The Dance-Houses.—What One Sees There. 271

CHAPTER XXXI.

THE MORGUE.

Its Growing Need in Gotham.—Its Appearance and Regulations.—Fascination of the Horrible.—Scenes Within and Without.—Apoplexy, Murder, Homicide and Suicide.—The Humorous Side of Ghastliness.   280

CHAPTER XXXII

ALEXANDER T. STEWART.

The Man of Money and Embodiment of Business.—His Past History.—A Merchant by Accident.—His Erection of the First Marble Building in Broadway.—His Up-Town Store.—His Fifth-Avenue Palace.—His Reputation for Generosity.—His Immense Wealth.—His Private Life.   289

CHAPTER XXXIII.

THE DAILY PRESS.

The Herald, Tribune, Times, World, Journal of Commerce and Sun.—Defects of the Metropolitan Newspapers.—Their Circulation and Characteristics.—Their Antecedents and Profits.—The Evening Journals.—What They Are and Do.   295

CHAPTER XXXIV.

THE WEEKLY PRESS.

Their Great Number.—The Illustrated Papers.—Remarkable Success of the Ledger.—The Sunday Journals and their Character.—Journalism as a Profession in New York.—Slenderness of the Compensation.—Needs of the Calling.—Its Overcrowding.   311

CHAPTER XXXV.

WILLIAM B. ASTOR.

An Exception to Most Rich Men's Sons.—His Great Care of his Father's Estate.—His Industry, Energy and Sagacity.—His Freedom from Pretension or Extravagance.—His Daily Duties and Domestic Life.—The Wealthiest Man in America.   319

CHAPTER XXXVI.

THE CONCERT SALOONS.

Their Rise and Sudden Popularity.—Various Grades of Music-Halls.—Danger of Frequenting Them.—The "Pretty Waiter Girls."—The Night Haunts.—The Vision of Dissipation.—Demoralizing Influence of Such Places.   326

CHAPTER XXXVII.
CORNELIUS VANDERBILT.

The Beginning of his Fortunes.—The Staten Island Perriauger.—A Purely Self-Made Man.—His Control of Steam Lines.—The Great Railway King.—Passion for Whist and Horses—His Extraordinary Wall Street Operations.—His Vast Income.—His Remarkable Vigor in Old Age. 333

CHAPTER XXXVIII.
BROADWAY.

The Street Cosmopolitan and Cosmoramic.—Its Architecture and Constant Throng.—Poetry and Philosophy of the Thoroughfare.—Its Resources and Suggestiveness.—Romance and Reality.—Love and Friendship.—Changes of Fortune.—All the World Flowing through that Channel. 339

CHAPTER XXXIX.
THE THIEVES.

Crime and Criminals.—Scoundrels Actual and Ideal.—Burglars, Hotel-Robbers, Shop-Lifters, Pickpockets and Sneaks.—Their Number and Mode of Operating.—The Art of Stealing and Science of Being Undiscovered. 346

CHAPTER XL.
SUNDAY IN NEW YORK.

The Change of the Week.—Silence of the Sabbath.—The Sacredness of Rest.—Different Modes of Enjoying the Day.—Excursions out of Town.—God in the Town and Country. . . . 355

CHAPTER XLI.
THURLOW WEED.

The Cabin Boy Becomes a Political Warwick—His Extraordinary Tact and Insight.—His Long Control of New York. Politics.—The Whig Triumviate.—The Commercial Advertiser.—His Adroit Management of an Obstinate Assemblyman.—His Income and Good-Heartedness. 365

CHAPTER XLII.
BLEECKER STREET.

Its Past and Present.—Its Variety and Oddity.—Its Strange Occupants. —Deception and Intrigue.—Dissipation and Death.—The Quarter of Artists and Bohemians.—Disturbance of Lodgers.—Great Freedom of the Neighborhood. . . . 372

CHAPTER XLIII.

NASSAU STREET.

Its Uniqueness and Symbolism.—Curious People and Phenomena.—Love and Loans.—Lager and Literature.—Confusion of Humanity.—The Old Book Stores.—Rambles Up and Down Dusty Stairways.—Back-Office Secrets.—Prolific Material for Novels. 381

CHAPTER XLIV.

THE HOTELS.

Americans not Domestic.—The Astor, St. Nicholas, Metropolitan, Fifth Avenue, New York, Brevoort and Barcelona.—Second Class Houses.—Gossip, Flirtation and Intrigue.—Hotel Life in Various Phases. 390

CHAPTER XLV.

WILLIAM CULLEN BRYANT.

Fame in the Metropolis.—His Poetry and Travels.—The Evening Post.—His Labors and Influence as a Journalist.—His Domestic Tastes.—A Hale and Hearty Patriarch.—A Congenial Companion and Clever Talker. 399

CHAPTER XLVI.

THE MARKETS.

American Extravagance in Living—Disagreeableness of Market-Going.—Liberal Supplies of Everything.—The Different Customers.—The Penurious-Wealthy. — Blushing Brides and Cheap Boarding House Keepers.—The Scale of Prices.—The Evening Market. 405

CHAPTER XLVII.

THE POST OFFICE.

The Old Dutch Church the Most Popular in Town.—Immense Business of the Metropolitan Office.—Anxious Inquirers and Insolent Clerks.—Letter-Writers and Letter-Getters.—The General Delivery.—The Different Stations.—Their Illegitimate Use. 415

CHAPTER XLVIII.

THE GAMINS.

Their Antecedents and Training.—Their Favorite Callings and Pleasures.—Persevering Boot-Blacks and Energetic Newsboys.—The Bowery Theatre Resort.—Decline and Development of the Urchins.—Natural Results of Bad Education. 424

CHAPTER XLIX.

THE DEMI-MONDE.

The Relation of the Sexes.—Man's Injustice and Woman's Wrongs.—Courtesans in the Metropolis.—Their Character and Calling.—Their Life, Love and Redeeming Traits.—Sad Pictures of Fallen Women. 434

CHAPTER L.

THE CLUBS.

Their Number in Manhattan.—The Most Famous Club-Houses.—Their Management and Membership.—How Women Regard Them.—The Century, Manhattan, Union-League, Travelers', City, New York, and Eclectic.—The Deceased Athenæum.—Journalistic Clubs.—Club Life in the Great City. 442

CHAPTER LI.

THE BEGGARS.

Their Nationality.—The Throng Increasing.—The Four Great Classes.—The Notorious Mendicants.—A New Order.—The Broadway Blindman.—The Old Hag near Fulton Ferry.—The Armless Frenchman.—The Canal Street Humpback.—The Noseless Pole.—The Mackerelville Dwarf.—Fortunes of the Vagabond Tribe. . . . 456

CHAPTER LII.

STREET RAILWAYS.

Their Supposed Origin.—Their Supreme Independence.—New York Made for them.—Magnanimity of the Managers.—The Charmed Life of Passengers.—Wonders of the Roads.—Haps and Mishaps of Travel.—The Hero of a Thousand Cars.—Every-Day Miracles. . 466

CHAPTER LIII.

THE PAWNBROKERS.

What They Represent and What They Are.—Under the Shadow of the Three Balls.—Messrs. Abrahams and Moses in their Glory.—The Watch, the Diamond Bracelets, the Keepsake.—Strange History of Pledges. 473

CHAPTER LIV.

CHILDREN'S AID SOCIETY.

The Boys and Girls' Lodging House.—How they are Managed and Supported.—Receipts and Expenditures.—The Emigration and Restoring System.—Industrial Schools. Refuge for Homeless Children.—Advatange of the Charity. 483

CHAPTER LV.
JAMES GORDON BENNETT.

The Child, Boy and Man.—His Education for the Church.—Struggles in America.—Choice of Journalism for a Profession.—Frequent Failures.—Establishment of the Herald.—Its first Success.—Peculiarities of the Man.—His sole Ambition and its Realization.—His private Life. 491

CHAPTER LVI.
THE CHINESE EMBASSY IN NEW YORK.

What One of the Number Thinks of the Metropolis.—His Experiences of American Life.—Puppies for Supper.—Peculiar Rats.—The City Directory as a Guide.—The Cause of Fires.—" Ghin Sling" in Various Trying Situations. 499

CHAPTER LVII.
JENKINSISM IN THE METROPOLIS.

The Peculiar Tribe.—Elaborate Description of a Wedding by one of the Fraternity.—The Bride and Bridegroom.—The Invited Guests.—Who they were, and how they Appeared.—Extraordinary Scenes at the Altar.—New Sensations at the Reception. . . 509

CHAPTER LVIII.
FASHIONABLE WEDDINGS.

What they Mean, and How they are Managed.—Ambitious Mammas and Submissive Daughters.—Mr. and Mrs. Fleetfast and their Connubial Career.—The Three Essentials.—Grace Church Brown.—Mockeries of Love. 516

CHAPTER LIX.
THE CITY MISSIONS.

The Five-Points Mission.—The Howard Mission.—The House of Industry.—Their Regulations and Advantages.—Attendance, Donations and Expenses.—Intemperance the Cause of the Evils. . . 523

CHAPTER LX.
THE TOMBS.

Origin of the Name.—The Inner Quadrangle.—The Tiers of Gloomy Cells.—Character of the Prisoners.—A House of Detention.—The Three Departments.—The Police Court and Court of Sessions.—Sunday Morning's Tribunal.—Notorious Criminals who Have been There.—The Gallows and its Victims.—Religious Exercises. 528

CHAPTER LXI.

THE MIDNIGHT MISSION.

The First Movement for the Reclamation of Fallen Women.—The Destitution of the Charity in New York.—The Asylum in Amity St.—Plan of Procedure.—Success of the Enterprise.—The Receptions.—Touching Scenes.—Repentant and Reformed Courtesans.—What the Charity Teaches. 535

CHAPTER LXII.

ASSOCIATIONS FOR THE POOR.

Effectiveness of the Charity.—Its Origin and Progress.—How it is Conducted.—Visits to the Tenement-Houses.—What is Undertaken and Accomplished.—The Spirit of Humanity at Work.—Beautiful Examples. 542

CHAPTER LXIII.

WORKING WOMEN'S HOME.

An Excellent Organization.—Mode of its Management.—Weeping Eyes Dried, and Wounded Hearts Healed.—Direction of the Institution.—Benefits Conferred upon the Poor.—Reaching the Source of Suffering. 548

CHAPTER LXIV.

THE MILITARY.

Fondness for Parade.—The National State Guard.—The First Division.—The Armories.—The Crack Regiments.—The Seventh.—Its Departure for the War.—The Great Sensation in Broadway.—Holiday Soldiers. 554

CHAPTER LXV.

THE FIRE DEPARTMENT.

The Old System and its Evils.—The Engine Houses in Times Past.—The Present Department.—The Steam Engines and Horses.—Their Advantage and Efficacy.—The Dead Rabbit and Decent Fire-Boy. 561

CHAPTER LXVI.

RACING AND FAST HORSES.

The Union, Long Island and Fashion Courses.—The Jerome Park—Fondness for Horse Flesh.—The Passion Growing.—Gentlemen's Stables.—Millionaires on the Road.—Vanderbilt, Bonner, Jerome and Fellows.—Money Invested in Blooded Stock.—Pleasures of the Turf. 568

CHAPTER LXVII.

GIFT ENTERPRISES AND SWINDLES.

The Many Swindles upon Countrymen.—Policy Shops.—Lottery Offices.—Infamous Devices.—The Rural Regions Flooded with Circulars.—Inability of the Law to Reach the Rogues.—How Mr. Greenhorn is Victimized. 575

CHAPTER LXVIII.

THE WICKEDEST WOMAN IN THE CITY.

Madame Restell the Abortionist.—Her Long and Shuddering Career.—Her Notorious Trial and Acquittal.—Her Dreadful Secrets and Practices.—Her Palace in Fifth Avenue.—Her Antecedents and Appearance. 582

CHAPTER LXIX.

MATRIMONIAL BROKERAGE.

The Brokers in the City, and their Manner of Operating.—Strange Revelations of Human Weakness.—Foolish Women and Hoary Simpletons.—Snares Laid for Feminine Innocence. . . 588

CHAPTER LXX.

HERALDRY ON THE HUDSON.

The Metropolitan Passion for Titles.—The Heraldry Office.—Manner of Conducting it.—Smithers in search of his Family.—Peculiar Mode of Making Genealogical Trees.—The Plebeian Magennises and the Norman Descent. Absurdity of Patrician Assumption. . 596

CHAPTER LXXI.

THE CHILD-ADOPTING SYSTEM.

How it is Carried On.—The Women Professionally Engaged in It.—Singular Disclosures.—Infants of all Kinds Furnished.—The Baby Market and its Fluctuations. 603

CHAPTER LXXII.

BANKERS AND WALL-STREET OPERATORS.

Daniel Drew, Brown Brothers, Leonard W. Jerome, James G. King's Sons, Jay Cooke, David Groesbeck, August Belmont, and Fisk & Hatch, 611

CHAPTER LXXIII.

CHARLES O'CONOR.

His Early Poverty and Industry.—His Inclination to the Law.—His Eminence at the Bar.—His Singular Political Opinions.—His Large Income and Forensic Capacity.—His Present Status. . 618

CONTENTS. 19

CHAPTER LXXIV.
JAMES T. BRADY.

His Legal Studies and Success.—His Enthusiasm for Ireland, and Popularity with the Irish.—His Deep Interest in his Clients.—His Perpetual Speech Making.—His After-Dinner Ardor. . . 622

CHAPTER LXXV.
FERNANDO WOOD.

His Past Life.—His First Election to the Mayoralty.—Double Disappointment of the Committee.—His Conduct and Character.—Personal Appearance and Influence. 625

CHAPTER LXXVI.
GEORGE FRANCIS TRAIN.

An Exaggerated American.—His Excentricities at Home and Abroad.— Book-making, Speech-making, and Money-making.—His Declaration that he is in no Danger.—Called a Fool.—His Supreme Egotism and Loquacity.—His Real Character. 629

CHAPTER LXXVII.
FANNY FERN.

Parentage.—Girlhood.—Marriage.—Husbands both Struggle with Poverty.—First Literary Earnings.—Connection with the Ledger.—"Fern Leaves" and "Ruth Hall."—Second Marriage.—Present Position. 633

CHAPTER LXXVIII.
TWO STRONG-MINDED WOMEN.

Susan B. Anthony and Elizabeth Cady Stanton.—The Revolution.—What the Woman's Rights Women Are and Demand.—Their Pen-Photographs. 636

CHAPTER LXXIX.
PETER COOPER.

History of a Self-Made Man.—His various Pursuits.—His Benevolence and Sympathy with the People.—The Cooper Institute.—His Honesty and Sterling Worth. 640

CHAPTER LXXX.
GEORGE LAW.

His Early Struggles.—Contracts the Beginning of his Fortune.—The George Law Markets.—His Personal Unpopularity and Common-Place Appearance.—His Day Gone By. . . . 642

CHAPTER LXXXI.
PETER B. SWEENEY.
His Political Power and Excessive Tact.—The Championship of the Ring.—His Large Wealth and Devotion to the Democracy.—The Manner of Man he is. 645

CHAPTER LXXXII.
DISTINGUISED CLERGYMEN.
Revs. Edwin H. Chapin, Henry C. Potter, Wm. Adams, Henry W. Bellows, Stephen H. Tyng, junior, Morgan Dix, F. C. Ewer, C. W. Morrill, Thomas Armitage, O. B. Frothingham, Archbishop McCloskey.—Samuel Osgood.—H. B. Ridgaway.—Rabbi Adler. . 647

CHAPTER LXXXIII.
JOHN ALLEN, "THE WICKEDEST MAN."
The Religious Excitement.—John Allen's Dance-House.—The Prayer Meetings in Water-Street.—Their Good Effect.—The Insincerity of Ruffians no Reason for Censure. 659

CHAPTER LXXXIV.
MARK M. POMEROY.
His Nativity and Wanderings.—His Career in the West.—La Cross Democrat.—His Establishment of a Daily in New York.—His Violent Political Course.—What he is and How he Looks. . . 663

CHAPTER LXXXV.
EMINENT BUSINESS MEN.
Grinnell, Minturn & Co., Horace B. Claflin, Howland, Aspinwall & Co., A. A. Law & Bros., E. S. Jaffray & Co., Harper & Bros., D. Appleton & Co., Jackson S. Schultz, Charles A. Stetson, the Lelands, R. L. & A. Stuart. 666

CHAPTER LXXXVI.
OUNG MEN'S CHRISTIAN ASSOCIATION.
Its Origin and Conductors.—Excellence and Influence of the Society.—What its Members have Accomplished.—Their Work During the War.—Their Hospitality to Strangers.—Result of their Labors. 677

CHAPTER LXXXVII.
PUBLIC SCHOOLS.
The Day and Evening Schools.—Girls' Normal Schools.—Evening High School.—Free Academy—Attendance and Aptitude of Pupils.—The System of Instruction and its Success.—Women Superseding Men as Teachers. 680

CONTENTS. 21

CHAPTER LXXXVIII.
DISTINGUISHED WOMEN.

Alice and Phoebe Cary.—Mary Clemmer Ames.—Kate Field.—Lucia Gilbert Calhoun.—Octavia Walton Levert.—Jennie June.—Mary E. Dodge.—Sarah F. Ames. 684

CHAPTER LXXXIX.
CITY CHARITIES.

Divers Institutions.—Ward's Island.—Hospitals.—Orphan, Deaf and Dumb and Insane Asylums.—The Buildings and Inmates.—Mode of Treating Patients.—Liberality and Benevolence of New Yorkers. 690

CHAPTER XC.
THE GREAT METROPOLIS.

Its Advantages and Disadvantages.—Improvements Everywhere.—Up-Town Splendors.—The Future of Manhattan.—The City Destined to be the Largest in the World. 697

ARCHITECTURAL CONTRAST.

BUSINESS CONTRAST.

CHAPTER I.

RICH AND POOR.

In the Metropolis, more than in any other American city, there are two great and distinct classes of people—those who pass their days in trying to make money enough to live; and those who, having more than enough, are troubled about the manner of spending it. The former suffer from actual ills; the latter from imaginary ones. Those lead a hard life; these an empty one. Those suffer from penury; these from ennui. Each envies the other; and both find existence wearisome, and difficult to endure. But the poor have the advantage in necessary honesty and earnestness; while the prosperous dwell in an atmosphere of insincerity and sham.

It is the custom to prate of the discontents of the rich. Yet we are all ambitious to share them, and to learn by experience the weight of purple robes and the sharpness of gilded thorns.

Our citizens who figure in the income list have no season of repose. When not engrossed in their business pursuits, (it is the misfortune of this Republic that few of its inhabitants ever learn to enjoy their wealth calmly until it is too late,) they are either planning campaigns at the watering-places and tours in Europe, or perplexing themselves with the most approved and distinguished manner of entertaining their fashionable friends in town.

They endeavor to leave such complicated affairs to women. But the women seek counsel of, and ever lean on, their masculine companions, and compel them, whether they will or not, to bear the burthen of leading a glittering, though hollow life, which rarely palls upon the feminine mind, occupied with externals, and reveling in appearances. So the Adams, even to the present day, pay the penalty of the temptation of Eve, and eat more sour apples than they do sweet ones, in the society of their irresistible charmers.

New-York is unquestionably the paradise of women. It is to the United-States what Paris is to Europe; and the fairer portion of creation, who dwell out of this vast and crowded City, remember their promenade in Broadway, their suppers at Delmonico's, their evenings at the Academy, and their drives in the Park, with a longing for their repetition that is almost akin to pain.

No where else, they fondly imagine, are such dresses, and bonnets, and shawls, and jewelry to be purchased; no where else can they be so generally admired; no where else can pleasure be found in such varied form.

Even Greenwood has its mortuary fascinations. The monuments look whiter there, the grass greener, the graves more genteel, the trees more droopingly sympathetic than in other cemeteries. And then the subterranean sleepers must have pleasant dreams of the excitements and sensations they enjoyed in the flesh on the island of Manhattan. When they die, they hope, in a sentimentally pious way, to take their last rest in such goodly company, and have winter roses strewn above them, that grew in hot-houses, and were clipped with silver shears.

Fifth, Madison and Lexington avenues, Fourteenth, Twenty-third and Thirty-fourth streets, Madison, Stuyvesant and Grammercy squares are among the chosen abodes of the fashionable and wealthy, who ever tend up town, and will soon make the Central Park the nucleus of their exclusive homes.

During the season, Saratoga, Newport, Paris and Florence are, for the time, dismissed, and home pleasures are alone considered.

Receptions, sociables and "Germans" are the social events of those modish quarters; and milliners, mantua-makers, hair-dressers, flower-venders, confectioners, and musicians, are busy from morning to night in lending their expensive assistance to the devotees of fashion in the arduous art of killing time elegantly.

Weddings, and their subsequent assemblies are at their height then. Hymen consorts with Cytherea, Juno and Bacchus, and supplies his torch with love-letters of the past, and capers nimbly upon hearts whence Mammon has expelled romance and the ideals of other days.

All New-York is in the midst of gayety and dissipation, and judging by surfaces, Eden is not far from the banks of the Hudson. Brilliant carriages, with liveried coachmen and footmen and sleek horses, dash up and down the avenues, depositing their perfumed inmates before brilliantly-lighted, high-stooped, brown-stone fronts, whence the sound of merry voices and voluptuous music comes wooingly out, through frequently-opened doors, into the chilly night.

One catches a glimpse of fair faces, and the odor of elaborate toilettes as pretty women hurry up the broad steps with kindling eyes and rosy lips, and disappear like beautiful visions amid the bewildering delights that are more seductive to, because they can only be conjectured by, the less fortunate wayfarers who are trudging to their humble homes, anxious and fatigued, and uncertain of the morrow.

Oh, the inequality of Fortune! It must be hard for the poor and distressed to believe that God is good, and Life a blessing, when they see every hour that thousands, in no way worthier, lie softly and fare daintily, while they go hungry and cold, and have no expectations of the better times that are always coming and never come.

Life at its best is seen in this splendid mansion, where all is warmth, and color, and richness, and perfume. The gilded drawing-rooms are crowded with a confusion of silks, and velvets, and laces, and broadcloth, and flowers, and jewels; and from the seeming-happy crowd arises a pleasant hum of low-toned voices, as if passion would never lift them, or pain make them discordant, from the cradle to the grave.

One meets there no shadows, no frowns, no haunting cares. All individuality is lost. Everything is toned down to a level of conventional similarity. All are maskers; and the maskers deceive themselves, as well as others, respecting their true character, and go through life, as through the revel, dully and dreamily,—believing they are happy because they are not sad, and that they are useful members of society because they attend church, and envy their neighbors, and pay their taxes punctually.

Probably there are hearts in the crowd distrustful if that be joy; but the wine is offered, and the music swells, and beauty beckons, and they float down the stream of pleasure, careless where it glides, and of the dark and fatal eddies that whirl below. The influence of the hour is to drown thought and stifle feeling; and he who can accomplish that will not suffer.

Dancing, and feasting, and flirting, and gossip bind the hours with fragrant chaplets, and the duties and purposes of life sink into a soft oblivion; while that is remembered only which is pleasant to bear in mind; and yields fruitage for self-love.

The night reels, like a drunken Bacchant, away; and the stars grow pale as the revelers depart with bounding blood and dazed senses to the embroidered chambers that hold sweet sleep in silken chains.

Life at its worst is visible not a hundred rods away. Yet to enter that wretched tenement-house, where the air is close and impure, who would suppose he was in the same city in which so much splendor and gayety are revealed?

A family in every room here, and sickness, and debauch, and poverty, and pain on every floor. Groans, and curses, and riotous laughter, and reckless boisterousness echo through those dingy halls, and steal up and down those greasy stairways, every desolate hour of the unwholesome day. Poison is in the atmosphere, and new-born babes breathe it before they suck their sickly mothers' sickly milk. Half a million of souls live in these pest-places. Vice, and crime, and death are their product, year after year; and, amid constant vaporings about Reform, Christianity, Progress and

Enlightenment, the yield is steady and the dark harvest growing.

Have any of those bright eyes that swim in self-satisfaction at the brilliant receptions looked within these dreary walls? Do the kind hearts that must throb warmly and sympathetically beneath the flowing robe and embroidered vest, hold knowledge of these silent tragedies that the poor of this Great City are actors in? The prosperous are not unfeeling; but they do not know what incalculable good they might do if they would rightly set themselves to work to relieve the wretched of their race. They have their round of pleasures, and they are full. They little think what responsibilities their wealth has placed upon them; what gods mere vulgar money might make them in potentiality of blessing.

Clouds and sunshine, corpse lights and bridal lamps, joy-anthems and funeral-dirges, contrast and mingle in New-York! Every ripple of light-hearted laughter is lost in its faintest echoes in a wail of distress. Every happy smile is reflected from a dark background of despair.

The Metropolis is a symbol, an intensification of the country. Broadway represents the national life,—the energy, the anxiety, the bustle, and the life of the republic at large.

Take your stand there, and Maine, and Louisiana, the Carolinas, and California, Boston, and Chicago, pass before you.

So the Bowery, and Wall street, and Fifth avenue, with their different figures and types,—each manifesting many, and many one. Beggars and millionaires, shoulder-hitters and thinkers, burglars and scholars, fine women and fortune-tellers, journalists and pawn-brokers, gamblers and mechanics, here, as everywhere else, crowd and jostle each other, and all hold and fill their places in some mysterious way.

Out of the motley million, each, however blindly, tries to better his condition; seeks his happiness, as he conceives it; and arrives at ruin or prosperity, ignorance or culture, health or disease, long life or early death.

Sympathy is the weight that drags us down in our struggle with the devouring sea. Cast it off, and we swim freely.

Selfishness is the friendly plank we grasp for safety. Holding it, we may reach the land, and then return with charity to help our shipwrecked fellows, and preserve them from the dangers from which we have escaped.

Alas, that those who reach the shore so rarely venture to sea again!

Tears and woe will come. Let us not go far to meet them. Take care of to-day, and the morrow will provide for itself.

Expect the best, and the worst will be less likely to happen. Believe yourself fortunate, and you have already robbed Fate of half its power to harm. What we mainly suffer from is the things that never occur; for the shadows of anticipation are more formidable than the substance of the actual.

The carriage is at the door, my friend. Shut up the shadow-book, and step into the light of the outer world. We will ride along rapidly while we can, and walk when we cannot ride; for we will go into the under-ground haunts, as well as the upper abodes of amusement and pleasure.

Through and into New York we will look with calm, yea, philosophic—eye; see its open and hidden mysteries at every angle; observe the places we enter, and analyze the people we encounter.

Regard all men and women as brothers and sisters, never to be hated, but only to be pitied in that they are less fortunate than we. Become great and universal democrats; and think nothing mean that is human; nothing wholly ill; no sin so enormous that sympathy may not reach and charity cover it truly and tenderly.

Leave Neræa to admire her beautiful eyes in the mirror; for it will be more flattering to her than her fondest lover. If she weep, she will soon dry her eyes; for tears she is aware dim their lustre. She is fair, and shapely, and elegant; but is no better in spirit and at heart, than the rude and homely Janette, who was born out of parallel with Nature. Janette went astray, since the path that lay before her was hard and crooked, as are so many ways of this World that we knownot whether to love or hate it, but which, after all, is the best we have seen.

CHAPTER II.

SOCIETY IN THE METROPOLIS.

New-York is quite as much the fashionable, as it is the commercial metropolis; for here are the age, the wealth, the caste-feeling and the social lines of demarkation that so largely aid in forming and sustaining what is known as Society. In the United States generally the duties we owe to society sit rather loosely upon "free-born Americans." But in New York they are such obligations as we feel called upon conscientiously to discharge, and do discharge upon pain of modish ostracism.

Fashion upon Manhattan Island will admit of no compromise with Reason, and refuses to listen to the voice of Common-Sense. She demands her fullest rights, and her devotees yield them with a zeal that savors of social superstition.

Fully half a million of our population are absorbed in a perpetual struggle to avoid physical suffering; while a hundred thousand, probably pass their lives either in being, or trying to be fashionable. That hundred thousand are very gay, and seem positively happy. Yet their woes and throes are innumerable; and their struggles with conventionality and gentility, though less severe, are as numerous as those of the half million with penury and want.

What our best society is will never be determined to the satisfaction of more than one of the cliques, or coteries, or sets that assume to represent it. Each and all of them claim they are it *par excellence;* and each and all go on in their own specific way, saturated with the conviction that they are the conservers and preservers of the finenesses, and courtesies, and elegancies of the fashionable elect.

No society in the world has more divisions and subdivisions than ours—more ramifications and inter-ramifications,—more circles within circles—more segments and parts of segments. They begin in assumption and end in absurdity. They are as fanciful as mathematical lines; and yet so strong that they can hardly be broken, and can rarely be crossed.

The grand divisions may be stated, though the subdivisions may not; for they depend on religious creeds, on community of avocation, on contiguity of residence, and a hundred nameless things. The grand divisions, like all that appertains to society, are purely conventional, wholly without foundation in reason or propriety. They depend upon what is called family, —on profession, wealth and culture,—the last considered least, because it alone is of importance, and deserving of distinction. Family, inasmuch as few persons in this country know who were their great grandfathers, puts forth the strongest claim and makes the loftiest pretension.

The old Knickerbockers, as they style themselves, insist upon it that they should have the first place in society; and, as most of them inherited real estate from their ancestors, that they were too conservative to sell, and too parsimonious to mortgage, they can support their pretensions by assured incomes and large bank accounts, without which gentility is an empty word, and fashion a mockery and a torment.

All the Vans and those bearing names suggestive of Holland, vow they are of the Knickerbocker stock, albeit it is said, some who were Smiths and Joneses two or three generations ago have since become Van Smythes and Van Johannes.

Be this as it may, the actual or would be Knickerbockers, are often the narrowest and dullest people on the Island, and have done much to induce the belief that stupidity and gentility are synonymous terms. They have fine houses generally, in town and country; have carriages and furniture with crests, though their forefathers sold rum near Hanover Square, or cast nets in East river; live expensively and pompously; display conspicuously in their private galleries their plebeian ancestors in patrician wigs and ruffles, that the thrifty old Dutchmen never dreamed of among their barrels of old Jamaica, or their spacious and awkward seines. They do all those showy things; yet are they degenerate sons of worthier sires, because they have one virtue less than they,—honesty,—and a defect,— pretension,—that puts the bar sinister upon all truly distinguished lineage. The Knickerbockers incline to entertainments and receptions where dreary platitudes pass for conversation, and well-intending men and women, whom nature would not bless with wit, fall asleep, and dream of a heaven in which they seem clever forevermore.

The livers upon others' means form the second class of our best society, without special regard to their genealogy. They sometimes boast that they do not work themselves, and reveal their vulgarity by the vulgar boast; but fancy that they have inherited gentleness of blood with the fortunes that came unearned into their possession.

Not a few of these have three or four generations of ease and luxury behind them; and consequently the men and women are comely, and have good manners and correct instincts; are quite agreeable as companions, and capable of friendship. To this division of the community, art and literature are largely indebted for encouragement, and Broadway and Fifth-avenue to many of their attractions.

These people patronize the opera, Wallack's, the classical concerts; furnish the most elegant equipages to the Park, and the most welcome guests to Saratoga, Newport and Long Branch. They wear genuine diamonds, and laces and India shawls; speak pure French and elegant English,—many of them at least; and are, on the whole, very endurable when they are thrown into contact with persons who value them for what they are, and not for what they are worth.

They are most injured by too much association with each other, and by lack of some earnest and noble purpose in a life they find it difficult to fill with aught beside frivolity.

The cultivatedly comfortable, who are the third and best representatives of our society, give it its best and highest tone from the fact that they are independent, broad and sensible. Successful authors and artists belong to this class, and all the families who have ideas beyond money, and consider culture quite equal to five-twenties. They lend a helping hand to those who are struggling in the sphere of Art, whether the form be marble, colors, sounds, or words; and believe that refinement and generosity are the best evidences of developed character. They give the most agreeable receptions in the city,—quiet gatherings of poets, authors, painters, sculptors, journalists, and actors occasionally,—without vulgar parade, or cumbersome form or wearisome routine. This class exercises a strong and marked influence, and is rapidly increasing; for, though really democratic, it is aristocratic in the true sense.

The new rich are at present stronger and more numerous than ever in New York. They profited by contracts and speculations during the War, and are now a power in the Metropolis,—a power that is satirized and ridiculed, but a power nevertheless. They are exceedingly *prononcé*, *bizarre*, and generally manage to render themselves very absurd; but, inasmuch as they annoy and worry the Knickerbockers, who have less money and are more stupid than they, I presume they have their place and achieve a purpose in the social life of Gotham.

These are the people who flare and flash so at the places of amusements, on the public promenades and in the principal thoroughfares, and whom strangers regard as the exponents of our best society, when they really represent the worst. They outdress and outshine the old families, the cultivatedly comfortable, the inheritors of fortunes, and everybody else, in whatever money can purchase and bad taste can suggest.

They have the most imposing edifices on the Avenue, the most striking liveries, the most expensive jewelry, the most gorgeous furniture, the worst manners, and the most barbarous English. They prejudice plain persons against wealth, inducing them to believe that its accumulation is associated with indelicacy, pretense and tawdriness, and that they who are materially prosperous are so at the price of much of their native judgment and original good sense. After two or three generations, even the new rich will become tolerable; will learn to use their forks instead of their knives in transferring their food to their mouths; will fathom the subtle secret that impudence is not ease, and that assumption and good breeding are diametrically opposed.

The mere adventurers are an itinerant class of New-York society, which flashes and makes a noise for a few months, or years, possibly, and then goes out, and is heard no more. They are of the new rich sort in appearance and manners, but more reckless, more tinseled and more vulgar,—because they are aware their day is brief, and the total eclipse of their glory nigh.

In the Spring we see their mansions resplendent and their carriages glittering oppressively through the drives of the Park and along the Bloomingdale road. In the Autumn, the red flag is displayed from the satin-damasked windows, and placards, on which are inscribed "Sheriff's sale," are posted on the handsome stables, where blooded horses stand ungroomed in rosewood stalls.

The adventurers live upon the top of a bubble which they know will burst soon, but which they design to enjoy while they can. They come here with some means or some credit, and go largely into an operation,—whether in advertising a patent medicine or "bearing" a leading stock, it matters little,—talk largely and coolly of their ability to lose hundreds of thousands without hurting them, but subsequently declare they have made as much; and on this plane of assurance contract enormous debts, and drive four-in-hand to the devil.

How many of these failures do I remember! How like a volcano they blazed, and at last hid their fires in smouldering ashes and unsightly cinders! They had a good time no doubt, in their own estimation, and relished the joke of cajoling the unfortunate tradesmen who played the sycophant for custom. They teach lessons, these adventurers, but give more expensive ones than they take, or are willing to pay for.

The sham and snobbery of our society are in the main indisputable, and far beyond those of any city in the Union; for there is a constant inroad upon the Metropolis of wealthy vulgarity and prosperous coarseness, from every part of the country, giving us more sinners against good breeding than we can conveniently bear, or should be charged with on our own account. Indeed, we have too much of the native article to require importation, and could better afford to part with what grows spontaneously here for the disadvantage of other less pretentious, but more deserving cities.

New-York society furnishes such themes for the satirist as no other place can, since its assumption and hollowness are greater, and its pretensions to superiority more insolent.

Wealth is good; but refinement, and culture, and purity, and nobleness are better. Everything not dishonest nor dishonorable merits a certain degree of respect and esteem, so long as it does not assume to be other than it is. But, when wealth claims to be virtue, or culture lineage, or purity elegance, or impudence genius, they all become vulgarized.

When will our American citizens cease to imitate Europe,—copying the vices of the titled, and omitting their virtues? When will they learn that thorough good breeding, as well as entire honesty, consists in daring to seem what they are, and in valuing manhood and womanhood above their accidental surroundings? Remember, oh worshippers of Sham, that you never impose upon others as you do upon yourselves, and that simplicity and truth are the bravest quarterings on the shield of genuine nobility!

The American gentleman and lady, strictly such are not to be excelled by the titled of any land; for they are the crownless kings and queens whose spiritual sceptres rule with a power of gentleness further and wider than the eye can see.

Even in our most artificial circles, the best and loyalest are to be found. Beneath the glitter of jewels and the costliest laces are bosoms full of sympathy and tenderness, and souls whose aspirations are after an ideal goodness.

There are fastidious men and dainty women who are better and gentler for their carpets of velvet and couches of down; who do good in unknown ways; who stand by beds of suffering and at the hearth of poverrty, and make them easier and lighter for their coming and their comfort.

Fifth avenue and Grammercy Park are not so far from the Five Points and the Fourth ward as is generally supposed.

Out of carved doorways, and down stately staircases, go elaborately dressed messengers of charity, and silken purses are unloosed by jeweled fingers to bestow alms to the needy and succor to the distressed.

Aye, even in the most heartless-seeming circles of Fashion there are saints in satin and angels in robes of the latest *mode*, that hide noble qualities no less than beauty of form, and yet suppress those qualities not at all.

CHAPTER III.

WALL STREET.

WALL STREET is the banking-house of the continent.

It is insignificant looking enough, with its crookedness and dinginess—its half-dozen blocks of grim, gloomy buildings. Yet its power is felt from Bangor to San Francisco, from Oregon to Florida; even across the sea, and round the sphere. Like the Hindoo deity, we see that it is homely, but we know that it is great.

We cannot afford to despise Wall street, strong as our will may be; for it holds the lever that moves the American world. We may despise its Mammon-worship; we may censure its corruption; we may decry its morals. But, unless fortune has filled our purse with ducats—and often not then—we are unable to escape its influence, or exorcise its spell. It is a great, established, far-reaching fact; and in its keeping are the curses and blessings that make up the weal and woe of life.

Upon that financial quarter rest the pillars of the money market, that mysterious something which no one sees and every one feels—strong as Alcides, and yet sensitive as the Mimosa.

All the cities, and towns, and villages of the country pay tribute to Wall street. All offer incense at its exacting shrine. All seek to propitiate it, that it may make a golden return. It is keen-eyed, broad-breasted, strong-armed, with a mighty brain and no heart—a Briareus without sympathy—a Samson without sentiment.

A stately church at one end, and a deep, broad stream at the other, are not without significance; for Wall street prays and looks devout on Sunday, and every other day of the week yields to its secular nature as the river to the ocean-tides.

All day and all night the stately spire of Trinity looks down upon the feverish, anxious street. All day and all night the East river floats softly to the sea. Humanity chafes, and frets, and suffers; but the shadows come and go upon the lofty pile, and fall upon the deep-green waters, and leave them all unchanged.

How many a worn and haggard face has looked up from the troubled thoroughfare for hope, yet found it not, in the direction of the heaven-pointing steeple, and thought of rest, but sought it not, in the bosom of the river!

Look at Wall street now, while the stars are shining down into its silence. You would not suppose it was turbulent and tremulous a few hours ago. It is still and placid as the battle-field after the battle. The strong houses are barred and bolted, and slumbering deeply for the struggle of the morrow. The great banks, whose names are known over all the land, and whose credit is firmer than their vaults, look like tombs at this hour. Their buried wealth no one guesses. It is supposed to be enormous; and yet it may have been long exhausted. The banks may be merely bubbles;

but they will float high and airily until panic pricks them, and they burst, spreading new panic in their breaking.

Oh, the mystery and uncertainty of Credit! Hard to create, the smallest circumstance destroys it. A moment of distrust shatters the work of years. An unfounded rumor unsettles what half a century was needed to establish. Breathe against it, and what seemed a monument of marble melts like a snow-wreath before the southern wind.

When the stars pale in the light of the morning, and the sun shimmers over the church and the river, Wall street still lies like a stolid sleeper—stirs not, nor appears to breathe.

Trinity's solemn clock tells the hours slowly and measuredly,—tells them remorsely, think they who have engagements to meet, and, lacking collaterals, are driven to financial desperation.

Nine strikes from the brown tower, and all along the streets the heavy doors open almost at once, and brawny porters look lazily out into the still, quiet quarter.

The capitalists, and stock operators, and gold speculators have not yet come down town. They are probably lounging over their luxurious breakfasts somewhere above Fourteenth street, though cashiers, and tellers, and book-keepers are at their desks, prepared for the business of the day.

The steps on the narrow sidewalks begin to thicken. Carriages set down handsomely-dressed men, young and old, opposite the sign-crowded structures.

The bulls and bears, fresh-looking and comely, with dainty-fitting gloves, artistic garments, and flowers in their button-holes, wheel into the street and hurriedly exchange greetings as they pass. The expression of their faces is changing. The regular fever of the time and place is rising. They are entering upon the financial arena, prepared to give and take every advantage that the Board of Brokers allows.

The tide of Wall street swells faster than the tide of the adjacent sea. The hum of voices grows into a war. Men hurry to and fro, and jostle, and drive, and rush in all directions, with eyes glittering and nerves a-strain, as if their soul were in pawn, and they had but forty seconds to redeem it. Doors slam and bang. Messengers, with piles of bank-notes and bags of coin, hasten up and down and across the thronged thoroughfares.

Short, quick, fragmentary phrases slip sharply out of compressed lips. You hear "Erie, Central, Gold, Forty, Three-quarters, Sell, Buy, Take it, Thirty days, Less dividend, All right, Done"; and these cabalistic words make a difference of tens of thousands of dollars to those who utter them.

Business is transacted largely and speedily, as though each day were the day before the final judgment and "margins" must be paid and "settlements" made before the next World opened a new stock exchange for the bulls that were blessed, or expelled from the Board the bears that had failed of salvation.

Every operator endeavors to outstrip his fellow. Device and deception, rumor and innuendo, ingenious invention and base fabrication, are resorted to. The greatest gambling in the Republic is going on, and the deepest dishonesty is concealed by the garb of commercial honor. No one asks nor expects favors. All stratagems are deemed fair in Wall street. The only crime there is to be "short" or "crippled." "Here are my stakes," says Bull to Bear. "Shake the dice-box of your judgment, and throw for what you like. My luck against yours; my power to misrepresent, and hide truth with cunning for the next thirty days."

"Dare you agree to deliver Reading, ten or a hundred thousand, on the first, at a hundred and three?" challenges Jerome, or Vanderbilt, or Drew.

"Have you the nerve to hold Hudson River next week at a hundred and twenty-five? Agree to deliver all you want."

A nod, and a note as a memorandum, and the trade is made.

The elegantly-dressed gamblers play largely, and hundreds of thousands are staked upon chances that shift like the wind. They live upon the excitement, as worn-out debauchees upon the stimulants that have grown necessary. Wall street is food and drink to them. They cannot spend their princely incomes; but neither can they perish of the ennui of honesty, of the inanity of repose. They can operate to what extent they choose. Wall street neither buys nor sells, as we should suppose. It merely pays "differences" when the day for delivery arrives. Two, ten, twenty thousand dollars make good the "differences," and the shares or gold are left untouched. "Corners" are the ambition and the dread of all. Originally designed for the uninitiated, the shrewder are often manœuvred into them; and now and then the heaviest operators are obliged to disgorge a million of their profits.

A "corner" is thus managed. A heavy capitalist or

a number of capitalists conclude to operate for a rise in Erie or Pacific Mail. They go into the street, and wish to buy a large amount of the stock which may be then quoted, say at 85 cents on the dollar. They find persons who agree to deliver it in thirty days at 86. Then the capitalists begin to purchase through brokers at the ruling price, and soon get all there is in the market, though so secretly that no one suspects they are the buyers. When the thirty days have expired the stock they have purchased is to be delivered. The parties who have agreed to deliver it say they will pay the curent rate; but the capitalists declare they must have the stock, and that they won't be satisfied with anything else. Then the parties try to buy it, and the demand sends up the stock rapidly. They send brokers throughout the banking quarter, and the scarcity with the pressing demand causes the shares to advance 10 or 15, often 20 and 30 per cent. in a single day. When it is at such a figure as the capitalists wish, they put their stock in the market, and sell it at the great advance from the old rate; thus realizing 15 to 20 per cent. on $5,000,000 or $6,000,000, perhaps $10,000,000, which will be between $1,000,000 and $2,000,000 profit by a single transaction.

The shrewdest of operators, like Daniel Drew and Leonard W. Jerome are reputed to have been made the victims of "corners," and to have lost fortunes in a day. But such as they are not often caught; the "corners" being formed for the less crafty and experienced. Often the capitalists consent to receive the difference between the price the stock was to be delivered for and its advance, and then sell the stock at the advance to persons who believe it will go still higher; thus making an enormous double profit.

Another favorite operation in Wall street is for the bears (the bears are those who want to pull down prices, and the bulls those who wish to push them up,) to withdraw a large amount of legal-tenders from circulation by borrowing money from the banks on certain securities, either railway shares or government bonds. The legal-tenders are not wanted, of course, but the bears lock them up, and the money market growing tight, the banks call in their loans. Persons who have borrowed on the securities are obliged to sell them to pay what they have borrowed, and forcing the sale of the securities, causes them to decline. That is what the bears seek; for they have agreed to deliver certain securities at a certain price and time. Say they have agreed to deliver New-York Central Railway at 105. The scarcity of money and the panic created thereby send Central down to 90. The bear who is to deliver $1,000,000 of the shares, thus makes $150,000 clear by his unscrupulous management. Every few weeks this locking up of bonds is resorted to by a few rich men who cause immense loss to others for the sake of increasing their own gains.

Nothing could be more dishonest than this operation or getting up a "corner." It is as disreputable as picking a man's pocket; yet Wall street not only allows, but admires and applauds it.

People who buy stocks or gold in the banking quarter usually put up "margins," that is one-tenth of the amount of stock bought. If a man wishes to purchase $10,000 worth of Hudson River or Harlem Railway shares he leaves $1,000 with his broker, who holds the stock. and charges his customer 7 per cent. per annum in ordinary times for the use of the money. If the shares fall 5 per cent. the broker notifies the buyer to make his margin good. If he don't do so, the broker sells the stock, takes out his interest and commissions, and returns the balance to the purchaser.

If the shares go up the buyer makes $100 every time they advance 1 per cent. The reason so many men lose money is, that they put up all the money they have as margins; and if the stock they purchase declines, though confident it will advance again, they have no more means, and their broker sells them out. Every day the margin men are obliged to let their stocks go when, if they could hold, on they would be certain to make something. But they are little fish, and in Wall street the big fish swallow the small ones all the year round.

The Stock Exchange and Gold Room are the scenes of such tumult and confusion that only members can comprehend the mysterious transactions. Excited, anxious faces, nervous fingers writing hurriedly with pencils in little books, clamor of voices, lifting of hands, becks and nods, are all the spectator sees and hears. He cannot even learn the rate of shares or coin amid the flurry and the noise. It appears to him like the struggle of overgrown children for tempting fruit that one alone can have. He is amazed and dazed, and cannot guess who has been bold, and who has held aloof from the avaricious scramble.

Three times every day stocks are called at the Exchange, and the members measure their brain and nerve, their capital and credit, one against the other. Shares are put up and put down, irrespective of values. Bulls and bears toss the prices as they would shuttlecocks upon the battledoors of their interest or caprice; and it is not uncommon for a non-paying railway to be fifty or a hundred above par, when a highly remunerative road is in the eighties or nineties.

Stocks are what the brokers make them, and their varying rate is determined by a "ring."

Wall street grows every day richer and more commanding, though fortunes are made and lost there every year that would buy the broadest dukedoms of Europe. Capital from abroad is constantly flowing to that great monetary centre; while private means are swelling to a degree that is not wholesome, financially. Operators can draw their checks for millions, and can "carry" such an amount of stocks as astounds the weaker ones of the street. The rich wax richer and richer, albeit, ever and anon, a monetary Nemesis pursues them to ruin, and brands "bankrupt" upon the brow that has braved the severest financial fates.

What a long and painfully interesting history might be given of the fluctuations of fortune that have marked the strange history of the street! What gigantic operators have ruled the quarter for years, and gone down at last,—gone down to poverty, to madness, to shattered health and self-inflicted death!

Pale ghosts, if Plato's theory be true, must stalk by night in the silent places of the banking bureaus, and long, with a longing that is their torment, for the pursuits they followed on this whirling planet.

Over non-success the pall of oblivion is thrown; for Wall street is too busy to hate, and too anxious to despise.

STOCK EXCHANGE,—BROAD STREET.

Whatever of energy and enterprise, financial daring and reckless speculation, lust of commercial power and mania for money-getting there is in the land, seems compressed into Wall street for half-a-dozen hours of the twenty-four. Out of it all grow advantages beyond the thought of those who lay wagers against circumstance. Wall street capital develops the country bounteously. The north, the south, the east and west go there for aid to hew, and build, and mine. If the bloated toad look ugly, its invisible jewel is precious. If Wall street have faults,—and they are many and grievous,—it has virtues not a few, and, outside of business, permits its heart to beat, and its hands to give, and its sympathy to heal.

Its great power is not always used unworthily; and the spire looking down upon it, and the river flowing by it, all day and all night, must have recollections of its goodness that would show the preciousness and poetry which are hidden in the hard environment of money.

CHAPTER IV.

THE POLICE.

New York is growing more and more like Paris in respect to the police. It is literally governed by them. They have almost everything in their own hands, and are prone to make the law a terror to all but evil doers. That they have entirely too much power is beyond question; and that they abuse it is a matter of hourly observation. But, like the World, they are improving; are much better now than they have ever been, and are likely to continue to develop upward.

It is common and easy to censure the police, who are neither estimable nor lovable, as a class; but, on the whole, they are about as good, or as little ill, rather, as can be expected considering their calling, character, and circumstances. We have no right to look for saintliness in blue uniforms and pewter badges, particularly when their wearers receive but $25 to $30 a week, and are necessarily demoralized by the very air they breathe.

The reputation of the tribe is bad; and men are rarely better than their reputation. They are compelled to associate with vulgarians and scoundrels of all grades; are exposed to every species of temptation; act unfavorably on each other, and have no restraining influences beyond their own intelligence, which is not very great, and their fear of exposure, which is not probable.

Like every other body, they have bad as well as good men; and I am inclined to believe the former are very much in the majority. Why should they not be? Who wouldn't deteriorate as a policeman? Six months on the force is enough to make Bayard a bully and Howard a blackguard. Therefore, all who resist the strong tendency of their vocation are deserving of extreme credit.

Some of the greatest rogues in town can be found among the so-called guardians of the public peace, and, on the other hand, a number of men who, in spite of temptation, association, and misrepresentation, have quick sympathies, generous impulses, and kindly hearts. The character of a metropolitan policeman can generally be determined from his physiognomy. Peter Smith you would trust instinctively; for his mild eye, broad forehead, and clear-cut chin will not lie. Dennis O'Grady you would avoid after dark; for you read treachery, brutality, cruelty, in the flat nose, the restless glance, the heavy jaw, the bull-like neck.

The police of New York number about 2,100, independent of the detectives, and are for the most part very comely physical specimens of the race. The force of the entire Metropolitan District, which includes the City, Brooklyn, Richmond, King's, part of Queen's and Westchester counties, has 2,566 men At their head is Superintendent Kennedy who has under him four inspectors, eighteen surgeons, forty-five captains, ninety-three doormen, ninety-one roundsmen, one hundred and seventy-seven sergeants, and twenty-one hundred and thirty-seven patrolmen. They are tall, erect, well-formed, able-bodied, chosen more for their muscle than their morals, for their pluck than their purity. They are regularly drilled, especial pains being taken with the Broadway squad, and form a very effective force for good or evil. They are capable of doing excellent service, as has been shown on numerous occasions, and with weapons in their hands, which they know how to use, make quite a little army of defense. During the August riots of 1863, they proved themselves men of determination and courage; fought the furious mob like veteran soldiers, and gave their lives to the preservation of public order and the restoration of the law of the land.

The Broadway squad, composed of about one hundred picked policemen, are noticeably good-looking. They are very neatly attired, and, though they have light duty, are very serviceable in assisting women and children across the crowded thoroughfares, directing strangers to different parts of the city, arresting pickpockets, and preventing street fights. They are the real autocrats of the highway, and the position is sought by all the members of the force; only the most intelligent and best-behaved being eligible to the place.

They have charge of street-incumbrances, and sign nuisances, and can regulate all such things as they choose. As Broadway is always blocked up and almost impassable from the causes named, it is fair to suppose the policemen are paid for their purblindness. Indeed, it is generally understood that bank-notes of any sort have a singular effect upon policemen's eyes.

They can't see beyond a ten or twenty-dollar note in the broadest light of day; and, after dusk, a bill of much smaller denomination not only obscures their vision, but affects their memory. They receive, doubtless, very liberal douceurs in that great avenue, and their perquisites must be far beyond their salaries.

The best class are usually Americans, men who originally entered the force because they could get nothing better to do, and who from long service have become attached to it from its alternately indolent and exciting character. They may not preserve their garments unstained, nor their hands unsoiled,—that is above policial power, perhaps—but their sins, if venal, are venial also. They do not lose their instincts of humanity nor their sympathy with suffering. They keep many an honest fellow from the hands of sharpers, many a virtuous country girl from the wiles of procuresses and the arts of debauchees.

They have abundant opportunities to do good, and when temptation the other way is not too strong, or nature too weak, they obey their better selves. Not unfrequently they prove themselves heroes in guarding honesty and innocence, and have yielded their lives to protect the defenseless and succor the distressed. They have time and again saved children and women from the flames at imminent peril to themselves; have snatched men from death and their sisters from worse than death, and been entitled by their deeds to the highest fame. Rarely has the chronicle been made; and, when it has, it has been forgotten a moment after.

The worst class, which is two, perhaps three, to one of the other, are generally foreigners, ignorant, brutal fellows, whom any elevation renders tyrants and bullies. They first obtained their place by partisan favor, though the present police are appointed by the Commissioners regardless of politics. They are in full sympathy and communion with all the rogues within sound of the City hall bell, and follow their calling purely to make money. They are fond of arresting innocent ruralists, charging them with some heinous offence, and frightening them out of their wits and pocket books at the same time.

They are approachable by bribes, and prone to serve those who pay the most. They release pick-pockets and burglars who divide; persecute unfortunate cyprians who refuse gratuitous favors; steal from drunken men; swear to anything; levy black-mail, and are guilty of any mean act their low minds can conceive of. They are usually on the scent of any misbehavior with which reputable persons are connected, using their knowledge to extort money by threat of exposure.

Glaring as their misconduct is, they are cunning knaves, and contrive to keep in office when decent men are removed. I have heard of scoundrels who are veterans in the force, and who won't quit it while there is a dirty thing to do, or a dollar to steal. They are strangely long-lived, too, on the hypothesis that Satan stands by sinners, and rarely have their brains blown out, or their throats cut, as they deserve, by the desperate characters with whom they come in contact. Such mishaps befall only the better class, who are more ready to expose themselves to real dangers.

The police-stations are 32 in number, in as many precincts, and are generally as clean and wholesome as such places can be. Their atmosphere, however, is repulsive at best, and a sensitive nature avoids them as it does painful scenes or horrid sights. Their patronage varies with the season and the occasion. In certain times of quiet not more than 200 arrests are made in the entire 24 hours; while at others the arrests will reach 600 or 800, or even 1,000. During the severe weather, lodgers, men and women who have no place to sleep, are very numerous. They huddle into the stations, ragged, dirty, shivering, either bloated or emaciated, and convey some idea of the poverty and wretchedness of the Great City.

Those who are committed to the stations are guilty of various crimes, among which drunkenness, disorderly conduct, and petit larceny are the commonest. When a first-class burglar, or a real incendiary, or an actual murderer is thrust into the lock-up, his presence creates a momentary sensation. The meaner prisoners want to catch sight of the rare monster, and peer at him through the iron bars. The policemen hurl rude jests at him, or curse him; while he either curses them in return, or sinks down on the rude bench in sullen indifference to his fate.

Now and then a bird of higher game is taken,—a bank-teller or book-keeper who has been embezzling or forging; a gentleman of position who has shot his sister's seducer or his wife's lover; a fashionable rowdy who has undertaken to break windows and watchmen's heads, with a charming indifference whether it is one or the other; a well-dressed man about whom strict orders are given, but whose offense is not stated. Such persons are usually treated with courtesy and distinction, for they have means and can pay for civility, and have a faculty of getting out that is impossible to vulgar sinners and law-breakers.

It is a sad and revolting sight to see the station houses emptying themselves in the morning. The prisoners are a few of the unwholesome and painful things the night hides, and the day keeps beyond vision. Bleared and blackened eyes, bloody faces, festering rags, horrid countenances, demonized brutes, hideous hags, guarded by policemen, and going to court, soon to be sent to the Tombs or Blackwell's island for the fifth, or tenth, or twentieth time.

How mechanically the policemen swear (half of them have no idea of the solemnity of an oath, so accustomed are they to that form of statement), and how indifferent they are to the scenes and characters before them! They are insensible, stolid, brutal, very many of the class, and laugh where others would weep. They consider crime and its punishment something of course, part of their business, and to be encouraged, inasmuch as their livelihood depends upon it.

Unfortunate the sensitive being who from some stress of circumstance falls into their hands. They will lacerate with looks, and stab with jeers, and never dream of giving pain. They have walked so much among thorn bushes and strong hedges they do not suspect the existence of the violets or daisies they are crushing under their feet.

The gross injustices of a police court, every week of the year, would fill a small volume if enumerated in detail; but they are usually practised upon paupers and outcasts, and no one cares for them. That they are unfortunate and friendless, is proof of their guilt, and their liberty is sworn away and their sentences fixed, without reflection or conscience. It is the policeman's duty to swear and the judge's to punish, and the sooner the duty is discharged the better, at least for themselves.

The detectives are a peculiar and distinct part of the police force. There are no less than 14 or 15 organizations (including about 400 men, with a few women) in the Metropolis, and its members are the shrewdest and most dishonest of the entire body. The organizations are divided into the central detective police, detectives of the separate wards or precincts, car-detectives, insurance and bankers' detectives police, national police agency, North-American detective agency, merchants' detective police, bureau of information, Matsell's police-detectives, hotel-detectives, divorce-detectives, United-States detectives, internal revenue detectives.

Their regular pay varies from three to eight dollars a day for "piping," "shadowing," "working-up," etc.; but they have such latitude in "contingent expenses," "special arrangements," and "individual enterprises" that no limit can be fixed to their profits. The chief detectives have a salary of $2,500 a year, but they make five or ten times that sum often, and frequently acquire a large property. Bank officers and persons having responsible positions in stores are watched, the moment the least suspicion is excited by their conduct; and, if they are using money not their own, they are always found out and reported, unless they happen to pay the detective better than his employer does.

There is a good deal of excitement and no little

romance in the profession of the detective. He must be very shrewd, understand human nature, be prolific of resources and inventions, cool, self-reliant, courageous, and resolute. He goes everywhere; adopts all disguises; plays many parts; combines, analyzes, manipulates, manages, and does work often that is a credit to his brain and a discredit to his principle.

Dickens, it is said, is very fond of consulting the detectives, who have helped him to many of his plots, at least in parts; and other novel-writers would do well to imitate the great master of fiction. The detective sees life and nature in its most peculiar and often interesting phases, and he has the capacity to unravel out of the tangled skein of his experiences threads of narratives as startling as truthful. Half they say would not be believed (they are fond of telling sensational stories); but, if they merely related the facts that come under their daily observation, the public would be incredulous.

They behold strange things unquestionably; see demons as angels, and angels as devils, and naturally learn to believe that what we call good and evil is merely a refraction of moral light passing through different mediums.

CHAPTER V.

THE SHIPPING.

The bay of New-York is not surpassed by any in the world for excellence and beauty. The bay of Naples is far more famous, because there have been more poets to sing its praises; but ours is quite equal, if not superior to the emerald crescent which has been set at the head of the jewels of the sea.

To appreciate fully the bay of New-York, one should go abroad, and remain a year or more. After wandering over Europe and Asia, he will return with the love of home and freedom strengthened in his bosom; and, sailing back to the great centre of the western world, he will catch sight of the spires looming up, like those of Venice, from the watery distance, and take in the picturesqueness of the bay, and all its varied charms, as he never did before.

There is a satisfaction, a sense of largeness and liberty, in a sea-port that no interior city can impart. By the side of the ocean one feels in communication with the rest of the World; on the outer surface of the Globe; at the pole of civilization. Inland, one seems out of immediate relation with the Universe; thrust aside from the current of events; washed up from the billows of busy being.

The chief advantage of New-York is its location.

A complete island, swept by every breeze, touched by ships from every clime, the great focus of wealth and trade, to live in it is to become attached to it, and grow broad by liberal influences from within and without.

One of the lasting attractions of the Metropolis is its shipping. I have always enjoyed wandering, or lounging, in West or Water streets, or on the Battery, watching the sailing of the ships, their riding at anchor, their lying idle at the busy piers. Nearly two hundred piers gird the island; and the vessels, receiving freight therefrom, and lying off in the rivers and bay, often number from fifteen hundred to two thousand.

From the south point of the Battery to the Harlem river, on both sides, and all round the island, in fact is one unbroken forest of masts. From them, the flags of every nation under the sun are flying; and many of the colors would not be recognized save by persons familiar with the ensigns of the world.

The cross of Great Britain, the tri-color of France, the eagles of Austria, Prussia, and Russia, the complicated arms of Spain, the crowned lions of Holland, the cross of Sweden, Norway, and Switzerland, the bars of Bremen, the crescent of Turkey, the checkered field of China, and even the crossed swords of Japan, may be seen floating in the air. Greece, Prussia, and Egypt are represented by the white cross, the lion-centred star and the stellar moons.

All tongues mingle on the piers and vessels as in olden Babel, but they are not confused. Every foreign ship has its interpreter, if he be needed, though many of the sailors, who have passed their lives on the sea, can speak enough of a dozen languages to make themselves understood. Every hour some craft is coming in from, or going out upon its long voyage. This for Liverpool, for Havre, for Marseilles, for Naples, for Constantinople, for Palermo; that for Hong-Kong, for Calcutta, for San-Francisco, for Yokohama.

With their immense and valuable cargoes, with their thousands of human souls, the ships trust themselves calmly to the treacherous deep, and, through countless storms and dangers, come back undaunted and unharmed. Men who have, all their lives, braved the perils of the ocean, die at last in their hammocks or upon the land they have so little trodden.

There is a species of fascination in watching the sea and the ships, in tracing them as they come slowly into sight; rise, as it appears, gradually out of the waves; or go down on the slope of the sphere, and fade away. We all say we believe the World round; but we do not practically. We can hardly conceive that those who left us a few months since are on the other side of the Planet, laughing or weeping directly under our feet. Even when we visit China, and reason and science assure us we have been with our antipodes, we do not realize it any more than that we have been beyond the grave in sleep.

The sailors are an interesting class. Their life is a hard and dangerous one, but they cannot be induced to quit it. They are the true cosmopolitans. Their home is everywhere and nowhere. They preserve their freshness of feeling, their relish of pleasure, their love of adventure always. They are children, and never grow old. They have sailed in all seas and dwelt in all cities; have pulled the pig-tails of Chinamen in Nanking; smoked with the Turks outside the mosques of Smyrna; drank tea with the Russians at Cronstadt, and whisky with the Irish at Cork.

Unsuspecting, unselfish, careless, they fall an easy prey to sharpers and swindlers. The moment they touch the shore, they are resolved upon a "lark." Their money burns in their pockets, and when it is spent they are as cheerful as before, and vastly more resigned to work. Always in trouble on shore, yet always in superabundant spirits, they know no medium between hard service and perfect self-indulgence. Half the duty of policemen in the Fourth and Sixth wards is to keep the sea-rovers out of mischief, and then they rarely succeed.

Liquor and loose women are all too much for poor Jack, and, after being robbed and beaten, he is carried off to the station-house, cursing his eyes, which deserve condemnation, since they are of little use to him in avoiding open pits. Often the master of the vessel is compelled to redeem Jack from bondage, and the unfortunate sailor can hardly see the receding shore through the clouds dissipation has spread before his eyes. Unlike the land-lubber, he does not promise reformation, and, unlike the same individual, he does not break his promise. He keeps sober on board because he can't get liquor. But he renews his New-York experience in the first port. The same tricks are played upon him; the same mishaps befall him, and with the same result. He goes rolling and blundering through life; regarding the whole World as a quarter-deck, and resting only when he is sewed up in his hammock, and cast to the fishes.

The emigrant vessels are curious studies. How strangely and puzzled the emigrants look as they come out of the depot at the Battery! They are entering, indeed, upon a new life, and America must seem to them like another world. The Irish are excited and nervous generally, an odd compound of timidity and boldness; but the air of freedom and even licentiousness they soon breathe, renders them defiant and aggressive.

The trouble with the natives of Erin is that there is no Purgatory between the Inferno of their own country and the Paradise of this, that would fit them for entering upon a broader and higher mode of existence. The change is too sudden, and they and those brought in contact with them suffer from it. They rarely understand their own interest. They are made the dupes of others, and their impulsiveness overrides their reason, and keeps them at constant disadvantage.

Having reached our hospitable shores, they stick, much against their interest, to the large cities, preferring menial offices to a prospect of independence in the country. No pestilence would drive them out of New-York. They would rather stay here, starve and die, than prosper in the territories. There are nearly as many of their fellow-countrymen here as in Dublin, and here they will stay, until Potter's field or the City Hall receives them.

The Germans are quiet, self-contained, half stolid, half wondering, when they land. They are more frequently imposed upon than the Irish; for the latter find adherents and protectors in their own countrymen, who have become American citizens, by the blessing of God and the ease of the naturalization laws. Usually they make brief sojourn in the Metropolis. They are agriculturally inclined, and wander off to the West to buy land and till their own soil. While their Milesian brothers are driving hacks, and digging cellars, and waiting on tables, the Germans are putting money in their purses and independence in their future.

The emigrant vessels are often torture chambers for the poor creatures who take passage in them. The officers neglect and abuse them shamefully, and one tithe of the injustice and cruelty practiced upon the strangers will never be known. Now and then there is an arrest, and a fine imposed upon a captain or a mate, or bail required. But there the matter ends, and the wrong continues.

The ill-treatment of emigrants is one of the most serious evils of this abounding-in-evil city; and few know the horrors of a passage across the Atlantic. The emigrants are not only deprived of proper food and air, but the men are robbed, the women debauched and not unfrequently beaten by scoundrels from whom no penalty is ever exacted.

The foreign steamers are well worth visiting on sailing days. You can see much of life among the better kinds of people there, particularly on the French and English vessels. Friends always flock to the steamers to see those departing. Excitement is a common ingredient in the adieux, and sorrow, by no means insincere, a concomitant of such leave-takings.

Step on board one of the Cunarders with me. Some prominent personage must be going abroad, for forty or fifty well-dressed women and a score of men are crowded around a mild, self-satisfied-looking individual who smiles patronizingly, and wears a white cravat. The women simper, and press close to him, and give him thousands of good wishes, and beg him to take excellent care of his health, and assure him they will pray for him while he is gone.

From the conversation, we learn that he is the Rev. Clarence Edmund Fitzdoodle. He has been worn down by labors of two hours a day, with a three-months' vacation each Summer, and has been prevailed upon to go abroad to heal his shattered constitution, and save his precious life. No one would suspect his ill-health. He looks round and rosy, and his rhetoric on Sunday is too weak to require any serious effort. He has an admirable appetite and digestion, and has never shown any particular weakness, except for worked slippers, and other pretty presents from his pretty parishioners. But they have declared he must go, and with the air of a well-fed and well-dressed martyr he resigns himself to their solicitations. He declares, however, he would sooner die in the pulpit (the cause of eloquence would improve if he should) than abandon any part of his duty. At this, his feminine worshipers vow he is a saint, and beg him to depart, with tears in their beautiful eyes.

Fitzdoodle goes, and has, you may be assured, a good time. He returns in six months, having drank more wine than was beneficial to him, and threatened with gout, which he ascribes to his severe studies of theological works while on the Continent.

Not far from this clergyman is a pretty brunette, who is parting with the "only man she ever loved." She tells Paul, while she leans on his arm, that her heart is almost breaking, and that she would'nt go, but that pa won't listen to her remaining behind. Paul is deeply touched, and so is Ida; and they look at each other through tear-dimmed eyes as the steamer moves off. The third day out Ida flirts with a young Englishman, and on the sixth forgets all about Paul, who is consoling himself with half-a-dozen other women, telling each one he doesn't care a straw for his departed dear.

On the French steamer a pair are devoting themselves to one another, and are really very fond. They are engaged, and on their way to visit all the wonders and beauties of Europe together, under the proper surveillance of their elders. James will kiss Mollie on deck by the star-light for the first three evenings, and, on the fourth, will hold her over the side while she is sick. A change in the situation, certainly; but they are to be married, and they might as well have some of the unavoidable prose before as after wedlock.

Here is a pale, but singularly sweet-looking woman, with her husband, and their friend—more hers than his, I fear. She is going away to break off her relation with the man she cannot wed, but must always love. He has advised her to the course, and hopes they may have a future yet. Perhaps they will. But while he waits for her letter, which is to tell him of her return, he gets the husband's note, and, opening it, discovers their future is beyond this World. She is dead; and hope comes not to the lover's heart—for three months at least.

Such is the shipping. We all send our little vessels out, and, to many of us, they never return.

CHAPTER VI.

THE ROUGHS.

A MORE despicable, dangerous, and detestable character than the New-York rough does not exist. He is an epitome of all the meannesses and vices of humanity, and capable, under pressure, of a courage desperate and deadly. He is Parolles, Bobadil, and Hotspur all at once,—a creature without conscience, a savage without the virtues of nature. He is not totally depraved, for total depravity is impossible; but his redeeming traits are so few, only the microscope of a broad charity can detect them. He is a social hyena, a rational jackal, utterly devoid of reverence or respect, whom education does not reach, and society cannot tame.

The metropolitan rough is usually American born, but of foreign parentage, surrounded by, and reared from his childhood under the worst influences,—all his brutal instincts stimulated, and his moral being suffocated, for want of wholesome air. Training he cannot get; education he will not have. He generally learns to read, however, by accident, and enjoys the knowledge in poring over obscene books, the *Clipper*, and the *Police Gazette*. He manages, too, by some mysterious means, to write a coarse kind of scrawl, which enables him to convey his plans to his brother-scoundrels when he is in the Tombs, or they are at Blackwell's Island.

Without education, he acquires a certain degree of intelligence that is almost unavoidable in the atmosphere of a great city; and his experience of the worst phases of life makes him cunning as a fox and cruel as a tiger. Long before maturity, he has developed all the instincts of a beast of prey, and, in the midst of a civilized community, he roams like a wolf among a herd of sheep.

The facial and cranial appearance of the rough goes far to establish the truth of physiognomy and phrenology. All the animal is in the shape of his features and head; but the semblance of the thinking, cultivated, self-disciplined man is very nearly lost. The cheek bones are high; the nose is flat; the lips are thick and coarse; the forehead low and receding; the jaws massive and protuberant; the neck thick and thewy; the head mostly behind the huge, prehensile ears. He is the exact species of animal from which a sensitive, intuitive organization would shrink, without knowing why. His approach in the dark would be felt as something dangerous. Dogs and children would avoid him, and detectives watch him on instinct.

How many of this class the Metropolis contains, will never be known. The rough, though gregarious, is mysterious. He is very vain, but he does not court popularity, nor seek to attract attention. Outside of his own degraded circle, he is not ambitious of distinction; for distinction increases the liability to arrest, and interferes with future operations.

Probably New-York can count its roughs by thousands, though they so burrow in the slums and dens of the town, that nothing but an earthquake will ever upheave them all. They delight in darkness; and yet they are so numerous and varied in character that many woo the day; brave the public eye; defy public justice. The Fourth, Sixth, and part of the Eighteenth wards are their favorite haunts, albeit no portion of the island confines them. They are water-rats and land-rats, river thieves and land thieves, pimps, confidence men, brawlers, burglars and assassins, as circumstance shapes and occasion demands.

They are reared in and trained to idleness and dissipation from their first years. They are fed on tobacco and gin from childhood. Ribald songs and the roar of swinish carousals, in place of maternal lullabies, echo in their infant ears. Living much in the open air, and fond of rude physical sports, they grow up stout and hardy, in spite of bad habits and pernicious nurture.

In their early teens, they find themselves lewd and lusty, thoroughly selfish and sensual, principled against work, predetermined to dishonesty and tyranny, all their worst passions in full play, and their sympathies and sensibilities latent, if not extinguished. In the midst of a great and wealthy city, they consider its inhabitants objects of prey, and discover on every hand the abundant means of knavish livelihood.

To bar-rooms and brothels they tend by a natural law, and soon come to regard ruffians, thieves and prize-fighters worthy examples of imitation and objects of envy. Any part of their brutal education that may have been neglected, is readily supplied in such places and by such companions. The more precociously shameful they are, the more they are flattered and coddled. Their first fight and first debauch are like the first honors of a college; and they mount higher and higher by sinking deeper and deeper into the slough of degradation.

Their earliest, as it is their latest, shame, is their connection with courtesans, upon the wages of whose prostitution they live, not only unblushingly, but boastfully. To those poor creatures they give the little affection they are capable of—paying for pecuniary support by abuse and outrage. To rob and beat in the morning, the woman whose arms they seek at night, is their idea of gallantry and chivalry; and they religiously believe that any departure from such conduct would result in the extinction of her love. Though they maltreat her themselves, they do not allow others the precious privilege. They are her champions indeed, when foreign foes invade or civil discords rise. And she, with the instinct of her sex, which neither neglect nor wrong can suppress, leans on, looks up to, and loves the brutal fellow who strikes her thrice for every kiss. Not a cyprian in the town but has her "lover" and protector in the shape of a rough, who, through laxity of law, has escaped the penitentiary, and, perhaps, the gallows. She cannot do without him, nor can he without her; though she is noble compared to him—aye, a saint by contrast. She is branded as an outcast; she could not return to purity if she would. He might reform and be accepted to-morrow; but he would not be honest if he could.

A popular recreation with the roughs of Manhattan is to attend picnics unbidden, and excursions which quiet and orderly people originate for rational enjoyment. They make their arrangements beforehand;

appoint a rendezvous upon the cars or boat, (they prefer the water journeys,) and keep peaceful until the place of destination has been reached. They either take liquor with them, or get it along the route; and, arrived on the spot, they proceed systematically to create a disturbance, which no amount of patience or forbearance can prevent. The more amiable the objects of persecution, the more resolved the roughs to make a row. In this country seekers of quarrel can always find it. Endurance ceases to be a virtue. Blows follow words, and the rowdies are in their natural element. They are on the spot in numbers, organized and armed, and carry things their own way by aid of superior strength.

The quiet men are brutally beaten and robbed. The women are terrified, but their screams are silenced by threats. They are extremely fortunate if they escape outrage, which part of the programme is generally followed.

Sometimes such entertainments are deferred until the return of the excursion. Then the train or boat is seized, and the rowdies do as they please; eluding or defying the police, between whom and themselves there seems often to be a perfect understanding.

One would not believe such things could happen, much less be repeated. But they do and are, season after season, and have grown so common as to cease to attract particular attention. That they would be possible anywhere else, now that the days of Baltimore plug-uglyism are over, I have not the remotest idea. New-York is the great centre of disorder and lawlessness, and her roughs the protected powers in her community.

The rough is not a regular or professional thief; nor does he generally consort with thieves. His chief affinities are bar-keepers, prize-fighters, harlots and ward politicians. He steals only when occasion requires, and commits crime when his ordinary means of revenue fail. He enjoys fighting when he is confident of victory, and relishes the beating of an inoffensive and unmuscular citizen as he does his morning cocktail. He is a trained and practised bruiser, and his youthful memories are of battles with boys for a drink of whisky. He knows all about "the ring" and its champions, and *Bell's Life* has for him all the charm of a romance. But for the accounts of prize-fights, it is doubtful if he would ever have learned to read; but, with such perpetual promise of pleasure, he nerves himself to the task, and accomplishes it.

All forms of combat please him. He would have enjoyed the ancient gladiatorial exhibitions like a true Roman, and would find as much happiness in a bullfight as a born Spaniard. Cock and rat pits are his delight, and the fistic ropes the summit of his ambition. A severe, bloody dog-fight, where one savage brute literally chews the other to pieces, fills him with enthusiasm; and that there are no battles to the death with bowie-knives, he considers the broadest mark of the degeneracy of the times.

No marvel he gloats over those inspiring accounts and cuts of the *Police Gazette*, wherein Lindley Murray is butchered in colder blood than the victims of burglars and midnight marauders. What pleasant dreams must be his, (does he ever dream?) and how sweet his reflections in tranquil hours!

An undetermined status is that of the rough; for

he is emphatically the creature of circumstance, so far as his degree of evil and crime is concerned. If fortune be kind, and courtesans liberal, he may never be more than an amateur thief, an enthusiastic bruiser, or member of the City Council. But if fate and women frown, he will become a professional burglar and a murderer, and, unless the gallows interfere, end his days among the Aldermen or in Sing-Sing. The sole objection he has to the greater crimes is, that they expose him to punishment, and sometimes compel him to quit New-York, which he ever cleaves to, knowing that nowhere else in the World is there such security for villains of the deepest dye. Municipal office is the half-way house between the rum-shop and the prison; and, if the rough can lodge there, he is plucked from dangerous precipices. Once chosen a servant of the people, or plunderer of the treasury, which is the synonym in New-York, his avarice is so aroused that he becomes conservative. The love of money clashes with the love of other evil, and his greed waxes so rapacious that prize-fights and petticoat-pensioning are gradually neglected.

All our roughs are eligible to municipal office by reason of peculiar training and moral character; and yet most of them miss their political destiny, and strike their penal one—or would if they got their deserts.

Strange, how few of our roughs, who are among the rarest scoundrels under the sun, are brought to justice! They lead the most infamous lives, and die quietly in their beds, and have obituaries written about them as "old and esteemed citizens." With age they grow cautious, even timid, and, instead of knocking down unsophisticated gentlemen from the country, at unseemly hours of the morning, they thrust their hands into the City exchequer, and are envied and applauded for their skill in stealing.

Hundreds of outrages are committed daily in this City, by notorious roughs; and yet the arrests are so very few as scarcely to deserve mention. True, the papers say the offenders are "known to the police;" and that may be the reason they are not disturbed in their career of iniquity.

Men are robbed in broad daylight; women are violated in the street cars; stores and dwellings are set on fire; houses are entered by burglars; corpses are thrown into the river; mysteriously murdered persons are sent to the Morgue. The roughs are the authors of those misdeeds, and are likely to be for years to come, without serious hindrance. Occasionally, for the sake of effect, one of them, like Brierly or Jerry O'Brien, is hanged, and the journals contain ghastly elaborate accounts of his execution. But others, even more guilty, are permitted to escape, and the saturnalia of crime go on unchecked.

No New-Yorker who goes his accustomed rounds, who frequents Broadway and the Avenue, the business and fashionable haunts, has any conception of the volcanic elements of vice that are smouldering in unvisited and unseen places.

The great, fierce beast pursues and finds his prey night after night; and yet he slays so silently that few are aware of his dangerous presence. But in that dreary garret, in that noisome cellar, in that gilded lazar-house, the beast lies, half serpent, half tiger, coiled, crouching, ready for the deadly spring. Go you there, and you will start before the cruel glitter of his eyes, and the savage growl that seems to tear mercy to pieces. But you need have no new cause of alarm. He has been there for years, as fierce, as hungry, as potent as ever. He is constantly unsheathing his claws, and striking his victim, but noiselessly as death. Only at long intervals does he dare to emerge into the open day, and roar defiance to the general peace and public security. Until we kill him outright, until the Metropolis is purified, he may awake us at midnight with his mingled hiss and roar, and strike and strangle us in the arms of Love, and on the very breast of Peace.

CHAPTER VII.

BLACKWELL'S ISLAND.

Thousands of people who live in New York have never seen Blackwell's Island; and quite as many, I venture to assert, cannot tell where it is. They hear it mentioned day after day; they know it is devoted to penal institutions, and somewhere in the vicinity of the Metropolis. But whether it is in the Sound, or East or North river, or in the Bay, they are wholly ignorant.

Time and again I have heard my fellow-passengers, residents of this city, inquire, while steaming to Providence or Boston through the East river, "What place is that?" as they passed the pleasant-looking spot. And they were much surprised when informed that it was the notorious Blackwell's island.

To the poor loafers, vagrants, and small rogues of the Metropolis, the Island, as it is called by way of distinction, is better known. They have learned its exact location and peculiarities by sad experience; and they are continually refreshing their memories by repeated incarcerations. I say the poor loafers and small rogues, for the prosperous and great ones are clad in purple and fine linen, instead of striped uniforms, and go to Long Branch and Europe instead of Blackwell's island.

Men not one-tenth as guilty as the dwellers amid

Fifth-Avenue luxury or Grammercy-Park splendors have passed half their lives on the island, at Sing Sing, and Auburn; and the wealthy and superior scoundrels have wondered meanwhile at the depravity of the poor.

A BLACKWELL'S ISLANDER.

The island, the lower end of which is opposite Sixty-first street in the East river, is one of the pleasantest spots, to the outward eye, in the vicinity of the Metropolis. During seven or eight months of the year it is as green, and cool, and picturesque a place as one could desire to linger in. The skies are so fair and spotless; the air is so soft and fresh; the water so smooth and clear around it, that it appears quite the ideal of a Summer resort. Few pass it on steamers without admiring it, and declaring what a charming abode those villains have; forgetting their own, perhaps, greater sins, and that the crime of the villains is only misfortune by another name.

The early history of the island is involved in mystery and tradition. It was a favorite pleasure ground with the Indians, it is said, and the early Dutch settlers celebrated their festal days there with a simplicity characteristic of their fatherland. In 1823 it passed into the hands of James Blackwell, an Englishman, who occupied it with his family as a farm for a number of years, and from whom it received its present name. About thirty-five years ago it was purchased by the City, and has since been employed as a prison for the violators of municipal ordinances.

The buildings are of gray granite, with a few frame

outhouses, well constructed, spacious, airy, and as comfortable as such places can be. They seem decidedly desirable at a distance, vastly preferable to the over-crowded tenement houses of the Fourth, Sixth, and Eighteenth wards, and induce one to believe that therein mercy tempers justice. But prisons are never handsome to persons confined in them; and he who imagines the island attractive can have his illusion dispelled by a short confinement.

The buildings are the hospital, workhouse, lunatic asylum, almshouse, and penitentiary. The indigent and the criminal have different quarters, but are treated in much the same manner. There is a species of worldly justice in this; for poverty is the only crime society cannot forgive.

The men and women are kept apart in all the buildings, though they contrive to elude vigilance and get together often, as is shown by the fact that children are born there whose mothers have been on the island for more than a year.

The paupers, and criminals, and lunatics vary in number from three to five thousand all told; and they increase every year, so that some of the departments are greatly crowded and unhealthy in consequence. The care of the paupers and criminals is as good as could be expected; but it is anything but what it ought to be; and flagrant acts of injustice, oppression, and even cruelty are not uncommon.

It is usual, in writing about superintendents, overseers, wardens, and turnkeys of charitable and penal institutions, to speak of them as humane and sympathetic, which they very rarely are. I have seen a good deal of this class, and I have often found them hard, unfeeling and tyrannical, and not unfrequently brutal and cruel to the last degree. Their position is not calculated to develop the sensibilities or refine the sentiments, and they do not enter upon their duties with any surplus of charity or tenderness. To expect the cardinal virtues of them is unreasonable. If they were fine or gentle natures, they would not be there; for saints do not gravitate to the custodianship of prisons and poor-houses, any more than vestals do to stews.

I seldom see men or women in such a place, particularly the former, without an instinctive shrinking from them. Their faces, their manner, their voices betray them generally for what they are. I cannot but pity the unfortunate committed to their keeping, subjected to their power.

The attachés of Blackwell's island are not exceptions. I have read their praises in the papers, from the pens of partial reporters; but those praises were for the most part either the blunders of ignorance or the result of premeditated misrepresentation.

The hospital is a stone building, 400 by 50 feet, and usually contains 200 to 400 patients suffering from every form of disease. They are fairly cared for; their beds clean; their diet wholesome, and medical attention good. They are ranged on little iron bedsteads in long rows, and are melancholy-looking enough; for little intelligence or moral culture illumines their pale and wasted faces.

The mortality among them is large, because they have abused themselves or been abused sadly by severity of circumstance. Many of them have been drunkards and outcasts from their birth; others have inherited broken constitutions and ancestral disease; and all have come into being out of parallel with nature—organization and destiny against them.

Death can have few terrors for them (it is always less fearful when near than at a distance); and I do not marvel they breathe their last with perfect resignation, or that they pass out of life cursing all that has been and is to come.

Sickness is ever painful. But sickness there, without hope, without means, without sympathy, without future, without friends, must be agony unrelieved.

Their logic must be this: What have they to dread from change? What other sphere can be worse than this to them? If God be powerful, He must gradually lift their burthens. If He be good, He will not punish them; for they have already suffered beyond their sin. And if He be not, then they will not be either. What then have they to fear?

The workhouse much resembles the other buildings. It is gray, granite, grim. Its inmates vary from 600 to 800, fully half of whom are women; though females would be the fitter word, inasmuch as woman suggests gentleness, tenderness, and lovableness,—qualities in which the island is deplorably deficient.

Persons are sent there for minor offenses, such as drunkenness, disorderly conduct, carrying concealed weapons, vagrancy, and the like. Very few of the inmates that have not been there again and again. They are sentenced for 30, 60, or 90 days, and at the end of this term they are discharged only to be brought back for a similar offense before the week is fairly gone.

A number of the men are employed at trades. They make clothes, or shoes or brooms; but most of them are engaged in quarrying or farming upon the island. They assist in repairing the different structures and raise vegetables for home consumption.

The women make hoop-skirts and braid straw; do the necessary cleaning, and wash and iron for the other prisoners and paupers. Many seem quite contented, and are very different creatures from what they are when intoxicated; intoxication usually being the cause of their commitment. Some of the men and women have been sent to the island 30, 40, even 50 times, and are doomed to die there. They have no restraining, no reforming influences; and they return to their old ways and habits by the same law that impels the tides of the sea.

The almshouse includes forty acres, almost a third of the entire island, and has 800 to 1,000 inhabitants; the men generally being in the majority. Both sexes are worthless creatures, and their surroundings remind one of the perpetual palaver of Mrs. Gummidge, whose constant apprehension was, that she would be "sent to the House." Their advanced age is particularly noticeable, and you wonder how such poverty and distress can have sustained life so long. They are with rare exceptions extremely ignorant; have been born to the fate they follow; have always had for familiar companions stupidity, squalor and sin.

Nineteen-twentieths of them are foreigners, the Irish being the most largely represented. And at least half of them came paupers to our shores. Not a few, however, were once industrious and honest, and have been prevented from earning a livelihood by loss of health or some accident that has maimed them.

The baby department attached to the alms-house has

usually about 200 little children who have either been taken there with their mothers, or found without parents. They are generally from a few months to two or three years old, and are great favorites with and pets of the aged, and even the younger women. Such is the maternal instinct of the sex that no deprivation, nor suffering, nor adversity, nor degradation can suppress it wholly.

Ill-natured stories are afloat that some of the infants are, strictly speaking, home productions; but those who are acquainted with the purity and continence of the attachés will not be slow to pronounce such stories vile slanders.

The penitentiary is an enormous building, and contains at present about 600 inmates—all masculine. They are employed very much as their companions in the workhouse, though they are more closely watched, and the discipline is more severe. They rise at 6 in the morning, and after breakfast, they begin their tasks and labor until nearly 6 in the evening. When they have taken their not very savory supper, they are locked up in their cells over night. They are attired in striped uniforms, and for refractory conduct they are put on bread and water diet and confined in dark dungeons. Most of the criminals are ruffians and thieves who have been committed for serious assaults, stabbing, shooting and stealing. They are a hopeless and graceless set, the greater part at least, and are usually fitted there for the higher honors of Sing-Sing.

Very many of them are quite young, and the generality in good health and of excellent physique. But their faces, especially their eyes, indicate their character, and strengthen faith in the truth of physiognomy.

You can see now and then, a strange mixture of cunning and boldness, of restlessness and desperation in their repulsive countenances, and you feel those men are capable of any crime under temptation or opportunity.

A strange, sad place is Blackwell's island. After going there you are relieved when you return on the ferry and feel the breeze from the sea blowing through your hair as if to purify you from the unwholesome atmosphere you have just breathed. You look back at the island, and all its beauty is gone. Never again does it seem picturesque; for you see through its outside down to its black and cankered heart.

CHAPTER VIII.

THE FIRST OF MAY.

The first of May, generally associated in this country with all the sweetness, and beauty, and gladness of spring, is in New York associated only with change of residence, and the countless vexations and disagreeablenesses of moving.

Elsewhere, children hail the day with delight, and mature persons look back to it with pleasure as a coronation of youth and a celebration of the heart. Here, we consider ourselves merely May Day's victims, despoiled of the flowers, and deem the occasion so ungrateful, that we expel it from the memory as far as possible, until its unavoidable return forces itself upon our attention.

Of all the days of the year, the first of May is the most hateful in the Metropolis. This City will never be quite happy until that date is either obliterated from the calendar, or the custom that deforms it be abolished. While the country goes Maying with floral chaplets and winged steps, and airy laughter, the Metropolis turns itself upside down; exchanges houses; is disheveled and disgusted, for at least a week of the month of beauty and of blossoms.

By what malignant and mysterious agency the custom of moving on the first of May was ever established in this unfortunate city, has never been accurately ascertained. It is supposed, however, to have originated, as did many other things, good and evil, with the early Dutch settlers here, who must have borrowed it from Satan or the demon of discord, for the especial affliction of unregenerate mankind. That such an inconvenient, unreasonable and expensive habit should have been continued to this day,· in the face of perpetual complaint and annual protest, is singular enough, and can only be regarded as one of the phenomena of life in Manhattan. The constant advance, however, in real estate and house-rents on this Island for five-and-twenty, particularly the last ten years, has had much to do with the perpetuation of the annoyance in all probability. Tenants have been unwilling to take a house, whose rent they deem exorbitant, and which, they are convinced, must be lower the subsequent year—for a longer period than a twelve-month. Every May they discover their mistake; but hope springs immortal in the human breast of house-renters, and every May they repeat their blunder, under the delusion that prices must sometime be reasonable, and that landlords must have consciences. When rents do fall, if that metropolitan milennium should ever be, then tenants will expect a continuous decline, and will be unwilling to occupy their dwellings beyond a single year. So until the end of this generation at least, New York is likely to be annually cursed with its May moving.

If Othello had lived in Gotham his reference to
—"moving accidents by flood and field
would have been more significant and impressive than it possibly could be in the romantic city by the sounding sea.

*   *   *   *   *   *

A privileged class, if not one absolutely blessed, is that which owns its houses. But, in New-York, to own a house is, to a man of ordinary means or ordinary prospects, much like the possession of Alladdin's palace. Few can hope for it; fewer still can realize that comfortable dream.

A good, convenient dwelling, with modern improvements, is worth a small fortune on this Island. Few can be had less than $20,000, and from that the price rises to the region of financial fable. Nineteen-twentieths of the people here might therefore as rationally expect to have Stewart's income, or be genuine heirs of Aneke Jans, as to find themselves holders in fee-simple of a private dwelling in any "respectable" quarter of the town.

The owner of a home anywhere within a radius of twenty-five miles of the City Hall is to be, and is, deeply and excusably envied, less perhaps for his material means than for the ever-present consolation which must be his, that he is not compelled to move on the first of May. That is one of the dearest and sweetest privileges of wealth near the confluence of the East and North rivers; and they who do not deem it such cannot long have dwelt in this American Bable.

During the three months between what is known here as quarter-day—Feb. 1—and moving time, I have seen amiable and self-disciplined persons, engaged in house-hunting, look sullen and angry as they passed the stately mansions of the prosperous,—wondering, no doubt, and indignant, that unequal Fortune had permitted those to live in New-York without exacting the usual penalty. "If I only had a house," is the burthen of a Gothamite's prayer, "that I could call mine, Wall street might fluctuate, and the World come to an end as soon as it pleases."

It must not be supposed that all prosperous citizens of New York own houses; for it is quite the contrary. Many whose incomes are as great as fifty and a hundred thousand dollars, rent and submit to the periodical nuisance of moving. Why they do this, is among the enigmas of humanity, since common sense and reason are against it. But they do: they often rent furnished dwellings at so extravagant a rate that they pay, every two or three years, a sufficient extra sum to buy their own furniture. Economy is not a virtue of the Metropolis, and thousands of its denizens live as if their chief purpose were to see how much money they could needlessly squander.

As a consequence, May moving is miscellaneous and democratic, confined to no class, restricted to no quarter. The whole island moves, from the Battery to Harlem, from Hanover square to Carmansville. On the first of that month, the Metropolis plays a colossal game of what children call "Pussy-wants-the-corner"; and the poor pussy who is left out after that day is compelled to move from town or into a hotel, until another opportunity is offered.

For two months, especially for a few weeks previous to the appalling first, New-York is searched for houses. Brooklyn, Jersey City, Weehawken, Hoboken, Hudson City, and all the suburbs for miles around, are explored by anxious and restless renters. Women, having more leisure, more patience, and more energy often, are generally the Iphigenias on whom house-hunting falls.

Poor creatures, their days and weeks, and no small part of their lives, are consumed in the endless seeking. They rise early and retire late. They visit real-estate agencies every hour. They pore over advertisements. They have visions of houses by day. They dream of houses by night. They walk, talk, eat, sleep and wake with houses. Houses, houses everywhere, and not a house to rent.

"Is it not pitiful,
In a whole city full,"

that shelter can not be had for love or money,— at least for any sum they can command?

Nearer and nearer comes the dreaded day, and no roof for the family long notified to vacate. What can its members do? What will they? Where shall they go? Time waits for no man. Houses present themselves for no woman. Each April our citizens and the newspapers declare a large number of New-Yorkers will have to go into the street, sleep in the parks, or move to the Catskills. But they do not somehow, and hence an increased faith in an overruling Providence.

"Everything will be got along with," is a colloquial consolation that all experience of life confirms. When the pressure or strain is too great, Nature yields, and a space is made in the World by another grave. Come weal or woe, tragedy or comedy, birth or death, our Common Mother regards it not. It is all the same to her. She looks calmly, unchangingly on, whether her children weep or smile, love or hate, rejoice or despair.

For weeks before the first every sort of vehicle capable of carrying furniture or household goods is engaged to move the unlucky wights of the Metropolis. That day is the carmen's harvest, and they profit by it by advancing their rates to a point to which nothing but necessity would submit.

People often begin for days before, and continue for days after, the first to transfer their goods and chattels to each other's houses. Jones moves into Brown's house, and Brown into Jones', and both are dissatisfied. Smith and Robinson exchange dwellings, and anathematize landlords and wonder what they were foolish enough to do so for. They vow they never will be guilty of such an absurdity again, and they are not—until next year.

Go into any street and you will find cars before most of the houses, where carmen and servants are quarreling in choice Celtic about the proper quantity of a load, or the careless manner of arranging furniture, while the mistress of the household stands on the stoop, or in the window, looking soiled and frowsy, anxiety in her face and a dust-cloth in her hand.

Windows and doors are open all along the block; tables, carpets, chairs, bedsteads, pier-glasses, pictures, are standing in the halls, on the steps, on the sidewalks, waiting for the next load. The houses have a generally dismantled, deserted, forlorn appearance, that is melancholy and oppressive. Domestics are visible taking down curtains, or rolling up carpets; while the feminine members of the household direct, and often lend a helping hand.

In the tenement quarters, the process of moving is conducted more speedily, because less carefully and methodically, and the poor have slender appliances either for happiness or comfort. Here, all is confusion. The carmen swear, and the movers reply in kind, and not infrequently a miscellaneous fight arises, in which most of the furniture is broken by its conversion into weapons, offensive and defensive. The corner grocery is periodically visited, and the stimulants used to assist in the task of moving not seldom prevent the need of moving, and necessitate the services of the surgeon and apothecary.

How poor and suffering humanity swarms in those tenement-houses! One sees dozens of families dripping darkly out of dwellings into which he would not suppose so many could possibly crowd. No wonder they want to go out of those unwholesome places. But they are going into others equally unwholesome. They pass from dirt to dirt, from poison to poison, from disease to disease, until at last Death, like a good angel, takes them away, and hides them forever in the garden of God.

The *genius loci* is evidently not the genius of America. We descendants and mixtures of Saxons and Normans, like the Romans described by Livy, carry our fortunes and destinies with us. We have no attachment to place. To us, locality has no interest or sacredness.

In this City, where all life is intensified, perhaps there is a fitness in this annual vacation of abode,— representing in excess the American restlessness and fondness for change. The blood of the old Norse sea-kings that is in our veins, makes the broad World our home, all lands and scenes our highways and pasture-fields.

Yet is there something sad in this cleaving to nothing, this tearing up of the heart, so to speak, before it

SHOE LATCHETS!

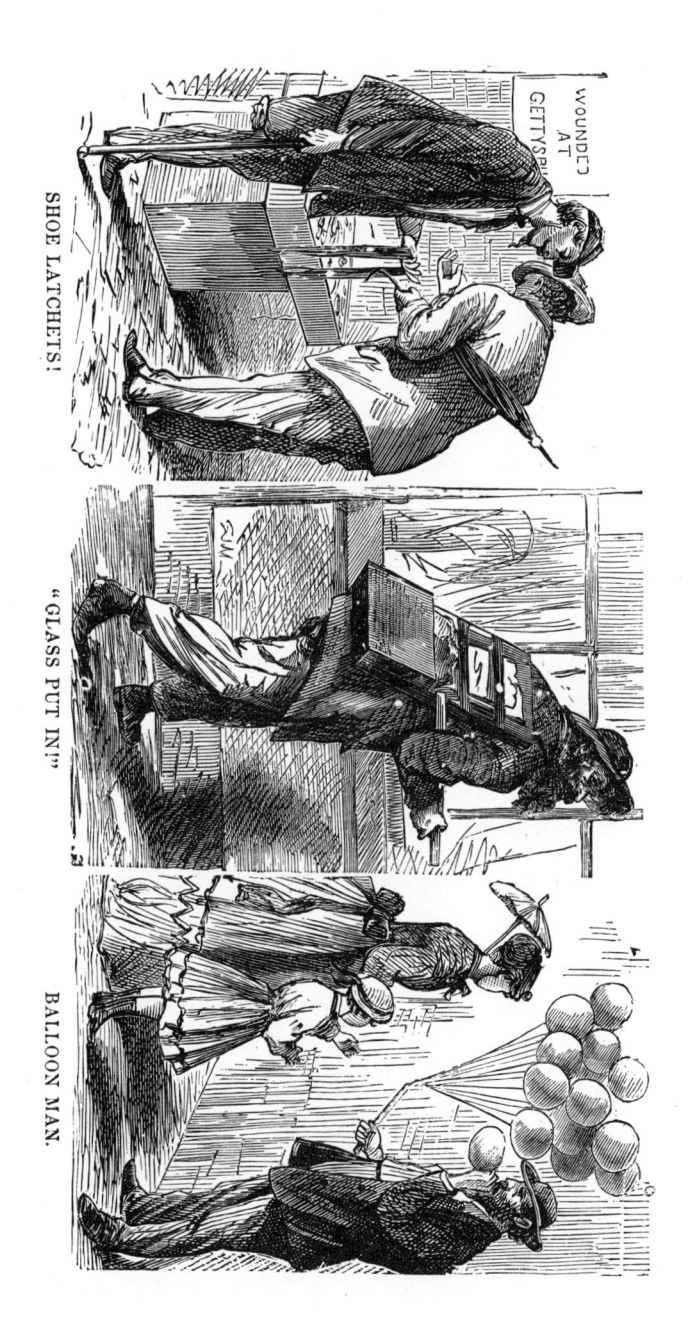

"GLASS PUT IN!"

BALLOON MAN.

The First of May.

has taken root anywhere. Every place must have associations; every dwelling its experiences and memories, often sweet, oftener bitter, yet seeming sacred through the light and darkness of gathered years.

In this moving from the spot we have called even for a year our home, where, perchance, the loved have died, or more painful still, love itself has perished; where the heart has throbbed with new joys, and the eyes been blinded with old griefs, there is a sorrow that cannot be all repressed. And when we pass the familiar house, now filled with strangers, it is not strange a vision of the past gleams like the light out of the windows, and makes us too sad for tears.

CHAPTER IX.

STREET-VENDERS.

THE wag who informed the rustic inquisitor about the object of his visit to the Metropolis that, if he liked the City, he intended to buy it, might well have been serious. He could easily have purchased the whole island and all it contained, if he had only had money enough.

The first impression one gets of cities, but particularly of New York, is, that everything in them is for sale. All the persons you meet seem bent on bargaining. All signs, all faces, all advertisements, all voices, all outward aspects of things, urge you to buy. The old woman in cheap and faded raiment, who spreads her gewgaws at the corner, is no more in the market than her smugly-dressed sister who rolls by in a carriage, with her daughter at her

UMBRELLAS!

side. "Pay me my price," says every vender, "and you shall have my wares, whether they be happiness or houses, love or locomotives, wives or wallets."

One would think the miles and miles of stores and shops of every kind would preclude the need or possibility of street-venders in the Metropolis. But those commercial skirmishers whose mart is the sidewalk, and who cover their heads with the sky, increase in numbers every month. They are the Bohemians of trade, the Bedouins of traffic. Like Æneas after the downfall of Troy, they carry their fates with them. All they ask of Fortune is clear weather and a crowded thoroughfare. They do not advertise, nor manage, nor manœuvre. They plant themselves on their instincts, according to Emerson's counsel, and the World comes round to them every twenty-four hours. No one would imagine the hundreds of street-venders could live here, and it is a perpetual marvel how they do. Many of them rarely seem to sell anything; and yet the fact of their remaining in their calling proves that it is remunerative.

The Broadway venders are the most noticeable and numerous. The curb-stone merchants and lamp-post dealers border the great thoroughfare from Morris street to Thirtieth, where the throng lessens into a line. Their wares are light, such as they can pack up at the earliest rain-fall, and retire with into unseen haunts. Their stock is perishable, and the native elements are its enemies.

Among the most conspicuous are the news dealers, who have all the daily and weekly journals published in the City that are supposed to have any general interest. Newspapers are an American necessity. A true American can dispense with his breakfast and dinner, or regular sleep, but not with his newspaper. If he go to business without having read the morning journal, he feels at a loss. Conscious of being behind his fellows, he avoids them until he can get into a corner and devour the main features of the news. Then he is armed with the latest intelligence; has his opinions, his prejudices, his sympathies; is prepared for the strife of the day.

The news-dealer knows how to arrange his supplies. A single glance takes in the contents of his stand. The more flashy his literature, the greater its display. The regular issues—*Herald*, *Tribune*, *Times*, *World*, *Sun*, and the rest—are folded modestly in a corner; so are the *Nation*, *Round-Table*, *Independent*, *Ledger*, *Harpers' Frank Leslie's*, and the better class of weeklies. But the *Days' Doings*, *Clipper*, *Sunday News*, *Mercury* and *Police Gazette* are flamingly arrayed, with their sensational contents cunningly revealed.

As the human tide descends, the heaps of papers rapidly diminish. There is no conversation between buyer and seller. The money is laid down, the journal taken up, and the change given, without a word. You might tell from the appearance of the purchaser what paper he wanted. This is a *Herald*, this a *Tribune*, that a *World* reader. You can see each one's particular need in his face. That affected person, with a slightly finical air, wishes the *Home Journal* of course. That crimson, sensual face is searching for the *Day's Doings* and its cheap sensations. This low brow and hard, cruel eye are in quest of the *Clipper*. This neatly-dressed, jockey-looking individual, seizes on the *Spirit of the Times;* and that dull, heavy fellow will have nothing but the *Police Gazette* and its hideous array of revolting crimes.

Flower merchants, usually girls and women, are the neighbors of all the hotels seven or eight months in the year. Their bouquets are pretty and cheap, but ill-arranged; and that they sell so many shows a love of the poetic and beautiful which money-getting cannot suppress. No city in the World has so many flower-buyers as New-York. Half Broadway wears them in its button-hole, and the other half gets them to illustrate the relation between women and flowers; for men who purchase often, purchase for a feminine market, you may be sure.

Here is the new-made husband. Every afternoon he carries a bouquet to his young wife, whose heart is in her ear while she waits for his coming. But it will not last long. When the honeymoon is over,—and it is sadly brief in most cases,—no more flowers, no more watching eyes, no more bounding hearts.

Here is the husband of ten years, the father of a little family. He buys flowers still, and for one he loves, but not his spouse. Passion, not sympathy, united him and his wife. Passion sated, the bond was severed, and a new affinity was found. The wife sleeps soundly while he lies in a rival's arms. She suffers not from jealousy or neglect; for she also is cured, and smiles at disloyalty which may one day be hers as well.

If we could trace the course of the flowers, it would be interesting. They go to sweet faces and soft bowers, are kissed by warm lips, and breathed upon by balmy breaths. They stand to many women for the love they feel, and which prompted their giving. They are treasured while they last, and regretfully thrown away. They are talked to in the silence of the night, and told dear secrets their bestowers do not share. The history of flowers is the history of hearts. Beautiful in their freshness and blossoming, they wither all too soon, and when withered are forgotten and thrust aside.

The flower-merchants are no more like their wares than musicians are like music. They see no special beauty in the blossoms. Neither color nor fragrance appeals to them. The flowers represent food and shelter only. The hard necessities of life leave no space for the culture of the ideal.

The toy-sellers are objects alike of contempt and wonder. There they stand, stalwart, healthy men, all the day long, blowing whistles or trumpets, handling scarlet balloons, jerking wooden figures, spinning tops on plates, twirling paper wheels, and crying in a deep, guttural tone, "All alive, all alive; only ten cents; beautiful invention; who would be without one?" They must know New-Yorkers to be the children that they are. How otherwise could they expect to sell such gimcracks to adults? The crowd sweeps up and sweeps down. No one seems to heed the peddlers of trifles, much less to buy. And yet they must have customers; for they are there to-morrow, and next week, and next year, neither emaciated, nor despondent, nor doubtful of their dignity.

It is marvelous they can rest content with such a life. They do not blush, nor stammer, nor apologize. They look boldly at the open day, and bellow like giants over their baubles. One would think it harder than cracking stone on the highway, drearier than confinement on Blackwell's island, darker than the shadow of the Morgue. But perhaps it is their place in the World. Some men are born to shape events, and others to sell toys.

Dog and bird-fanciers are common in Broadway and elsewhere. They are foreigners usually, as are most of the street-venders, and have a patient, stolid and unexpectant look. They ask no one to purchase; but they stand in the sunshine, with puppies in their arms, and cages in their hands, as if trusting to the instincts of the dumb creatures for appeal. I have seen kind-hearted men glance at the gentle eyes of the dogs and the hard faces of their keepers, and buy out of sympathy and pity. The birds appear happier than their holders. They flit about and sing, and yet seem grateful when they are sold, as southern slaves were wont to do when they passed from the ownership of a hard master.

Women are usually the customers of that class. They are always wanting pets, and they will get them with money if they come not of themselves. The feathered bipeds are quicker of sale than the stouter quadrupeds, and often exchange the open street for dingy rooms and upper attics, where they forget their song and perish from neglect.

The Chinese, who deal in candy and cigars, are conspicuous among the street-venders. They have a strangely lonely, forlorn, dejected air. They rarely smile. They are the embodiments of painful resignation, and the types of a civilization that never moves. Their dark, hopeless eyes, their sad faces, high cheek-bones, square, protuberant foreheads, remind you of melancholy visages cut in stone. They sell cheaply, and their profit is in pennies. They live by what an American would starve upon; for they are the most saving and economical of their kind. The closest Germans are spendthrifts to them. They have no care for comforts, or cleanliness even. They occupy garrets or cellars in Park or Baxter streets, and dawdle their way through meanness, and filth, and isolation, to an unbought grave.

Miscellaneous wares, such as cravats, suspenders, tobacco, nuts, fruits, cheap jewelry, are disposed of by the peripatetic school. Its members have no stand. They roam up and down Broadway, and, with an instinct of physiognomy, detect the appetites and requirements of passers-by. Men, women and children lead that life. There are scores of them; and they all subsist somehow, though their entire stock, sold at the maximum rate, would not pay for a day's board at a Broadway hotel. They are satisfied with their slender gains, apparently. They look calm and contented, compared to the prosperous ones who hurry anxiously and nervously along. They adapt themselves to their conditions, and, expecting little, get it, and are not disappointed.

The old-clothes hawkers do not frequent the better portions of the town. They go where their cast-off garments will find a sale. They carry sacks, and cry in an unintelligible way their second and third-hand wares. They are ever ready for a trade. They will exchange an old hat for a broken pair of boots, a one-armed coat for threadbare pantaloons, and see a bargain where there are merely rags. Whether they have hats, or shoes, or gowns, or bonnets, for they vend the

CHINESE CANDY DEALER.

attire of both sexes, they announce their goods in the same tone, and in the same unintelligible syllables.

Who are their customers? Thompson, Greene, Mulberry, James and Cherry streets, much of the Fourth and Sixth wards, part of the Eighteenth, Mackerelville, Corlear's Hook,—three-quarters, perhaps, of the whole Metropolis.

Park Row and the Bowery are favorite localities for street-venders of the cheapest sort. They offer every kind of low-priced article, from a dog-eared volume to a decayed peanut. They furnish impromptu dinners and breakfasts for a shilling; prepare oyster-stews while you take out your pocket-book, and bake waffles while you determine the time of day. They dispose of frozen custards and sour milk, sweetened, for ice-cream; soda-water without gas; lemonade without lemons; songs without sentiment; jokes without point; cigars innocent of tobacco, and all manner of shams, making sales profitable by niggardliness.

Indeed, those quarters are the best adapted for street-venders, who in Broadway rarely find purchasers except among strangers and the transient class that believe they must buy something when they come to the Babel of Manhattan.

CHAPTER X.

THE FERRIES.

ABOUT twenty-five ferries connect New York with its surrounding cities and towns, which are divisions of the Metropolis as much as Harlem, Yorkville, or Carmansville. Nearly half a million of people whom Manhattan holds, and makes life and fortune for, dwell within a radius of five miles from Printing House Square as a center. The fifteen or sixteen towns clustering along the Bay and around the North and East rivers, are merely the human overflow of New York's inundation.

Brooklyn, never thought of here, apart from the Metropolis, has a population of 300,000, and is the third city in the United States. Jersey City, Hoboken, Hudson City, Bergen, are good-sized towns; but they have no distinct existence. They are absorbed by the great Centripetal power of Gotham.

Of the ferries nine are to Brooklyn, from Catharine Slip, foot of Fulton, Wall, Jackson, Whitehall, New Chambers, Roosevelt, East Houston and Grand streets; two to Hoboken, foot of Barclay and Christopher streets; two to Jersey City, foot of Courtlandt and Desbrasses streets; two to Hunter's Point, from James slip and foot of East Thirty-fourth street; two to Staten Island, foot of Whitehall and Dey streets; two to Green Point, foot of East Tenth and East Twenty-third streets; Hamilton avenue ferry, foot of Whitehall street; Bull's Ferry and Fort Lee, pier 51 North river; Mott Haven, pier 24 East river; Pavonia, foot of Chambers street, and Weehawken, foot of West Forty-second street.

The most crowded are the Fulton, Wall and South ferries to Brooklyn, and the Courtlandt street to Jersey-City; though all of them do a very profitable business, and consider their privilege, or right, better than exclusive ownership in a mine of gold. They do not say so openly; for all corporations that make large sums of money put forward the assumption of benefiting the public for a very small consideration.

It is singular how disinterested monopolies are. Instead of confessing that they have no souls, they declare they are all soul. They are the embodiment of generosity, chivalry, self-sacrifice. Their controllers exist only for the people. They suffer to serve the masses. They shed tears of blood when the dear public is not pleased with their magnanimous labors. They sympathize with it, with full stomachs and fuller purses.

Half a million of people living outside of, and most of them doing or having business in, New-York, make the ferries the sole means of communication with the island. It is not difficult to perceive that the different companies must realize handsomely from their investments. It is calculated that 250,000 to 300,000 persons come and go upon the ferries every 24 hours, and that they make a clear profit of about $1,000,000 per annum.

The fare to Brooklyn is two cents; to Jersey-City, Hoboken and Weehawken, three; to Staten-Island, ten and twelve cents; and to other points, in proportion to distance. The rate is low, but the aggregate receipts swell to tempting sums in the course of a season.

About 4 o'clock the ferries begin their regular trips, though some of them, as the Fulton and Courtlandt and Barclay streets, run all night, and their passengers increase until 9 or 10 o'clock in the morning. Then they fall off until 3, or 4, or 5 in the afternoon, when the refluent tide sets in.

People generally rise according to their necessities. The poorer the man the earlier he gets up. To lie in bed is one of the privileges of wealth. The operator who saunters leisurely into Broad street at noon is believed to have been fortunate in his speculations, and can borrow money at a lower figure than if he became visible at 10. But the wight that hustles about Exchange place at 9 o'clock is regarded with distrust, and his broker calls in the loans made to him unhesitatingly the week before.

When the coming dawn drops her gray mantle over the mists of the rivers, the gardeners and farmers, from Long-Island and New-Jersey, drive their carts and wagons, loaded with fruits and vegetables and farm products, upon the ferries, and wend their way to Fulton, Washington, Catharine, Essex, Jefferson and Tompkins markets. Many of them are Germans, particularly the gardeners,—patient, thrifty, plodding, ever on the alert to catch the worm that creeps where pennies are to be gathered. They are accompanied by their wives, or mothers, or sisters, or daughters. Women from fatherland work side by side with the men, and look anxiously at the sky to see if the weather promises fair, for storms seriously affect sales, and therefore disturb the Teutonic heart. In two hours the ferries are freighted with market wares. Then they carry over a few belated venders, who look vexed and sour because of their own delay, and are inclined to vent their feelings upon others, while the odor of fruits and vegetables is blown away by the sea breeze.

Farmers and hucksters are succeeded by a throng of mechanics with their flannel and check shirts, with buckets and begrimed appearance—many of them going from their tenement-house homes in the Great City to the grim factories trembling and throbbing along the half-awakened rivers.

Occupation is healthful, but toil is unwholesome; and the daily hard tasks that cannot be lessened or deferred leave their marks upon those overworked men. They are not satisfied with their lot. Why should they be? Why should they be enslaved for a mere livelihood, for the privilege of continuing an existence they have neither the leisure nor the means to enjoy?

Six days in every week it is the same—ten hours of toil, engrossing and consuming toil, when they in no sense belong to themselves,—the dragging home of their tired bodies, heavy and often unrefreshing sleep, and the compulsory return to the hateful labor which yields them only bread. Even their wives and children are sources of anxiety as much as of comfort; for they can see no period, however remote, when freedom and ease will be theirs.

They are honest and industrious, and ought to be happy, no doubt. But I question if they are. I know I could not be, if I were they. They do not give the impression of supreme felicity, but rather of men who have duties to perform for others, and who would be glad when they could lie down and sleep forever.

Until 7 o'clock the stream to the factories in the great and small cities flows turbidly. Then it stops, and the shirts of passengers begin to whiten and raiment to improve.

The mechanics are followed by salesmen, accountants, clerks, most of whom are young and seem hopeful. Life is before them yet, and this World has not been shorn of its illusions. They have views of financial success, of partnership, of high reputation on 'Change, of princely incomes. They talk glibly of "our firm," its prospects, its trade, its profits, and deem themselves fortunate in their positions. They are learned in their vocation, and business is the spirit of their being.

Occasionally you observe among them an older and a wiser head. He is alert, but listens and looks, and smiles half sadly, half satirically. He once had ambitious expectations; fed himself on the sweet fruit of his own imagining, and wrought at the shadows until they seemed substance. His ambition was filled; his expectations deceived him.

At five and fifty he is a clerk still, with a large family, and $1,200 a year. A perpetual struggle his life has been, with little compensation in it. He has been told by clergymen, and journalists, and authors, since he could understand English, that honest industry is always ultimately rewarded. His reward is two sick children, an invalid wife and debts that torture him because he cannot discharge them. He has found that integrity brings curses more than blessings. He might have been wealthy but for devotion to principle. Successful merchants deem him a simpleton. He does not share their opinion; but he knows he is wretched.

When the expectant underlings have been transferred to the Babylon which is now rattling, and smoking, and steaming, and roaring, their superiors come upon the scene. They are rather grave, but they have a self-satisfied air, like men who have striven and won. They are middle-aged, mostly. They have incipient crow's-feet about their eyes, wrinkles at the corners of their mouth, flecks of grayness in their hair. They are confidential clerks, with salaries of five or six, perhaps ten thousand a year, in the great houses in Church street or West Broadway, or special partners or leading salesmen, with a percentage on profits. They are in comfortable circumstances. They have incomes independent of their positions. They can afford to think of others, and grinding poverty does not compel them to be mean. Externals appear well to them. They feel the sunshine, even if the heavens be overcast, and the air is sweet, though it comes from New-York.

The masters rarely flash upon the sphere before 11 or 12; but they tread almost on the heels of those only a little less than themselves. They are truly of the fortunate in the worldly sense. They are the senior members of the prosperous firms; the men who have much to get and little to do; who walk or ride over to their counting-room; superintend and give council for an hour or two; lunch at Delmonico's, and over a bottle of Chambertin, or Côté d'Or, discuss with their wealthy rivals the effect of the trade of

Japan upon the United-States. They should be contented and satisfied, at least in money matters. But they are not. They are more anxious to increase their fortune, though their present income is far beyond their largest expenditures, than they were when it was below a hundred thousand. They have physical ailments and domestic infelicities which they would get rid of at the price of all their 5.20s. When the gout twinges, and their brain reels with presaging apoplexy, they wonder why their riches can't preserve them from such attacks, and fancy they would surrender fortune for youth and health. But they would not. The loss of what they would never need would drive them half mad; for the masters are the slaves of Mammon and servants of self-interest.

If they poured out their secret sorrows, perhaps we would not exchange our poverty for their great gains. But we all have secret sorrows, and they are easier to bear with plethoric purses than empty ones; for, say what we may, the heart aches less on a satin sofa than on a pallet of straw. And Araminta's arms are fairer when luxuriously indolent and spanned with diamonds than when bared to the drudgery of the kitchen. And Amy's kisses sweeter from her poetry-pronouncing lips than if they were drawn down habitually from lowness of spirit and abject circumstance.

David Ducat, Sr., president of the Sapphire bank, and founder of the great importing house of Ducat, Doubloon & Co., is sorely distressed because David, Jr., is drinking himself to death, and his dearest daughter Julia *will* meet that profligate verse-maker clandestinely. But he need not be inconsolable. He has a family lot in Greenwood, and, if harm come to Julia, the scamp will marry her, for she is one of only three children. On the whole, things might be worse; and the credit of the house never stood better.

One tribe goes early to the ferries from this side, and lingers until the solid men have descended to the piers—the tribe of newsboys. They rush frantically down to the ferry-houses before the first arrow of light is shot across the sky, and fill the fresh morning with clamor about the *Times, Tribune, Herald, World* and *Sun.*

The first comers generally want the *"Staats Zeitung"* or *"Journal"* or *"Demokrat,"* though a number buy the *Sun;* some the *Herald* and *World.* The second-class have no eye for any other paper than the *Sun*, laud the quartos as the urchins may. But when the original sun flames up the east, and burns down upon the waters, the neglected large dailies grow into favor. Even the *Times* and *Tribune,* which were dull stock at first, find ready purchasers from well-dressed and thoughtful-looking men. One division of the newsboys keeps guard upon the boats, permitting no one to pass without yelling in his ears the news of the morning. Other divisions deploy as skirmishers, and dash through Brooklyn, Jersey-City, Hoboken, Astoria, Ravenswood, East New-York; board the morning trains; hurry into every nook and corner and lonely street of the surrounding towns and villages, and sell out before the leisurely part of the Metropolis has stirred in its bed.

The refluent wave rises about 3 P. M., and it washes and surges for four or five hours far more than the advancing swell of the morning. One would suppose, if he took his stand at the different ferry-houses, that

New-York was emptying itself before a devastating plague. Down Broadway to Wall and Fulton, to Whitehall and Courtlandt streets, sweeps the mob of home-seekers, reckless of vehicles, careless of each other, driven by one idea—that of reaching their destination in the shortest possible time.

In that rush all classes are mingled, lawyers and ladies, physicians and clergymen, merchants and beggars, pickpockets and philanthropists, authors and prize-fighters, bar-keepers and artists, courtesans and prudes, zealots and atheists, side by side, intertwisted, interlocked, brushing each other's garments, breathing each other's breaths. The ferries are black with people, and ultra professional reporters in the throng think what a magnificent sensation they might write out if the boats would blow up or sink suddenly.

Long before the vessel touches the pier boys and men measure the distance with their eyes, and leap off at serious risk to themselves. When the chain is thrown down half the masculine passengers are out of sight, and no one is hurt. We Americans are an agile and carefully calculating people, after all. If any other nation were as reckless as we, it would have distressing accidents by the dozen every day in the year. We seem to know what we can do, and do it. We are born to narrow escapes, but we rarely fail.

In the evening we have from over the river the amusement-goers, and later, their return; and the boats are full until 11 or 12 o'clock. At the latter hour the ferries stop generally, though, as I have said, the Fulton, Courtlandt and Barclay street boats run at stated intervals all night. The passengers are few after the nocturnal noon, and at the weird hours that

THE FERRIES.

precede the dawn the few who cross the rivers regard each other with suspicion. Journalists imagine exhausted printers from the same office to be highwaymen; and printers fancy the man whose "copy" they have set a thousand times a moon-struck fellow, waiting for a favorable moment to leap overboard.

The ferries furnish good studies of human nature. He who likes to read character, and trace personal history from outlines of suggestion may find occupation and interest on the rivers and the bay at all hours and all seasons. Every kind of people will sit before his mental pallet, and unconsciously resign themselves to his rambling brush.

FORT LAFAYETTE.—BURNED DEC. 1868.

CHAPTER XI.

GREENWOOD.

GREENWOOD is one of the first places strangers visit. New Yorkers are more indifferent about the famous cemetery, because, perhaps, they know they are certain to go there soon or late. They have reason to be proud of it, however; for it deserves its reputation, and is a charming place in which to sleep eternity away.

It is both poetic and philosophic to make pleasant the last resting-place; to rob death of its thousand nameless terrors and give it the appearance of an unbroken calm of the emancipated spirit,—the taking home to the bosom of Nature and her silent sympathy the souls that have been o'er wearied in the struggle with life.

Graveyards may be sad; but there is a sweetness in their sadness, and the deep suggestions of infinite rest, which the lightest heart, in the midst of its highest happiness, forever craves. There is balm for many wounds in the strolling among low mounds, and the listening to the airy voices that are ever whispering of peace.

A gay Gaul who made a visit to New York some years ago, thought it singular enough that the hackman he asked to drive to the pleasantest places in the vicinity should carry him to what he called the Père la Chaise of America. "Strange people, these Americans," he reflected; "they think death delightful."

The hackman's nature was deeper than the Frenchman's. The one was a worldling, the other a philosopher, and a man of taste as well; for Greenwood is, excepting the Park, the pleasantest place in the neighborhood of the Metropolis.

Just about a quarter of a century ago, Greenwood, containing over 500 acres of beautiful, rolling and varied land, was opened for burial purposes; and since then it has been steadily increasing in attractiveness and picturesqueness of effect. During that period, nearly 140,000 persons have been interred there, and many of the finest specimens of art which the country can show, have been erected as monuments to the memory of the dead. Vanity, the strongest passion of humanity, not only lives beyond, but rears itself in fantastic marble above, the tomb. Many of the monuments have cost from $10,000 to $100,000; and marble and truth have been tortured to transform the vices of the living into the virtues of the dead.

A ramble or a ride through Greenwood is delightful, especially in Spring, when the earth has put on its fresh greenness, and the flowers are in their first blossoming, or late in Autumn, when vegetation is dying in prismatic beauty, and the brown and crimson leaves are floating off to the calling of the sea. Its walks and drives, and lakes and groves, with the distant view of the Island City, the beautiful Bay, and the ocean stretching away into cloud and sky, form a panorama hardly equaled on the Continent.

No wonder it is a popular place of resort. No one sensible to beauty or the charms of Nature, can fail to experience a joy of vision as his eye sweeps for miles around, over land and river, over sound and sea; catches the far-off spires, the highlands of Staten Island, the Palisades of the Hudson, the forests of masts among which Manhattan is buried, and the countless water-craft steaming and sailing in every direction from the vast centre of commerce to every port and clime beneath the sun.

No other cemetery at home or abroad—and Europe boasts much of some of hers—has such advantages of position, such variety of prospect, such richness of ocular effect.

I am not surprised so many sentimentalists go to Greenwood to idealize Love, and Life, and Death, and seek the realization of all poetry in their own hearts. I rarely visit the place that I do not meet the loving and the loved wandering pensively and sympathetically through the pleasant walks, or sitting magnetically together, discoursing in low voices of the mystic thing which makes the World go round. The quietness and pensiveness of the place suggest the fiercely-tender passion, which is always sad, and render the heart dangerously susceptible to its mysterious promptings.

If you seek, good reader, the love of a fine woman, who has thus far been unwon, invite her to Greenwood, and, in the presence of the dead, and while the hand of Autumn is shaking down the variegated leaves, tell her you are wretched; that only through the light of her eyes comes hope; that you have longed for years to be at rest in the grave, but that love for her has given you new life; that the World cannot be hollow which contains her—with other kindred sentimental-isms—and, trust me, you will find her hand stealing to yours, the tears to her eyes, and her head to your heart.

That will open the door to her hard bosom, and you can enter it unchallenged, and sit thereafter, long as you please, upon the throne of her self-love, in the high court of her self-admiration.

"Carry not your melancholy and your wooing too far," says a cynic at my elbow. "I knew a persevering gentleman who did so, and the result was, his charmer became his wife, and charmed no more."

If Wall street owned Greenwood, it would daily quote graves in demand, funerals active and death easy. It rarely happens the cemetery is without a funeral cortege, and at least a score of laborers are ever opening graves.

The tears of affliction are always falling; the sob of bereavement is always heard; the wail of stricken hearts is always rising there. And yet, nowhere does the sunlight fall more softly; the birds sing more sweetly; the flowers smell more fragrantly. They are wiser than we purblind mortals: they see beyond, and know the whole.

From 15 to 20 interments are daily made in Greenwood; and already a number nearly equaling the entire population of some of our largest cities lies under the soil, sacred forevermore in at least 1,000,000 mourners' eyes,—eyes which may be dry to-day, but will be wet again to-morrow.

A dark train is always passing over those green undulations; and the laughing sight-seers are hushed when, at the sudden turn of the walk, they come upon weeping friends about a new-dug grave.

Many a pair of the wandering sentimentalists I have named have forgotten for the moment their fancied woe while they heard the earth fall hollowly upon the coffin-lid which shuts out forever and forever the face that was dearest in all the World.

How use doth breed a habit in a man! The gate-keepers, grave-diggers, undertakers, hearse-drivers, see in the agony of the bereaved only a phase of nature, as they do the clouds in the sky, or withering leaves on trees. They have had their own woes, and will have them again, and cannot afford to sympathize with those external to themselves; for the sympathetic are ever bearing burthens that do not belong to them. The great gates which seem to say, "Abandon love, all ye who enter here," are not less sympathetic than their keepers; and both look stonily upon the funeral pageants as they pass, and have no heart to answer to that low, stifled wail which is the note of despair.

Observe the funerals. They are many and different; some pompous and pretentious; some plain and unassuming, with more freightage of grief than the loftier ones; for prosperity hardens, and splendor, which hides, also lessens pain.

This is an ambitious cortege. The coffin is rosewood and mounted with silver, for the dead man was very rich and little loved. The weeds of his widow and nearest relatives are very deep and costly; and those kinsfolk look as if they deemed it their duty to mourn, which, like many other duties, is most difficult to discharge.

Are they thinking of what they have lost; of a gentle smile forever withdrawn; of a loving heart forever still? They are thinking less of what has gone than what has been left,—of bequests and legacies, of pleasures they will purchase and vanities they will gratify. In their secret hearts, they rejoice that he is dead. His death was the kindest thing he ever did for them; and, were he conscious once more, they would thank him for quitting a life he was too selfish to make useful and too sordid to beautify.

Another comes. The deceased was an old man; but the widow is young, and fair, and fashionable, for she loved her husband not. She tried long and hard; but who can compel the heart? And, when esteem was half mistaken for affection, the one great love which woman never feels but once, often as it may be repeated, and counterfeited, swept like a consuming fire through every fibre of her long-starving soul. Prudence, duty, loyalty, were reduced to ashes by the intense flame, and blown to every wind by the gusts of passion. And yet it burned on, burned when the lamp of the other's life went out; burns when he is lowered into the earth. Conscience pricks; remorse stings; but, looking up, the widow meets the tender eye of the living and loving man for whom all this deception and perfidy have been, and the whole Universe has nothing for her but that one tender gaze.

Few carriages make up this train, and few mourners are in them. But the tears they shed are genuine, and the grief they show comes from their inmost souls. Wife and mother was she to the fullest; and, when she died, a place was made vacant that cannot be supplied. Years hence, he and his children will entwine her dear name with their prayers, and Heaven will seem near when her spirit is invoked.

In that coffin lies a girl, of eighteen, so young in

years, so old in sin; and her funeral is the contribution of her riches in shame. How old the story, but as sad this hour as when the first woman fell! No natural protectors; with beauty that tempted and passion that deceived, it was as natural she should err as the o'er-ripe fruit should drop or the breezes blow. After two years of wantonness, she still could love, and deserted by a common creature whom the poor courtesan had made a god in the profane temple of her heart, she lifted her hand against her life, and slew it.

What made Romeo and Juliet immortal, and set Werther to the music of his kind will not hallow a nameless grave. Yet love is love, throbbing below the coronet or trembling in pariah's garb; and the Eternal Love will always recognize it, and bless it for its being, and see that no part of it shall ever perish.

In that little group mourns one who has no social privilege to mourn, whose love would be reckoned sin (as if to love could ever be a sin) in books of creed and canons of the Church. But he loved her better than a brother, a father or husband, and yet was none of those. It is pity it is so; that circumstance, and destiny will not flow in the channels of inclination, or bubble up in the springs of sympathy.

Does the next, or any succeeding sphere set right the wrongs and cross-purposes of this? Ask the ocean of its tides, and the stars of their occupants; but they will not answer any more than that question can be answered. Yet it is good to believe all is for the best; for belief is consolation, and consolation strength.

A bachelor friend, who has seen a good deal of the World, and of that peculiar portion known as women, once told me one of his sentimental experiences while we were lounging in Greenwood.

"Five years ago about this time," he said, " I was sitting near this spot with a very pretty and romantic girl, who had long declared she loved me, and who, though blessed with a wealthy father, would have married me and my poverty, and defied all her relatives, if I had permitted her to make such a sacrifice.

"I was quite fond of her, as men of sensibility and gallantry usually are of women who love them devotedly, and the fact that I could not make her my wife rendered our relation more poetic than it would have been had we been engaged. She was rather delicate, and her friends feared she had a pulmonary affection. She thought she would not live long, and the day we sat together here she looked pale, and more lovely than ever. The Autumn leaves were falling round us, and with her head leaning on my breast, she said, with tears in her eyes: 'I feel, darling, that I am dying. I believe that the next year's leaves will strew my grave. But I shall rest sweetly if I can dream in Heaven that you still love me.'

"My heart was touched as it never was before," my friend added. "I fancied at that moment that I loved her devotedly. I was tempted to say, 'Be mine, darling, before the World. If we love each other, we shall have wealth enough, and contentment that fortune cannot buy.' But I remembered the day would come when neither of us would feel so; that no passion, however ardent, can survive meager breakfasts, and cold potatoes at dinner. So I kissed her tenderly; dried the dew of her tears on the rose leaves of my lips (I was sentimental then); and told her she would be some man's lovely wife when I was at supper after Polonius's fashion.

"She looked a sad rebuke at this, and shed more tears, which I kissed away again, and we wandered into less lugubrious themes.

"We retained our sentimental attachment until the War broke out. I went to the field, and after a few letters our correspondence ended.

"When the struggle was over, I came home, and one of the first carriages I noticed in the Park contained my quondam inamorata, a middle-aged man, rather vulgar, though very prosperous-looking, and two bouncing children in charge of a French-Irish *bonne*.

"One glance told the whole story. I perceived that the sentimental drama had ended as a comedy, with marriage; and I laughed, as I had often done before under similar circumstances, at the prose denouement of the rose-colored episode. I learned a few days after that my sweet Saloma had accepted a husband, of her parents' election, who had made a fortune by a Government contract, and who did not know whether Dante was a Dane or a Dutchman, and certainly did not care.

"I was glad she had done so well, and gladder I had not been unwise enough to make her matrimonially miserable. I drank a glass of wine at dinner every day for a week to her connubial happiness—it was barely necessary to toast her health then—and, meeting her at the opera a fortnight after, she remembered my face, but had forgotten my name—the name of the man she had vowed she loved better than her own soul, and who was all the World to her, and something more.

"Women are fine rhetoricians," remarked my friend, "but I think they place a small estimate upon the World and their own souls."

Another story about the cemetery. A merchant of wealth lost his wife, of whom he had seemed to be very fond, and who had borne him several children. He followed her coffin to the grave in tears, and showed more violent grief than it is usual for men, even in the greatest affliction. His friends pitied him, and declared him a model of domestic devotion; some even doubting if he would long survive the partner of his bosom. Their surprise and indignation may be imagined when he married the governess of his children, the third day after the funeral.

Those who claimed to know, said he proposed to her on the way home—they rode together in the same carriage—and that she, after a fit of weeping and a tumultuous protest against the haste and indelicacy of the proceeding, under the circumstances, accepted him, and had a clear understanding about the amount of the settlement he would make upon her.

Many members of his set cut him directly, and his premature marriage excited so much feeling in his circle that he found it convenient to go abroad and stay for two years. When he returned, his dead wife's friends had grown indifferent to, or forgotten her wrongs, and received the second wife with welcome, as if nothing had occurred to disturb the old social relations.

The merchant understood human nature. Go away for two years, and people will forget almost anything, their dearest friends not excepted.

When you read all the inscriptions and epitaphs,

believe them true, and wonder not how it happens that the grave is the great saint-maker. You may think, when the predicted resurrection comes, that most of the risen, on reading their tombstones, will be convinced they were put into the wrong graves. But do not say so, lest you be deemed a cynic, or a truth-speaker, which is much the same.

Console yourself with the reflection that whatever life you lead, your virtues will blossom in the dust; that men who carve in marble are privileged to lie; and that, being fairly out of everybody's way, and incapable of coming back, your worst enemies will hardly take the pains to remember they hated you.

But as for those who loved me? ask you. Never mind them, Sir Egotist, and they will not disturb themselves about you. Love has often done men more harm than good in this World; but in the tomb it will do you neither one nor the other; for the grave-grass heals the deepest wounds that love has ever made.

THE MALL, CENTRAL PARK.

CHAPTER XII.

THE PARKS.

If New-York has its festering tenement-houses, it has also its wholesome parks, and these are, in some sort, its redemption. No city in the Union has so many breathing-places, and the Metropolis, in spite of its crowded population, its municipal mismanagement, its poverty, its vice and its squalor, is probably one of the healthiest great centres of civilization in the World.

It is not a little remarkable, in a City where every square inch of ground is prized as gold, that so much real estate in the most valuable part of the island should have been appropriated to the public use. We owe much to the early moulders of Manhattan for their liberality, and much to the good sense and judgment of those who first suggested the purchase of the Central Park.

Altogether, we have as many as twenty squares or parks; but a number of these are private, and others are being converted to business uses, which is not greatly to be regretted, since we have the Central, including and overshadowing all. The best-known, exclusive of the Central, are the City Hall, Union, Madison, Stuyvesant, Washington, Tompkins, Gramercy and Manhattan.

The time-honored, once famous plaza, the Battery, has

long been employed as an emigrant dépôt; St. John's is now used as a station by the Hudson River railway; Tompkins' square has been allowed to run to waste; Grammercy has become private property, and is kept carefully locked up the greater part of the time.

City Hall, Washington, Union, and Madison are really the only public grounds, and they have been so much neglected that they have lost most of their attractions. Since they have been placed in charge of the Central Park commissioners, however, it is believed they will soon be made to resume something of their old freshness and beauty.

The down-town enclosures have of late years, especially since the opening of the Central, been given up to disreputable loungers, children and nurses—those of our citizens who needed recreation and fresh air going to *the* Park to find them. The smaller open spaces add to the pleasantness and picturesqueness of the Metropolis; but they are more for ornament than for use, and so completely swallowed up by the Fifty-ninth street *rus in urbe* as to be undeserving of special mention.

Many of New-York's pretensions are absurd, as every sensible person knows; but it has a right to boast of the Central Park, (and it does, too,) for it is indeed an honor and a glory. It is hardly surpassed by any in the old world, and will in time surpass the celebrated Hyde Park of London and the Bois de Boulogne of Paris. Every year adds to its attractiveness, and when its groves have grown and its countless projected improvements been completed, it will well deserve the name delightful.

With nearly a thousand acres of elaborately laid out

grounds, with its charming walks and drives, its lakes and grottoes, its caves and casino, its mall and bridges, its rocks and rustic arbors, it would be a temptation and a pleasure to any one, but most of all to the busy million who inhabit this busy island, and who are shut away from fresh breezes and green fields by the presence of poverty or the demands of interest.

The great advantage of the Park is, that it is open to all, and that the poor enjoy it more than the rich, who can go where they like, and purchase what the Central gives gratis.

No sight is more pleasant there than the laborer or mechanic, on Saturday afternoon or Sunday, with his wife and children, luxuriating in the mere absence of toil, and drinking in the breezes from the sea which cannot find their way into the close tenement quarters he calls his home. He gains new health, new hope, new heart there, and dares to believe, while Nature is whispering to him on every side, that he may yet emancipate himself and those he loves from the meanness and hardness that environ him. His good resolutions are strengthened there; and who shall say that men who have dissipated their earnings, and robbed those dependent on them of such comforts as were needed, have not, under the clear canopy of the sky, away from dust, and tumult, and distraction, felt the better and truer life, and turned to it with earnestness and laudable ambition? No doubt the Park does moral as well as physical good; for there is closer connection between what is known as sense and soul than philosophers have discovered, or theologians have dared to believe.

The Park is noticeable in one respect: It is the only well-governed part of the entire island. The corruption, the political trading, and the malfeasance in of fice that characterize the "authorities" of New-York, seem kept out of that particular territory by honest cherubim, imported from some other locality, who guard the gates with unseen swords. Of the commissioners, wonderful to relate, no one complains. They have never been accused of, much less discovered in, appropriating the public funds, or defrauding the municipal treasury in any way. Yet they are mortal and live in New-York. So the age of miracles is not over, and the millenium may yet be hoped for.

On pleasant afternoons the Park presents a brilliant appearance, and reveals not only the worth and wealth, but the pretension and parvenuism of this aristocratic-democratic city. One would hardly believe he was in a republican country to see the escutcheoned panels of the carriages, the liveried coachmen, and the supercilious air of the occupants of the vehicles, as they go pompously and flaringly by. Some of these persons are so conspicuously emblazoned and tawdrily attired that one may well doubt if meanness and vulgarity do not lie behind their elaborate tinseling. And, if he inquire, he will discover his doubts are confirmed. He will learn that the *nouveaux riches*, the people who are from not only humble, but vulgar origin, who lack culture and generosity of character, are most anxious to hide their past with purple, and veneer their lacking with pretense.

Those two carriages following one after another are singularly alike, and so are the occupants. The women are fleshy, gross, and very showily dressed. They imagine they resemble duchesses, (some of the most vulgar-appearing ladies in Europe are elderly title-bearers;) but they look more like the devil, as he is popularly supposed to look, with unrefinement oozing out of their every pore, and good breeding blushing behind their backs.

One carriage contains the wife and sister of a contractor who made a fortune during the war by defrauding the government, and who ten years ago played "friendly games" with marked cards. They now envy the wind that comes between them and their new nobility, and believe they are "genteel" because they are rich.

The other carriage bears a brace of unfortunates whose mode of livelihood is no mystery in Mercer street, and whose pigment cannot hide the secret of their shame. The newly rich women imagine those fallen sisters leaders of fashion, and privately long for an introduction and an invitation to what must be very exclusive receptions. If told of their mistake, how indignant they would be, and how ungrammatically they would deny that they supposed "those horrid creatures" to be ladies.

Here comes a plain carriage, with a plainly dressed pair. Neither the man nor woman is handsome, if regularity of features mean that; but their faces are intellectual and spiritual, and their eyes seem to mirror truth, which is beauty as well. Their coachman has no livery. They wear no diamonds. They are free from all appearance of affectation. They are of the kind which parvenuism would consider nobodies at first sight,—persons who wanted to be something and could not succeed.

Deeply deluded they who judge so. That man and woman are husband and wife in the true sense. Though wealthy and moving in the very best circles of society, they wedded for love, and lost not caste by it, for they themselves make the genuine caste. If there be such a thing as gentle blood in this confused democracy of ours, they have it. But they do not talk of it. They do not tell you, unless by accident, who their grandfather and great-grandfather were; for they know that true refinement and breeding need no trumpets.

As an offset to that contented and single couple is another, who are their friends, and drive by them in a turn-out putting theirs to shame. The second couple are fond of display, but are educated, good-hearted, highminded. They are far from satisfied, however. The childless wife loved a poor man, whom she could not therefore wed; and so, with characteristic perversity, wedded a man she could not love.

She has paid the penalty, as all do who violate nature, which is, if rightly understood, the only sin. Year after year she represses every loving impulse of her heart, and starves her tender soul in the midst of material plenty.

Her partner rather than her husband, has an ample fortune, but a broken constitution and feeble health. There is no enjoyment for him. He knows the woman who sits opposite with vacant eyes has no sympathy with him. He has sought pleasure in society, in travel, in the excitements of business; but it came not. The old pain, the feeling of exhaustion, is with him always; and he waits with such patience as he can command for the end. "Oh, yes, that will be a relief," he thinks, "for the dead do not suffer and to be comfortably dead is a blessing after all."

The hard-working mechanic that looks up at the pale face, and sees the handsome carriage, envies him who has such abundant wealth. And the man of means looks down at the toiler with the ruddy flush in his face, and the stalwart form, and envies what he himself has lost.

Ever thus with life. We envy the seeming, ignorant of the actual. We murmur at our own lot, and yet would shrink from exchanging destinies with those standing apparently above us, and wrapped in self-content.

To him who pines for pecuniary success, who has been rudely buffeted by fortune, there is, if he be generous, satisfaction in knowing while he stands or walks in the Park, that there are so many more blessed than he. He can count by the hour the line of carriages that dash by him, radiant with smiles of the inmates and emitting odors of prosperity; and rejoice that they have gained what he has missed. If he be ungenerous, he can think of the skeletons in perfumed closets at home; of the one desire longed for above all others, and never to be gratified; of the vacuity of the heart that will not be filled, put into it what chinking coin we may; of the absence of the sympathy we all need, since gold will not buy nor adversity destroy it; of the sweet hope of to-morrow, without which life is only breathing beneath a pall.

Let him think of those things, surely sad enough, and consolation will be born of thought,—a little consolation, which will not be lost, but which will be succeeded by a broader feeling. A higher philosophy will come, that each human creature must work out his own destiny as best he may, and with such forces as are his; that Envy is more than useless; that Duty as we conceive it, alone. is precious; and that, within less than a century, nothing in the present can yield us pleasure or give us pain.

The Park has its lessons; and, though envy may be the first feeling of him who goes there poor and unsuccessful, a certain content will come after he lingers and reflects on what passes before him. He will see in due time that all that glitters is not gold; that while health and self-respect remain he has no reason to complain of fortune or despair of the future.

MASS MEETING, UNION SQUARE.

CHAPTER XIII.

THE BOWERY.

The Bowery is one of the most peculiar and striking quarters of the Metropolis. It is a city in itself; and a walk from Chatham square to Seventh street reveals a variety of life second only to Broadway itself. It is the Cheapside of New-York; the place of the People; the resort of mechanics and the laboring classes; the home and the haunt of a great social democracy.

Within a single block of Broadway, it is sufficiently unlike that great thoroughfare to be in another State or section of the country. The buildings are different; the people are different; the atmosphere, the manners, the customs are different. The few blocks separate it from Broadway as a Chinese wall; and opposing Tartary rages but disturbs not, within reach of the human voice.

When one turns off from Broadway at Park Row, struggles through Chatham street, and toils into the Bowery, he cannot be so absorbed as not to be unaware of the change. Every place and step remind him of his wanderings.

The human sea on which he floats is more noisy and tumultuous. The waters are less clear. More drift and sea-weed are on the surface. The dash of the waves is more irregular; their murmur hoarser; their swell more unbroken.

The Bowery is more cosmopolitan than Broadway even. It contains more types of persons; more nationalities; a greater variety, though less contrast, of characters.

The vast Globe seems to have emptied itself into that broad curve, lined with buildings of every kind, new and old, marble and brick, high and low, stone and wood.

Germans are so numerous there, one might fancy himself in Frankfort or Hamburg. Irish so abound that Cork and Dublin appear to have come over in the vast ships lying at the not distant piers. Italians prattle, in Ariosto's language, of the beauty of bananas and the importance of pennies. Frenchmen jabber; Spaniards look grave; Chinamen stand sad and silent; colored men stare vacantly, or laugh unctiously, in that singular hub-bub of humanity.

Order, and form, and caste, and deference, shaken and confused in Broadway, are broken into fragments in the Bowery, and trampled under foot.

"Who are you? "I am as good as anybody;" "The devil take you;" "We are for ourselves; Look out for your own," are written in every passing face, and flaunting sign, and tawdry advertisement this side of Cooper Institute and Tompkins market.

No respect for persons in the surging Bowery. You may be the President, or a Major-General, or be Governor, or be Mayor, and you will be jostled and crowded off the sidewalk just the same as if you drew beer at the Atlantic Garden, or played supernumerary at the Stadt theatre.

Broadway has some idea of what is known as behavior. Perhaps the Bowery has too. But it does not carry the idea into practice. It treads on your heels; turns molasses, or milk, or liquor over your clothes; tears your garments, or whirls you into the gutter; yet never asks your pardon, or explains in the least.

If you want manners, you should not be there. You must submit to the customs of the quarter, or fight, if you are aggrieved. In America, fighting is always a proposal to be received, and is generally welcome to some one within sound of your challenge.

When the denizens of Broadway straggle into the Bowery, they are easily recognized as Greeks in Constantinople. They are evidently not at home. Elbowed and run against, they look up in surprise, and seem to expect some kind of apology. If they murmur, an oath is thrown back at them, or a withering contempt for their conventionalism and consequence.

"If you disapprove of our ways," says the Bowery, with defiant chin and arms akimbo, "go over to Broadway. They make you pay for manners there. Here you can have plainness and naturalness for nothing. We'll drink or fight with you. But we won't feign or flatter. It isn't our style."

The Bowery is practical as well as blunt. It is a great retail mart. Every block is filled with tradesmen, and showmen, and tricksters. It has its own theatres, and hotels, and literature, and business, and pleasures.

Its object is not to sell to the public what the public wants, but what it does not want. Hence unfortunate dealers, and aggressive clerks, and flaming advertisements and posters, that assure you in many ways you are a fool if you neglect the golden opportunity for the first and last time presented.

To believe a tithe of what huge cards, and oppressive signs declare is to feel your fortune secured, and the kindest gods struggling to crown you with their choicest blessings.

You can buy anything in the Bowery—buy it cheap, and find it very dear. Brass watches, warranted to be gold; frail goods, made strong by oaths; spurious jewelry, shining with affidavits; old clothes, scoured to brightness with much care and more promises,—all these are to be had there in profusion, and confusion withal.

In what ruin all Bowery dealers are determined to involve themselves! What sacrifices they are resolved to make! What religious consecration is theirs to the pleasure and the benefit of the deeply-adored public! How solicitous are they to secure to the needy community bargains at all hazards!

Externally, they live only for others. Really, they live only upon others. They measure their shrewdness against the meanness of their customers. They practically believe honesty is the worst policy and that he who cannot cheat deserves to be cheated.

The Bowery knows its patrons. What would insult a Broadway *habitué*, and drive him off in indignation, holds and wins the frequenter of the more democratic thoroughfare.

The Bowery takes the ground that no man or woman knows what he or she wants, and that it is the mission and the province of the shop-keeper to enlighten such ignorance. Desire must be created; articles must be urged. Given the customer, the tradesman is a simpleton who cannot manage the sale.

I have often wondered, and at last smiled, at the

method of the Bowery merchant, which is much in this fashion.

Woman—Have you got any calico like this (showing a piece)?

Tradesman—Any quantity; but you don't want it. I'll show you—

Woman—I want something to match. I've—

Tradesman—You're mistaken, madam. You don't want such old-fashioned goods as that. Of course you don't. No woman does. It's absurd to s'pose so. Look at that piece, madam. A regular beauty, and cheap as dirt. Sold that yesterday for a dollar. Will let you have it for six shillings. Not another such bargain in New-York.

Woman—But it isn't like what—

Tradesman — It's just what you want, my dear madam. Why, I can see in your pretty face that it is. Suits your style 'xactly. When you put it on, your husband will declare you never was so lovely.

Woman—I haven't got any husband.

Tradesman—Of course you haven't. But you will have when you buy this dress. That's what I meant. See that, now. Why, those colors would catch any chap. They're elegant, and so very low, madam. Remember, I said six shillings. They cost five and sixpence at the manufactory; can show you the bills. You've too much sense and taste to refuse that at the money. Don't hesitate. It's your last chance. How many yards? Nine? Better take eleven. That's right. Boy, bring the yardstick. What kind of trimmins? Perfect beauty made up. You're a lucky woman this day. Only six shillins. What a splendid bargain!

Scene, a boot-store. Enter a modest-looking mechanic; made humble by oppression and over-labor doubtless.

Mechanic (with timid air)—Want to look at pair of cheap boots, if it isn't too much trouble.

Dealer—Trouble, indeed? We don't intend to be troubled. We 'xpect to make people buy who come in here. Don't we, Jake (to a rough-featured salesman a few yards off)? Yes, sir; we'll fit you, sure."

Mechanic—I just wanted to look to-day. I'll call again—

Dealer—No, you won't. Set down. On that stool there. Try these. They don't fit? The devil they don't? Never was better fit; was there, Jake? You don't know anything about it. Come, come, old boy. Pull out your pocket-book. Let her bleed for $7. Can't wear 'em out. You must have 'em. Not money enough now? Then leave $3, and drop in ag'in. That's right. Name? Robert Murray. All right. Keep 'em for you, my man. Good mornin'.

The descendants of Abraham are abundant in the Bowery. They deal in old and new clothes, in watches and jewelry, and advance money upon pledges,—the three vocations to which Jerusalem ever tends in America. They are ever on the alert. They detect a good customer as a pointer does a bird. They especially covet the men whom the ocean-breezes bear to the port of New-York, and the winds of Fate drive into the Bowery on stormy days.

The dark-eyed, dark-visaged fellow behind the glass case perceives a sailor rolling towards him, and fastens the mariner with his eye and then by the sleeve.

Shark—Vant to buy a goot vatch, mein fren'?

Sailor—Dun no, messmate. What ye got to sell? Might buy, p'raps.

Shark—Ah, dare's te nichest vatch vat ever vas. Sheep as you ever saw. Take it for dirty tollars. All gold; full sheweled; sholid as a rock. Isn't it a peauty? Misther Ishaacs, de broker, round de corner, lends feefty tollar on it, but must have de moneys. He veel give you more as tat any times. You have a barg'in, my fren'. Dat vatch all gold, full-sheweled, for dirty tollar. O, O, how sheep!

While the sailor looks into the case, the Hebrew slips the gold watch into a drawer, and takes out another, galvanized. The latter he hands to the unsuspecting seaman, who puts his treasure in his pocket, and rolls off. He will never know the fraud, for he is bent on a cruise through the Fourth ward. He will get drunk in a dance-house and be robbed of his valuables, the galvanized chronometer among the rest.

Perhaps Mr. Simons so reasons, and justifies himself accordingly; though Mr. Simons' conscience is not one of the things that trouble him often.

After nightfall, the Bowery is more crowded in the vicinity of Canal street than during the day.

When the tide has run out in lower Broadway, it is rising in the Bowery. Then its theatres, and concert saloons, and beer-gardens, and cock-pits, and rat dens are in full flame.

Rude bands torture melody; great lamps glare; sidewalk venders cry "Hot-corn," "Roasted chestnuts," "Nice oranges." Dishonest auctioneers bellow from smoky rooms about cheap wares and low prices to the crowd that goes swaying by the door. The famous "Red House" is at the top of its tumultuous trade, with its mountebanks in harlequins' attire, and shrill voices wooing the Bowery to buy.

People of both sexes are streaming in and out of the beer gardens,—often consisting only of a few benches and withered boughs,—and the soft music of a Lanner waltz or a Rossini overture comes rippling out over the turmoil of the street, like the light of the moon over a dreadful deed.

The theatres—German and English—are drawing their respective audiences. American newsboys and mature mechanics are discussing the dramatic horrors they expect to witness, and laughing in anticipation of the dreary drolleries of Tony Pastor's opera-house, where the mob is tickled and good taste disgusted for soiled postal currency in small amounts.

The Bowery *habitués* enjoy themselves, somewhat coarsely, but thoroughly I suspect. They laugh uproariously at the theatre and in the minstrel-halls and concert-saloons, and show their appreciation of the frequently indelicate humor by punches in the side of their neighbors, or mashing down of well-worn hats over perspiring brows. They work hard by day; laugh loudly and sleep soundly at night, and let the morrow provide for itself with true philosophy.

They have not much to live for, but they have less to leave behind when life is over; and so anxiety for what is not concerns them little. They have good appetite and digestion, and they so fill their hours with work that conscience cannot keep them awake; and, moreover, they whose toil is constant are not troubled by that invisible and uncertain monitor.

Conscience is somewhat of a luxury; and he who can keep it has means to silence it when clamorous.

The type of the quarter, known as the Bowery boy, is nearly extinct. He is seen sometimes, in degenerate form and with shorn glory, about the famous theatre, and in the cock and rat-pits near Houston and Grand streets. But his crimson shirt, and his oiled locks, and his peculiar slang, and his freedom of pugnacity, and his devotion to the fire-engine are things gone by.

The places that knew him know him no more. He was a provincial product, the growth of a period. The increase of the city, the inroad of foreigners, the change in customs, and especially the disbanding of the volunteer fire department, swept the Bowery boy from his fastenings; and he is a waif now under many names—a thief at the Five Points, a blackleg in Houston street, a politician in the Fourth or Sixth ward, a sober-settler in the great West, or a broker in Wall street.

The Bowery boy proper has passed away. But the Bowery frets and cheats, and does good and ill, and has its wheat and chaff, and is a curious study still.

CHAPTER XIV.

FORTUNE-TELLERS.

THE age of superstition has not passed, nor will it ever pass altogether.

The proof of this is in the fact that hundreds of persons, usually women, are supported here by the pretended possession of supernatural powers. Those pretenders call themselves spiritual physicians, clairvoyants, seers, astrologers, wizards, oracles. But they may all be classed under the head of fortune-tellers; for their attraction is in their claim to divine the future, and anticipate destiny.

The fortune-tellers of the Metropolis reside mostly in Division street or the Bowery, though they are scattered over the town in every direction—advertising their location and their special powers in the morning issues of the *Herald*. These revealers of fate, as I have said, are generally women, albeit there are men who find it profitable to play the charlatan in that way—coining a livelihood out of the credulity of the million.

To read the absurd advertisements of the fortune-tellers, one might imagine he had slipped back two or three centuries in time. One marvels how persons can be found capable of believing the transparent and worn-out nonsense about seventh daughters and seventh sons, the influence of Mars and Venus, and the strange signs in the house of life—taking the mind back to the days of Paracelsus and Caliogstro, before Positivism had overthrown the theories of dreamers and the delusions of madmen. One cannot understand with what interest and curiosity such advertisements are read; how the poor and the distressed grasp at the smallest straws, hoping for the far-off shore of peace and comfort, even while the death-waters are gurgling in their ears.

Men long for wealth and power; women for love and beauty. Facts and reason influence those; feeling and imagination these. Hence women can never quite divest themselves of superstition. Their hearts make them believe in miracles, and they are never entirely sure the handsome prince they read of in the fairy tale, or the hero they worshiped in the delightful romance may not come to them some day, and claim them for his own.

The would-be witch or gipsy who says she can tell a woman, if unwedded, who her husband will be—or, if a wife, when she will be a widow, and when married again—appeals to her sex as no argument and no philosophy can. Consequently the patrons of fortune-tellers are naturally feminine, and are to be found in all grades of life—in servant-girls, in seamstresses, in shop-girls, and in the daughters of wealth and fortune.

They are all alike in their affections—all dreamers and idealists; sympathetic through their sentiment, and sentimental through their sympathy; clutching at the rainbow of happiness as if its mistiness were matter.

Strange to an unprejudiced mind, that the wonder working creatures who know where treasures are buried, where prizes may be drawn, and how fortunes are to be made, should not convert their knowledge to their own advantage. But they will not; at least they do not.

While living in dingy rooms in unwholesome neighborhoods, scant of food and raiment, they inform others of the royal road to wealth, but decline to journey that way themselves. They are devoted to their divine science. They are directors to the goods of the World, of which they must not partake. Their souls are very rich with wisdom. Their hands must not be full of lucre.

This is Division street, where architecture and cleanliness are despised. The houses are old, and soiled, and unwholesome. Many families live in each dwelling. Retail shops abound in the quarter; and all look dusty, stinted and starved.

Second-hand furniture establishments, porter-houses, quack-doctors, green-groceries stare with rheumy eyes at each other across the narrow thoroughfares. Rags and rickety signs flutter and flap in the unsavory wind. Poverty, and trickery, and misfortune abide there evidently.

Division street is one of the walls to which the weak and woe-begone are driven in life's hard battle, fought over again every day.

At many grim doorways are smoky, besmeared signs, such as "Fortunes Told;" "Madame Belle, Astrologer;" "Ida May, Clairvoyant;" "Temple of the Unknown;" "The New Oracle;" "The Great Arabian Physician;" "Signora Saviltari, Italian Conjurer;" and others of a still more striking character.

Perhaps at the entrance of these abodes of the mystagogues, stands an uncombed, unwashed boy—as unweird and unmysterious as can be imagined—with misspelled circulars inviting the public, especially you, to learn the secrets of the future—whom you will marry; when you will die; how you will grow rich—and whatever your restless spirit hungers to know.

You go up the uncarpeted staircase, and pause before a begrimed door, behind which a tin or painted sign informs you, the oracles of the gods are dispensed. You are ordered to knock or ring; and you do so, with no other shrinking than that which is inspired by bad air, and an unmistakable hatred on the premises of soap and water.

You are ushered in by a colored woman, who requests you to be seated, and says her mistress will soon be disengaged. You place yourself upon a hard, wooden chair, whose back has the lumbago, and whose legs are infirm, and look around while you are waiting.

Nothing but bare walls and a strip of rag carpet in the little ante-room. You hear a murmur of voices on the other side of the thin partition, perhaps a monotonous shout, and soon the sound of a bell, and the sable portress appears, and you are invited to enter the presence of the priestess, who unfolds your destiny for a dollar in currency, whatever the fluctuation of gold.

Disappointment greets you as you enter. You see no paraphernalia of the occult art. No skulls, nor bones, nor crucifixes, nor black hangings with triangles or circles wrought thereon in crimson or in white; no retorts, nor strange vessels with amber-hued philtres; no large, dark volumes with iron clasps; no owls, living or stuffed; no wand or instrument of magic.

Even the sorceress is artistically a failure. Neither Ayesha nor Kefitah is she. The tall, lithe figure, the dark, piercing eye, the deep, solemn voice, you look and listen for in vain.

The priestess is only a gross, fleshy slattern; and she gives out—must I confess it?—such an odor of onions and gin that you are convinced she is more mortal than mystic. Perhaps she is an Assyrian or an Arabian, for she speaks very imperfect English, and with a nasal accent that was never born of Delphos.

She looks at you with blood-shot eyes, and says with energy, "One dollar, sir, for gintlemen;" takes up a greasy pack of cards, and proceeds to tell your fortune.

"Here's a black-haired woman and a light-haired woman. Both of 'em is in love with you very bad. Both of 'em wants to marry you. The light-haired woman's jealous like; but t'other'll be yer wife sure."

"I'm already married, madam, and to a second wife."

"Then the black hair'll be your third. Yis, yis, I see. Here's a fun'ral. Somebody's goin' to die. That must be your present wife. Yis, she won't live many months, I see in these here cards."

(I've known some men to look elated over this dismal intelligence, and depart, after giving the fortune-teller an extra dollar, without waiting to hear more.)

"You're goin' to travel, and git a letter from a dark-haired man who seems drunk; for he's upside down in the pack. Some of the men you've knowed, take too much wunst in a while, don't they?"

"I did not come here to impart confidences, madam."

"Oh, well, you needn't be snappish. It's so, anyhow; for the cards tells it, and they isn't mistak'n never. Let me see. Here's trouble for you—great trouble about money. You or your friends is goin' to lose somethin'. Some of 'em's goin' to be rich, too, though you don't believe it. There'll be a death, too, in your family. Yis, here's a coffin and a hearse."

"Is my wife to die twice?"

"No; it will probably be one of your children."

"I haven't any children."

"Not born in wedlock, perhaps, but a love-child you mayn't know nothin' about. You know those kind of things happens."

"Confound it, madam, I'm a member of the church."

"Church-members is mortal like the rest of us."

"Well, I've heard enough for my dollar."

"If you'll pay another, I'll tell you how to get rich. Just dip your finger in that ere tumbler on the shelf, and you'll——"

The remainder of her sentence is lost by the closing of the door, which you slam behind you, disgusted as you descend to the unpleasant street.

On your way down, you meet two servant girls, with a kind of awe-struck appearance, and at the front door, a pale seamstress who is taking her last dollar—she was two whole days earning it—to the gross impostor up stairs.

In the Bowery, above Prince street, a more pretentious type of the fortune-teller may be seen. Her surroundings are better, and her charges higher.

"Consultations five dollars, and strictly confidential," her advertisements read. "Patronized by the most fashionable people in New-York," too. That is something; for one's future is likely to be better when told with that of the prosperous.

Handsome carriages often stop a few blocks off, and the liveried coachmen wait while their mistresses, under pretence of visiting the poor, run into the fortune-teller's abode.

Much ceremony there, and an effort made to be impressive. The rooms are clean and spacious. The principal one is fitted up like a cabinet, and dimly lighted. What was wanting in Division street is procured in the Bowery.

Necromantic symbols are abundant. The sorceress was formerly an actress, and understands stage arrangements and the effect of character-costuming. She dispenses with cards. She asks her patrons their age, their place of nativity, the complexion of parents, the number of children; inquires about moles and marks upon the body; looks into eyes, and examines palms; speaks enigmatically, and assumes the profoundly mysterious, until most of her feminine visitors are convinced she is a perfect witch, and prepared to believe all she tells them.

In a symbol-covered black or crimson robe, which she first wore in some spectacular drama, with a stuffed serpent about her neck and a crown of tinsel on her head, she talks of the natal planets, of Ormuzd and Ahrimanes, of the powers of darkness and the angels of light, of the influence of the stars, and the destiny of mortals; turns a sort of planetarium; handles a skull; burns a powder in a lamp until the cabinet is filled with white and crimson lustre; assumes to consult a horoscope; buries her face in her hands; mutters gibberish, and reveals what the "supernal agencies" have whispered to the "daughter of the inexorable Destinies."

Fortune-Tellers. 145

A dozen of these impostors ply a prosperous trade by their mummery. Feminine residents of Fifth avenue and Twenty-third street go to the theatrical magicians with full faith, and have their lives shaped not seldom by what is told them amid stage surroundings.

Singular as it may seem, men of business, men who deal with facts and figures, who despise imagination and laugh at romance, visit such fortune-tellers, at times, to be told of the future.

Wall street operators invest five dollars to determine if they shall buy gold for a rise, or sell Pacific Mail short.

Ship-owners inquire the fate of vessels over-due, before they obtain extra insurance.

Church dignitaries, who pretend to believe in nothing the Bible does not teach, question the oracles of the Bowery, touching the lucky number in the April lottery.

Our Gradgrinds are often more superstitious than novel-reading school-girls; and the men who despise the fancies of poets, are deluded with the shallowest tricks.

The trite and homely proverb which says, "Cheating luck never thrives," seems to be verified in the persons of our fortune-tellers. They make money in various ways. They are purchasable for any purpose almost. They act as accoucheuses and abortionists on occasion. They will consent to be procuresses, if sufficient inducement be offered; will assist in crime, and hide criminals, whenever their palms are crossed with silver. Yet they are generally very poor.

They are most ascetic in assumption; talk of fasting

and abstemiousness and spirituality as needful to their solution of mysteries and penetration of the future.

Practically they lead loose and sensual lives; have coarse appetites and coarse pleasures, until age sets in and avarice suppresses other passions.

As a class, fortune-tellers are unprincipled, improvident and profligate. Wickedness is rated by what it can pay, and a full purse makes atonement for the commission of sin. Like gamblers and cyprians, what they gain they do not keep. Ill come, soon gone.

It is darkly whispered that fashionable women often seek the fortune-tellers, not to learn what will be, but to consult them upon what has been; that the determiners of the future interfere with the results of the past, and array themselves against Nature, instead of allying themselves with her to the fullest.

The life of the fortune-teller is hard. If she sins, she atones by penury, and ostracism, and isolation. She subsists by her wits, and subsists poorly. She shuffles through her meagre and cheerless years, an object alike of suspicion and of contempt. All her pretended gifts avail her nothing. Her calling is a satire on herself. Advertising her power of blessing, no blessing comes to her; and she exchanges her draggled gown at last for the coarse shroud that covers her with charity, and shuts her away from woe and want forever.

Many of the seers and clairvoyants are not only abortionists, but they are procuresses and the agents of bagnios. They are often directly employed by blacklegs and debauchees to secure for them some pretty and unsophisticated girl—one from the country generally preferred—and liberally paid in the event of success.

The scoundrels visit the fortune-tellers, and leave several of their photographs, informing the hags what they want, much in this wise:

"Can't you get me a nice girl, madam [all of their kind are madams]—a really plump creature that has lately come to town?"

"Well, I don't know. It's a very difficult and dangerous job. The police might find it out. We're all watched, you know; and if——"

"I'll make it worth your while, I've got money enough. You must know I 'run a bank.' Here's $10 to begin with. Get a girl that suits me, and you shall have five times as much."

"Well, since you're such good pay, I'll try it; but I won't promise positive. I'm afraid you're partic'lar. What kind of eyes and hair, light or dark?"

"I don't care so much about that. I'd rather have a black-eyed woman; but it doesn't make much difference, so she's nice and young. You know a pretty girl, I'll warrant. I'll trust you. Shall we call it a bargain?"

"Yes; but mind, mister, I don't promise positive; and then you must promise that you won't do anything to make a row, and get the police after me; for you know I'm a hard-working woman, and get a living honestly."

"Of course you do, madame; so do I. When shall I call? to-morrow?"

"O Lord, no! You don't suppose we can find willin' beauties every minute, do you? Come in 'bout a week. Or, give me your number, and I'll drop a line to you. I'll do my best; but I won't promise; and remember, I won't have any fuss. Soon as I get on the scent, I'll tell you."

After this dialogue, which I refrain from making as vulgar and brutal as the speakers do, the faro-dealer goes away; feeling assured, to use his elegant language, that "he's got a good thing of it."

The very moment a young woman appears who can boast of any comeliness, and who seems friendless or ingenuous, the seer plies her so adroitly with questions as to discover all she wishes to know. She perceives that the desire to be loved is in her heart (in what woman's is it not?); so she talks to her of her prettiness, and of handsome gentlemen who would be very fond of her, if they only knew her, etc. Then the girl's fortune is told, and the man who is to love her is described according to the photograph. The lover is praised to the skies, and the girl is told to come again to have everything revealed that can't be revealed then on account of the position of the planets, or some such flummery.

Meantime the seer sends for the lecher, and he continues to meet the victim, who finds the prediction fulfilled, and considers it her destiny to adore the scoundrel. He flatters her; declares his passion; makes an appointment with her; prevails upon her by his arts; uses wine or opiates, and makes her wholly his before she has fully recovered from her bewilderment. In a few weeks the villain abandons her, and she either destroys herself, or seeks to drown memory and conscience in a life of shame.

Few persons are aware to what an extent this species of debauchery is practiced. Many of the proprietresses of houses of prostitution are in league with the fortune-tellers, and pay them for every poor creature that falls into their clutches through the supernatural agents. The police understand this, as they do most of the villainies of the city; but they are often made blind and deaf.

God help the poor woman who comes to this sinful City penniless and unbefriended! He may temper the wind to the shorn lamb; but He protects her not from the villains who beset her path on every side.

CHAPTER XV.

THE BOHEMIANS.

THE term Bohemian, in its modern sense, has been erroneously applied to gipsies—the wandering, vagabond, aimless, homeless class, who, coming originally from India, it is believed, entered Europe in the fourteenth and fifteenth centuries and scattered themselves through Russia, Hungary, Spain and England.

In Paris, more than a quarter of a century ago, the name was given to the literary and artistic people, who were as clever as careless; who lived in to-day, and despised to-morrow; who preferred the pleasure and the triumph of the hour to the ease of prosperity and the assurance of abiding fame. Henri Murger, in his *Vie de Bohème*, first gave a succinct and clear account of the peculiarities, habits and opinions of the true Zingara; lived the life, and died the death, he had so eloquently described as the disposition and destiny of his class.

Since then, all persons of literary or artistic proclivities, regardless of conventionality, believing in the sovereignty of the individual, and indifferent to the most solemn tone of Mrs. Grundy, have received the Bohemian baptism. Journalists generally, especially since the War correspondents during the Rebellion received the title, have been called Bohemians all the country over, and will be, no doubt, until the end of the century.

Bohemian, particularly in New-York, has indeed come to be a sort of synonym for a newspaper writer, and not without reason, as he is usually no favorite of fortune, and his gifts, whatever they may be, rarely include that of practicality. His profession, enabling him to see the shams of the World and the hollowness of reputation, renders him indifferent to fame, distrustful of appearances, and skeptical of humanity. He sinks into a drudge, relieved by spasms of brilliancy and cynicism; rails at his condition, and clings to it tenaciously. Bohemians, however, are older than Henri Murger, or the fourteenth century, or the Christian era. Alexander of Macedon, Alcibiades, Aspasia, Hypatia, Cleopatra, Mark Antony and Julius Cæsar, were all Bohemians—splendid and dazzling Bohemians, the best of their kind, the highest exponents of the antique school, of magnificent powers, and melancholy, but picturesque endings.

The Bohemian now-a-days is popularly supposed to be a man of some culture and capacity, who ignores law and order; who is entirely indifferent to public opinion; who disregards clean linen, his word or his debts; who would borrow the last dollar of his best friend, never intending to repay it, and glory in dishonoring his friend's wife or sister.

That is the common idea; but I am glad no such class exists, however many individuals there may be of the kind. It certainly is not true of journalists, who are quite as honest and honorable as members of any other profession, and who continue poor enough to prevent any suspicion to the contrary.

The Metropolis does contain a number of wretched men, ill-paid—mostly foreigners—who act occasionally as reporters for the daily and weekly papers, and who are driven to every shift, and out of every shirt, by press of poverty and the exigency of circumstance. They are not journalists, however, any more than stage-sweepers are dramatic artists. They are to be pitied, though, in spite of their faults, for which society and temperament are in the main responsible.

The original Bohemians, in this City and country were fifteen or twenty journalists, the greater part of them young men of ability and culture, who desired, particularly in regard to musical and dramatic criticism, to give tone and color to, if not to control, the public press, not from any mercenary consideration, but from an earnest intellectual egotism. They had their rise and association about twelve years ago, and flourished up to the commencement of the War, which broke up the Bohemian fraternity, not only here, but in other cities.

At their head, as well by age as experience and a certain kind of domineering dogmatism, was Henry Clapp, Jr., who had been connected with a dozen papers, and who was one of the first to introduce the personal style of Paris feuilleton into the literary weeklies. He was nearly twice as old as most of his companions; was witty, skeptical, cynical, daring, and had a certain kind of magnetism that drew and held men, though he was neither in person nor manner, what would be called attractive.

Soon after the inception of the informal society, he established the *Saturday Press*, to which the brotherhood contributed for money when they could get it, and for love when money could not be had. The *Saturday Press* was really the raciest and brightest weekly ever published here. It often sparkled with wit, and always shocked the orthodox with its irreverence and "dangerous" opinions.

Clapp kept up the paper for a year, when it was suspended. After its death he twice revived it; but its brilliancy would not keep it alive without business management, and it was too independent and iconoclastic to incur the favor of any large portion of the community.

The third attempt to establish the *Press* failed about three years since; and Clapp, bitter from his many failures, now lives a careless life; writes epigramatic paragraphs and does the dramatic for one of the weeklies. He is stated to be over fifty; but his mind is vigorous as ever, his tongue as fluent, and his pen as sharp.

E. G. P. ("Ned") Wilkins, of the *Herald*, was another prominent member of the fraternity, and one of the few attachés of that journal who have ever gained much individual reputation. He was a pungent and strong writer, at the same time correct and graceful, and had the requisite amount of dogmatism and self-consciousness to render him acceptable to his guild and satisfactory to himself. When he promised far better things than he had ever performed, he died, leaving no other record than the file of newspapers—the silent history of countless unremembered men of genius.

William Winter, who came here from Boston, after graduating at Harvard, because he believed New-York offered the best field for writers, was a contributor to the *Saturday Press* and other weeklies; composed many clever poems, and did whatever literary work he could find at hand; supporting himself comfortably by his pen, and gaining considerable reputation, particularly as a poet. A few years ago he married a literary woman and has not since been much of a Bohemian; for Hymen is an enemy to the character, and domesticity its ultimate destroyer. He is now dramatic critic of the *Tribune*, and a very hard worker; deeming it a duty to perform whatever labor comes to him without seeking.

Edward H. House, for years connected with the *Tribune*, was a fourth friend of Clapp and also a *Saturday Press* contributor. He has quitted journalism, at least for the time, and made a good deal of money, it is said, by sharing the authorship of some, and being the agent in this country of all of Boucicault's plays. House is a good fellow, handsome, well-bred, winning in manners; is still a bachelor; does little work and gets a good deal for it; and enjoys himself as a man of the World ought.

Fitz James O'Brien, who made his début in the literary world, as the author of *Diamond Lens* in the *Atlantic Monthly* ten years ago, and who was a generous, gifted, rollicking Irishman, was one of the cardinals in the high church of Bohemia, until the breaking out of the War. He entered the field and distinguished himself for desperate courage until he was killed in Virginia and forgotten. O'Brien had a warm heart, a fine mind and a liberal hand; but he was impulsive to excess and too careless of his future for his own good.

Charles F. Browne, having been made famous through his "Artemus Ward" articles while local editor of the *Cleveland* (O.) *Plaindealer*, and come to the Metropolis, where clever men naturally tend, worked to advantage his droll vein for the *Saturday Press*, *Vanity Fair* and *Mrs. Grundy*. He was a pure Bohemian, thoroughly good-natured, incapable of malice toward any one, with a capacity for gentleness and tenderness, like a woman's, open-handed, imprudent, seeing everything at a queer angle, and always wondering at his own success. He drew about him in New-York a number of the knights of the quill; gained their esteem and affection, and left a vacancy in the circle and their sympathies when his kindly soul went out across the sea.

George Arnold was a very clever writer in prose and verse, a regular contribntor to the *Saturday Press*, and remarkable for his versatility. He had many gifts; was good-looking, graceful, brilliant. His easy, almost impromptu poems, full of sweetness and suggestive sadness, have been published since his death, which took place three years ago, and been widely admired. He sang in a careless way the pleasures and the pains of love, the joys of wine, the charm of indolence, the gayety and worthlessness of existence in the true Anacreontic vein. From such a temperament as his, earnest and continued exertion was not to be expected. Like Voiture he trifled life away in pointed phrases and tuneful numbers; but gained a large circle of devoted friends. At three and thirty he slipped out of the World which had been much and little to him, and left behind him many sincere mourners who speak of him still with words of love and moistened eyes.

William North, a young Englishman,—he had quarreled with his parents who were wealthy, and come to this country to live by his pen,—was also of the Bohemian tribe. He found the struggle harder than he had anticipated; for, though a man of talent and culture, he lacked directness of purpose and capacity for continuous work. His disappointment soured him, and poverty so embittered his sensitive nature that he destroyed himself, leaving a sixpence, all the money he had, and the "Slave of the Lamp," a manuscript novel, which he had not been able to sell, but for which the notoriety of the mournful tragedy secured a publisher.

Mortimer Thompson, who had become a popular humorist under the sobriquet of "Doesticks," and who was at the hight of his popularity, was a Bohemian in those days, and consorted with the clever crew. He was then a member of the *Tribune* staff. Since that time he has been a war correspondent; had various changes of fortune, and no longer enjoys his old fame. He still lives in New-York, however, and does the drollery for some of the weekly papers over his old *nom de plume*.

Charles Dawson Shanly, a well-known littérateur, Harry Neal (deceased), Frank Wood (deceased), contributors to *Vanity Fair* and other publications of the time, Charles B. Seymour, now dramatic critic of the *Times*, Franklin J. Ottarson, for five and twenty years a city journalist, nearly all of which he has spent in the servive of the *Tribune;* Charles Gayler, a playwright; John S. Dusolle of the Sunday *Times*, and others were members of the fraternity. They met frequently at Pfaff's restaurant, No. 653 Broadway; had late suppers, and were brilliant with talk over beer and pipes for several years. Those were merry and famous nights, and many bright conceits and witticisms were discharged over the festive board.

The Bohemians had feminine companions at Pfaff's frequently. There was Ada Clare, known as here then as the queen of Bohemia, and of course a writer for the *Saturday Press*. She was of Irish extraction; a large-hearted eccentric woman who had property in the South, but lost it during the War. She afterward published a novel, "Only a Woman's Heart," said to have been a transcript of some of her own experiences, and went upon the stage. The last heard of her she was playing in a Galveston (Texas) theatre, and had been married to the manager. There was a pretty little creature, known as Getty Gay, probably an assumed name, and Mary Fox, both actresses; Jennie Danforth, a writer for the weekly journals; Annie Deland, still on the boards, and Dora Shaw, who was the best Camille on the American stage. The ill-fated Adah Menken, also went to Pfaff's occasionally; and altogether the coterie enjoyed itself intellectually and socially as no coterie has since. But all that has passed now.

The War, as I have said, interfered with Bohemian progress. Many have become apostates now, and others deny all connection with the fraternity. The order in its old form is practically extinct; but without the distinguishing name or any organization, but better, and higher, and freer, and purer, it exists, and does good, though it may be invisible, work.

I might give a long list of city writers and journalists well known throughout the country, who are Bohemians in the best sense, but who dislike the title because so many unworthy persons have made the name repulsive by claiming it as theirs.

Certain reporters are largely of the pseudo-Bohemian class, and do more to degrade journalism than all the worthy members of the profession to elevate and purify it. And for the reason that the former are impudent, sycophantic and unprincipled, while the latter are modest, independent and honorable. If newspaper proprietors would adopt the wise policy of employing good men at good salaries, the disreputable class would find their level and cease to be a nuisance, at least in the vicinity of Printing-House Square.

The true disciples are men and women who are charitable where the World condemns; who protect where society attacks; who have the capacity and courage to think for themselves; the earnestness and truthfulness to unmask shams; the faith to believe sin the result of ignorance, and love and culture eternal undoers of evil and of wrong. They honestly discharge every duty and every debt. Their ways are pleasant and their manners sweet. They are misunderstood because they are in advance of the time, and have comprehensive views the great mass cannot take.

Such Bohemians are found in the pulpit, on the bench, on the tripod; and every day they are increasing the area of Thought, the breadth of Charity, the depth of Love. Children of Nature, they go not about with solem faces, declaring after the common fashion, the degeneracy of the age and the wickedness of humanity. They have a hope and creed born of reason and spiritual insight; believing that God and Good are identically the same; that Progress is onward and upward forever and ever.

CHAPTER XVI.

THE LAGER-BEER GARDENS.

The difference between a lager-beer saloon and a lager-beer garden among our German fellow-citizens is very slight; the garden, for the most part, being a creation of the brain. To the Teutonic fancy, a hole in a roof, a fir-tree in a tub, and a sickly vine or two in a box, creeping feebly upward unto death, constitute a garden. Perhaps their imagination is assisted by their potations, more copious than powerful, which enable it to conjure up groves and grottoes, and walks, and fountains that are not there in reality. Be this as it may, the Germans accept what is called a garden as such, and neither criticise nor complain of its striking inadequacies.

New-York, probably, has a German population of one hundred and fifty to two hundred thousand; and it is a part of the social duty of every one of these, if not a point in his worldly religion, to drink beer,—the quantity varying with the intensity of his nationality. Germans and beer are related to each other as cause and effect; and, one given, the other must follow of necessity.

Manhattan, from the battery to Harlem bridge, is covered with beer-saloons and gardens. They are in longitudinal and lateral directions, in the broad thoroughfares of Broadway and Third avenue, and in the out-of-the-way and narrow quarters of Ann and Thames streets. The whole island literally foams and froths with the national beverage of Rhineland; and, from sunrise until midnight, (Sunday excepted, if you have faith in the Excise Law), the amber hued liquid flows constantly from more than ten thousand kegs, and is poured into twenty times as many thirsty throats, and highly-eupeptic and capacious stomachs.

There must be in New-York three or four thousand lager-beer establishments, kept and patronized almost exclusively by Germans, who tend to beer-selling in this country as naturally as Italians to image-making and organ-grinding. These establishments are of all sizes and kinds, from the little hole in the corner, with one table and two chairs, to such extensive concerns as the Atlantic garden, in the Bowery, and Hamilton and Lyon parks, in the vicinity of Harlem, not to mention their superabundance in Jersey-City, Hoboken, Brooklyn, Hudson-City, Weehawken and every other point within easy striking distance of the Metropolis by rail and steam.

Of course, Sunday is the day of all the week for patronage of such places, for Teutonic recreation and bibulous enjoyment; and hence the bitter opposition to the Excise Law on the part of the Germans, the greater part of whom are Republicans, but who are not less hostile on that account to the Republican measure. They are determined to have beer on Sundays, and are making every possible effort to render the odious law inoperative by declaring it unconstitutional. They have opened their purses wide, which they rarely do unless terribly in earnest, to regain what they believe to be their rights; and they will never cease agitating the question until permitted to absorb beer when, where, and to what extent they please.

The question, Will lager-beer intoxicate? first arose, I believe, on this island, and, very naturally too, considering the quality of the manufactured article. I have sometimes wondered, however, there could be any question about it, so inferior in every respect is the beer made and sold in the Metropolis. It is undoubtedly the worst in the United-States—weak, insipid, unwholesome, and unpalatable; but incapable of intoxication, I should judge, even if a man could hold enough to float the Dunderberg. It is impossible to get a good glass of beer in New-York, and persons who have not drank it in the West have no idea what poor stuff is here called by the name.

One would suppose the vast body of Germans in this City would insist upon having excellent lager; but they do not. They seem quite satisfied with the thin, semi-nauseating liquid that tastes generally as if it were the product of aloes, brown-soap and long-standing Croton; and are not nauseated over its excessive absorption.

Peradventure they regard it as they do their "gardens,"—idealize it completely. Their palate tells them it is a wretched cheat; an insult to the German sense of appreciation; an indignity offered to their digestion. But their imagination makes it what they like; and they drain their glasses with the flavor of their fancy moistening their lips.

The Germans are an eminently gregarious and social people, and all their leisure is combined with and comprehends lager. They never dispense with it. They drink it in the morning, at noon, in the evening and late at night; during their labors and their rest; alone and with their friends; and yet we never hear of their floating away upon the swollen stream of their own imbibitions, or of their ribs cracking and falling off, like the hoops of barrels, from over-expansion. The chief end of man has long been a theme of discussion among theologians and philosophers. The chief end of that portion who emigrate from Fatherland is to drink lager, under all circumstances and on all occasions; and the end is faithfully and perseveringly carried out.

The drinking of the Germans, however, is free from the vices of the Americans. The Germans indulge in their lager rationally, even when they seem to carry indulgence to excess. They do not squander their means; they do not waste their time; they do not quarrel; they do not fight; they do not ruin their own hopes and the happiness of those who love them, as do we of hotter blood, finer fibre, and intenser organism. They take lager as we do oxygen into our lungs,—appearing to live and thrive upon it. Beer is one of the social virtues; Gambrinus a patron saint of every family,—the protecting deity of every well-regulated household.

The Germans combine domesticity with their dissipation,—it is that to them literally,—taking with them to the saloon or garden their wives and sisters and sweethearts, often their children, who are a check to any excess or impropriety, and with whom they depart at a seemly hour, overflowing with beer and *bonhommie*, possessed of those two indispensables of peace—an easy mind and a perfect digestion.

Look at them as they once were, and will be again,

in Lyon or Hamilton park, on a Sunday afternoon or evening. They are assembled at the popular resort to the number of four or five thousand,—men, women and children, persons of every grade and calling, but all speaking the same language and liking the same drink, which perhaps, more than aught else, makes them a homogeneous and sympathetic people. How entirely contented, and even joyous, are they! The humblest and hardest toilers are radiant with self-satisfaction, as if there were neither labor nor care to-morrow. They drink, and laugh and chat energetically and boisterously, as if they really relished it, and smoke, and sing and dance, and listen appreciatively to music, day after day, and night after night, never tiring of their pleasures, never seeking for a change.

Their life is simple, and included within a little round. Dyspepsia and nervous disorders trouble them not. Every day they labor; every night they rest, laying a solid bar of sleep between the days; each year adding something to their worldly store; always living below their means; thrilled by no rapturous glow; disturbed by no divine ideals; speculative, but calm; thoughtful, but healthy; comfortable, but thrifty; resolved to have and own something, if years are given to them, and making their resolution good in real estate, brick houses, and government securities.

How can they enjoy themselves so? think the pale, taciturn, eager-looking Americans at the table opposite. What do they find to talk about so volubly, and laugh at so loudly? How eloquent and witty they must be!

Neither the one nor the other, you will discover, if you listen. They are simple as Arcadians. Little things amuse, trifles interest them. The commonest circumstances, the mere mention of which would weary you, my American friend, are subjects of protracted discussion; and they roar over what would seem to you the merest insipidities. You may be as witty as Voltaire and sparkling as Rochefoucault to your companions. They only smile and look bored again. The most expensive wines stand untasted before you. The great glory of the night, and the beauties of Beethoven and Mozart fall upon you and your friends unmoved; while your German neighbors drink them all in with their lager, and burst into rapturous applause

Subtle influences those of race and temperament, which nothing can change! Ours is a melancholy brotherhood over whom the Starry Banner waves, and we have purchased our freedom and progress at the price of much of our content. Lager delights you not, nor Limberger either; and the centuries-distant blood of Œdipus is in your veins.

It is a goodly sight to see the Germans, who eat and drink, but eat as they do everything else, with a purpose. No elaborate dainties, no *recherché* viands, no delicate *entremets* for them. Brown-bread and caraway seed, sweitzerkase and Limberger, which no nostril or stomach out of Germany can endure, solid ham, Bologna sausage and blood-puddings appease their vigorous appetites, and preserve their ruddy health; while pipes of strong and by no means choice tobacco yield them all the repose they require.

What a racket they keep up in the pauses of the music, even while it is being played. Food, and drink, and talk, and laughter, hour after hour. They raise their voices; they grow red in the face; they gesticulate; they strike the tables; they seem on the point of mortal conflict; and an American who knew them not would believe murder was about to be committed.

But it is only their way. They are merely discussing the last masquerade, or the claims of Sigel to military reputation. Another round of lager—each person pays for his own glass—will mollify any asperity that may have arisen. Another plate of sweitzer will change the theme, if it be an unpleasant one, and a cabbage-leaf cigar will dissolve into thin air the last traces of ill-temper.

The Atlantic Garden is a favorite resort of the Germans, and one of the noticeable places of New-York. It is all under cover, and capable of accommodating twenty-five hundred or three thousand people. It has a large bar-room in front, and smaller ones inside; a shooting gallery, billiard and bowling saloons, a huge orchestrion, which performs during the day, and a fine band that gives selections from celebrated composers during the evening. The entire place is filled with small tables and benches, which are crowded every evening with drinkers and smokers. A confusion of ringing glasses, of loud voices speaking German in high key, of laughter and strains of soft music, float up through tobacco smoke to the arched roof until midnight, when the musicians put away their instruments, the lights are turned out, and the vast place is locked up.

The Atlantic is the most cosmopolitan place of entertainment in the City; for, though the greater part of its patrons are Germans, every other nationality is represented there. French, Irish, Spaniards, English, Italians, Portuguese, even Chinamen and Indians, may be seen through the violet atmosphere of the famous Atlantic; while Americans, who have learned to like lager—even that made in Gotham—and who are fond of music, sit at the little tables, and look like doomed spirits beside their round-faced, square-browed, jolly neighbors. Much may be had there for little, which is less recommendation to the Americans than to the Germans; and they who desire cheap concerts—one may sit there all the evening without a single glass of beer, if he is so minded—can have them every evening in the year.

With all their industry, and economy, and thrift, the Germans find ample leisure to enjoy themselves, and at little cost. Their pleasures are never expensive. They can obtain more for $1 than an American for $10, and can, and do, grow rich upon what our people throw away. They are odd compounds of sentiment and materialism, of poetry and prose, of generous emotion and narrow life, of affection and selfishness, of dullness and shrewdness, of romance and practicality, of opposites of many kinds, but altogether blending into praiseworthy prudence, honesty, industry and enterprise. They are always endeavoring to improve their condition; and, from their constant self-seeking, they soon acquire property, carefully educate their children, ally their descendants to those of Anglo-Saxon blood, and in a few generations become as thoroughly American as the Americans themselves.

CHAPTER XVII.

THE CHURCHES.

The churches are a power in New-York. They are excellent in themselves, and but for them the City would be much worse than it is; for they have a restraining influence upon the community, and compel Vice to pay a certain deference to Virtue.

The Metropolis has about five hundred churches, of almost every denomination under the sun, and the value of the entire church property on the island is estimated at $300,000,000. Much of the most desirable real estate here is owned by ecclesiastical societies, and additions to it are constantly being made. Trinity corporation alone is said to be worth $60,000,000, and yet its members feel so very poor that they frequently solicit charity, and never ring the chimes on secular festal days without compelling the City to pay for the discordant and painfully monotonous tintinnabulation.

The architecture of the churches is an ornament to New-York, and the grounds surrounding them are among the handsomest here. Few private churches can afford to occupy so much space as the religious edifices do,—perhaps because the orthodox who are truly charitable reverse the expression, believing they lend to the poor by giving to the Lord. It is certainly creditable to the churches that they are willing to retain such ample inclosures, even in the heart of the Metropolis, instead of selling them, as is so often done elsewhere. There must be some faith in and some reverence for religion when it is superior to pecuniary interests; for the purse-strings are often drawn so tight as to strangle the soul.

Broadway, Fifth avenue, Twenty-third, and other principal streets can boast of the finest and most expensive churches in the country. Their elaborateness and elegance are not confined to sect either; for the Presbyterians, the Episcopalians, the Baptists, the Methodists and Catholics vie with each other in rearing showy temples in honor of their God. They evidently think His sense of beauty equal to His sense of mercy, and that prayers from gilded altars will be more likely to propitiate Him than if they ascended from homely pulpits. The early Christians believed otherwise, and the groves were the first temples of the Deity; but theology, like other things, must advance and change, and the most sacred creed can not be wholly conservative.

No reasoning mind can doubt the excellent influence of churches, whatever their denomination, upon most natures; and though there may be, and doubtless are, those who are a law and religion to themselves, requiring neither form nor restraint, confirmation, discipline and example are of vast importance and benefit to the mass of believers. That religion is often employed as the cloak of sin proves nothing against religion, but merely the disposition of humanity to hypocrisy. It is to be regretted, however, that religion has grown so much a matter of fashion and respectability as to furnish targets for the satirical arrows of skeptics and of scoffers.

Especially is this the case in New York, and it is becoming more and more so every year. Hundreds of persons of both sexes deem themselves privileged to sin all the week, if they attend Divine service on Sunday. They seem to imagine Jehovah attracted by glare, and pomp, and lavishness; and His eyes so dazzled by material splendor that He cannot, or will not, perceive their most palpable defects. They imitate the French nobleman of the ancient *régime*, who declared the Lord would think twice before He concluded to damn a personage of *his* quality.

"Purchase or rent a pew," the church fashionable appears to say, "and you shall be absolved from wrong-doing."

"Be rich and much shall be forgiven you."

"The way of the transgressor is hard; but the way of the poor man is harder."

"It is easy to obtain a pardon of heaven when you get it in a Bible with gold clasps."

Look into the stately granite edifice. But before you do so, see if you are in proper guise. You wear a suit of fashionably cut black; your boots fit neatly; your gloves are fresh, and of Courooisier's make; you have the odor of jasmine on your person; you can enter unquestioned and sanctified, particularly if you are *distingué* in appearance, and look like a person of substantial means. The portly, oleaginous, rather pompous sexton will beam upon you, and show you to a seat with alacrity. There is a species of gentleness and courtesy engendered by Christianity, you think, as you receive the honors of the temple. While you are so occupied, a pale, quiet-looking man enters, in a threadbare suit, though "gentleman" is written in his face, and over all his form. The above sexton scowls at him a moment, and turns away. He walks nervously and blunderingly up the aisle. No one opens a pew-door for him. He glances around uneasily, and his color deepens as he turns and walks out. He is not a man. He is of the peculiar class styled "persons" by upper servants in the fashionable avenue.

He certainly must have been a stranger; otherwise he would have known better than to obtrude upon a fashionable congregation in Broadway. He probably mistook it for Sixth avenue, where the Creator listens to invocations from His creatures regardless of their apparel.

This church with its congregation is a pleasant vision. No wonder the people repeat the litany so gently, and after the manner prescribed by Mrs. General. They are too prosperous to feel the need of worship. They give the idea of patronizing the Deity, as if they said, "Good Lord, we approve of Thee while Thou assurest us steady and liberal incomes. Be careful and watch over our interests. Make the society of Heaven exclusive if Thou would'st have us come there. Don't permit the vulgar to profane it. If they do, we must withhold our presence, and that would grieve Thee, poor God, who wert made for us alone, as Thou knowest in Thy wisdom."

How precise and elegant is everything and everybody in the church! The music is executed faultlessly, and after the style of the Academy. You forget the words and place in the skillful execution of the trills and bravuras.

"The members of the choir sing well," you whisper to your neighbor.

"Why should they not?" he answers. "They are paid very liberally for it," as if he designed intimating to Providence that He should appreciate the favor done Him.

The pastor is daintily dressed, and reads the prayers with arduous affectation and an almost total omission of the R sound. He shows his delicate hand to advantage, and uses his perfumed handkerchief gracefully, and exactly at the right periods.

The worshipers are costumed as carefully as if they were at the opera. The building is thoroughly ventilated, and redolent of the soft, almost voluptuous, odor which emanates from the toilets of refined women. They look devout with a mathematical uniformity and precision. They fare sumptuously; they pay their minister $10,000 a year, and are acceptable in the sight of Delmonico and the Deity.

How pious appears that elderly man! Well he might; for his remaining years are few, and the most profligate can give to the service of Heaven the little period in which sin is a physical impossibility. And yet he is a Sabbatarian merely. To-morrow he will falsify and cheat his best friend in an operation in Broad street. His colossal fortune has been built upon misrepresentations—upon the adroit tricks which plain people would call stealing.

Yonder handsome woman is earnest in her orisons. The tears are under her eye-lids; her white forehead is wrinkled with intensity of emotion. She is praying that her love, who is across the sea, may return to her safely, and kiss her fashionable anxieties away. Of her disloyalty to her husband—who, with head resting devoutly on his hands, is reflecting on the last fall in "domestics"—she thinks not; for long custom and much passion have reconciled her to her sin.

This sweet-faced girl is peering through her open fingers in envy at the bonnet of her next-pew neighbor, which is twice as pretty as her own, and which, to employ her own phrase, she is dying to possess. She forgets her Bible and her prayer-book in her absorption upon that "sweet hat," and all her religion would not enable her to forgive the "creature" for her good fortune in securing the dainty pattern.

One of the pillars of the church, as he is called, should be called one of the sleepers; for, with his head resting on his hand, he has for the past half-hour been unconscious of his whereabout. Casuists have said, "Man cannot sin in sleep." Perhaps that is the reason so many virtuous souls slumber through Sunday service.

Let us go further up town, to even a more liberal church, to which, a cynical wit has said, "No man who loves his wife, or a woman who loves her husband is admissible." Without aught that can be termed a creed, many of the bravest and truest spirits gather there every Sabbath, and gain strength and consolation from the teachings of their skeptically Christian clergyman. Most of his congregation believe more in good works than in faith; and yet the best of them are weak, and fail of their intent, as all of us must do, strive as we may.

The organ peals through this crowded temple, where many are kneeling, even into the street. The robes are rich; the incense is aromatic; the music is choice.

How entirely devout do these humble worshippers appear? They bend almost to the marble pavement; they seem to agonize with repentance. Unquestionably they are contrite. They resolve to sin no more; and to-morrow they violate half the commandments.

The spirit may be strong; but the flesh is weak. Is it not so with all of us, whatever our belief? What is life but misdeed and repentance, and repentance and misdeed? It may be true that we do what we must, and call it by the best name we can.

The Metropolis is not favored, according to its size and pretensions, with particularly able or eloquent divines; though if you take the word of each congregation, there are as many men of genius in the pulpit as there are churches.

Ministers in the City, thought to be as gifted as Chrysostom or Thomas Aquinas, have power to put persons troubled with nervous disorders more profoundly to sleep than a dormouse in mid-winter. Some have good thoughts and much learning; but they spoil all by their manner, and they would, though they had the thought of Shakspeare and the style of Plato.

Pulpit oratory has long been peculiar, not to say vicious, mainly from the fact that clergymen have feared to become theatrical.

So far as I have observed, there is no imminent danger of the clerical profession falling into that fault.

Let them not be alarmed. They can change their style greatly, and yet never be suspected of dramatic tendencies. Let them be convinced without a revelation from Heaven, that strained pronunciation, and drawling, and the twisting of syllables out of their recognition, are no more agreeable to the Eternal

Father than naturalness and the common graces of elocution.

If we have so much fashionable religion in New-York, we have more that is earnest, true, devoted. We have men and women whose lives are a long sacrifice and offering of their highest and best for the good and happiness of their fellows.

There are humble and wayside temples of God, where elegance is not the price of virtue, but where charity is so regarded still.

We have men and women devoid of all sentimental and sensational sensibilities, who, in silent ways, bind up wounded hearts, minister to the needy, (and they are of many and different creeds,) and quarrel not with those seeking their own way to Heaven—believing all true Christianity consists in doing unto others as ye would that they should do unto you.

If great hypocrisy, and untruth, and insincerity be masked with religion, there are virtues hidden in it so deeply that only he who seeks for good in all, with a sympathetic spirit, can find them, and all the purer and meeker for their concealment and unsuspected being.

CHAPTER XVIII.

THE THEATERS.

What is known in dramatic circles as a metropolitan reputation or success, and the need that an *artiste* should be indorsed here before acceptance by the "provinces," seems to have become positively indispensable. There is incalculable advantage in making a first appearance and gaining favor here; and the advantage is not merely apparent, it is actual. It enables agents and managers to make engagements elsewhere; and the country is always anxious to know the character and extent of the reception in New-York.

New-York almost always includes fifty to a hundred thousand strangers from every quarter of the Union; and these compose the great body of our play-goers and amusement-seekers. Even when cultivated and fastidious, they are in no mood or mind for criticism on such occasions. They rush to the theater to get rid of themselves,—to kill an evening; and their satisfaction is a foregone conclusion. It matters little to them whether it be Wallack's, Tony Pastor's, the Academy, or the San Francisco Minstrels,—an elegant comedy, a new opera, a leering ballet-girl, or a Virginia break-down. They go to enjoy themselves, and they do, without regarding the entertainment artistically, or analyzing the source of their gratification.

New-York has usually about twelve theaters, or

places where lyric and dramatic entertainments are given; and they are so well patronized generally, that if their managers do not become rich, it must be because of their improvidence. Four of our theaters, not to speak of Barnum's Museum, were burned within a year.

Barnum's museums, both the old and the new, were serious losses to the country people, who regarded them as the loudest-roaring lions of the town. The famous establishment at the corner of Ann street and Broadway, where the *Herald* now stands, was for years the center of attraction for our rural cousins, who felt after they had looked on the "one hundred thousand curiosities" the great showman advertised, and had visited "the lecture room," that the best of the City had been seen. When it was burned, and the daily journals printed burlesque accounts of the conflicts of the stuffed beasts and the thrilling achievements of the wax figures, many of our rustic friends believed the narratives sincere; throbbed with intense sympathy, and mourned over the irreparable loss.

The Academy has been rebuilt, and new and better dramatic temples will supply the place of the others. New theatres are now either in process of erection or projected; so there is slender prospect of any diminution of histrionic entertainments in the City.

The Academy, though incomplete in its interior arrangement, is much of an improvement on the old opera house, and may be considered a graceful and elegant cage for our Tuscan birds of song. Taste for the opera, like that for olives, is generally acquired— the result of culture; and, during the past ten years it has grown popular, not only in New-York, but in other cities.

NEW YORK PILOT BOAT.

BARNUM'S MUSEUM, 1860.

The early embarkers in lyric enterprises had hard fortunes and grievous failures here; and Max. Maretzek's recent success has not been very brilliant. He came to America very poor, and according to his account he has been losing money ever since. How a man who had nothing to begin with can constantly be declining in means, and yet have a comfortable income can be determined only by the musical scale peculiar to the Continent.

The opera in New-York though thoroughly appreciated, and enjoyed, is supported as much for fashion as for art's sake. At least one-third, if not one-half, of the boxes are nightly filled by persons who would not go there if it were not the mode, and if it did not give them an opportunity to indulge their love of dress.

To have a box at the opera is considered as essential by pretenders to the *haut ton* as to have a house on Fifth avenue, or a pew in Grace church. Consequently one sees men and women in full dress boring themselves mercilessly in Irving Place or Pike's Opera House night after night, and declaring they are delighted, when they cannot distinguish a cavatina from a recitative. Those indifferent to the opera at first come to like it after a while, if they have any ear for time or tune, and even to have a passion for it at last; so that fashion may finally create what it originally affected.

Operas have been better and more effectively presented during the past few seasons, and this community has become sufficiently cultivated and discriminating to demand a certain degree of excellence in the lyric drama.

Pike's Opera House has been called the handsomest theater in the world, though a little more simplicity in its interior would be desirable. Its vestibule is beautiful and imposing, and the auditorium, when lighted, is brilliant in the extreme. The Opera House somewhat resembles the Grand Opera at Paris, and is much finer than the famous La Scala at Milan or the San Carlo at Naples, which are great, dreary, dingy, uncomfortable houses that few persons admire after having visited them. It is very remarkable that Samuel N. Pike, a comparative stranger, should have built with his individual means an opera house at an expense of nearly $1,000,000, when a crowd of wealthy New-Yorkers were with difficulty induced to put up the Academy of Music, even with the privilege of occupying the best seats by virtue of being stockholders.

Pike is certainly enterprising and generous to the verge of audacity; for he is the only man in the City capable of expending a great fortune on what at the time of its expenditure gave little hope of return. He has lately sold his Opera House to the Erie Railway Company for an advance on its cost; but the theater will be retained, it is said. I fear it won't be, unless it is found to be a good investment, which is not probable, so far is its location—Eighth avenue and Twenty-third street—removed from the fashionable quarter. I sincerely hope the Opera House won't be disturbed, for New-York cannot afford to be deprived of so elegant a temple of art.

For Booth's new theater, Fifth avenue and Twenty-third street, large promises have been made. It is not yet finished; but it will be superior, no doubt, to any other theater in the United States. Edwin Booth has built it, little regarding the expense, with all the improvements that the older theaters lack. It is designed by the young tragedian for his home of the legitimate, especially the Shakspearean drama, and will, it is expected, do much to resist the tendency of the time to merely sensational plays.

Wallack's is, and has been for years, the best theater in the United States, and is quite as good as any in Europe outside of Paris. It is devoted almost entirely to comedy, and has no "stars," as that term is usually employed, but the most capable and best-trained company that can be selected at home or abroad.

Plays without any particular merit succeed, because they are so carefully put upon the stage, so fitly costumed and so conscientiously enacted. It is more after the style of the French theaters than any other in the country. The old stage traditions and time-honored conventionalisms are given up there. Mouthing, ranting, and attitudinizing are not in vogue; and men and women appear and act as such, and represent art instead of artificiality.

It is commonly said that New-York goes to Wallack's; and so it does more than to any other place of amusement. But lovers of good acting from every section usually avail themselves of a sojourn in the city to witness the artistic representations at that theater.

The Winter Garden, burned more than a year and a half ago, has not been, nor will it be rebuilt. It has occupied a very prominent place in the drama of New-York. For its absurd name (given, perhaps, because there was nothing in or about the house to suggest either a garden or Winter,) it is indebted to Dion Boucicault, who translated the title from the well-known *Jardin d' Hiver* in Paris. It was formerly Tripler hall; then Boucicault's theater; then Burton's; then Laura Keene's; and some years ago passed into the hands of William Stuart, a clever Irishman, at one time on the editorial staff of the *Tribune*, and author of the famous but violent *critiques* on Forrest which appeared in that journal many years ago.

At the time of its destruction, the theater was mainly owned by Edwin Booth, who, with some of the most famous *artistes* of the day, such as Forrest, Brooke, Anderson, Carlotte Cushman, and Jean Marie Davenport, made the place historic. After Wallack's, it was the best conducted theater in town, which seriously feels its loss. The star system was generally adopted and followed there; and the extreme popularity of Booth caused his engagements to extend through the greater part of the regular season.

Niblo's Garden, another of the inaptly named, is probably the oldest of the Broadway theaters. It was once a garden; but it, as well as Niblo himself, disappeared so long ago that the time when they were is forgotten. It has had numerous managers, but none more prosperous than the present, Jarrett and Palmer. Their engagement of the Parisian ballet was particularly fortunate for their exchequer; for its success far exceeded the most sanguine expectations. For seventeen months it crowded the theatre, the largest in Broadway, every night, and realized to each of the managers about $100,000.

Classic tragedy and sparkling comedy are very well in their way; but, when brought into competition with voluptuously-formed dancing girls, who seem to wear little else than satin slippers, with a few rose-buds in their hair, the legitimate drama dwindles into insignificance. What appeals to our intellect is entitled to our esteem. What appeals to our passions carries us by assault.

Niblo's is the coolest and handsomest theater, the Academy excepted, in the City, and, during the lavish display of saltatory nudity, was by long odds the most popular.

The Olympic was built by Laura Keene; was afterward very successful under Mrs. John Wood, and has done well since, under varied management. It ranks fourth among New-York theaters, but is not at present distinguished for anything in particular.

The New-York has catered to the lighter tastes of the public, and with a remunerative result. This theater is very small, was formerly Dr. Osgood's church, and was opened by Lucy Rushton, who had an ample *physique*, but no discernible dramatic talent. and failed because mere avoirdupois was not monetarily magnetic in Manhattan.

The Théâtre Français, in Fourteenth street, was, as its name implies, designed for Juignet & Drivet's French comedians; but it was not prosperous with them. It was opened year before last with an English opera company, who did so well that its members fell to quarreling, and disbanded in the midst of a season. Ristori made her triumphs there; and of late devoted to opera bouffe, it has been very successful.

The Broadway is Wallack's old theater, and is one of the most inconvenient in the city. Maggie Mitchell, Heckett, John E. Owens, and Barney Williams and his wife often play very successful engagements there.

George Wood disposed of the Broadway some time ago to Barney Williams, its present lessee and manager.

The notorious old Bowery, once the temple of the legitimate has long been surrendered to the blue fire and bowl and dagger drama. The New Bowery was burned a year ago, and will not be rebuilt. The Stadt is a large, barn-like house, where the Germans applaud Schiller and Kotzebue over lager and Limberger.

It is needless to refer to the Bowery, for its reputation and peculiar school of acting have become national. It still preserves its fame; and sanguinary bandits and desperate assassins die to fast poison and slow music over and over again, to the delectation of newsboys and the enthusiastic peanut-lovers of the East side.

Dawison played his remarkable parts at the Stadt, and drew such audiences as the theater very rarely attracts. It has all the appearance of a continental theater, and it is with difficulty, when inside of it, that one resists the impression that he is in Berlin or Vienna once more.

Wood's Museum and Metropolitan Theater is further up town than any other, being at the corner of Broadway and Thirtieth street. When it first opened with a ballet troupe it did well, but was ill managed, and failed. George Wood, formerly of the Broadway, leased it, and with a burlesque English singing company, in which Lydia Thompson and other actresses, more comely than modest, are conspicuous,—he is filling the house nightly.

There are other theaters and numerous halls in the

city where theatrical entertainments are given; but those named are the principal, and convey an idea of the drama as represented and supported in the Metropolis.

The defects of the City theaters are their general discomfort and lack of ventilation. Nearly all of them are so close and hot, when crowded, that enjoyment of the performance is marred, if not destroyed, by difficulty of wholesome respiration. Especially is this so when the weather is at all warm; and that a hundred women do not faint nightly, suggests that feminine swooning, is to a certain extent, a matter of election and predetermination.

The nominal price of admission is seventy-five cents; but for secured seats, or in other words any seats at all, you pay a dollar and a dollar and a half; and are fortunate, should there be any special attraction, if you are not compelled to buy tickets of speculators at a very considerable advance on the regular rate. The speculators are a nuisance, which the manager assumes to oppose; but he is often suspected of being in league with them, and dividing the profits of extra charges.

Theatrical people are peculiar and much misunderstood. Their life is very laborious; and yet it has fascinations few members of the profession are able to withstand. They are strangely misrepresented, and to their disadvantage, by those who know nothing of them but by the excesses or dissipations of a few and the scandalous stories told of dead celebrities. They work very hard generally, but are much better paid than they used to be. Subordinate actors and actresses receive $20 and $25 a week; the leading men and women $75; soubrettes $50, and the ballet girls, as they are called, $8 to $10. Many of them support aged and infirm parents and relatives; make daily sacrifices for love and duty; are heroic in a humble way as few outside of the profession are capable of believing. They live two lives. The life of the stage is quite apart from the practical one, and often as real as that which demands food and raiment. They forget many of their troubles and hardships before the footlights, which are to them the radiance of their ideal world. They are made peculiar by their mimic being; but once entered upon a theatrical career, they follow it through every variation of circumstance, and cleave to it with an earnest interest and perfect sympathy that ought to insure them the independence they seldom gain. Their trials are many, their temptations strong; and yet there is often such beauty in the lives of the humblest, that a narrative of facts would sound like a romance. They are very migratory except at two or three of our City theaters; playing here this season and next season in New-Orleans, San-Francisco, or Montreal. Good actors are always in demand; but there is such a difference of opinion respecting merit, so much in circumstance, that they who strive hardest and are most deserving not seldom subsist from hand to mouth, and become such wanderers they never know the sense of rest, the satisfaction of independence, or the sweetness of home. He who casts stones at them knows them not, and forgets what pleasure they have given him when life looked fair and the heart was young.

The narrowness of the managers is shown in their unwillingness to engage actors or actresses who have not made their reputation in New-York, pretending that their success in "the provinces" is not based upon ability, and that they would fail when exposed to the severe test of metropolitan criticism. Some of the artists who cannot get engagements are better than those who have won laurels in New-York; and not a few who have struggled for years to make an appearance in the City have, when the opportunity was afforded, taken the town by storm.

Eliza Logan, Matilda Heron and John E. Owens are instances of this. James E. Murdoch, for years the best genteel comedian in the country, could never, if my memory serve, obtain an engagement here, because he was deemed a western actor.

The people of New-York generally know about as much of the great West as they do of the Siberian steppes, and are somewhat surprised when they hear that the citizens of Chicago and Cincinnati wear gloves, and use napkins at table. It is not improbable that the Gothamites will increase their knowledge before the century is over and learn that the "provincialists" in some things are equal to the self-sufficient "metropolitans."

CHAPTER XIX.

THE "DEAD-BEATS."

"DEAD-BEAT," though by no means elegant, is rather an expressive term, probably of English origin, meaning entirely spent, exhausted, broken down, bankrupt, and finds its synonym in our slang Americanism, "played out." "Dead-beats" are hardly natural to the soil and surroundings of the Republic, and must have been primarily an importation. But, once transplanted, they flourish and multiply here as they could not abroad; for nowhere else could or would they receive such sustenance and encouragement.

New-York abounds in dead-beats. They are found in every profession and calling, in every kind of society, in all manner of disguises. No set is so exclusive, no vocation so earnest, that the dead-beat does not enter it. He is irreverent, obstinate, audacious. He rushes in where angels fear to tread. While Capacity, combined with Modesty, holds back and blushes with diffidence, Self-Assertion and Impudence, which are the heart and brain of dead-beatism, crowd forward and steal the prize.

The eminent dead-beat is he who is not found out; who half imposes upon himself as well as others; who has come to believe, at least partially that he is what he has so long pretended. The pulpit, the bar, journalism, art, the medical profession are full of such. But only the keen-eyed few perceive them. To the great mass they are the appointed oracles and the ministers of Fate.

The Rev. Ambrose Arrowroot has an extended reputation for learning and for eloquence. Men laud and women languish for him. But he is only a plausible hypocrite and fair-faced muff, that his biased congregation have dyed gorgeously with the crimson splash of their praise.

Peter Pettifogger, Esq., brandishes green boughs of language, devoid of strength and sap, before judges and juries, until fatigue disarms criticism. He harangues crowds with noise and egotism, and they accept him as a new Chrysostom.

George Washington Jones writes columns of presumptuous verbiage year after year, until he proves the public a great ass, and is enrolled on the list of cotemporaneous fame.

Angelo Smith, designed for a sign-painter, executes marvels of bad taste on canvas, and calls them art. Sciolists echo him; fill his purse with sequins, and his little soul with conceit.

Dr. Machaon Mercury kills people in the dark, and prates of science. A quack and charlatan, he looks solemn and sapient, and his patients gain confidence. Nature heals them, and they praise and pay the pompous trickster.

Such dead-beats require elaborate treatment. To expose them would be to shatter our idols, to transfix many of our dearest friends. We prefer those of a lower grade, who know what they are; who have developed backward; who, having ceased to cheat themselves have resolved to cheat the World.

The adventurers, the Jeremy Diddlers, the fellows who live by their wits, are the ordinary representatives of the class whose highest career is on the island of Manhattan. These are the ultra Bohemians, in the worst sense of the word; the men of defective organization; the preyers upon the good nature and faith of their own kind; the persons who hold that the World owes them a living, whether they strive to earn it or not. Work is vulgar to them; deceit, and falsehood, and knavery commendable, or at least excusable on the ground of the inequality of fortune. All men deserve alike in their creed; and they who are defrauded of their birthright are privileged to get from others what has been denied to them.

No doubt there are thousands of people here who rise in the morning without knowing where or how they will get their breakfast or dinner, or where they will lay their heads at night. Most of those would work if they had the chance; but a large proportion would not so demean themselves while a livelihood is to be obtained by social stratagem or unblushing imposture.

The genuine dead-beat exists by falsehood and by borrowing. He is an artist in his way; intelligent, observing, with a knowledge of human nature and an insight into character. At the first glance, after he has had sufficient experience, he knows his victim; determines how much victim can spare; understands the mode of reaching victim's sympathies. As success after success crowns the adventurer's efforts, he feels a pride in his power and tact, and regards getting money out of a man very much as a general does an advantage over the enemy, or a libertine the conquest of a woman. He comes to consider his calling as legitimate as any other. He earns his fee by his adroitness, as a lawyer by his argument, a physician by his diagnosis, an author by his last volume.

Dull, plodding men are disposed to be honest. They have not the temperament or the resources needful to an adventurer's status. If unprincipled enough to adopt the profession, they could not prosper in it. They lack the appliances, the expedients—are incapable of making the combination and arranging the plan of attack.

Something akin to genius is required for the avocation—a union of valuable qualities that would yield profit if properly directed. The dead-beat is almost always a person of decided capacity, with something omitted in his mental or moral composition, or against whom the tide of circumstances has too strongly set.

Beau Brummel was a clever specimen of an accomplished dead-beat; Beau Hickman is a poor example of the lowest form. Capt. Wragge, in Wilkie Collins's "No Name," united the talents and the virtues of his profession.

The dead-beat cannot complain of monotony in his life. His variations and contrasts are like those of a woman's temper. In the morning he flushes with hope; in the evening he pales with disappointment. But he never surrenders hope, which is his spiritual pabulum. His exterior undergoes striking changes. You meet him smartly dressed to-day. Next week he looks shabby as a resident of Mackerelville. At this moment he is lavish of money. When next you meet him, he is penniless as the old-time printer used to be on Monday morning. At times he is unpleasantly tipsy; at others he is somberly sober. All conditions and moods join in him. The August sun and December frost dwell together in his being.

The dead-beat is usually the embodiment of good nature, polite, and desirous to conciliate every one. He cannot afford to offend the humblest member of the community on which he subsists. His list of acquaintances is interminable. He recognizes and remembers you at once. He thinks he has met you at a great many places where you have never been; but at last fixes upon some fact of your life, and pursues you with it.

He has the highest opinion of you, and so informs you. He flatters you grossly or delicately, according to your appetite. He discovers your foibles, your particularly weak spot, in a few minutes' talk. If you have lectured at Cooper Institute, or Chicago, or San Francisco, he recalls the occasion; for it made a distinct impression upon his mind. He was delighted, and he wonders, great as your reputation is, that you are not more fully appreciated.

If you have written anything, he considers it, on the whole, the best thing of the kind he ever read. He is so observant that he bears in memory the young woman you last drove with in the Park. And, though tastes differ, he hazards the opinion she has more beauty, and elegance, and style than one usually finds, even in the best circles of society. He has often wondered, with your capacity, and culture, and opportunity, you don't push your fortune. He scorns to flatter anybody; he is a person of candor, even though it give pain. But he shall always consider you a man of great capacity, different from others—too original and sensitive, perhaps, to succeed, but with a deal of power—more deserving of fame than nine-tenths of the fellows who have schemed themselves into a name.

After all that, you are more than human if you don't begin to believe there's something in D. B., though he does talk a great deal. And when he intimates a desire for a small loan, you grant it with alacrity, and feel the obligation is on your side.

If you are a merchant, or a politician, or a muscular Christian, he will tell you of your skill in buying and selling, your understanding of the people, or your dexterity in the brutal art of bruising. He will fit his color to your sample, however rare the shade.

The dead-beat, though you think you have seen him every day for a month, has always just been, or is just going, somewhere. A number of people are anxious for him to do this or that; but he is in grave doubt. Jones has not money enough, and Robinson is hardly as liberal as he might be. And then what's the use of a fellow who is in demand constantly taking the first offer?

He invites you to drink, and discovers he has left his portemonnaie in his other coat. He asks you to call on families of position, but defers the visit if you accept. He relates his flirtations with the youngest daughter of the wealthy banker in Exchange-place; and informs you confidentially of the row he had with old Sturgeon, because his young wife was so devoted to—he won't say who or what, but "you understand, old boy."

The dead-beat haunts the hotels, the places of amusement, and the principal streets. He is ever on the alert for some dear friend—he has more friends than all the Veneerings—but will walk with you if you're not in haste. He has a singular faculty of meeting you about dinner or lunch time, and is forever leaving something at home. He is a regular barnacle. He won't be disturbed or shaken off. He sticketh closer than a brother, though you abuse him like a brother-in-law. His friendship for you is greater than that of Nisus for Euryalus, or Alexander for Hephæstion. He will talk, and drink, and eat, and sleep with you until he has borrowed your last dollar, and then advise you to be more careful of your means.

These strange creatures are usually made what they are by evil passions, by indulgence in some vice. If they kept sober and didn't gamble, their pride would come to their aid, and give them strength to lead true lives. Their course is all downward. They frequently become bar-keepers, low blacklegs, runners for gambling houses, and even for bagnios. What we call sin, perpetually goes backward, tends below. Their career is brief and melancholy. If they do not die suddenly, they slip away and disappear in space. Probably they fly off from the great centre of the Metropolis, and revolve in the orbits of the country towns.

I have known men of fine talents, with excellent opportunities and beginnings, fall to the under plane of dead-beatism; and their career was thenceforth downward, until the coroner's inquest told all that was left of their history.

Their first mistake was in endeavoring to obtain something for nothing; in cherishing the delusion that the race of life was to be gained by standing still.

They spent more than they earned. They borrowed, and borrowed, until they grew used to borrowing, and careless of payment. That was the dangerous step; for they lost confidence in, and respect for, themselves the moment they surrendered conscientiousness about debt.

I remember a reformed beat who unfolded his experience, which extended through five years. He "got behind" at faro, and borrowed to make up his loss. In a few weeks he had borrowed three thousand dollars; pawned his watch and jewelry; overdrew his account in the office, with not a farthing in prospect. Then he began to drink to excess; lost his situation; grew desperate; borrowed of every one he saw; gambled more; prospered pecuniarily for a while, but discharged no old obligations. At that time, he was boarding at a first-class hotel; could not pay his bill, running through six months; was invited to leave; stole off one night with his baggage; went to another hotel, with same result; then to private boarding-houses—fashionable ones at first; mackerel-eating and coatless people at table, with soiled hands and unsavory odors, at the last.

All his old acquaintances cut him; father refused to help him; besought strangers for small means; got into the gutter; the days and nights were hideous and confused like nightmare dreams. He gravitated to a gin-cellar in Water street, and received lodging and food to drug the liquor of predestined victims; took money from the drawer; was beaten half to death by the proprietor of the vile place; sent to hospital, where delirium, added to his wounds, laid him at the door of death. For weeks he knew nothing; but, as he recovered partially, familiar faces stole through his feverish dreams; familiar voices sounded in his ear. Better and better by degrees; and one morning, waking stronger than ever, he felt her kiss—the kiss of his mother—on his forehead; and the face of the World was changed before that good, sweet, sympathetic face of man's first, and last, and best, and dearest friend.

His fight with the ruffian had found its way into the newspapers. His mother, in a distant city, having seen the account, came to New-York, saved him, and returned him to a new life.

To-day he is prosperous; a happy husband and father; and, better still, charitable to all who err or walk in the downward way. His advice never to borrow money, without paying it, is good, for debt is the beginning of dishonor.

Money may be vulgar, but it is needful. So long as men are conscientious in the payment of the money they owe, they will be in the discharge of social and spiritual obligations. Who would be free, independent, contented, should avoid debt. The debtor is enslaved. Debt imposes a burthen upon him that prevents his walking upright and wholly honest in the light in which Peace is found.

CHAPTER XX.

THE ADVENTURESSES.

To KNOW an adventuress, and to find her out, is always a wound to the masculine self-love that is slow in healing. All men of the World who have traveled have met adventuresses, and have sometimes been deceived by the clever creatures, though their vanity may disincline them to such confession.

What American that has lived abroad, or wandered there, but has met, in Paris, or Berlin, or St. Petersburgh, at Biarritz, or Ems, or Wiesbaden, some artful and interesting woman, with a romantic history and a sentimental soul, who has drawn him into sympathy and love with her for at least a season! Perhaps circumstance has intervened between her and discovery, and her gallant has come home to think of the dark-eyed countess or the blonde baroness, who was imprudent to be sure, but imprudent because she so wholly loved.

"Ah!" sighs my bachelor friend, "Mina was a charming creature; and I have often thought it unwise not to have thrown her stupid Saxon husband overboard, that delightful night on the Adriatic. That might have changed my destiny. Poor, dear Mina! I wonder where she is now. How devotedly she loved me! I should be inhuman if I did not remember her with fondness."

It is well for my friend's vanity he does not know where and how Mina is. Since he knew her, she has had many husbands and lovers,—the terms are synonymous with her,—and, if she could recall him, she would laugh at his folly, and declare, in her pretty German-French way, that men are very easily deceived.

Most of our sex who know anything about women think they know all, and are disposed to believe themselves interesting to any she they deem worthy of attention. Upon this knowledge of men, upon their weakness respecting women, adventuresses found their career. They attack men's purses through their vanity or passion, and are usually successful because of the feebleness of the point of attack. Very skillful spiritual anatomists are the members of the deceptious sisterhood. They soon find the available place, and carry the assault, less from strength without than weakness within.

The larger the city, and the more cosmopolitan, the broader and better the field for feminine operations. And New-York, with its vast variety of people, its easy freedom and indifference to country conventionalisms, is a proper pasture for women of this sort. They are more numerous than is supposed in the Metropolis, which is their centre and radiating-point. They are drawn here by the attraction of numbers and wealth. They migrate to "the provinces" in times of dullness and adversity, and return when fortune promises fairer.

The number of adventuresses in New-York can be

reckoned no more than the number of dishonest men; but they can be counted by hundreds if not thousands, for they are often seen where no one would suspect.

The unfortunate creatures who pace Broadway after nightfall, anxious to sell themselves to whoever has the means of purchase, are adventuresses in their worst and most obnoxious form. But they are not of the class I mean; for they are driven by a terrible necessity, and lost thereby to every sense of shame. They are in the very shambles of the senses, and hold no masks before their wretched infamy.

The adventuress, strictly such, earns all her success by seeming to be what she is not; by an adroit assumption of virtue she can hardly remember to have had.

A walk up Broadway or Fifth avenue, a visit to the Academy during the opera season, a drive in the Park, a sojourn at the watering-places, during the Summer, will always reveal to the discriminating a number of full-blown, perfectly-developed adventuresses, who, to the many, are fine ladies and leaders of fashion.

Theophrastus failed to mention the adventuress among his "Characters," for the reason that she belongs more to the romantic than the classic, the modern than the ancient school. She is peculiar, and not discernible except to the practiced and below-the-surface-seeing eye. She is usually either young, or capable of making herself appear so—often near the middle age, but so fresh in semblance and agreeable in manners that she loses her years in proportion to one's acquaintance with her. If not positively pretty, she has a noticeable face, a graceful figure, excessive tact, and knows how to use her tongue. What more, especially when it is remembered she has surrendered the inconvenient thing we call conscience, could or would a woman need to measure herself against the World she is resolved to cheat and profit by?

The moral faculties are very essential to a well-balanced organization; but they are sadly in the way of achievement sometimes, and the person that throws them overboard is the first to reach the port of prosperity.

Our heroine is self-poised, self-disciplined, incapable of being taken unawares or at disadvantage. She has strength and resources: she understands the power and efficiency of impudence and of inflexible determination never to be put down.

Some of her ethical and social tenets are:

Believe every man a fool until he has proved himself otherwise; and even then distrust his wisdom more than your power to deceive him in the end.

Tell half-truths when there is fear of discovery; for half-truths disarm those that are whole.

Always remember that a falsehood well adhered to is better than a truth poorly defended.

Never trust a woman with what you would not have repeated.

Bear constantly in mind that men are to be won and held through their senses and their vanity. When one is satisfied, stimulate the other.

Never make confession. It is glorious to die at the stake, if you can perish with a lie on your lips.

The adventuress seems to prosper. She is usually well and expensively dressed; has jewels and money; though in straitened circumstances, she seeks the pawnbroker, and secures advances from her mercenary uncle,—the last relative from whom we can obtain a loan. Her fortune varies like that of a gamester; and she is as improvident. A true epicurean, she lives in to-day, and trusts Mercury for to-morrow. She thinks Destiny will care for those who care not for themselves, and that the fabled Devil never abandons his own. No doubt she suffers dreadfully at times; but she looks cheerful; and, when anxiety wears her pale, she lays on the rouge, and devises new schemes to ensnare.

Our large hotels furnish the best sojourning-places for adventuresses, who can always be seen there. Those women do not stay long in one house usually; for they are unwilling to be too conspicuous or well known. They go from the Astor to the St. Nicholas, from the St. Nicholas to the Metropolitan, from the Metropolitan to the Fifth Avenue, and in turn to the Clarendon, Brevoort, Everett, Union-Place and Westminster—wherever men and money are to be found. By way of episode, they enter the fashionable boarding-houses; but the field is narrow there, and the espionage and gossip of their own sex is not to their liking.

They are often the most attractive women at the public houses. They know how to dress, and they have good manners. There is nothing rustic, or awkward, or disagreeably bashful about them, albeit they appear too easy sometimes for good-breeding and too free for entire modesty. They elicit your attention at breakfast and dinner; assume graceful and picturesque positions in the drawing-room; let you overhear a piquant phrase as if by accident; and make you believe, if you are vain, that they feel an interest in you, by certain half-averted glances and stealthy looks.

The adventuress is almost always alone, unless she is accompanied by a child, too small to be troublesome and too young to be observant, which gives her an air of respectability, and surrounds her with the sanctity of maternity. She is ever waiting for somebody, or going somewhere, or expecting something. She has expectations from the future, which the future is slow to redeem. She never lives in New-York, nor do any of her relatives. They dwell hundreds of miles distant, for some mysterious reason; sometimes in New-England, sometimes in the West, sometimes in the South; and are very difficult to hear from. They are persons of culture and position, and particularly attached to their kinswoman,—rather narrow and puritanical, perhaps, but amiable and affectionate to her broader self.

The adventuress is generally a widow, but sometimes a wife, (never a maid, either actually or by assumption), the history of whose husband, living or dead, is circumstantially narrated. When her husband is with her, he is said to be a very jealous and excitable, even dangerous man, who displays extraordinary capacities for being absent when he is not wanted,—quite unusual, I have heard, in husbands of a less dubious character. It is recorded, however, that he does make his appearance most inopportunely, and that his wrath is so great at unavoidable discoveries that it can be mollified only by liberal disbursements of private exchequer. He insists on blood at first; but finally compromises on lucre,—informing the wounder of his honor that such a thing must not happen again.

Since the War, widows have been more abundant than ever. They have lost their husbands in the struggle, sometimes on the side of the North, but usually on the side of the South. They hail from Charleston, and Savannah, and Mobile, and New-Orleans, frequently from the interior, and they are waiting for the release of their estates. They have been to Washington, and have friends there looking after their interests. They have suffered a great deal in various ways, especially from poverty; but they will soon be in affluent circumstances again.

War-widows are to be regarded with suspicion, particularly when from the South, and possessed of confiscated plantations; for their kisses sting like adders, and their hands are greedy of gold. Victims of such may be reckoned by the hundreds. Hotel-proprietors, as well as hotel-guests, have discovered that investments through sympathy are unproductive, and that cotton is not king, but the queen of deception ofttimes.

Year before last the crop of Southern widows was superabundant; and mine host was so often cajoled by them that, if they failed to pay their board promptly at the end of the week, he gave them full permission to go elsewhere. They went from the Stevens House to the St. James, pausing at all intermediate places because of the lamentable condition of public confidence. Their baggage and wardrobes were seized, and they would have been turned into the street had not men been found who had faith and folly.

Examples of interesting poverty are not unfrequent among adventuresses. They make the acquaintance of some kind-hearted man, and inform him of their straitened circumstances. They have failed to receive remittances, and can not pay necessary bills. If he can lend them a certain sum, they will return it in a few days. They show letters to substantiate their statements. He lends and obtains payment, if at all, in coin more tender than legal, and the loan is increased, and a liberal relation of debtor and creditor established.

Sometimes the woman declines to receive money unless the lender will take her watch and jewelry as pledges for payment. But what man of gallantry in America can do that? He naturally grows indignant, and inquires if he looks like a pawnbroker. She has made no blunder. She was as well assured by her knowledge of character that he would not receive her trinkets as that she would receive his money. She converts herself into a charming fountain at this juncture; and the more he seeks to turn off the water, the more brilliantly it plays.

Those eloquent tears have quite overcome him. He consoles her sentimentally, and her debts are his—until he finds her out.

When lovers and money become scarce, the adventuress frequently sends suggestive advertisements to the *Herald*, or answers some she finds there, in which "young and handsome," "comforts of a home," "agreeable companion," "with a view to matrimony," are the alluring baits. She often rents houses, and takes lodgers or boarders, and lays siege to one after the other, until their purses are no longer available. She agrees to accept a situation in a private family as teacher; to do copying; to transcribe accounts; to assist in literary labors; soliciting or granting interviews that terminate in almost anything else.

Adventuresses travel on the cars and steamers running out of New-York in the capacity of "unprotected females," and soon make friends whom they convert into remunerative lovers. They tell marvelous stories (what man could ever tell a story like a woman, so plausible, so interesting, so delicately flattering, so deliciously false?) veined with seeming ingenuousness and hued with sentiment.

Men listen, and believe, and succumb; for their vanity prompts them to believe, and passion dulls their reason.

The loudest logic is unheard before the small voice of desire, and the strongest resolution melts beneath the softest kiss.

Not a few of our adventuresses make annual pilgrimages to the watering-places and Washington, where they reap a better harvest even than in New-York.

At the national capital they have always been a power; for there intrigue is at a premium, and well-managed incontinence in women more potent than principle, more effective than zeal.

What men will not do for truth, for patriotism, for justice, for plighted word, they will for the fascinations of a petticoat and the follies of a night.

At the Summer resorts, the adventuresses give zest to the commonplace flirtations, and lend a dash to the monotony of life there, that is long remembered by coxcombs who plume themselves upon the prodigious conquests they have made. Such fellows would be mortified, indeed, if they knew of their predecessors in pleasure. But they don't; and it is well they are less wicked and more foolish than they suppose.

Unnatural, unwomanly, repulsive as is the life of an

adventuress, she appears to enjoy it; and she does (for we all justify, soon or late, our conduct to ourselves;) but she has days and experiences that are dark and bitter to bear, and the storms of her being break upon her unseen heart. Hardened and selfish as her career renders her, she retains possibilities of good, and dread of evil when it takes new form; is capable, after all her miserable make-believes and hideous deceptions, of generosity and sacrifice, even of disinterested affection and beautiful devotion.

With all her wanderings, and weaknesses, and errors, she has something of the angel left, and above the crumbled ruin, written in colors of light, may be read the word, Woman, still.

CHAPTER XXI.

THE BOARDING-HOUSES.

LIFE in boarding-houses, especially in New-York, is as different from life in hotels as residence in the Fourth and Eighteenth wards. The better class of hotels are generally comfortable, often luxurious; but boarding-houses, of any sort, call them by what enticing name you may, are never more than endurable, and rarely that.

People seldom go to boarding-houses save from necessity. Poverty, not choice, directs them thither; and they stay there for the same reason so many men have remained in the territories—because they have not the means to come away. Boarding-house existence is a doom and distress here. Men are born to it, and, through narrow circumstances, compelled to continue it when every instinct and taste revolt at it.

Woe to the mortal obliged to drudge in the Great City through all the months of the year, and unable, toil as he may, to emancipate himself from the tyranny of boarding-houses. Like Ixion, he is bound to the ever-revolving wheel. Like Tantalus, he is promised satisfaction that never comes. Work at his business; annoyance in his home—the only one he has—he vegetates through existence, and dies at last consoled by the hope that in the next world boarding-houses are impossible.

Boarding-houses here include so many varieties that no social Agassiz could enumerate them. They extend all the way from the extensive establishment in Union square, where boarders must be specially recommended, to the sailors' staying-place, where robbery is a system and murder a variation. Generally, however, they may be divided into two great classes—those that aspire to be genteel or fashionable, and those that do not. Having gone through the former, few persons would have energy or curiosity enough to continue their experience. They would conclude that the upper strata contained all that is worth knowing, or that humanity is capable of bearing.

The fashionable boarding-house is the characteristic, and, phenomenally considered, the interesting class which chiefly claims consideration. The boarding-house of such pretension is of fair and of promising exterior and in the best quarters of the City. But it is of the Dead Sea apple complexion; and they who would not find ashes and bitterness must not go beneath the surface. Fourth, Eighth, Tenth, Fourteenth and nearly all the cross streets, with such neighborhoods as Union, Madison and Stuyvesant squares, bloom with fashionable boarding-houses, to which men who work with their hands, and are incapable of paying at least $12 or $15 a week, are inadmissible.

They are usually kept by women who have made the business a study and an economy; who have, by long experience, learned the expansive power of every dollar, and the fullest value of every fraction of postal currency, with the rare cheapness and advantage of pretension.

Widows for the most part preside over the destinies of boarding houses, having been driven to that occupation by stress of fortune. Whatever their original gentleness, generosity and womanliness, their perpetual struggle with life and the countless perplexities and anxieties of their situation, make them hard, selfish, sour and narrow. They see the sphere at only one angle, and that the most acute one. Their whole thought, and feeling, and aspiration is embraced in making both ends meet,—in solving the ignoble problem, "How shall I live?"

Any cosmopolite knows a boarding-house proprietress at a single glance. She has emanations that reveal her at once, much as she varies in form. She is generally very thin and haggard, in worn and threadbare attire, with a cold, yet nervous and anxious manner, as if all her blood and sympathy had gone out of her with the last payment of rent. Or she is large and fleshy, tawdry in dress, with high cheek-bones and high color, sharp, gimlet eyes, staring at every man as if he were a delinquent boarder, and at every woman as if she suspected her of an intrigue, and were determined to get at her secret. She is always looking for bargains in furniture, millinery and provisions, and vaguely expects that, when the World comes to an end, she will be able to buy it cheap, and have the only genteel boarding-house in either hemisphere.

When you enter a tall, handsome brown-stone front, exactly like its next door neighbor, where the Wall street banker or Beaver street merchant resides in the midst of velvet carpets, ormolu clocks and classic bronzes, you cannot help but be surprised. The drawing rooms look dismal; the furniture worn and scanty; the stairways treacherous and untidy; the walls soiled and of marvelous acoustic property. Nothing like comfort or content anywhere, but the opposite of what you mean when you talk of home.

Probably you see a table set in the back parlor, and, if it be Winter, a feeble semblance of a fire, that must be dreadfully skeptical at times of its own existence; for, like the lodger in the fourth story, it is always going out. Everything that meets your eye is thin and unreal, save the landlady, who weighs two hundred, and stands in hourly dread of her own appetite. Though by no means lovable, you cannot but admire the extreme shrewdness she manifests when you talk of becoming a boarder. She drives you into every financial corner, and gives you to understand you can obtain no advantage over her. You might as well try to buy treasury notes at a discount of Simon Israels in Chatham square, as make anything out of her. Her whole expression says, "Ive seen men like you before. I'm an unprotected woman; but you can't impose upon me."

She shows you through the rooms, and informs you of the genteel character of her boarders. ·She never takes any one that she doesn't know all about. She prefers nice people to common people, even if the latter have money. She has been well reared herself, and would have been wealthy still, if poor, dear Mr. Dobbs hadn't gone on the paper of his friends, and lost his entire fortune. (Dobbs I know personally. The only fortune he had was the ill-fortune of marrying the present Mrs. Dobbs. She led· him such a crooked life that he took to brandy straight, and walked off the dock one night in preference to walking into his wife's bed-chamber.)

She gives you a biographical account of all her boarders; declares you ought to know them; that you would be delighted with them; that her house is like a home; that she has frequently thought of giving up the business, but that her boarders wouldn't let her. Her young men, she believes, really love her, (no accounting for tastes, you remember, though your incredulity isn't great enough for that,) and would be quite inconsolable if she ever should give up. She ventures the opinion that they would marry if they couldn't board with her.

You reflect which of the two evils will be the greater; conclude to enlist under the petticoat-banner of Mrs. Dobbs; and disregard matrimony and fresh butter forevermore.

At the table, all the boarders meet. They are very punctual, having learned by familiar hunger that to him who has an appetite delays are dangerous, and, if often repeated, will be fatal. Boarding-house life enforces punctuality, though it does not satisfy the palate. But what are the senses to the social virtues?

The boarding-house is fashionable. Pray bear that in mind, and let the fact console you for any shortcomings in the larder or any peculiarities of the landlady.

You have all the courses at dinner—soup, fish, pastry and dessert—but scantily served, ill-cooked and uninviting, though on unexceptionable crockery and well-washed tablecloths. The meals are long drawn out, not because there is much to eat, but because the waiters are few and slow of motion. Dinner especially is a prolonged agony, in which a deal of commonplace talk is made to supply the precepts of Blot and the dainty abundance of Delmonico.

If a new comer, you are introduced to Mr. Wiggle, salesman in Franklin street; to Mr. Newcomb, a law student at Columbia college; to Mr. Pritchard, a reporter on a morning paper; Mr. and Mrs. Humdrum, newly married, who came from Hartford, and who still deem it necessary to make love to each other in public, because their instinct tells them they will soon cease to do so in private. Miss Ridgway, who gives music-lessons and sings sentimental songs over the tuneless piano in the front parlor, but who believes she must find a husband ere long, is presented and seeks to captivate you with her milk-and-water eyes. Several others are there, but they are too insignificant to remember, and too much occupied with getting something to eat to waste opportunities in conversation.

During the entire week—dinner is reserved for the flow of soul— you are interested to perceive how many words can be spoken without ideas, and what amount of giggle is required for every silly speech.

The theaters, the opera, the newspapers, the gossip and the scandal of the town, interspersed with the report of the alarming price of provisions from Mrs. Dobbs, and wonderings how she shall get along, (evidently intended, from her oblique looks at Wiggle and Newcomb, to be understood personally,) are diluted and distilled through an hour or two of hunger waiting on appetite.

Several of the masculine boarders tell their singular experiences of last night or last year, albeit you cannot see wherein they are singular, and are consequently considered stupid by the narrators from your bland expression of face. Miss Ridgway declares men are such deceivers; that they now love every woman they meet; that they have n't a particle of heart; and that no girl can believe them now-a-days. By way of rejoinder, a Mr. Luffy, who is rejoicing over an incipient pair of mutton-chop whiskers, and who fancies he is like Don Giovanni because he has found favor in the eyes of the chamber-maid and the cook asserts with a loud laugh that life is played out; that love's a nice thing to talk about in the country, but that it won't go down in New-York.

Everything has an end and the dreary dinner is no exception. The boarders go to the parlor and talk more nonsense than at the table. Miss Ridgway asks Norma to hear her, and tells Robert she loves him, at the piano, though it is very doubtful whether Norma or Robert care anything about her. Some members of the company stroll out; some fall asleep, and others seem to feel a real interest in each other.

Humdrum sighs for billiards and departs in search of them; while Luffy, profiting by the husband's absence, tries to be gallant to the wife, who draws away her hand, and tells the youth to his whiskers he is a fool. The disappointed Faublas blushes very red, and is so crestfallen that he seizes his hat, and, going down Broadway, consoles himself with a "pretty waiter girl" in the Louvre. He returns home at two in the morning, with a bad hiccough—a general impression that "those d—d houses" are trying to crowd him off the sidewalk, and with a particular conviction that he'll break Mrs. Humdrum's heart for the rebuff she gave him. "Yes (hic)," he says to the unsympathetic lamp-post, with a wave of the hand, "when she longs (hic) for the shelter of these arms, I'll (hic) cast her off forever."

Mrs. Humdrum, after the exodus of Luffy, retires to her room in a high state of indignation; but opens her door to Mr. Hicks, her husband's employer, who has called to see her lord and master on particular business; and, by way of showing her confidence in the gentleman, puts her head on his shoulder, and asks him if he thinks a woman can love two men at the same time.

At 9 o'clock Mrs. Dobbs is left alone in the parlor with a Mr. Jones, one of the silent men at the table, who now finds his tongue, and vows he adores her with his whole soul. She leans upon his paletot, and says she likes him for his delicacy of feeling, (perhaps she would be glad to say the same of his appetite), and hopes he won't come home drunk any more.

Jones' private history is, that he has no money, and is too dissipated to keep a situation. Largely in arrears for board, he pays court to the landlady, (at her age and weight, she considers the love-making complimentary, and as a kind of off-set to his indebtedness;) occasionally borrowing five dollars of her, returnable in kisses savoring of tobacco and lager-bier.

Miss Ridgway has two devoted admirers. One she receives in the afternoon, and the other in the evening; giving them good reason to believe she worships both of them. Neither of them has proposed as yet; but it is quite time they did. She would accept both, if she had no fear of the law against bigamy; for she has solved the problem that seems to trouble Mrs. Humdrum.

Certain it is that Miss Ridgway, and Mrs. Dobbs, and Mrs. Humdrum are not prudent women; but they make up for any lack in that direction by saying extremely ill-natured things of their feminine acquaintances, who do not act half so badly as they. That is a woman's compensation, and should be accepted from the injustice with which it is made.

Mrs. Dobbs has a great many boarding-houses on this island, and Miss Ridgway and Mrs. Humdrum are generally to be found there, though they are called by different names.

Clœlia and Pulcheria board there too; but they do not like it a whit. How can they help themselves? They are pretty, and good, and discreet; but Plutus answers not their prayers; and he above all other deities emanicipates mortals on the island of Manhattan.

The refined, and generous, and hungry souls who are, from want of money, obliged to dwell in boarding-houses, are to be profoundly pitied; for your boarding-houses, even the best of them, are a wretched make-believe, and a social evil only the sufferers can completely understand. Persons who keep them, and through whom they are kept, deserve sympathy. Boarding-houses are unnatural, and the result of an over-crowded civilization. Every one must pity the man born with a soul above a boarding-house, who is still compelled to keep his body there, with an appetite he cannot appease, and through circumstances he cannot control.

CHAPTER XXII.

HORACE GREELEY.

HORACE GREELEY is, in all probablity, the best known man in America. No remote corner of the Republic that has not heard of the editor-in-chief of the New-York *Tribune*. His name is repeated in Arkansas as an exorcism to mosquitoes, and even New Zealand is not unmindful of his fame.

He has been written about more than any American of his time, and is a standing theme for gossips who indite letters from New-York. James Parton made his first fame by his biography of Greeley, which he has recently completed to the present time, and which, in revised form, has recently been issued from the press.

Much as is known of Horace Greeley as a journalist, politician and reformer, he is little understood as a man. All sorts of tales are told of him, and, as he is extremely eccentric, many of the most extravagant stories are widely believed. His absent-mindedness is largely insisted on, and I have often heard it stated with gravity, that he keeps a boy in the *Tribune*, especially to inform him, at a stated hour, whether he has eaten his dinner, and what his name was when he entered the office.

Those personally acquainted with Greeley are as much amused as he no doubt is, by the absurd gossip respecting him; for they know that shrewdness and uncommon sense are among his most marked characteristics.

Horace Greeley was born on the 3d of February, 1811, in Amherst, N. H., of very poor, and, necessarily, therefore, very honest parents. Of his hard work on his father's sterile farm; of his early precocity; of his devouring of books when he was obliged to read by the light of pine knots; of his apprenticeship —very unlike Wilhelm Meister's—to the printing business; his severe struggle with fortune; his wandering from one village paper to another, both his biographer and himself have told at length.

He came to New-York in August, 1831, a pale, thin, awkward country boy, looking like Smike, and though over twenty, he seemed at least five years younger. I have often heard him described as he wandered up and down Nassau, William and Chatham streets, in his worn shoes and short trousers, his flimsy hat and thin, flaxen hair, all his worldly goods in a handkerchief at the end of a stick, thrown over his shoulder, seeking for work, work at any price, and determined to get it; believing then, as now, that in work and by work all things are accomplished. He had only $10 in his pocket; but he had faith in his industry, his patience, his energy, and that faith was a fortune beyond calculation.

For ten years he set type and wrote, connecting himself with various newspaper enterprises, and always failing, but never losing hope, until, on the 10th of April, 1841, he issued the first number of the New-

York *Tribune*, himself selecting the name that has grown famous, and which, as a mere name for a truly democratic paper, has no equal in the World. The *Tribune* was something new, and far in advance of any daily paper of that time in tone, breadth and force; its key-note from the start being humanity, a fair chance for all men. I never realized how excellent a paper it was in the beginning until I looked over its early files; and I can't help thinking that it was, considering the great advance in journalism since, much abler and more interesting in its first years than it is now.

From the day he started the *Tribune*—the darling of his journalistic heart, to which no other darling is comparable—to the present time, its editor's career has been one of unflagging labor. One may well say of him what Clarendon said of Sir Walter Raleigh— he can toil dreadfully. He has a mania for work that persons of luxurious temperament can hardly comprehend. I have often fancied that by such constant occupation men like him either work out any discontent and bitterness they may have, or so revenge themselves upon themselves for the dissatisfactions of life. The amount of work Greeley accomplishes every year is something incredible. He finds his chief happiness in work, as other men do in recreation.

Every day that he is in the City—and he never leaves it except on urgent business, or to keep an engagement to speak or lecture—he writes at least two columns for the *Tribune*, not to speak of his contributions to various other publications, which, I presume, average six columns' space of his paper each week. He speaks and lectures fifty or sixty times a year, and makes, every month, a trip to Albany or Washington, to regulate, according to his own views, the affairs of the State or Nation. He writes, with his own hand, fifteen to twenty-five private letters a day; pores over the papers like a man who is paid for it; reads all the books of any note that come out, whether of philosophy, history, poetry or romance; and sees more people on every conceivable and inconceivable business than any man on the island of Manhattan.

When he was writing his "American Conflict," he found it necessary to conceal himself somewhere to prevent constant interruption. He accordingly took a room in the Bible House, where he worked from ten in the morning until five in the afternoon, and then appeared in the sanctum, seemingly as fresh and as anxious to write as if he had been on one of his theoretical fishing expeditions for a number of weeks.

When people use the stereotyped phrase "I want to see a man," I am sure the anonymous individual is Horace Greeley, who is certainly the most sought and inquired-after person in New-York.

Beggars of all kinds, politicians of all schools, reformers of all types, counsel-seekers of all degrees of weakness, are in perpetual pursuit of Horace Greeley. So much is this the case that, some months ago, his sanctum on the editorial floor was demolished, and a den prepared for him in the impenetrable recesses in the vicinity of the counting-room. Some thousands have attempted to find him there; but as the last heard from them was a mingled groan and malediction, amid the howling darkness of the press-room, it is believed they paid the penalty of their rash curiosity.

Horace Greeley's home, to which he goes every

Saturday, and where he spends twenty-four hours, is at Chappaqua, on the Harlem Railway, about twenty-five or thirty miles from the City. He has a pleasant and highly cultivated farm there, of some forty acres, in which the eminent journalist has spent most of his earnings, and which will not pay him on the investment, more than one cent on each one hundred dollars. With the return he is entirely satisfied, as he considers that his money has been devoted to the cause of agriculture, one of H. G.'s favorite hobbies, and in which he has always taken the deepest interest. His farm is a fancy farm in the completest sense; and those who ought to know say that every beet and turnip he raises is worth, so far as his outlay is concerned, twice its weight in gold.

At Chappaqua he amuses himself by chopping wood —that is what he conceives to be recreation—and playing at digging ditches, with kindred light pleasures, while the daylight lasts. Sunday morning he returns to town, attends Dr. E. H. Chapin's (Universalist) Church, of which he is a member, and after the service bursts into his den down town, and for the next six hours makes diagrams of Boston in ink, and calls them editorials.

Horace Greeley married in his youth a pretty and intelligent New-England girl, whom he found teaching school in North-Carolina, and by whom he has had three children. His boy, of whom he was passionately fond, and who was an extremely precocious and promising child, died years ago, and has ever since been mourned by his father, with a grief that has hardly yet been comforted. His two daughters, Gabrielle and Ida, aged respectively nine and eighteen, are said to inherit much of their father's intellect and their mother's strength of character.

The editor-in-chief of the *Tribune* has always been very charitable, and, until within a few years, was in the habit of giving money to whoever asked for it. It is said he has, as a miscellaneous alms-giver, parted with $50,000 to $60,000 since he started the journal of which he is naturally ambitious to be known as the founder.

His personal appearance, carelessness of dress, (he is always neat, and has a Beethoven-like fondness for the bath,) passion for politics, vagaries of conduct, frequent irritability and alleged injustice to his friends, require no chronicling. He has all through life shown an unswerving devotion to principle, and, though by no means free from faults, this generation, and generations to come, will do him the justice to say that no man of his time has done more for humanity, or to educate the people to a sense of right, than Horace Greeley. Like the naughty woman mentioned by Aretino, he is (according to his political opponents) always ruining himself; but each ruin seems to establish him more firmly in the confidence of the people. They believe in his earnest endeavor to do right, and to lead where his understanding of truth directs him. Whatever his defects, he could not wisely exchange his prospects for immortality with those of any man in America.

CHAPTER XXIII.

FIFTH AVENUE.

Of the fifteen or sixteen avenues of the City, Fifth is known as the Avenue by way of distinction. It is, by all odds, the most handsome and exclusive street of the Metropolis—the only one that has thus far resisted the encroachments of trade and railways, and defied the peculiar regulations of our municipal government. Every few months an innovation is attempted upon the fashionable thoroughfare, which has too much strength, through its wealth, to submit to any vulgar alteration in its settled courses.

Fifth avenue exclusiveness must be purchased at large prices; for it always offers temptations to private speculators and corrupt legislators. It even prefers fashion to fortune, for the reason that it has more of the latter than the former, and it would rather be over-generous than under-genteel.

"Let me alone; let me be as I want to," says the Avenue to outside barbarians, in nervous anxiety, its hand upon its purse, "and I will pay without stint the most exorbitant of demands."

Street railways are the periodic terror of the Avenue. Though loud threats are made to put them there, there is little danger of their establishment; for the prosperous quarter knows better than Walpole that few men fail to be convinced by monetary arguments.

Who has the most money wins in New-York, where the long as well as the short race is to the fullest purse.

Whenever a house is for sale or rent in the Avenue, its residents feel a profound interest in the character of the inmates that are to be. They dread lest the mansion may be converted to unworthy uses; lest they may be hourly shocked by a plebeian neighbor who is what they themselves were twenty, or five years, or perhaps a few months before. Their vigilance is sleepless in this regard, still they have often been compelled to buy out common tradesmen, and ambitious courtesans, and enterprising blacklegs, who had purchased an abiding place in the socially sacred vicinage. There have been those whom bank accounts and bank checks could not persuade. Madame Restell, the notorious abortionist, and gamblers by the score, and cyprians by the dozen, have penetrated into the street, and cannot be gotten rid of for largess or for logic.

Yet the energy and munificence of the Avenue, in the endeavor to keep out the unanointed, is commendable from its stand-point, and in another direction, would be productive of no little good.

It is a defect of our perception that we expend our strength against the current of events.

It is the habit of New-Yorkers to style Fifth avenue the first street in America. So far as wealth, and extent and uniformity and buildings go, it probably is. But in situation, it is far inferior to many thoroughfares I might name. Beginning at Washington square, it extends above Harlem; and, far as Fifty-ninth street, it is almost an unbroken line of brown-stone palaces. The architecture is not only impressive, it is oppressive. Its great defect is in its monotony, which soon grows tiresome. A variation, a contrast—something much less ornate or elaborate—would be a relief. Its lack of enclosures, of ground, of grass plats, of gardens is a visual vice.

Block after block, mile upon mile, of the same lofty brown-stone, high-stoop, broad-staired fronts wearies the eye. It is like the perpetual red brick, with white steps and white door and window facings for which Philadelphia has become proverbial.

One longs in the Avenue for more marble, more brick, more iron, more wood even—some change in the style and aspects of the sombre-seeming houses, whose occupants, one fancies from the exterior, look, think, dress and act alike. One might go, it appears, into any drawing-room between the Park and old Parade-ground, and he would be greeted with the same forms; see the same gestures; hear the same speeches.

The stately mansions give the impression that they have all dreamed the same dream of beauty the same night, and in the morning have found it realized; so they frown sternly upon one another, for each has what the other wished, and should have had alone.

The slavish spirit of imitation, with poverty of invention, has spoiled the broad thoroughfare where we should have had the Moorish and Gothic, Ionic and Doric order, Egyptian weight with Italian lightness, Tudor strength with Elizabethan picturesqueness.

It is a grievous pity that where there is so much money there is so little taste.

The sum of Fifth avenue wealth is unquestionably far beyond that of any street in the country. The dwellings cost more; the furniture and works of art are more expensive; the incomes of the inmates are larger and more prodigally spent than they are anywhere else on the Continent.

The interior of the houses is often gorgeous. Nothing within money's purchase, but much that perfect taste would have suggested, seems omitted. Few of the mansions that do not reveal something like tawdriness in the excess of display. The outward eye is too much addressed. The profusion is a trifle barbaric. The subtle suggestions of complete elegance are not there.

Still, to those who have suffered from the absence of material comfort, or to those whose temperaments are voluptuous and indolent, as most poetic ones are, a feeling akin to happiness must be born of the splendid surroundings that belong to the homes of the Fifth avenue rich.

What soft velvet carpets are theirs; what handsome pictures; what rich curtains; what charming frescoes; what marbles of grace; what bronzes of beauty; what prodigality of prettiness! The soft, warm, yet fresh odor of luxury comes from every angle; fills the corridors, and the delightful chambers, where sleep seems to be hidden beneath the spotless pillows of lace, steals out of the half-open library, where hundreds of morocco volumes stand silent with the treasures of time and mind in their keeping; creeps up and down the stairways, like the breath of flowers blown by the gentle wind.

Whatever the senses could ask, or culture require, or fancy crave, might be had in the walled paradise of those splendid homes. Dishes so delicate as to tempt the most surfeited appetite; wines rich enough to woo an anchorite to their tasting; music Mozart, and Mendelssohn, and Beethoven to cheer and soften, to strengthen and console; tomes of bards and sages to lift the thoughts to ideal possibilities—all these are to be found there. Fair harvests may be gathered every minute of the day or night; and he who takes not up the golden sickle in the fragrant field, is more to be pitied than he who sighs for flowers in a sterile waste.

Too sad for tears is the bitter fact that everything palls; that the highest and best satisfies only for a time. They who live in the midst of such splendor grow so familiar with it that they value it not. They are spared a certain number of wants, but others are felt that may not be supplied. The spirit is not satisfied with junketings; the vacuities of the heart may not be filled with shows of pleasure or the tinsel of display.

It is good to be rich; but it is better to be contented.

"Remove the banquet where Sympathy will not come," says every starving soul some time in its progress, "and spread the humblest board where Love may sit."

See that fair woman, robed like a queen—beauty in face and form, and grace in every motion.

What has she to sigh for? What can she need, with wealth, and position, and friends, and a generous heart?

Nothing that she has; everything that she has not. Her generous heart, that should have been her blessing, has proved her bane. Her husband is not her love, and never was. She is wife in name merely; and to be such is to be accursed with seeming. She is married, not wedded; bound in law, though not in affection.

She obeyed Fashion's dictates, and Nature exacts the penalty.

How she longs, in her splendid desolation, for the love of children that do not come for all her longing! How she thrills in sleep with the kisses of the babe that kindly dreams send to her, and presses the airy cherub to her unnursed bosom! The tender eyes open, and the happiness has gone. *He* sleeps heavily at her side, and she shrinks away from the dreaded touch that always wakes her like a shock.

O, the woe of those whom Man has joined together, and God does not put asunder!

Tall and dignified is the handsome-looking man who sits abstracted at breakfast, over the morning paper, and whom the money-article does not even attract. His spouse seems cold, and his children distant, grouped at the oval table amid the silence of unsympathy that tells what words cannot. He has speculated, and traveled, and gratified such ambitions as most men have. But they are empty in this hour—the still, introspective, conscientious hour, which none of us can wholly escape.

He remembers the landscape that he loved to look upon fifteen years before—the creeping river, and the distant village, whose spires winked through the twilight; and the lithe form that slipped away from his arms until it rested on the grass, and the little head lay still in sleep upon his lap.

He remembers the coming out of the stars, and the bending down of kissing lips to the brown hair, and the walk homeward, when the milestones would not stay apart, and the struggle between the fascinations of the great city and the narrow life in the humble town, and the surrender of love to stronger lures.

Alas, he left his happiness behind, and learned the truth too late!

It is with all of us as it is with him and her. We miss the way of life because human destiny is dark. We discover where our peace was when we can no longer grasp it. We ask for the beautiful vase we dashed to pieces in our petulant mood. We yearn for the impossible, and think it dearest because it is impossible.

Our hearts will not bear examination. Our experiences may not be told, for they are bitter, and teach nothing even to ourselves.

Let the World spin down its grooves, and let us spin with it, and cry amen to others' prayers, and praise the shams that are put upon us every day of the year.

Come out of the houses that are not homes. Come into the street—the crowded Avenue where life overflows, and drowns disturbing thought.

What a glitter of carriages! How the well-groomed horses beat the pavement, hour after hour, all the way to the Park! Those men and those women daintily dressed, wreathed in smiles, are not like him and her we saw within those handsome walls.

Oh! no; *they* have no skeletons in their gilded cabinets. The festering wound is not behind those clustering gems. We none of us have woes to speak of to the many. But the stern angel who bears about the key of sympathy, unlocks velvet doors that lead to haunted chambers and to charnel vaults.

The brown-stone fronts, with all their likeness, admit very different guests.

The people who live side by side in the pretentious Avenue, know each other not. Knickerbocker and parvenu, the inheritor of wealth and the architect of his own fortune, the genuine gentleman and the vulgar snob, reside in the same block.

One house is visited by the best and most distinguished; the house adjoining, by men who talk loud in suicidal syntax, and women who wear holyhocks in their hair, and yellow dresses with pink trimmings. Here dwells an author whose works give him a large income; over the way, a fellow who has a genius for money-getting, but who cannot solve the mysteries of spelling.

Into this plain carriage steps a self-poised, low-voiced, sweet-faced woman, while, just opposite, a momentous "female" throws herself into a new landau, and orders the coachman in showy livery, to drive to "Tiff'ny's right straight before all them di'monds is gone."

On the sidewalk, Mrs. Merrit passes quietly; and her perfect air of good-breeding is not altered by the high tones of "Mrs. Colonel Tufthunter," who says to the *bonne* at the door, "*Prend garde du ma infante jusque je revins.*"

At this the *bonne*, who chanced to be born in Paris instead of Dublin, looks blank, and replies in good French, which her mistress no more understands than did the maid her mistress' barbarisms.

Some of the most spacious and expensive mansions in the Avenue always have a deserted look. Only the occupants and servants appear on the high, carved stoop; only the carriages the master of the establishment owns, stop before the door.

That family purchased a house in the Avenue, but Society has not accepted its members. They have nothing but a new fortune to recommend them. They must bide their time.

The first generation of the unrecognized fares hard. The second is educated, and the third claims lineage; prates of "gentility," and frowns upon what its grandparents were.

To get into the Avenue, and into its Society, are different things.

They who struggle to enter certain circles are not wanted. Those who are indifferent to mere fashion are in request; for not to seek, socially, is usually to be sought. Destiny appears willing always to grant what we do not want, and determined to withhold what we do.

Very many of these houses have histories that would furnish abundant themes for the old-fashioned, three-volume English novel. Every day that passes within them would supply comedy and tragedy, one or both, if they who know would tell. One meets there, any time, women looking so pure their faces would almost contradict facts, yet part of their lives, if revealed, would repel their dearest friends. Those women are good and bad, as we understand the terms. Their faults would shock, and their virtues win us. With our foot we might spurn; with our hand we should caress.

Men we encounter in the Avenue have the angel and devil commingled in their being. They are neither so faulty nor so faultless as is believed. They are half divine, yet wholly human. They represent the World. Circumstance drives, Temperament binds them.

Fifth avenue has its shams, and follies, and evils. But go there or elsewhere, and, when we have pondered deeply enough, we shall see that Charity ends what Sympathy begins.

CHAPTER XXIV.

HENRY J. RAYMOND.

HENRY JARVIS RAYMOND was born in this State, in the little town of Lima, on the 24th of January, 1820; his father being a small farmer, whom Henry assisted in the field while a mere boy. He is said to have been a very hard worker for a little fellow. He hoed potatoes and planted corn like a veteran, and riding horses and driving cows were his favorite recreations.

He very early manifested a fondness for reading, and before he was eleven years of age had consumed all the books within a radius of ten miles of his father's home. Henry attended the Academy of his native village, and in his fifteenth year taught in the District school. After continuing in that capacity for eighteen or twenty months, he went to the University of Vermont, and graduated in 1840. Very soon after, he came to this City and began the study of law, supporting himself in the meantime by teaching a select school for young ladies, and by writing for a weekly literary paper known as the *New-Yorker*. In his first teens he had shown an aptitude and passion for writing; and while at the Academy and while teaching school in the country he composed verses and plays of a very superior order for one of his years. A remarkable versatility was his even then; and it was observed that he could take almost any view of a subject and write on it with facility and apparent earnestness. In the debating societies, too, to which he belonged, he could espouse the affirmative or negative of a question, and support one as ably as the other. Sometimes—so runs the rumor—he would become confused in his arguments, and leave his hearers at the end of his speeches very much in doubt which side he was on.

The more Raymond learned of law the less he seemed to like it, and the more he wrote for publication the fonder he became of it. A few years in a law office made him conclude journalism was his forte, and when Horace Greeley established the *Tribune*, Raymond went into the office as associate editor at the princely price of $8 a week, working on an average about thirteen or fourteen hours a day. H. G., who is a perfect fanatic concerning labor, and who thinks that a man only ordinarily industrious is a mere drone, actually urged Raymond not to work so much; and he is the only person the editor-in-chief of the *Tribune* has ever found it necessary to remonstrate with on that account.

Raymond was a capital reporter, and distinguished himself in that branch of journalism, at a time, too, when reporting was a rare art.

He served two years on the *Tribune*, and then connected himself with the *Courier and Enquirer*, where he continued for several years. In 1847 he became a book-reader for the Harpers, doing also different kinds of literary work, and remained with them ten or twelve years. During his connection with the *Courier and Enquirer* he had a controversy on socialism with Horace Greeley (the latter defending, and Raymond attacking, it) which was carried on with zeal and ability on both sides, and attracted a great deal of public attention.

In 1849 he was elected to the State Legislature by the Whigs, and was very conspicuous in debate, for which he had unquestionable talent. The peculiarity of his school days was repeated in public life. He seemed by the force of his own argument, to convince himself of the truth of the opposite side from that he espoused. He was re-elected after his term had expired, and having twice served the State he went abroad for his health, which had become delicate, and remained a year. In 1854 he was chosen Lieutenant Governor of the State, and was very recently sent to Congress. He is now out of politics so far as the filling of offices is concerned, and he is reported to have said that he will keep out, having learned at last that a newspaper requires all a man's time, and that the profession of a journalist is the highest and most influential of any in the land.

September 8, 1851, the first number of the *Times*, which had been for a long while in contemplation, was issued—Raymond upon it as editor-in-chief—and it is said he had over twelve columns of his matter in the initial issue. The *Times* was published at first for a cent and afterwards increased to two cents. It was well received from the start, though $90,000 were sunk in the concern before it began to make any return. Of late years it has grown quite profitable, and though its circulation varies considerably its regular profits are about $80,000 per annum.

Raymond is a very fluent and easy writer, and it has often been stated in the office that if the days were a little longer he would write up the whole paper.

Paragraphs, reviews, dramatic and musical criticisms, sketches, general editorials, political leaders, all are alike to him. He is, no doubt, the most versatile writer on the New-York press. One of his most remarkable performances was his article on the death of Daniel Webster. It filled nearly fifteen columns of the *Times;* was written at one sitting, and in the incredibly short space of twelve hours.

Almost every one remembers the article which appeared in the *Times*, some years ago, in which "the elbows of the Mincio," "the sweet sympathies of youth" and other incoherent phrases were strangely blended, making a mass of ridiculous confusion that gave it the title of "the drunken editorial." As it was printed while Raymond was in Europe, and after he had figured prominently as an energetic fugitive at Solferino, the *Herald* and other papers charged its authorship upon him. He never knew anything about it until he came home; and then learned the entire history of the article, which is as follows:

One of the staff, a clever but erratic fellow, now on the *World*, was in the habit of dining out, and drinking so freely at times that when he came to the office at a late hour his MS. was very uncertain. Consequently the foreman had orders to look closely at Mr. ——'s copy, and see if it were safe. If not, to leave it out. On the eventful night the eccentric personage came in, flushed with wine, but sat down and wrote a few "takes" very clearly and intelligibly. The regular foreman examined the first part, pronounced it "all right," told his foreman to follow copy, and went home.

The heat of the room very soon acted upon the

journalist, who mixed up his rhetoric alarmingly. The assistant obeyed orders literally, no doubt relishing the heterogeneous editorial, through that passion for waggery so characteristic of printers. In the morning the article appeared, a very rhapsody of nonsense, to the great amusement of the readers and the horror of the editors.

Raymond is small in stature and slight, has dark hair, gray or light hazel eyes, a thin, nervous face, with dark side-whiskers, and is quick and energetic in movement. He dresses neatly, but not extravagantly; has pleasant manners; talks fluently and rapidly, and has quite the appearance of a busy man of the world. He would be thought a merchant, by strangers, or, perhaps, a stock-broker, rather than a literary man or a journalist.

He was married while quite young; has five or six children, the eldest a son in his eighteenth year. He has made journalism profitable; his income being probably $20,000 to $25,000. He lives very comfortably, having a house in town and one in the country. His wife spends much of the time in Europe, and he himself has made four or five tours of the Continent. He is the author of several books that have had a large sale, and will probably write a dozen before he has surrendered active duties.

Raymond is very sociable; likes company exceedingly, and when he has nothing to do, which is seldom, enjoys conversation and story-telling as well as any journalist in New-York. He has a great fund of anecdotes, knows exactly where the point of a story lies and when it is reached. He is fond of theatrical entertainments; has a keen relish of the good things of life; is in no sense an ascetic or a puritan, but much of a practical optimist, who thinks the World was made for our enjoyment, and that work is necessary to pleasure no less than to health. He is very well liked by his brother journalists, and has a large circle of friends.

A great deal has been said of Raymond's inconsistency and trimming. He certainly varies his political course a good deal, but he is sincere in his variations. In conversation with a friend he once spoke of his ability to see two sides of everything. "I always try," he said, "when one side is presented to look at the other, and in turning it round, I am instinctively inclined to favor the reverse of the side I have first examined." This is the true key, no doubt, to Raymond's vagaries, as they are called. They belong to his temperament, and are part of himself as much as the color of his eyes or the curve of his spine.

CHAPTER XXV.

THE BATTERY.

The Battery is a kind of connecting line between New-York past and present. No other place in the City, probably, has so many associations, or is so prolific of historic and personal memories. Yet no one can visit the extreme southern point of the island of Manhattan without feeling something like pain at the departed glory of the Battery, the shorn beauty of that once delightful look-out to the picturesque bay and the ever-suggestive sea.

The Battery was laid out nearly a century ago, and is associated with many stirring scenes of the Revolution. The early heroes and fathers of the country trod its ground, when Washington's headquarters were within a stone's throw of the spot; and there the enemies of the then unborn Republic at one time pressed their victorious feet. After our independence was secured, the Battery was converted into a public promenade, and was, for half a century, what the Central Park has since become to the Metropolis. For years there was no other lounging or bathing place; and there the fashion and wealth of the City disported themselves in pleasant weather, and drank in the ocean breezes which swept our scanty commerce to and from our thinly settled shores.

There walked, and talked, and laughed our mothers and grandmothers, and even our great-grandmothers, who had seen Washington review his little army on the Battery; who had waved their handkerchiefs when Lafayette was received there; who had looked with patriotic and admiring eyes upon Montgomery when he lifted his hat to them, and the salt sea-breeze stirred his clustering hair.

What foreigner of note who has ever paid us a visit, what American of celebrity, has not walked on the Battery, and watched the sails of the receding ships flashing in the distance, as the sunlight caught them, like the wings of great gulls that seem to live gracefully upon the troubled deep? Benjamin Franklin has reflected there, and observed the gathering tempest which spoke to him in thunder, that was then an unrevealed law of science. Bryant, in his youth, may have caught the idea of *Thanatopsis* and the *Hymn to the North Star*, while listening to the wash of the waves, and the faint calling of the far-off sea. Emerson has gazed with his calm eyes across the broad bay, and gone home to his quiet Concord study, and written with the Atlantic's murmur in his ear, and reproduced it in his dreams of destiny and visions of the future.

Long after the City Hall Park and Union Square were popular places of resort, the Battery kept its hold upon the affections of the citizens and strangers; and to-day, dismantled and deformed as it is with unsightly objects, it is the most pleasant resort in New-York. It is a pity it has been converted to common uses, and permitted to run to waste; for its delightful view is unimpaired; the vessels and water-craft of every kind come and go, and the bay laughs with its green dimples, as they did when Bowling Green, surrendered completely now to shipping offices, was the Belgravia of the town.

When Jenny Lind came to America, so adroitly advertised and bepraised that many of the credulous believed her half an angel, she filled Castle Garden with her first notes. And when the florid and self-conscious Jullien gave his initial monster concert in the United States, the crash of his hundred instruments grew mellow as it fell from Castle Garden over the waters that curled about the walls of the Battery.

After that, Castle Garden lost its prestige. Artists no longer honored it with their efforts, and enthusiastic audiences no more awoke its echoes with their applause.

New-York had retreated too far from the Battery, which was then made an emigrant depot; and now only lovers of nature and a few strangers wander in its neglected walks, watching the ships, and listening to the sea, as of yore, conscious that the ocean and the sky must be ever fresh and fair.

The Battery is the first glimpse seven-eighths of the emigrants from Europe catch of the New World; and they must remember it always, therefore, with its bleak and barren appearance, looking bleaker and barrener to them for their expectation of finding this country a perfect Paradise. It is interesting to watch these strangers as they step for the first time upon free soil, and breathe for the first time the atmosphere of the model republic.

They must have deemed it singular, a few years ago, to behold on the grounds of the Battery, all the appearance of the oppressed lands they had left behind—barracks of soldiers, armed men, the movement of artillery. But that, fortunately, was only a pause in the giant's growth, a convulsion of the elements that cleared the air.

Every week about a thousand Europeans arrive at the Battery, and are distributed throughout the wonderful country where they have hoped to find happiness and wealth growing on every tree. Mostly Germans and Irish, who have rarely seen large cities, save in passing through on their trans-Atlantic journey, they seem lost in surprise and pleasure, while they go gaping and staring up roaring Broadway, jostled and bewildered by thousands of well-dressed men, bent, apparently, on missions of life and death.

Not strange that they are confused when the great thoroughfare bursts upon them. It must be a revelation, a sensation, an era, the realization of some fantastic dream; and as they stand at the corners, or are shouted at by hackmen and truckmen, no doubt they are endeavoring to determine to their own satisfaction if they are really awake.

We Americans, all more or less cosmopolitan, can hardly comprehend how great and sudden must be the change to the poor, oppressed Irishman, or patient, plodding German, who has lived all his life so hard and narrowly that comfort and liberty, as we understand them, are almost unknown. To take us out of our sleep, and drop us down in Jeddo, or Canton, or Damascus, or Alexandria, would be little compared to the removal of a half-intelligent foreigner from a rural village of the continent to the heart of New-York.

When the emigrants first set foot on the Battery they are compelled to run the gauntlet of sharpers and rogues, generally foreigners like themselves, whom too much and too sudden liberty has demoralized beyond hope of reformation. The graceless scamps lie in wait like beasts of prey for the unsuspecting and ignorant strangers, and, whenever the police do not prevent, pounce upon and plunder them recklessly of their slender savings. The knaves assume to be officers of the Government; charge them a sum for their initiation to the country; a price for their luggage, and then steal it; carry them off to wretched boarding-houses, where they are robbed again, and beaten if they protest; play all manner of dishonest tricks upon them, until they often pray in their hearts, I suspect, that they were comfortably back in their humble homes.

Poor creatures! it is the fiery ordeal they are compelled to pass. But they soon find those willing and glad to deliver them from the knaves into whose hands they have fallen; and from that hour the star of fortune rises above their new horizon.

How many times I have watched the groups of emigrants wandering about the Battery, and fancied their ideas and feelings in the new land to which they have come.

Men, women and children, how oddly they look; but not half so oddly as we to them, I suspect.

An intelligent foreigner once told me the first impression he received of the country was, that every man here wore a clean shirt; which was only another way of speaking of the neatness, and wholesomeness, and prosperity of the people at large. I presume the extensive scale upon which everything is done by, and the apparent comfort and wealth of, the Americans, must be the first idea that the emigrants receive, particularly when they pass up the main aisles of the City. If they were to walk through the Fourth, or Sixth, or Tenth wards,—many parts of them, at least,—they would suppose they had not improved their prospects by crossing the ocean. For there the squalor, and poverty to which they have been accustomed, if they have lived in European cities, must strike them as familiar sights.

The different nationalities represent their different traits of character on their arrival. The Irish are excited, sanguine, merry and belligerent on the smallest provocation; indeed, the atmosphere of the Republic seems to generate bellicose qualities. Our Hibernian brothers are the only people under the sun who fight for the pure love of the thing, and who seem to like a man the better after a few knock-downs, either given or received.

The German is staid, quiet, sober, when he lands, and remains so to the end. He is fond of company, capable of great self-enjoyment; but he is moderate in his pleasures, and thrifty to the last degree. He does not make much money, but he rarely spends it, and grows wealthy after a while by a rigid economy.

The Scotch are somewhat like the discreet Teutons, with more tact and perspicacity. They prosper materially if any avenue be opened. If there be not, they probably open one themselves. They are canny as the proverb makes them,—resembling the Germans in their fondness for companionship and social pleasures.

The French are still French. They adhere to each other, and sigh for Paris. When they can, they return to France, and wonder what is the use of any other place but its gay capital.

The Italians run to plaster casts, and organs, and monkeys and fruit, for the most part,—congregating in the same quarter, and dragging Italy across the sea as best they may.

Yet America affects them all insensibly; enlarges them; deepens them; elevates them. They rarely—I never heard of a single instance—regret the day they come, or the hour they arrive here, and they usually remember the Battery with a tender affection.

THE BATTERY IN 1861.

CHAPTER XVI.

THE GAMBLING-HOUSES.

THE instinct to gamble is strong in humanity. It needs development only, in the shape of circumstance, to convert hermits into hazarders, and gownsmen into gamesters.

Every man is conscious of this, and avoids the opportunity and its temptations. However, they find him often when he avoids them too sedulously, and he yields, as women yield when passion masters their hearts.

Such gambling is gambling in the restricted and proscribed sense—the hazarding of money against cards or dice. With a larger and truer meaning, all men are gamblers. All life is a great game. Power, love, wealth, reputation, are the stakes we play for, and Death wins all.

Trade and business of every species are gambling under another name. The successful merchant and banker are esteemed and honored in life, and epitaphs, false or fulsome, written over their graves. They who deal with paste-board and ivory are christened "black-legs," and "virtuous society" places them beyond its pale. The Wall street gambler is crowned with laurels, and the no more dishonest gamester of Houston street with the cypress of reputation. One wears the

Brahmin's sacred robes; the other the Pariah's garb, and yet their spiritual caste is the same.

The character of America and Americans generates a spirit of recklessness and adventure which is the parent of gambling. We feverish Anglo-Saxon-Normans, or whatever we may be, lay wagers of our peace, and hope, and life itself against destiny and death, and accept the result with the indifference of philosophy or the calmness of despair.

Here in New-York, where all life is concentrated, and a year crowded into a month, the prompting to gamble comes in with the breeze from the sea. The pulses of expectation and ambition rise and fall with the tides that wash this crowded strip of a million struggling souls.

Fifth, and Lexington, and Madison avenues gamble as well as Wall, and Broad, and New streets. There socially; here financially; but all with dice they fancy loaded.

In the Metropolis, it is estimated there are nearly 2,500 gambling places, (as gambling is generally understood,) from the gorgeous saloon, where tens of thousands are gained and lost, in single nights, to unhealthy and dingy cellars, where besotted beggars play for pennies, and are satisfied to win the purchase of the poison that maddens, but is slow to kill.

The "respectable" and fashionable establishments are mostly in Broadway, though Fifth Avenue, and Houston, and Grand and Pine streets, and the Bowery exhibit the pugnacious tiger with show and pretension to those inclined to war with him.

The fierce animal, never averse to combat, and never to be slain, roars all over town; seeks his victim under the shadow of churches, and in the full glitter of fashionable display. He lies in cosy and luxurious jumbles of satinwood and velvet, and they who do not seek him rarely suspect his presence. Yet they who search can always find; and guides are not lacking to direct strangers to the favorite haunts of the striped beast. He looks handsome at first. His claws are sheathed, and he lies supine in drowsy symmetry, and rubs his yellow head in playful softness against the caressing hand. But he is treacherous as savage, and the unwary who woo him most he rends the cruelest.

All the way from the battery to Thirtieth street, gambling saloons are thrust carefully out of sight in the upper stories of buildings of stone and marble, which thousands pass every day without dreaming of their existence. They have no outward sign to the many; but to men about town they are known at a glance. They usually have large gilt numbers on glass over doors leading through small vestibules to another door with a bell handle at the side, and a faithful porter behind. Any one can step into the first door from the crowded street, and no one will know where or how he has disappeared.

The faintest sound of the bell brings a peering face through a lattice, and after a moment's scanning, unless the visitor or visitors have something suspicious in their seeming, the inner door opens, and a hall and stairway lead to the apartment where every man's money is as good as another's until it is lost, and then it is a great deal worse.

If the weather be cold or inclement without, the new scene to which you have been introduced is a pleasant contrast. It gives, suddenly or completely, shelter, warmth, and comfort; pervades the mind with a sense of ease and pleasure, and luxury; prompts you to stay longer than you had intended

The rooms—there are usually two or three, sometimes more—are brilliantly lighted and expensively furnished. Curtains of satin and lace, sofas of velvet or silk, mirrors from ceiling to floor, carpets of crimson and white, carved sideboards sparkling with decanters and goblets, and swimming with liquors and wines, tables spread with china and silver, and dishes of appetizing odor are there.

You can recline on lounges, or smoke, or drink, or read the papers or magazines, or examine the pictures on the walls as long as you will without expense. Everything is free to *habitués* of the saloon, though the proprietors expect you to show your appreciation of their hospitality by a little patronage now and then. But they do not ask you. In the adjoining room fortune holds high carnival, and promises fairly to be kind.

Forget she is feminine, and not to be trusted overmuch. Go to her boldly, for boldness wins her as it does all her sex, and see if she repay you not with golden favors.

That is not counsel. It is the whisper of avarice in the heart, the greed of gain, the seductive voice that tells of wealth without labor, and pleasure without pain.

The adjoining room is open. It is closed to none. Enter; and, if you do not play, perhaps the game will interest you. Such your thought and prompting, and you go in.

This department is more quiet than the others, where men were talking, and smoking, and laughing.

The men are young and old; but all are well-dressed, rather overdressed, as they are generally in New-York. They stand about a cloth-covered table, on which cards are fastened, and put down circular pieces of ivory, known as "chips," while a hard-faced fellow draws the cards corresponding to those on the cloth from a silver box, and throws them to the right and left.

One pile is the banker's, the other the better's; the game being faro, of course. If you have put your "chips" on the card whose corresponding one falls on your pile, you have won; if on the banker's, you have lost.

The game is very simple and seems fair; and it is the fairest of gambling games. Yet the advantages in favor of the banker are such that he must always win in the long run. Faro banks are broken sometimes. But hundreds of betters must be broken before one bank can be. The temptation, even to gamblers, to bet against the bank, is so strong that they often make affidavit before notaries and witnesses to abstain from staking their money on that side of the table, as they say, for six months, or a year, or a lifetime even.

The difference between the professional and amateur gambler is very marked. The latter is anxious, pale, nervous; his voice is unsteady and hoarse; and he calls often for wine or liquor. His whole soul is in the game. His eye watches it with a quivering glow. He smiles with a sickly smile sometimes, especially when he loses largely; but the counterfeit would not deceive a child.

The professional's face is cold and fixed as marble. The closest scrutiny could not determine if he was winning or losing. With the same stolid indifference he takes in and pays out the money, even if he owns the bank. He is often a dealer only, on a regular salary; but, whether dealer or banker, no one would conjecture from his countenance.

I have seen bankers lose their last stake, and the puff of their cigar was as regular as when they had gained $20,000 in half an hour.

A gambler at Baden Baden lost immense sums to a dark-browed Spaniard, whom the superstitious fancied in league with the Evil One, and, when he passed over the last *rouleau* of gold, he quietly said, "The bank is broken," stepped aside, and blew out his brains.

The patrons of the bank are, as I have said, of different ages. The beardless youth, the man in middle life, the gray-haired, wrinkled man are there, drawn by the same fascination. The majority of those present are past middle age; for love of money survives the love of pleasure.

No one can enter a fashionable gambling-house in New-York, unless he has learned the World thoroughly, (the knowledge is not sweet, though it be profitable) without being surprised at those he meets there, without some disturbance of his faith.

That young man, known to be dissipated, spoiled by the over-indulgence of a wealthy but unprincipled father, you expected to see at such a place. It is natural enough a badly-reared youth, with a bad example before him, should seek to gain the means for a still more lavish expenditure. Any one can read his destiny. A few more years of waste and riot; probably a conventional marriage, without abandonment of mistresses; death from *delirium tremens*,—printed, in the morning paper, congestion of the brain—a funeral sermon in a Fifth avenue church extolling the virtues he laughed at in life; a hearse and mourning carriages trailing to Greenwood; a comely widow and few tears.

But that sleek, venerable-looking man you did not think to encounter. You say you have seen him with gold-clasped hymn-book, bending low and repeating audibly at Trinity. No doubt. That was Sunday. This is Thursday; and the best of fashionable Church members may be wicked one day of the week.

Flushed and pale by turns is the person opposite. He has been there regularly for three months past; and he has lost of late thousands of dollars, though fortune favored him at first. His salary is but $1,500 in the Petroleum bank. He is assistant teller, and he makes his account good with memorandum-checks that never can be paid. Possibly he will pay the debt by paying the one he owes to nature. Desperation is upon him, and discovery imminent; but the Hudson is deep, and flows not far away.

The silence is impressive about the table, save when a short quick oath is breathed by a loser, or the voice of laughter comes from the supper-room, where the jingling of glasses is heard. Men come and go, and until long after midnight the game continues—betting often growing heavier with the advancing hours. Those entering are usually hot with drink, and bet carelessly and blindly, and are lucky not seldom. Those departing look wan and wretched, for they have lost everything. They dash down a glass of liquor, as they go out, to drown memory, and Broadway greets them as before; but all is changed.

Hundreds of these faro banks, splendid, fascinating dangerous, are in every fashionable and frequented quarter, particularly near the hotels and theatres. They have regular attachés, who are either salaried or receive a certain per centage for the strangers they induce to enter the gilded hells. Those decoys are very energetic and persevering. They frequent the hotels, restaurants, bar-rooms and places of amusement; make acquaintances by pretending to have met the strangers somewhere before; inviting them to drink, to take a walk, to step in and see a friend, and all the well-known rest.

Strange, men can be so easily duped. But they can. The oldest tricks seem to become new every day. The pretending-to-be world-wise walk into open pitfalls with open eyes. Many of the gambling-saloons are conducted as honestly as such places can be. But more are mere pretexts for plunder. Strangers are drugged, and, when consciousness returns, they have been robbed. At many, professional bullies manufacture quarrels, and steal under appearance of fighting.

In the First, Fourth and Fifth wards, desperate characters are to be found, with dirty cards and bloated faces, prepared for burglary and murder, but preferring the easier task of swindling.

In the low bagnios of Greene, and Mercer, and Thompson streets, cards, and dice, and "sweat-cloths" can be had for less than the asking.

In the William street and Bowery concert saloons, monte, and vingt-un, and roulette, and rouge-et-noir, and, of recent months, coulo and keno, have been played, and are still.

Sailors' boarding-houses in Water, and Pearl, and West streets, employ runners to seize mariners, who are robbed and beaten, and have no redress.

All over the island, gambling goes on. But the most dangerous places are the fashionable saloons in Broadway and in the vicinity of Union and Madison squares. Where champagne sparkles, and gamblers are elegantly dressed and have good manners, the first temptation is offered, and the first steps downward are covered with velvet, so soft that the falling footstep awakes not the most timid fear.

The proprietors of the fashionable gambling-saloons in New-York live like princes, but usually spend as they go. They have incomes reckoned by tens of thousands; but their mistresses, and horses, and luxurious establishments, and hazards leave them but little at the close of the year. Some of them are men of education and family; but generally they are of vulgar origin, and have learned those characteristics of gentlemen—coolness and self-possession—only as a necessary accompaniment of their perfidious calling. They appear well often. But, taken beyond their depth, they betray the coarseness of their nature, and the meanness of their associations.

CHAPTER XXVII.

HENRY WARD BEECHER.

IF the country contains any man in or out of the pulpit more popular, in the strict sense of the term, than Henry Ward Beecher, I do not know him. That he is regarded more as a man than a clergyman, is shown by the fact that, in speaking of him, the prefix of "reverend" is rarely applied to his name. Indeed, there seems to be something inappropriate in the title, intimately as Beecher has been associated with the clerical profession all his life. He is the representative of the liberal American mind rather than of the Congregational church; of humanity rather than of a creed: hence his reputation and influence.

Henry Ward Beecher was born June 27, 1813, at Litchfield, Conn., graduated at Amherst, Mass., in his twenty-first year; studied theology under his father, the celebrated Lyman Beecher, at Lane Seminary, near Cincinnati, Ohio, and in 1837 was placed in charge of a Presbyterian church in Lawrenceburg, Ind. He remained there only two years, having been called to Indianapolis, where he continued until 1847. His sermons were from the beginning marked by freshness, boldness and originality, and attracted so much attention that he was induced, after spending ten years in the West, to accept the pulpit of Plymouth Church, Brooklyn, of which he has ever since been the pastor. Though he lives in Brooklyn, he is so identified with New-York that he could not, with fitness, be omitted from this volume.

The Beechers are unquestionably a gifted family, and some of them have shown something very like genius and an inclination, if not determination, to follow their own thoughts and express their own judgment. Common traits are visible in Lyman, the father, and in the children, Edward, Henry, Harriet and Catherine. They are all strong-minded, brave-hearted, firm-souled; and their peculiarities have reproduced a new form of the old epigram, that mankind is composed of the human family and the Beechers.

At school Beecher was not remarkable for application or diligence. He was bright, but, on the whole, rather indolent, so far as routine studies were concerned. He was a perpetual reader, and exceedingly fond of Nature. Often, when he should have been conning his lessons, he was wandering in the woods, or lying beside streams, devouring some one of the numerous volumes he was more ready to borrow than return. Several of his professors predicted he would never amount to anything, and others that he would come to some bad end. They were false prophets, as they generally are; for their knowledge is of books, not of men. They are prone to believe any youth who does not put his soul into Greek hexameters and conic sections, and fails of punctuality at chapel service, is tending to irremediable evil. Beecher did not, I am glad to say, graduate with the highest honors of his class, as the stereotyped expression is. On the contrary, he barely got through; and if he had not gotten through, he would have been little grieved, for he always held the deepest wisdom to be in communion with Man and Nature, through whom God is revealed.

Lyman Beecher had, from Henry's childhood, designed him for the church. He was not alarmed by the eccentricity of the youth, for he had deep faith in the boy's good sense, stability of character, and disposition to do right. He was proud of him, too; believed him a genius because he was a Beecher, and the son of his father, and preordained, therefore, to walk in the true ways of the righteous.

Henry Ward had no natural appetite for theology; thought seriously of being a sailor, a traveler, a physician, a public speaker. But his filial affection and the earnest wishes of his father determined his course, and sent him to Lane Seminary. He showed there many of the eccentricities of Amherst. He roamed over the beautiful hills about Cincinnati, sometimes even on Sunday; and it is rumored that he "profaned" the sacred day by reading poetry and novels. He was heterodox, too, in his liking for feminine society—girls, especially those of a superior age (clever and precocious boys are usually attracted to women of twice their years) having always interested him, and drawn him even from the books he read with the sweetness of conscious interdiction. In spite of the rather stiff and sombre character of Lane Seminary, Beecher seems to have had quite a good time there, and he still preserves very happy memories of the days spent at Walnut Hills. Many of the residents of the neighborhood recollect him as a merry, light-hearted youth, as unlike his fellow-students, and as free from formality and seriousness as if he had dropped down at the Seminary from the planet Mercury or Venus.

There has always been something a trifle grotesque, to my mind, in Beecher's being a Congregational minister, not because Beecher is so peculiar, but because he is so unlike all other divines of that church. For more than twenty years he has filled the Plymouth church pulpit, and has constantly advanced what, in any other man, would have been deemed the most startling and pernicious heresies. He has escaped condemnation and expulsion by his honesty and audacity. His boldness of utterance has frightened the timid into silence, and the thoughtful into admiration. Every one has deemed him sincere and zealous, and has accepted his breadth and toleration as the advanced conditions of a higher Christianity.

Beecher must have startled his flock at first; for its members were very different when he took charge of their spiritual direction from what they have since become under his teachings. But he has shown supreme tact and admirable discretion; his fine instincts revealing to him what he could and what he could not say, and when the opportunity was ripe for a theologic *coup d' état.*

I can imagine with what an uncomfortable feeling many of his spiritual brothers and sisters must have heard his first invitation to all who believed in Jesus Christ to take the sacrament. They have grown used to him now. He has educated them up to a height from which they would once have looked down dizzily. He has led them along unconsciously until they hardly know over what an immense space they have traveled. The floods they feared, and the precipices they dreaded, were found to be flowing by picturesque banks, and commanding beautiful views, whose existence they had been unconscious of.

I do not wonder many people say Beecher does not and cannot believe in his creed. He is too broad for it; but he does an immense deal of good in an orthodox pulpit that he could not do in any other. He knows that; he is dimly conscious of a pious fraud; but he thinks the end justifies the means. He satisfies his conscience by the conviction that he is broadening all theology, and by degrees making it and Christianity one and the same thing.

They who hold such opinions are mistaken. Beecher is sincere and earnest beyond question. He is broader than his church is usually regarded, but not broader than his interpretation of its dogmas. He expounds the truths of the Bible for himself instead of being bound by the explanations of others; and no one will say Humanity and Christianity are not on his side. He is a natural man, in perfect health, and therefore cheerful, buoyant, hopeful. He does not fancy himself pious because he is bilious, or devoted because suffering from dyspepsia.

Beecher has been compared to Spurgeon; but one suggests the other only by contrast. Beecher seems odd, for he is what few men in the pulpit are, an individual. He is eccentric without affecting eccentricity, and his peculiar oratory is so different from the starched common-places and narrow theology of some divines that I do not marvel it is captivating alike to the ordinary and the cultivated. He does not believe his office is sacred unless he fills it with living work and vital faith in humanity; and he does not claim for his position what he, the man, fails to yield to it. Other preachers lose the man in the profession. Beecher loses the profession in the man; and this, I suspect, is more than all else the secret of his clerical success.

Beecher was one of the founders of the *Independent*, the most lucrative religious paper in the country. He was for years its *de facto* editor, and contributed to it a series of fresh, racy and vigorous articles signed with an asterisk, which were afterwards published in book form under the title of the "Star Papers," and had a wide sale. Several years since he dissolvod his connection with the *Independent* on account of his numerous employments, sacerdotal and secular.

Hardly any man dwelling in the metropolian district is more industrious than he. He has an appetite for work that is hardly appeasable. However much he does he is dissatisfied because he does not do more. Between his sermons and church duties, his correspondence and lectures, his general literary work and his travels hither and thither, he has little time he can call his own.

He has written and completed a number of able and eloquent volumes, and is now engaged upon a "Life of Jesus," which will be his most elaborate and finished work. He will not complete it probably for several years, but when he does, it will necessarily attract great attention, be sharply criticised and generally read. The opinions of such a man as Beecher on Christ are worth hearing, especially as he has said that he can only understand God through his Divine Son; that Eternal Goodness, Justice and Mercy are made clear and certain through the suffering and atonement of the Savior of Mankind.

"Norwood" has done much to popularize Beecher's mode of thought and his views on religion. Though not a novel according to the rules of art, it is very interesting as a record of the author's opinions and sympathies. The fact that he was about to write a novel, troubled a part of his congregation at first; but he is always troubling its most orthodox members, and they soon reconciled themselves to what they have come to believe his inevitable waywardness. The publication of "Norwood" in the *Ledger* increased the circulation one hundred thousand, so that Robert Bonner could well afford to pay $30,000 to its author.

With the exception of John B. Gough, Beecher is probably the most popular lecturer in the country. He did not lecture last season, nor will he this, albeit he can make $10,000 every Winter he consents to appear before lyceums.

He took a deep interest in politics after the question of slavery entered into them. In 1856 he addressed mass meetings in favor of the Republican candidates, and continues to be a stump speaker whenever he believes he can benefit the cause. He was untiring in his efforts to strengthen the North during the rebellion, and it is said, after Sumter was fired on, he was with difficulty prevented from taking up a musket in defence of the country. He was only kept out of the ranks by his friends proving to him logically that he could be of infinitely greater service in influencing public opinion with his voice and pen than in acting as a private soldier.

Beecher has a good income, much of which he is

reputed to expend in charity. Last year he returned about $40,000, the greater part of which was, no doubt, from "Norwood." His salary as pastor of Plymouth Church is $10,000 or $12,000, and he earns quite as much in other ways. He has an amiable and devoted wife and several children, one of whom, his eldest son, served as a captain of artillery during the War, and another who is now entering Yale college. He has a very pleasant and comfortable home in Brooklyn, full of pictures, books, Scripture mottoes and sunshine. Everyone knows how he looks; that his face is quite as physical as spiritual; that he is always in robust health, and that in his fifty-fifth year he appears like a great, fresh-hearted boy released from the school of tradition for a Summer holiday of good-fellowship and common sense.

CHAPTER XXVIII.

THE RESTAURANTS.

To a stranger, New-York must seem to be perpetually engaged in eating. Go where you will between the hours of 8 in the morning and 6 in the evening, and you are reminded that man is a cooking animal. Tables are always spread; knives and forks are always rattling against dishes; the odors of the kitchen are always rising. Is the appetite of the Metropolis ever appeased? you think. Whence come all the people to devour all the food that is displayed in every shop between Whitehall slip and Central Park.

In West and Water streets, as well as in Broadway and Fourteenth, the appetite is tempted, though in more or less delicate ways. The whole island appears covered with oysters and clams, and the destiny of its inhabitants to eat is clear. We are forced to believe no one can be hungry in New-York, which seems to contain food enough to supply the entire nation. This must impress the emigrant as the land of plenty, the great store-house of the World. And yet hundreds daily pass the richly-furnished restaurants and heaps of prepared provisions, without the means of gratifying their hunger.

One advantage of New-York is that a man can live here very much as he chooses. He can live fashiona-

The Restaurants.

bly and luxuriously for from one to five hundred dollars, or meanly and poorly for six to eight dollars a week. The latter method very few Americans adopt unless compelled by absolute necessity; and not then very long, for laudanum is not dear, and the rivers are very deep.

The City contains five or six thousand restaurants and eating-houses of different kinds. Nearly all of them do a successful business, and many make their proprietors rich in a very few years. They vary as greatly in their appearance and prices as in the character of their patrons. They range from the elegance and costliness of Delmonico's and Taylor's to the subterranean sties where men are fed like swine, and dirt is served gratis in unhomœopathic doses. There, are silver, and porcelain, and crystal, and fine linen, and dainty service. Here, are broken earthen-ware, soiled table-cloths, and coarse dishes. In Fourteenth street, you pay for a single meal what would keep you for a week below Chambers street, and give you dyspepsia withal unless you have the stomach of an ostrich.

One wonders how even this great City can support so many eating-houses. It could not but for the great distance between the business and residence quarters, and the consequent necessity of the commercial classes dining or lunching down town. Nearly three-quarters of the restaurants below Canal street owe their support to that fact; for as soon as the mercantile tide sets northward, their trade is over for the day.

Nowhere else in this country do men live so largely at restaurants as in New-York. Nowhere else are lodging and eating so completely and strictly divided.

Probably 150,000 of our population rent rooms up town, and get their meals down town. They adopt that mode of existence because they are not able to live at hotels, and they are unwilling to put up with what is termed, by an ingenious figure of speech, boarding-house accommodations.

Eating is done in the Metropolis with the haste of Americans intensified. From 12 o'clock to 3 of the afternoon, the down-town eating-houses are in one continuous roar. The clatter of plates and knives, the slamming of doors, the talking and giving of orders by the customers, the bellowing of waiters, are mingled in a wild chaos. The sole wonder is how any one gets anything; how the waiters understand anything; how anything is paid for, or expected to be paid for. Everybody talks at once; everybody orders at once; everybody eats at once; and everybody seems anxious to pay at once.

The waiters must be endowed with extraordinary, and the cooks with miraculous, power of hearing. How could any one expect them to comprehend, "Ham-eggs-for-two-oyster-stew-coff and-ap-pie-for-three-pork-beans-ale-cigars-for-four-beef-steak-onions-porter-cigar-for-five-mut-'n-chop-mince-pie-black-tea-for-one," all pronounced in one word, in various keys and tones, with the peculiar recitative of eating-houses?

It is a curious sight to witness the skirmishing, as it is termed, in Park row, Nassau or Fulton streets, about the hours named.

A long counter is crowded with men, either standing elbow to elbow, or perched on stools, using knives, and forks, and spoons; talking with their mouths full; gesticulating with their heads, and arms, and bodies;

eating as if they were on the eve of a journey round the World, and never expected to obtain another meal this side of the antipodes. The hungry are constantly satiated,—constantly going; but others, as hungry, as feverish, as garrulous, as energetic as they, are always coming to supply their places, and continue the chaos of confusion as before.

If misery makes strange bed-fellows, restaurants in New-York create singular companions. Men meet there who never meet anywhere else. Faces become familiar at a table that are never thought of at any other time. You know the face, as that of your brother, or father, or partner; but, when it turns away into the crowd, you never suspect, or care, or conjecture where it goes, or to whom it belongs.

I heard an old *habitué* of restaurants say the other day, "There's a man I've been seeing for twenty years at Crook's. Yet who he is, or what he does, or how he lives, I have not the remotest idea. I wonder who the devil the old fellow is? But I suppose he has the same curiosity about me."

It is interesting to enter the restaurants now and then, and observe the faces, the manners, the general bearing of the frequenters. How full they are of opposites and variations! They are very different from what I often take or mistake them.

I remember thinking that that milk-faced, pale-eyed man, in such plain and well-worn attire, with such a humble air, was a poor clergyman who was probably compelled to work for a pittance during the week for one of the religious journals, and was firm in this idea until, coming down-town one evening, I observed my old friend in the hands of the police, who were dragging him to the Tombs. He was one of the most desperate burglars in the City, and had for years escaped detection. The day after his commitment he was found in his cell, hanging by the neck, one of his suspenders about his neck, stone dead,—glaring defiance out of his glazed eyes at defeated justice.

There was the hard-visaged, cruel-chinned person, who ate like a cormorant. A sinister expression was in his eye, which would not meet yours, strive as you might to catch it. I was convinced he was a scoundrel —a sneak-thief, perhaps; that he beat his children unmercifully, and ruled his poor, frightened wife with a rod of iron. He subsequently proved to be a Williamsburg clergyman, and was esteemed a saint by his congregation.

The slovenly, abstracted, care-worn looking mortal whom I fancied a carman or a porter, and whom I was often tempted to give a dollar to, so woe-begone and overworked did he seem, revealed himself to me as one of the richest men in New-York. His daily income was more than all I was worth, including my lands along the Guadalquivir and my castles in the Pyrenees.

Strange, all this. Is physiognomy at fault; or is it truer than we think?

Seated on that stool is the editor of an ultra republican paper; and, as he cuts his slice of roast beef, his elbow touches the arm of the democratic high-priest, who claims to dictate the course of the party in New-York. They have abused each other for years in print; and now they nod to each other, and drink a glass of ale together, and separate, each to tell his readers how unprincipled the other is.

Opposite one another at the small table, are two literary men whose names are familiar as household words all the country over. They recognize each other's faces, but neither has the most latent suspicion that his neighbor is the famous poet, or the author of half a dozen of the best known books in America.

That handsome, carefully dressed man of fashion lights his cigar by the cigar of the pensive artist. They have not met before, and yet their warm friendship for the same metropolitan beauty who has just come back from Paris, ought at least to make them acquainted. At the door they pass her husband, and the artist is unconscious who he is. But the other grasps his hand, and presses it as if the husband were very near his heart. Do men ever really like the husbands of the wives they love?

When evening comes and the business of the day is ended, the down-town restaurants are closed, and those up-town have their active season. Then Curet's, and the Café de l'Universite, and Taylor's, and Delmonico's thrive, particularly toward midnight, after the theatres and the concerts and the operas are over.

The up-town restaurants furnish quite a contrast to those in the lower quarter of the City. They have no confusion, no bustle, no jostling, no door-slamming. Ladies elegantly and elaborately dressed go with their escorts to upper Broadway and Fourteenth street; go in handsome equipages, amid flower and toilette odors, and with all the suggestive poetry that night lends to a fine woman, intoxicated with her own sweetness, and the consciousness that she is lovable to every sense.

Late suppers, and rich wines, and low voices, and delicious flattery are dangerous, dear madam, even if you think it not. And he who is so gallant and so refined, so tender and so generous—such a contrast to him you vowed to love when your heart revoked the vow—may be more to you than you dream.

It is hard for a man to be a married woman's friend, and only that. Yet every woman declares he shall never be aught else; and, while she declares, is deceived, and learns nothing by her deception.

How few of the fashionable wives that sup up town after the play or the opera, sup with their husbands! Their husbands may be there; but they are with other women. Etiquette is opposed to the consorting of the married in public; and one might be excused for believing the custom founded on nature, so liberally and gladly is the custom followed.

It is an old fashion, but good, nevertheless, that persons doomed to live together should love each other. Society has changed that, I am aware; but society makes dreadful mistakes sometimes, and, for its own convenience and interest, wrecks the happiness of individuals not seldom.

"Do not moralize. The World is well enough as it is. We must take it as we find it."

So says my married friend who smokes his cigar contentedly at home, while his pretty wife flirts at a brilliant reception, with "one of the best fellows in the World."

Well, I won't moralize. If he is satisfied, why should I complain?

CHAPTER XXIX.

MANTON MARBLE.

Though Henry Mackenzie is known in literature as the author of "The Man of the World," he is not, so far as is ascertained, a progenitor of Manton Marble, called here by the same title.

Marble is the youngest of the editors-in-chief of the Metropolis, and compared to the rest, is rather a new man. He was, I believe, attached to the staff of the *Evening Post* for a number of months, but first emerged from his obscurity when the *World* newspaper was established, if my memory serve, in 1860 as a one-cent religious paper, so painfully pious that it would not publish theatrical advertisements.

Marble was born, I am informed, in Rhode Island, and graduated from Rochester University in his nineteenth year. It is presumed that he inherited little more than a good classical education, and that he early sought to earn his own livelihood. He had at first some ambition to become a lawyer, but discovered in himself so strong a bias for writing that after contributing for a while to the Providence papers, he concluded, though unheralded and unknown, to remove to the metropolis of New England and seek his fortune there. He had written enough to awake the admiration of his youthful friends and to gain confidence in himself. Long before he quitted college he was accounted unusually clever with his pen, and is said to have written the theses of his less capable fellow-students, and to have shown as much variety as activity in compositions of his own.

Arrived in Boston, where the citizens are so much engrossed with Greek and Latin that they rarely have leisure to study English, Marble went into the office of the *Traveller* and asked for an engagement.

"What can you do?" inquired the editor.

"Almost anything."

"Have n't you any specialty?"

"No. I'll try my hand at any kind of writing."

"Have you brought letters of recommendation?"

"No. I think a man's work is his best recommendation. All I want is a chance. I have determined to adopt journalism as a profession, and I have concluded to begin here."

"You are confident, at least, my young friend; and I like your manner and directness. Have you ever tried dramatic criticism?"

"I shall try it when you have assigned me to some duty. I feel quite at home in theatricals."

"Very well. Forrest plays 'Lear' at the Boston Theater this evening. Go there, and let us see what you can do."

Marble attended the performance, and wrote at the close two columns of very able and exhaustive criticism upon the play, its historic character and its representation by the American tragedian." For so young and inexperienced a writer the critique was remarkable, delighted the editor, and pleased the City of Notions. Marble was engaged the next evening upon the regular staff, and continued the office for two years. He subsequently connected himself with other papers at the "Hub;" but finally out-growing Bunker Hill and Boston Common, he came to Broadway and the Central Park.

He went upon the *World* as a general writer at a salary, I have been told, of $30 a week, and rapidly rose in the establishment until he was made editor-in-chief. The paper changed hands, character and politics, was revolutionized half a dozen times; from religious became secular and then political; was mildly Conservative; grew Republican; waxed Democratic— feebly at first, ferociously at last; and amid all those changes Marble held on, and developed with them into the latest form and freshest shape.

What his politics were originally, no one seems to know. It is said that at college he cherished few convictions, but left his mind free to embrace what at any time appeared best. The Republicans declare he is, or ought to be, with them; but that he has temporized, and followed where his interests led. Such statements are gratuitous. It is fair to presume that Marble knows, at least, on what side he wants to be, and he certainly has a right to choose his party and his principles among the variety prevalent at the present time.

If Marble is individually what he is professionally, a man of the world, he is a shrewd and successful one; and it is nobody's affair what he privately thinks or believes. He says daily through his columns that he is an ultra Democrat, and as such the public is bound to accept him and his paper.

When Marble went into the *World* he was not supposed to possess anything, and he now has a large interest in the journal he controls, report making him owner of more than one-half of all the shares, which can hardly be worth less, for his portion, than $150,000. He has manifested tact and energy in getting hold of the stock, and lifting himself from a mere salaried subordinate to the chief-editorship. He receives a salary for his services of $6,000 a year, and his present income from his shares ought to be at least $10,000 to $12,000 more.

The financial history of the *World* has been varied. It sank money with persevering liberality for several years; $300,000 to $350,000 having been swallowed up in its fluctuations between theologic sanctity and pugnacious partisanship of the most confirmed character. The paper is on a paying basis now, and its profits last year are stated to have been about $25,000, with a prospect of a material increase during the current year.

Marble, though still young, is not a hard worker in the sense in which Greeley and Raymond are hard workers. He manages and directs the fourth or editorial page alone, leaving the other departments to the care of subordinates. He writes most of his editorials, not long nor frequent usually, in his own library up town, where he lives very comfortably, if not luxuriously, sending his manuscript to the office, and receiving proofs at home. He was married four or five years ago to a lady of fortune, whose death he has recently been called upon to mourn.

Marble is a man of fine culture, being well versed in intellectual philosophy and transcendental metaphysics. He has read Hume and Hamilton, Buckle and Mill, Spencer and Comte, and has dallied with

Kant and Schelling, Fichte and Hegel, as much as an active journalist conveniently can unassisted by mental cobwebs and vats of lager beer. He is about forty, and though he looks materially older than he did at the beginning of the War, he would generally be considered handsome. Indeed he may lay more claim to personal comeliness than any New-York editor of prominence, and his manners and presence are very good and prepossessing. He is under the medium size, rather too heavy for his stature, has dark eyes, black hair and deep olive complexion.

Marble is, it is said, a descendant of the Puritans, his ancestors having been residents of New England for three generations. He is quite picturesque in appearance. If he were attired in a velvet doublet with slashed sleeves, a conical ribbon-crossed hat put upon his head, a guitar slung to his back, a carbine placed in his hand, and he himself set down in the midst of the Roman campagna, he would be mistaken for an Italian bandit of the romantic school.

Marble is an active politician, a prominent member of the Manhattan Club, and, for a journalist, a man of elegant leisure, cultivating the graces, more than most of his guild, and believing that continual toil does not include all the virtues, or make compensation for every sharp annoyance and feverish trouble of existence. He is something of an epicurean withal, and wisely holds that while the uses of labor are sweet they need the acid of repose to give them the relish that does not pall.

CHAPTER XXX.

THE FIVE POINTS

NOTHING indicates the moral improvement of New-York more than the change the notorious locality, the Five Points, has undergone during the past ten years. It is bad enough now—bad as it can be, one who saw it for the first time would think; but, compared to what it was fifteen years ago, it is as a white-sanded floor to the Augean stable.

The Five Points, formed by the intersection of Worth, Park and Baxter streets, is within a stone's throw of Broadway; and yet there are thousands of persons born and reared here who have never visited the famous and infamous quarter. Though the place has strangely changed, its reputation is nearly as vile as ever—showing how much easier it is to keep a bad name than to obtain a good one. The notoriety of the Five Points is not only national; it is trans-Atlantic. Londoners know it as well as St. Giles; and strangers ask to be shown to it before they visit Fifth avenue or the Central Park.

Deformities, after all, seem more interesting than beauties to the masses. Most men would rather look at a great criminal than a distinguished reformer;

would prefer the head of Probst the murderer, at the Museum of Anatomy, to the child-like face of Horace Greeley, in Printing-house square.

The Five Points is the festering nucleus of the Sixth ward, which, for nearly half a century, was much the worst in the City; though the Fourth now successfully disputes with it the palm of vice.

The moral suppuration extends far beyond the Points, into Mulberry and Mott, Elm and Centre, Pell and Dover, James and Roosevelt streets. Within half to three-quarters of a mile to the north and south-east of the Points, poverty and depravity, ignorance and all uncleanliness, walk hand in hand, with drunken gait and draggled skirts. Wherever one turns, his gaze is offended, his sensibility shocked, his pity and disgust excited at once.

The Five Points presents the other side of life, the unpleasant and painful side, which we think to banish by ignoring. Going there, we are brought face to face with the sternest and most revolting facts of civilization, and compelled to admit, much as we may wish it otherwise, that education and advancement can never be more than partial.

How vice always creeps under the hedge where virtue blossoms fragrantly! The Five Points is merely a background to Broadway and Fifth avenue—a background most of us are unwilling to see, but which exists, nevertheless, in all its hideousness.

The Points does not peer out at us in its polluted ugliness, as we walk or ride self-satisfied up town; and we take good care to shun such haunts in our every-day life of indifference, interest or pleasure.

Turning out of glittering and crowded Broadway

through Worth street, nearly opposite the New-York hospital, two minutes' walk brings us to the Five Points, with its narrow, crooked, filthy streets; its low, foul, rickety frames; its ancient, worn-down, unsavory tenements; its dark, mephitic green-groceries; its noxious liquor dens; its unsightly cellars; its dingy old clothes and old furniture establishments; its muck, and mire, and slime, reeking, rotting, oozing out at every pore of the pestiferous place.

The worst parts of London, and Constantinople, and Lisbon are concentrated there. Your senses ache, and your gorge rises, at the scenes and objects before you. Involuntarily your handkerchief goes to your nostrils, and your feet carry you away from the social carrion into which you have stepped. But if, like a young student in the dissecting-room, you have come to see and learn, you will stay your flying feet.

The first thing that impresses you, is the swarm of children in every street, before every house and shop, and at every corner; children of all ages and color, though the general hue inclines to dirt. The offspring of vice is prolific as the offspring of poverty, and both are there. From the coarse or cadaverous infant in its hard-featured mother's arms, to the half-grown girl or boy, unkempt, unwashed, unrestrained, the period of early youth is represented. Even maternity is not sacred or tender there. No soft light in the mother's face, as she gives nourishment from the gross, all-exposed bosom to the already infected babe.

What should be the innocence of childhood is banished from those purlieus of impurity. Those boys and girls have no childhood, no youth, no freshness, no sweetness, no innocence. They have never eaten a mouthful of wholesome food; inhaled a breath of untainted air; heard the tones of a pure affection. They are accursed from their birth; formed to evil by association; bound to vice by a chain of necessary events they cannot break. Pity them, then; but hate them not; and rejoice that to you fortune has been less unkind.

All along the sidewalk, unless it be cold, lounge, sit and stand men and women, out of whom all the gentleness of humanity seems pressed. You cannot see anywhere a face that woos or holds you. You do not hear a voice that touches you with its tone. Hardness, and grimness, and filthiness are in the people and the places, spread up, and down, and across every visible thing.

How can any mortal live there? you think. It seems a physical impossibility in such an atmosphere, with such surroundings.

See the group near the corner. That gray-haired crone, clad so slatternly that you shrink from passing her, talks in a hoarse, harsh voice to the young mulatto woman who leans against the broken door-way with a dirty pipe in her mouth, and leers at you as you go by.

A stalwart, cruel-looking negro sits on the dirty door-step, and calls to a white child to get him a dram from the opposite grocery—offering a penny for the service.

A young man, not nineteen, perhaps, but looking far older from the deep lines in his face, and the scowling expression about his brows, curses a boy who peers out of the window above, and calls him by names that one may not print. The boy answers in kind. The twain seem anxious to outdo each other in profanity and obscenity. You fancy murder may be there until you hear, rather than see, their horrid laugh. They are really friends,—such friends as the Points alone can create. They are indulging in pleasantry. They are in their most amiable mood; and soon they join each other for a hideous debauch.

Old and young of both sexes, are mingled everywhere. You would hardly know the men from the women but from their beards and dress. In the women the distinction of sex is merely physiological. They swear, and drink, and fight like the most brutal men, often exceed them in coarseness and cruelty; for women who have once violated their nature have the redeeming virtues of neither sex.

Germans are not rare in the quarter; but they are usually thrifty. They are buying and selling for profit; and after a short time they move to better neighborhoods to set up bar-rooms and groceries.

Italians are numerous; for they are indolent, sensual and reckless of the future. They have no bias against dirt or vice. They love mendicancy, and monkeys, and musical instruments when they can be turned to practical account. Give them pennies, and garlic, and liquor—those of the lazzarone class who dwell there—and they will not ask for other comforts.

Some of the most brutal and desperate men of the locality are English. They are generally thieves, shoulder-hitters, or burglars,—sometimes murderers,—and end their lives in prison or in the gutter. They would die on the scaffold had not New-York a prejudice against hanging its greatest scoundrels. When they have done something that deserves hanging, they are chosen members of the City Council or Board of Aldermen.

Negroes are scattered through the Points, though most of them, from a long bleaching process, have become more Caucasian than African in their lineage. From this constant intermixture with other races, they have nearly died out, and are far less numerous than they were a few years ago.

One rarely sees a genuine black man or woman in the quarters; mulattoes and quadroons have supplied their place.

Before the War, some of the most desperate characters were negroes. A number of them were shot and stabbed to death; others, strange to say, were hanged, and more, not understanding the peculiarity of Metropolitan justice, were seized with needless alarm, and ran away; foolishly believing other places might be as safe for notorious criminals as our own dear New-York. Had they been more intelligent, they would have known the folly of their flight.

Rum-selling is the principal business at the Five Points; and it is said there is a groggery for every hundred adult male inhabitants. Everybody drinks, even the children. If they did not, they would not stay there. They have to keep themselves down to that unnatural level by increasing their bestiality through artificial means.

"Fences," or places for buying stolen goods, are very common. There are generally second-hand stores and pawnbrokers' shops combined, where a little money is lent on a good deal, and where anything is purchased without the asking of impertinent questions.

Retail groceries, where poor provisions are sold dear, and liquor vended by license or in secret, emit noisome odors at every corner.

Beyond these three branches of trade, commerce has few representatives. One wonders how so many shops can be supported. They could not if they had honest dealings with their customers. But honesty is not even assumed in Baxter street neighborhoods. All classes steal; and they who are cheated last and most, steal anew to right themselves,—a simple code of mercantile ethics that should commend itself to the more complicated one, Wall street.

The dance-houses, though they no longer share the glory of the past, are still a feature of Five Points society, and nowhere else can so vivid an idea of them be obtained. Strangers and New-Yorkers often visit dance-houses for curiosity; but they take the precaution to go armed, and under the direction and guidance of a policeman. Even then they sometimes get into trouble, and have been attacked and hurt before they could be rescued from the thieves, and harlots, and desperadoes among whom they have gone.

The dance-houses are kept by the lowest and vilest of the Five Points residents, and the dancing is usually in cellars, or in back rooms, or on ground floors. Black and white, males and females, of all ages are admitted free.

A cracked fiddle or two are supplied; and whoever will accept a partner steps upon the floor, and goes through the figures of a rude quadrille or waltz, until the musicians stop to drink, and the dancers to get breath.

If a man dance with one of these unfortunate creatures who calls herself a woman, he is expected to buy her a glass of liquor. The bar has its profit thereby, and the proprietor is paid for keeping up his establishment.

Hour after hour the grim and grinning cyprians dance and drink, and drink and dance, with thieves and burglars, sailors and bar-tenders, cracksmen and murderers, until they are overpowered with liquor, and sink down into brutal oblivion; or, on the alert for stealing, they wait for their companion's unconsciousness, and plunder him of his valuables.

Such orgies are revolting to the last degree; for there is no assumption of decorum, no pretense of the commonest decency.

There you see vice laid naked in all its deformity; and consequently, to all but those bred in its bosom, it is too repulsive to be dangerous, and too loathsome to be attractive.

Few of the curious care to witness Five Points life, or any of its phases, a second time. And they who have seen it once must doubt when they have gone away, that such shameless sin, such unrelieved grossness can be daily and hourly indulged in and enjoyed by those whose race and kind claim kindred with their own.

CHAPTER XXXI.

THE MORGUE.

The morgue in Paris has long been one of the objects of mournful interest that strangers and sight-seers visit. The morgue in New-York, since its establishment, little more than two years ago, has been one of the lions, though a dead lion, of the City, and attracts alike the curious and the sympathetic to its shadows.

The Metropolis alone has a morgue, though all the great American cities need, and will doubtless have one ere long. The cases of "Found Drowned," "Mysterious Death," "Nameless Tragedy" and the like are constantly increasing in this country, particularly in this City, and the want of a morgue was felt here years before it was instituted. Suicide has grown so alarmingly prevalent in the United States within a few years that our people threaten in undue season to equal, if not surpass, the Japanese in self-destruction. The English and French no longer enjoy a monopoly of throat-cutting, drowning and suffocation by charcoal. We Americans kill ourselves for all manner and no manner of reasons; and we seem to find many more pretexts for leaping off the precipice of time than the people of other lands.

Everything is in extremes here—the people, the climate, the conditions. We are the most nervous and intense the most eager and earnest, the most sanguine and sensitive, at once the most hopeful and melancholy nation on the Globe. We are constantly staking our future and our destiny on the cast of a die; and, when we lose, no wonder the thought of self slaughter rises in our minds. We are ever inclined to measure ourselves against Fate; and when Fate wins, the click of the pistol, or the stroke of the razor, or the leap into the water, settles all scores.

Moreover, our heterogeneous population, our gathering to our republican bosom the refuse and outcast of every soil and zone, naturalizes here each variety of crime, and makes murder the chronicle of the hour.

For such a peculiar condition of a peculiar society, where all races, rude and cultivated, toil and weep and strive, the morgue is needed—the sad epilogue after the dark curtain has fallen upon the tragedy.

M-o-r-g-u-e you read in prominent letters over the lowest door of the Bellevue hospital on the upper side of Twenty-sixth street, near the East river. The letters are gilt; but they seem set in deep shadows as you look at them, like lights burning in vaults of the dead. One might imagine the morgue had been located so near the broad, deep stream that the mysterious dead in its keeping might float to the door of the sombre place. In the still night the murmurs of the river, and the flow of the tide, sound strangely and mournfully in that quiet neighborhood. They seem calling for the unknown corpses under the waves to come to the morgue and be recognized.

The morgue will disappoint you when you enter it. It will remind you of a subterranean vault from its smallness, quietness and dampness. The room devoted to the purpose is not more than twenty feet square, divided by a glass partition, an exact imitation of the famous dead house in Paris.

One compartment, that to which the public is admitted, is entirely bare. Nothing on the checkered brick floor, nothing on the hard, strong walls but the rules of the morgue.

In the other compartment beyond the glass partition are four marble slabs, supported upon iron frames. Upon those slabs are exposed the bodies, entirely nude, except a slight wrapping about the lower part of the abdomen, of the unfortunates who have been found dead. Gutta percha tubes, suspended from the ceiling and connected with a reservoir, drop water steadily upon the foreheads of the corpses as they lie there, to keep them cool and fresh, and prevent decomposition until they are either recognized or removed for burial. The bodies are usually kept for twenty-four hours. If claimed by friends or acquaintances, in that time, they are delivered up with the clothing they wore, and such articles as they may have had on their person. After that period they are interred at the expense of the City, the usual absurd coroner's inquest having been held—rather to show, it would appear, how stupid the living are than how mysterious the dead—and their raiment and effects kept for six months in the event of their possible identification.

The number of bodies at the dead-house varies greatly, but increases steadily every season. Sometimes the four slabs have each a lifeless occupant, though that is seldom; and at others two or three days pass without the entrance of a corpse into the morgue. The average number of bodies is, about two hundred a year; and ten years hence, I doubt not they will be twice as many. Many of the bodies, perhaps the greater part, are never identified; nor is it singular when it is remembered how many hundreds there are in this vast City who have neither abiding place nor friend.

The majority of the corpses bear marks of violence, and are discovered in the water. Probably one half of the persons found have been murdered, and one quarter of them have committed suicide. The other quarter includes accidental drowning, falling dead in the street, run over by street-cars, and other vehicles and the natural casualties of city life.

Strange histories and startling tragedies lie within the life and death of those brought to the morgue. If all they thought, and felt, and endured, and suffered, could be known and written, romancers would not need to tax their invention and ingenuity for plots, situations and catastrophes. Truth is stranger than fiction; for that is original, and this only a copy. If those cold, mute lips could only speak from the still heart, still as the white marble beneath it, every living heart would thrill to the utterance as it never has over Shakspeare, or Poe, or Dickens.

A visit to the morgue is attended with something of the fascination the horrible has for even the finest of us. We like to linger there in spite of the repulsion of such a place. We are held, as when in the presence of the dead, by an indefinable magnetism, more painful than pleasurable; and yet we stay. What a flood of suggestions pours in upon us as we contemplate the naked figures through the glass! Who were they? What were they? Who loved them? How did they die?

What were their antecedents? Where are they now? —are the questions every mind asks, and no mind can answer.

That is the figure of an old and genteel-looking man. His hair is gray, but soft and fine. His flesh is white, and firm, and smooth, as if he had lived comfortably and been well cared for. His clothes are fashionable and expensive. A valuable watch and $500 in money were found on his person. He could not have been murdered. He could hardly have killed himself. How came he there? He was a wealthy gentleman from the West.

He was staying at the Fifth Avenue hotel, where his daughters are still expecting him. While walking through Twenty-third-street, in perfect health, he reeled beneath a stroke of apoplexy, fell on the sidewalk and died in three minutes. Habits of indolence and luxurious living have exacted their penalty. No one knew him. He was carried to the morgue.

To-morrow morning's papers will chronicle the "sudden death." His daughters will read the description, hasten to the morgue, pale and frightened, weeping and trembling; go home with his remains, and forget him in a month.

The blood still oozes from the gash in this head. The face of the man lying on the slat is bronzed and scarred with hard lines, as if he had led a life of toil; had had strong passions, and indulged them. Nothing was found on his person. His pockets were turned inside out. The body was picked up on one of the East river piers, as if it had been dropped there by one who intended to hurl it into the water, but had been frightened and hurried away.

The suspicion is correct. The dead man was a sailor. He had come from Liverpool, and with his wages in his pocket entered a low den and dance-house in Water street, was gotten drunk and an attempt made to rob him. He was powerful and resisted bravely. He struck the ruffian fiercely in the face, until anger added to avarice made a demon of the robber, who seized a hatchet and buried it in the victim's skull. No further struggle then. All still as death, for it was death. Then the fear of detection, the effort to hide the murder in the river, and the failure through sudden alarm.

But the murderer goes unpunished. A dozen murders have been committed on his premises, and no one has yet been convicted. There have been arrests, but nothing has been proved. The law is lax, and in New-York justice is represented only in marble upon the cupola of the City Hall.

It is folly to say "Murder will out." It will do nothing of the sort. More murders are unknown than revealed. Without reward there is little hope of recovery, and after a few days no one thinks of the most horrid crimes. The community demands a victim to-day, but to-morrow its sympathies are excited as its indignation has been. "He has not harmed me," says each one; "let him go for all me."

"Found dead, with a bullet through the brain," reads the item in the *Tribune*, and adds that no clue to the murder or murderer has yet been discovered. The body remains at the morgue for twenty-four hours without recognition. He is a foreigner, apparently French; looks like a mechanic; silver watch in his vest pocket; few dollars in his wallet; money evidently not the object of the deed. Two weeks pass. A wretched, hollow-eyed, half-starved man is picked up drunk in the Bowery. He is incoherent, raves, dreams terrible dreams.

Suspicion is awakened. The police look up the antecedents of the unfortunate, and it is shown he is the murderer of the Frenchman. When accused, he makes confession; says he does not want to live. His story is, that he is English, a resident of Birmingham. He saw the Frenchman first five years before, and the two became friends. The Gaul was poor, penniless indeed, and the Englishman took him to his home; gave him shelter, money, procured him a situation. The ungrateful scoundrel seduced his friend's wife; eloped with her; deserted her eventually, and came to America.

The husband vowed revenge; had no other purpose; followed the villain to these shores. Three months after arrival in New-York he met the Frenchman in a concert saloon; invited him to walk out, and shot him dead in the street.

Imprisonment and trial follow. The culprit has neither friends nor money, and should not, therefore, have indulged in the luxury of taking life. He is convicted and hanged in the Tombs yard. Another legal murder, far worse than the crime, is added to the disgraceful list.

In America we rarely execute men who take life for domestic honor. No man occupying the rank of gentleman can be hanged in the United States, outside of New-England. But with poor fellows and foreigners it is quite different. Ropes run smoothly about plebeian necks.

Suicide. Her features are regular, her limbs well formed. The gentleness and calmness of death have come to the worn and dissipated face turned upward to the ceiling of the narrow room. She must have been young, not more than twenty, I should judge; and yet dead by her own hand! The faint, peculiar odor of laudanum is about those full but colorless lips. She was found lifeless in a garret she had rented the day before, in a miserable tenement house in Rivington street. She had given no name. She had paid for the room a month in advance; had gone out but once, and then they had found her as she now lies. She left a rude scrawl, misspelled and scarcely legible: "Tel George I done it at laste. I coudent liv without him. I knowd I couldent. Lov is the caus."

It is the old story—old before Cheop's time. Even in the heart of that uneducated, untrained, friendless, abandoned girl, Love, after years of prostitution, had found lodgement and consecration. She would have led, at that late day, a true life, had it been possible to her; for love means purity and loyalty, even to the vilest. But he, the unworthy object of a sacred passion, deserted her; and she rubbed her dark memory from the face of Nature. Who says the age of romance and poetry is over, when common courtesans die every day for the love their loathsome calling would seem to make them incapable of feeling?

The ghastly morgue has, like everything else, its humorous side.

Out of this elegant carriage steps a pretty girl, in elaborate toilette, with pale, tear-stained cheek. She looks eagerly through the glass, and sees not a single body. She inquires if a young man, describing him as an Apollo, has been brought in; and the person in charge replies: "No, Miss, we haven't had nothin' this two days. Bizness is gettin' mighty dull." So the girl goes back to the carriage; tells the liveried coachman not to mention where she has been, and is driven off.

Poor sentimental child! She has just had her first lover. He didn't come to see her last night, and they had had a little quarrel the evening previous, and she fondly believed he had destroyed himself on that account. Charles is really drinking champagne furiously at Curet's with a college chum, and has quite forgotten all about the quarrel, and "darling Dora" beside.

It is not uncommon for women to seek their lovers at the morgue, though that is the last place they are likely to find them. But men rarely suspect their mistresses of self-destruction, perhaps because there *is* such a close connection in feminine minds between love and laudanum.

Wives who have dissipated and eccentric husbands visit the morgue frequently in search of their dead lords. Is their visit prompted by their wishes, or their fears?

The morgue is melancholy, but has its uses. You and I may meet there, reader, and no more recognize each other dead than living.

CHAPTER XXXII.

ALEXANDER T. STEWART.

More than any one else in America probably Alexander T. Stewart is the embodiment of business. He is emphatically a man of money—thinks money; makes money; lives money. Money is the aim and end of his existence, and now, at sixty-five, he seems as anxious to increase his immense wealth as he was when he sought his fortune in this country, forty years ago. Riches with him, no doubt, have become ambition, which is to be the wealthiest man in the United-States. For ten or twelve years William B. Astor has been his only rival, and it is now uncertain which of the two is the greater capitalist. Astor owns more real estate; but Stewart has the larger income.

Stewart has never been communicative about his early life, and those curious in respect to it are generally rebuffed in their inquiries. It is known that he is a native of Ireland, having been born near Belfast, though he claims to be descended from a Scotch family. He is of Scotch-Irish extraction, with the determination, perseverance and energy that marks such stock, and must of necessity have sprung from the heroic defenders of Londonderry, as all the Scotch-Irish, risen to any eminence, have done before and since his time.

In his eighth year Stewart lost his parents, and was reared by his maternal grandfather, who intended to educate him for the Methodist Church, of which he himself was a devout member. The boy is reported to have shown very early a resolution to be first in whatever he undertook, and to have been foremost in his class at Trinity College, Dublin, where, like every true son of Erin, he graduated with honor. He was then in his eighteenth year, and his grandfather being dead he was placed under the guardianship of a Quaker. Not liking Ireland he concluded to seek his fortune in the New World, and came here in 1823 with letters of recommendation to some of the best families of Friends in the City. He was a teacher at first, and persons now living remember when they sat under his instruction.

He either did not succeed in his calling, or did not relish it; for after ten or twelve months of teaching he entered a mercantile establishment, though without any natural bias for trade, his friends say—a statement to be received with liberal allowance. He had an interest of some kind in the house, and accident, it is said, made him a merchant; for his partner died suddenly and left the entire responsibility of the business upon the young man of two-and-twenty. He then determined to devote himself to trade, and returning to Ireland sold the little property he had there; bought a lot of laces with the money, and came back to New-York.

His store was a very small, dismal one in Broadway, opposite the City Hall Park—it is torn down now—but by close application, skill and taste in buying, and by fair dealing with his customers, he soon secured a very good trade. His judgment of goods was excellent, particularly of fine laces, and he made a practice of buying at auction and retailing to much advantage. He soon gained the patronage of a number of wealthy and fashionable families, and so established a prestige that he has never lost. His terms were reasonable; his word could always be depended on, and four or five years after setting up for himself he was on the high road to independence.

His small store had by this time become inadequate to the accommodation of his numerous customers, and he accordingly purchased the lot in Broadway between Reade and Chambers, then occupied by the old Washington Hall, at about one-fifth of what it is now worth. He erected upon the site his present store, the first marble building in the great thoroughfare. Stewart's "marble palace," as it was long called, was the admiration of the town and wonder of the country, and so distinctive that the proprietor has never put up a sign.

In the new store Stewart secured a large wholesale trade, and soon grew to be one of the heaviest importers and jobbers in the City. For the past fifteen years he has done the largest business in this or probably in any other country, and it is still increasing monthly.

His other up-town establishment, corner of Tenth street and Broadway, is his retail store. He built it seven or eight years ago, and has just extended it to embrace almost the whole square. It is two hundred feet front on Broadway and Fourth avenue, and three hundred and twenty-five on Tenth street, includes nearly two acres, and the structure, six stories in height, is the largest dry goods store in the World.

The third architectural achievement of Stewart is his private residence, or what is designed to be such, in Fifth avenue, corner of Thirty-fourth street. It is a huge white marble pile; has been four or five years in process of erection, and has already cost $2,000,000. It is very elaborate and pretentious, but exceedingly dismal, reminding one of a vast tomb. Stewart's financial ability is extraordinary, but his architectural taste cannot be commended.

Numerous stories are told of the merchant prince, some to his credit, and more to his discredit; but it is doubtful if any of them are quite true. He is said to be very generous on one hand, and extremely mean on the other. He has often given munificently to public charities, but of his private contributions little is heard; whether because they are not made, or because he does good by stealth, I shall not undertake to say.

During the famine in Ireland he purchased a ship, loaded it with provisions and sent them there. On the return voyage he filled it with young men and women, and obtained situations for them before they had reached this shore.

During the War he gave at one time to the Sanitary Commission a check for $100,000, which was obtained in this way: Some one having asked him to contribute, he said he would give as much as Vanderbilt. Vanderbilt, on being approached, agreed to give as much as Stewart. Stewart then sent the applicant back to Vanderbilt, who, in a fit of annoyance, drew on his banker for $100,000. Stewart kept his word, and the Commission was $200,000 richer by the operation.

Respecting his wealth, it is difficult to estimate it. It is set down at $30,000,000, and even as high as $60,000,000. His income varies greatly. It has been less than $1,000,000 and as much as $4,000,000 a year; the amount depending upon the activity of trade and the fluctuations of the market. Every once in a while it is reported in the country that Stewart has failed; but in the City his failure is known to be impossible, as he has always made it a rule to buy for cash.

He has the reputation of being strictly truthful. He has but one price, and all his goods are what he represents them to be; and to those two things he is understood to attribute his success. He has three partners, William Libby here, Francis Warden in Paris, and G. Fox in Manchester, England, and foreign depots in Manchester, Belfast, Glasgow, Paris, Berlin and Lyons. He supervises and conducts his whole business, and works eight or ten hours a day, not unfrequently toiling over his private ledger on Sunday. He is a member of the Episcopalian Church—St. Mark's, corner of Tenth street and Second avenue—and regular in his attendance. He is a slave to business, rarely allowing himself any recreation. His happiness is in his accounts and profits, and to be the great merchant of New-York is his comfort and his pride. He lives in a plain house in the Avenue opposite his unfinished marble mausoleum; sees little company; has a wife, but no children, and must on the whole have a cheerless old age.

Stewart is a commonplace man in appearance, of medium height, slight in figure, thin-visaged, sharp features, sandy-grayish hair and whiskers; enjoys good health, and on close inspection has a shrewd, searching look which reveals his true character. He is well preserved and very vigorous for his age. He makes calculations for twenty years more of life, and clings to his immense fortune as if he should draw compound interest on it after death. Without children, with no future beyond the few years that yet remain, all his existence is an unbroken round of anxious toil, not many who may covet his wealth would, if they knew them, envy his surroundings.

CHAPTER XXXIII.

THE DAILY PRESS.

GREAT newspaper establishments are interesting to everybody but the persons connected with them.

The New-York offices, from their central and commanding position, have long been subjects of gossip and objects of curiosity. Out-of-town people who make visits to the large establishments in Printing House Square; penetrating the mysteries of the press, composing and editorial rooms, and, possibly, catching a glimpse of Greeley, Bennett, Raymond or Bryant, think themselves fortunate, and speak of the fact, for years after, as a memorable event.

Though all Americans read newspapers, not many have any clear notion how they are made. They have no idea of the amount of labor and capital required for the publication of a leading daily in the Metropolis. Indeed, its interior management and economy is a sealed book to them, which they are very glad to open whenever opportunity offers.

The expense of a great morning daily here is much larger than is usually supposed. The *Herald* has been the most liberal in the getting of news, though of late it has grown more economical, regarding some of its past expenditure as wasteful and superfluous. Still, whenever important intelligence is to be had, the *Herald* is more willing than any other journal in the country to pay for it. Its daily expenses have been estimated at $20,000 a week, sometimes more, sometimes less; and that is not far from the cost of the other quarto morning papers. The *Tribune* spent $969,000 year before last, and cleared only $11,000. It would be a fair estimate to reckon the cost of publishing one of these journals at $800,000 to $1,000,000 per annum.

The force employed upon one of the quartos is from four to five hundred persons, including clerks, compositors, pressmen, feeders, newsmen, proof-readers, reporters and editors.

Each paper has an editor-in-chief, who dictates the course and policy of the paper, and who decides all questions having reference to its editorial conduct.

The next to him in rank is the managing editor, who, in the absence of the chief, is supreme, and who attends to all the details, the engagement and dismissal of sub-editors and correspondents, with power to regulate salaries, and determine character of service. He is responsible to the chief, and his subordinates are responsible to him.

The night editor is a very important person. His position is arduous and responsible, as he has charge of the making-up of the paper, determining what matter shall go in and what stay out. He remains at his post until the journal is ready to go to press, between 2 and 3 o'clock in the morning, generally, though he sometimes stays till daylight. He goes upon duty at 7 in the evening, so that his hours of labor are commonly seven or eight.

The foreign editor deals with the foreign news and correspondence; writes editorials upon European politics, and is authority upon all matters belonging to his department. He is usually a foreigner himself, and conversant with several languages.

The financial editor is usually independent in his place, being, in most cases, a stockholder, or having some proprietary interest in the concern. This position is the most sought after of any on a paper, and is consequently filled by a man who can command influence; who has means, and is well known in banking circles. Financial editors generally name their successors before death or resignation—either of which events is improbable—and believe the place too good to be permitted to go out of the family. They write the daily money articles, and have facilities for pecuniary success that no other journalist in the office has. Nearly all of them make money, the amount of their salary being of secondary importance. Most of them grow rich through certain interests they are allowed to cultivate in Wall street. I recall the financial editor of a leading daily, who retired after a few years of service, with $250,000, all made by his position, and another, not long dead, who left a fortune of $300,000. To be a money-writer is considered to be on the direct road to wealth; and the road is seldom missed.

The city editor controls the city news. All the reporters are under him. He directs their movements, making out every day, in a large book, the places for them to go, and the amount of matter they are expected to furnish. The managing editor holds him responsible for the city department, and he sees that the reporters discharge their duty on pain of dismissal.

The principal dailies have day editors, who have charge of the office during the day; see visitors in the absence of the manager; receive or decline communications, and direct the affairs of the office from 9 or 10 o'clock in the morning, to 5 or 6 in the afternoon.

The literary editor or reviewer writes the literary criticisms; receives all the new books that are sent to the office, and notices them according to their merit or demerit. He is an autocrat in his department, and is a man of many and varied acquirements, and correct and scholarly tastes. George Ripley, of the *Tribune* stands at the head of the reviewers of the City and country, by seniority, culture and experience.

The art, dramatic and musical critics are indispensable to a newspaper. Their title implies their office. They are supposed to understand thoroughly what they write of, and to be in every way competent, though between them and the persons criticised, there is usually a remarkable difference of opinion. Some of them are very accomplished gentlemen, and others much less able than they would like to have it supposed.

Then there are translators, of course, who speak and write French, German, Italian and Spanish. One translator I know, is master of twenty different tongues, and speaks correctly every language but his own. Each large daily has from twelve to thirty reporters. Some of them report law cases, police matters and fires exclusively; while others devote themselves to Brooklyn, Jersey-City, Hoboken, Weehawken, and other adjacent towns. The city editor has a number of general reporters, some of them stenographers, who are assigned by him to duty. Their labors vary from two to eight hours a day. At times they have very light work, and again they toil like beavers. When occasion demands, extra reporters, who are always numerous, are employed, and are paid for their special work.

The editor-in-chief of the *Tribune* is, as every one knows, Horace Greeley; and the managing editor—he has been less than two years in the position—is John Russell Young, formerly of Philadelphia. The editor-in-chief of the *Herald* is, of course, James Gordon Bennett, and the managing editor, James Gordon Bennett, jr., when he is in the office; several of the other editors supplying his place if absent. Of the *Times*, Henry J. Raymond is chief, and Stillman S. Conant manager; of the *World*, Manton Marble chief, and David G. Croley manager; of the *Sun*, Charles A. Dana chief, and Isaac W. England manager; of the *Journal of Commerce*, David M. Stone chief, and J. W. Bouton manager; of the *Evening Post*, William Cullen Bryant chief, and Augustus Maverick manager; of the *Commercial Advertiser*, Thurlow Weed chief, and Chester P. Dewey manager; of the *Evening Express*, James Brooks chief, and Erastus Brooks manager.

Those are all the old papers; and of the new ones, *Evening Telegram*, *Evening Mail*, *Evening News*, *Evening Commonwealth*, *Democrat* and *Star*, the chief and managing editor is generally the same person. They are small papers, and their departments less numerous and complete than those of the long-established journals.

The press-room of the morning dailies is a great curiosity to many persons. They like to see the huge ten-cylinder Hoe press throwing off sheets at the rate of 16,000 an hour, but printing them on only one side at a time. The Hoe press, it was supposed, was the highest reach of mechanical skill; but recently a new press, the Bullock, has been invented, and threatens to displace its rival. The Bullock is very small and compact; prints on both sides; requires but one feeder, and saves much expense. The paper is put in in one long roll, and the wonderful machine cuts the sheet of the right size, and throws it out a perfectly printed journal. The Bullock works quite as rapidly as the Hoe, and is said to spoil fewer papers. It has so many advantages over Hoe's, that it ere long promises to take its place in most newspaper establishments in this country and Europe.

Ten or twelve years ago, the New-York papers began to stereotype their forms, thereby saving the wear of the type, and in other ways, fully 20 per cent. upon the old plan. Each office has a stereotyping room, and the process is as follows. The forms are made up on curved plates. When the type is all set, a pulpy preparation of paper is pressed upon them, and it is of such consistency as to keep the mold of the type exactly. Into this mold liquid type metal is poured (it does not burn the paper because of its moisture); and a solid plate formed as if the original type were all welded together. This plate is put upon the press, and the impressions of the journal made. The forms of the *Tribune, Herald, Times*, and recently the *World*, are all stereotyped.

The metropolitan journals, considering the natural and acquired advantages they enjoy, are not all they ought to be. And yet, they are as a class, superior to those of any city in Europe. In fact, outside of London, and the *Times*, they have no rivals there; for the Paris, Berlin and other Continental journals, though able in some particulars, amount to little as a journalistic whole.

The London *Times* has obtained a power and influence in Europe that no one journal could obtain in the United States. It stands almost entirely alone; and its opinions and predictions are looked to with an interest, and carry a weight, which we Americans, accustomed to think for ourselves, can hardly understand. Its editorials from first to last, are the strongest, clearest, and best written on either side of the Atlantic. Those in New-York are often as good, sometimes superior; but, on an average, fall below the standard of the "Thunderer."

The leaders of the *Times*, with its correspondence and parliamentary reports, make up its excellence. With all its ability, it is heavy and unenterprising and would not be successful in this country, where we demand more variety and lightness, more humor and much more news.

A defect of the metropolitan dailies is, that they too closely imitate the English papers in excess of foreign news and overfulness of reports—giving matters really of little general interest, to the exclusion of what is more important. Americans naturally care far less about European affairs than the Europeans themselves; but our daily journals do not seem yet to have discovered the fact. The result is that we have long letters from abroad, often with little mention of the condition of things in our home cities and territories.

Condensation is not one of the journalistic virtues

of New-York, especially in telegrams, which every day fill several columns, when all they contain might better be expressed in one-fourth of the space.

The use of the telegraph originally was to transmit news of importance; but of late it seems to be to give unimportant news significance. That is sent over the wires which, but for such sending, would not be printed at all.

It is very common for our night editors to omit an item of city news to give space to something much less interesting that has been received by telegraph. They appear to think it of no consequence that a New-Yorker has broken his neck, but of the greatest that a laborer on a Western railway or a freedman in Texas has been killed by a locomotive or a ruffian

When our dailies comprehend that what Americans are most interested in is America, we shall be, journalistically, much better off.

Newspapers seem to imagine themselves as much privileged to misrepresent their circulation as fops their follies or cowards their courage. Hence it is very difficult, if not impossible, to give the exact circulation of any daily; though, inasmuch as I have made diligent inquiry, and have what should be trustworthy sources of information, the figures I give in round numbers ought to be nearly correct. The circulation of the best known morning and evening papers I estimate as follows:

Herald	70,000	Evening Post	9,000
Sun	50,000	Evening Express	7,000
Tribune	40,000	Evening Mail	6,000
Times	35,000	Commercial Adv.	3,500
World	25,000	Journal of Commerce	2,500

Of the new papers I have no means of judging. The *Star* (morning), *Democrat* (morning and evening), and the *Telegram* and *News* (evening), claim to count their circulation by tens of thousands; while the figures of the *Commonwealth*, also evening, I have not heard stated.

The circulation of the dailies has greatly decreased since the close of the War. The leading quartos ran up on some days of the Rebellion, when accounts of battles were received, to over a hundred thousand, the sales even reaching one hundred and fifty thousand in twenty-four hours.

During the present year, the circulation of the *Tribune*, *Sun* and *World* has gone up more rapidly than that of their cotemporaries. The *Herald*, increases steadily, with occasional fluctuations.

The *Herald* much as it is condemned and abused is, on the whole, the most enterprising and best managed newspaper in the City. James Gordon Bennett unquestionably understands the philosophy of journalism and the secret of popularity. Without any particular convictions or fixedness of principle himself, he gives no one else credit for them; and therefore thinks the best thing is to render his paper acceptable to the largest class of people possible.

That he does without regard to consistency for which he has no respect; and thus freed from the ordinary restraints that develop, but often hinder mortals, it is not strange he has achieved great material success.

Something over thirty-three years ago Bennett, in a dingy, subterranean office in Ann street, issued the first number of the *Herald*, a small, inferior-looking sheet, doing all the editorial work with his own hand;

and to-day he has the most wealthy daily in the United States.

The great fire in December, 1835, was fully and graphically reported in the *Herald*, the first time such a thing had ever been done or even attempted, in the country; and the remarkable enterprise of the journal on that occasion brought it into general notice, and gave it a reputation for news that it has never lost.

Bennett says he publishes the *Herald* to make money (he might have added for his own glorification), not for the benefit of philosophers, which is a hit at the *Tribune*. Privately he does not assume to control or mold public opinion, but to follow it; and he generally manages to be about twenty-four hours behind it, that he may publicly declare he has anticipated and created it. The *Herald* is consistent only in its inconsistency, and its determination to be on the strong or popular side of every question. By miscalculation or misunderstanding, it sometimes gets on the unpopular side; but, the moment it discovers its mistake, it leaps to the other with noticeable alacrity.

Bennett understands that a daily newspaper is emphatically a thing of to-day, and that the mass of people care very little for what it has said yesterday, or may say to-morrow. Consequently, he issues every number as if there never had been, and never would be another, and so prospers. Its rivals declare the success of the *Herald* a libel upon the general intelligence. Perhaps it is; but its success, great and growing, is an undeniable fact, from which any one may draw his own inferences.

The *Herald* makes a feature of sensation of some part

of its news every morning; and, if there be no important news, creates its appearance by typographical display. Its matter is carelessly prepared, for the most part, but altogether acceptable to its readers, and therefore what Bennett approves.

The *Sun* is the oldest morning paper in town except the *Journal*. It made a good deal of money for its original proprietor, Moses Y. Beach. He disposed of it eight or ten years ago, and the purchasing parties unable to manage it, lost heavily, and were glad to sell it to Beach again. The *Sun* during the Beach period was the organ of the workingmen, and the advocate of their interests. It was a penny paper until the depreciation of the currency made it necessary to advance it to two cents. For many years it had the largest circulation of any daily in New-York, and may have again.

Last January the *Sun* was revolutionized by its sale to Charles A. Dana, representing a number of wealthy stockholders, of whom he is one. It was removed from Fulton and Nassau to the reconstructed buildings corner of Nassau and Frankfort streets, formerly occupied as Tammany Hall. The *Sun* deserves its name; for it has the reputation of the brightest daily in the City. It is independent, high-toned, liberal and perfectly good-natured. Its editorial corps consists of a number of highly cultivated gentlemen and in its freedom from bitterness, party rancor and one-sided judgment is an example the larger papers might imitate to advantage. The *Sun* abounds in graceful and vigorous articles, and is characterized by a playful irony so subtle often as to escape detection by many of its readers. It adheres to its ancient motto, and "shines for all."

It is said to be very prosperous, and it certainly deserves all its prosperity.

The *Tribune*, in spite of its crotchets and occasional violence, has wielded and still wields a greater influence than any other daily in New-York. An anti-slavery paper twenty years ago—the cause was most unpopular then—it has lived to see the "peculiar institution" abolished, and its own principles triumphant.

The *Tribune* is so identified with Horace Greeley, that it is difficult to tell what it would be without him. He is so intensely personal, and capricious often, that he is constantly furnishing clubs to his antagonists to strike the causes he defends with such ability and earnestness.

The original stock of the *Tribune* was a hundred shares of a thousand dollars each (Greeley began the paper with a thousand dollars of borrowed money) and the shares are now worth more than six thousand dollars. It has made money, but not nearly so much as it ought to have done, the consequence mainly of being under the control of a board of free-voiced stockholders, who always interfere with the government of a journal. A newspaper should be an autocracy, and to the fact that the *Herald* is such, much of its success is owing.

The *Tribune* is able, probably the ablest daily in the City, for it has always had more capacity and culture on its staff than any other paper, though it has not always used its means or strength wisely. It aims to be more a vehicle of opinion than of news, and its editorials are allowed to crowd out interesting intelligence almost every day; albeit most of its readers would, I suspect, prefer facts, which are universal, to leaders which are, after all, only the expression of an individual. There is no good reason why the *Tribune* should not be the most interesting newspaper as well as the ablest journal in the City. Until good old Horace Greeley is gathered to his fathers, and some man succeeds him who can be made to believe his daily opinions are not vital to the salvation of the Republic, I look for little change in the great radical organ of the New World.

The *Times*, which has been accused of political instability, has shown decided improvement recently, and is a very readable paper. Its editorials generally are well written, though not so vigorous as those of the *Tribune*. Its correspondence, its news, and its literary department are very creditable. It was started as a penny paper by the Harpers, and sank $80,000 or $90,000 before it began to pay for itself. Since then it has been pecuniarily successful; has been for years a stock company, though its shareholders have no voice in its direction, which is entirely under the control of Raymond, one of the best journalists in the country.

The *World*, for the money it spends and the force it employs, is probably the best conducted paper here. Its political editor and director, Manton Marble, is a very forcible and graceful writer, and a shrewd and energetic manager. Ultra-democratic in its politics, it is a formidable and tireless enemy of the *Tribune* and *Times*, and its editorials are not excelled in strength and plausibility by any in New-York. It is unquestionably the best made-up daily in town; and, though frequently positive, even to bitterness, it is never weak and rarely inconsistent.

The *World* was begun as a religious journal, and

after various changes, during which it is said to have sunk $300,000 or $400,000, it became the organ of the democracy in the Metropolis, especially of the Manhattan club, and has long been on a paying basis.

It imitates the *Herald* too closely in its news and correspondence to be in quite good taste. It is determined to make the most of what it has, and is so wedded to sensation that its chief fault is overdoing.

The *Journal of Commerce* is one of the old Wall street journals, has retained some of its influence and all of its prosperity. It is eminently respectable, and well edited, though it does not enter into competition with the morning quartos as a newspaper. It is the organ of the wholesale merchants and importers, and has made a fortune for half a dozen of its proprietors. It is the oldest journal in the City, and was, twenty years ago, one of the most enterprising. It long ago retired into comparative obscurity, contented to receive its ample dividends, and leave the strife of journalism to younger heads and more ambitious hearts.

The *Star* is an offshoot of the old *Sun*, and assumes to be its legitimate successor. It was started by several attachés of the Beach journal, and is very much what that was in appearance, tone and character. It has not yet completed its first year. It began as a penny paper, and is now sold for two cents. It does not belong to the Associated Press, nor do any of the evening journals except those heretofore named. The *Star* is vigilant and persevering in watching the rights of labor and laborers, and its future prospects are reported to be good.

The *Democrat* is the new ultra-democratic journal set up here a few months since by Mark M. Pomeroy of the famous *La Crosse Democrat*. First it was an evening, now it is a morning paper. Its editor and proprietor claims to have met with remarkable success, and to be firmly established in the good will of the toiling millions.

The influence of the evening is naturally much less than that of the morning journals; the *Post* being the ablest and most influential of the entire number. It is carefully edited, though its elder and best-known conductors spend much of their time in Europe. Its columns are fastidiously free from indelicacy or pruriency, and it well deserves to be considered a family newspaper.

The *Commercial Advertiser* is interesting and new life has been given it by Thurlow Weed. Its proprietors have not shown much disposition to make money.

The *Evening Express* is managed with tact and economy by the Brooks Brothers, who make an excellent newspaper and $40,000 a year.

The *Telegram*, a kind of evening edition of the *Herald*, is owned by James Gordon Bennett, jr., is lively and full of news, and sold for two cents.

The *Evening News* is the property of Benjamin Wood, and the only penny paper in town. It seems to have a very large circulation, and those who ought to know declare it profitable. It is given over to police news and every variety of crime, and no doubt suits its readers exactly.

The *Evening Commonwealth* is but five or six months old, a Republican two-cent paper, very dignified and conscientious, though not so vivacious or forcible as it might be. It is said to be gradually but steadily creeping into favor.

There are three German morning dailies; *State Gazette*, *Democrat*, and *Journal*, and one German evening paper, the *Times*. There are two French morning journals, the *Courier of the United States* and the *Franco-American Messenger;* and these end the list of the dailies in the Metropolis.

There never has been a time when the City had so many evening papers; and it is probable they will interfere with each other so strongly that some of them must yield to the struggle for existence before long, and go down to early, though not unlamented graves.

PRINTING HOUSE SQUARE.

CHAPTER XXXIV.

THE WEEKLY PRESS.

FEW persons who live out of, or even in, New-York are aware of the number of weekly papers published in the City: indeed, I venture to say no journalist here can name half of them. They are devoted not only to news, literature, agriculture, amusements, art, music and crime, but to various interests and kinds of business, and, all told, amount to about one hundred and fifty. Among the secular weeklies, the best known are *Harpers' Weekly*, *Harpers' Bazaar*, *Frank Leslie's Illustrated News*, *Round Table*, *Nation*, *Ledger*, *Citizen*, *Home Journal*, *Leader*, *Weekly Review*, *Sunday Mercury*, *Sunday News*, *Dispatch*, *Sunday Times*, *Literary Album*, *Anti-Slavery Standard*, *Revolution*, *Clipper*, *Spirit of the Times*, and *Police Gazette*. Of the religious press, the *Independent*, *Examiner*, *Evangelist*, *Methodist*, *Observer*, *Tablet*, *Liberal Christian*, *Christian Advocate*, *Christian Inquirer*, and *Church Journal* are most prominent.

The *Ledger* is the most popular of the weeklies, having at present a circulation of over three hundred thousand. Robert Bonner, the proprietor, was at one time a poor printer-boy, who made his journal famous, and the source of a large fortune, by extremely liberal advertising. It is a story-paper, and one of the very best of its kind. Bonner employs the best talent he can command, particularly the celebrities, at munificent rates. Almost every writer in the country has either contributed, or thought of contributing, to the *Ledger*, at his own prices. Henry Ward Beecher's "Norwood" was a good acquisition to the *Ledger*, increasing its circulation fully one hundred thousand.

Bonner may sometime engage Louis Napoleon, Garibaldi, the Tycoon of Japan and Pio Nono, for his thought by day, his dream by night is whom he shall next secure as a contributor to the *Ledger*.

The majority of the paper's readers are women and young people—it is intended for a family journal,—though many men of culture con its columns regularly.

All newspaper publishers owe a debt of gratitude to Bonner, inasmuch as his eminent success is the strongest evidence of the advantage of advertising.

The illustrated papers number a dozen, probably; the best being *Harpers' Weekly*, the *Bazaar* and *Frank Leslie's*. Harpers' publications rank highest, especially in the literary department, and have the largest circulation. The *Weekly* and *Bazaar* claim a circulation of over one hundred thousand each, while *Leslie's* is about sixty or seventy thousand. Both have made a great deal of money, and every year adds to their profits.

The *Round Table* and *Nation* are, as literary and critical journals, the ablest in the country; in fact, almost the only ones that hold any rank or deserve any reputation. The *Round Table* has more piquancy and variety, the *Nation* more force and solidity. Both have had a hard struggle, but are now said to be on a sound and paying basis. They employ some of the ablest pens in the Metropolis and New-England, and are edited with conscientious tact and zeal.

The *Revolution*, published and edited by Susan B. Anthony and Elizabeth Cady Stanton, is an able and energetic exponent of women's rights, and radical on all subjects. It is too ultra for most people; but it is, no doubt, doing a needful work by elevating the character and stimulating the independence of women.

The religious papers are published in the interest of the different sects, and, very naturally, each is the favorite of the church it represents. The *Independent* is the most independent in character as well as in name, and the most profitable. It is published by Henry C. Bowen, formerly a Broadway merchant, and is said to yield him $50,000 to $60,000 a year. Theodore Tilton is its principal editor, at a salary of $7,000 a year—one of the highest paid in New-York. The *Methodist*, *Observer*, *Examiner* and *Liberal Christian* are the ablest, and make the largest returns to the proprietors.

The *Citizen* gained considerable reputation through its late editor, General Charles G. Halpine, better known as "Miles O'Reilly." He was a clever, rollicking, careless, good-hearted Irishman, a kind of scribbling Dugald Dalgetty, who had the knack of flattering people into good humor with themselves and good feeling for him. He obtained his first notoriety by a series of adroit and ludicrous tricks, and was elected to a municipal office, worth $40,000 a year, which he held at the time of his sudden death.

The *Citizen* is often aromatic and generally readable. Its circulation is not large, but, as it has the City printing, it is, no doubt on a firm financial foundation. It is half political, half literary, and seems to flourish.

The *Home Journal* has manifested more signs of life since the death of N. P. Willis, with whom it was for many years identified. It claims to be an elegant journal of polite society, and has recently wrought the Jenkins vein to advantage. The latest follies of Fifth avenue are always chronicled with fervor and fidelity in its columns.

The Sunday papers, such as the *Mercury*, *News* and *Police Gazette*, are sensation journals of a curious sort, to which a murder is a benison, and an intrigue a godsend. They deal with what the dailies will not mention, or print in brief, enlarging with keen relish and elaborate pruriency upon details that delicacy would eschew.

They reprint all the sensational facts and gossip they can find in the country press, or exhume from the licentious haunts of the City. They are widely read, of course, and are, for the most part, profitable. The better class of the community do not read them, unless they happen to contain something extraordinary racy and wanton, when curiosity overcomes the scruples of conscience and the dictates of decorum.

Another class of weeklies are those styled literary, which publish highly-colored stories, with absurd incidents and impossible characters of the Rinaldo Rinaldini, and Alonzo and Melissa class. No educated person would believe a market for such matter could be found; and yet publications like the *Literary Album* and *New York Weekly* have a circulation of seventy or eighty thousand, and make their proprietors rich. It costs little to print them; the original stories being written by some impecunious hack, at the rate of one or two dollars a column, and the slender editorial compounded with paste and scissors. Such journals are circulated almost entirely in the country, few persons in the City being aware of their existence.

The worst class of weeklies are the *Police Gazette* and the publications devoted to prize-fighting, criminal news and flash intelligence. They are abominably written, and illustrated with hideous cuts, enough to frighten Ajax or Diomede, and are read with avidity in Greene, Mercer, Water and Houston streets. Bar-rooms and bagnios, gambling saloons and rat-pits patronize them, and consider them the most entertaining and instructive journals in the World.

The profession of journalism, though possessed of a strange species of fascination, which holds those once embarked in it, and draws back to it the men who have endeavored to escape, is, considering the culture, training and devotion it requires, the least remunerative of callings.

Journalists who follow their profession zealously for years, find, after they have worn themselves out in its arduous service, that their prospects are no better than when they began. They have not saved more than enough to meet their daily expenses, and, when they can no longer work, they are set aside as of no further use, and fresh and younger put in their place. Republics may be ungrateful, but they are far less so than newspaper publishers, for the most part men of money rather than culture, without sympathy with those who toil their lives out for a salary hardly equal to that of a good mechanic or an accomplished cook.

Any other business, faithfully followed, gains in value with years; and he who retires from it can sell its good will for a bonus. The bonus of not a few improvident journalists has been a legacy of unpaid debts, and a funeral at the expense of their friends.

Journalists in the Metropolis are more poorly paid, strange to say, than in many of the other and smaller cities. The best of them, those of large experience and long service, rarely receive more than $30 or $40 a week; while the price for reporters is $15 to $25— seldom the latter.

A few men are compensated liberally; but they are well known, and are generally paid for their reputation, or because they have proprietary interests in the concern to which they belong. Frederick Hudson, formerly managing editor of the *Herald*, received $10,000 a year; but he had grown up with the concern, and he broke his constitution by his ceaseless toil. Horace Greeley's salary is $7,500 as editor-in-chief of the *Tribune;* but he is its founder and a large stockholder, and has a national and trans-Atlantic reputation. The managing editor of the *Tribune* has $5,000; but it is not two years since the salary was raised to that figure; and those who know anything of the mode in which a man in such a position in a stock concern is badgered and bedeviled, will willingly testify that the price is not extraordinary.

Most of the New-York sub-journalists are compelled, so great is the price of living, and such the smallness of their pay here, to do outside work to make both ends meet. When one has to pay $2,000 for a respectable house to live in, and gets but $1,400 to $1,500 for his services, the need of increased exertion, especially if he has a large family, is not altogether undiscernable. In consequence, if he is clever, he makes a sort of galley-slave of himself, and does the labor of three or four ordinary men. He contributes to the magazines or weeklies; corresponds for the country press; reads for the book-publishers; translates from the German or French the noticeable works in those languages, and fills up his leisure hours by writing a comedy or a novel, for which he receives a few hundred dollars and all kinds of abuse.

The New-York journalist is fortunate if he has the ability and industry to do all this, and more fortunate if he has the opportunity; for the Metropolis is overcrowded with writers of every description, impecunious *littérateurs*, broken-down scribblers, and unsuccessful authors.

You can engage men here to compose an epic, a tragedy, or a romance; indite an ode, a sonnet, or a madrigal; waste ink and paper on any subject, for much less than you could an attorney's clerk to copy the same things. Talent, learning, and even genius, if you will permit the great unappreciated to place their own estimate upon themselves, are more common here than scandal in boarding-houses, or bad morals in French novels.

At any rate, the supply of writers of ability and culture, is much greater here than the demand; and there is no commoner mistake than for young men who have a suspicion, shared by few others, that they are among the intellectually elect, to imagine New-York needs them, and is suffering from their absence. If any such are doing well where they are, there let them remain.

This great City is overcrowded, overburthened, over-supplied. There are vain and egotistic dullards enough here now, ill-fated fellows who live by wits none too bright before they were overstrained, and who will go down to their graves with the conviction that the World would not recognize their gifts. Do not increase the number, my self-sufficient brothers of the quill. Stay at home, and go to Heaven in your own quiet way; and remember that he who tells you so speaks by the card, and styles himself, with the characteristic egotism of his egotistic class, sometimes Sir Oracle, and sometimes yours truly.

CHAPTER XXXV.

WILLIAM B. ASTOR.

WILLIAM B. ASTOR is a very noticeable exception to the rule that the sons of rich men squander what their fathers spent their lives in earning. Economy and thrift are hereditary virtues in the Astors, and the immense wealth that old John Jacob accumulated is likely to remain in the family for generations.

William B. Astor's life is little, but his property is great. His chief distinction is that he is John Jacob Astor's son. As such he is known; as such he will be remembered. If it require, as has been claimed, as much capacity to take care of money as to make it, then the son is equal to the father. William B. has been preserved by his temperament from all extravagances and excesses. He has the cool head and calm blood of his German ancestors, to whom irregularity was unknown and temptation impossible.

Associated in business with his father from his early years, he learned his habits and followed his example. The power and benefit of money being one of the first things he was taught, it is not strange he has remembered his early lesson through all his years. Instead of diminishing the wealth he inherited, he has largely increased it, and has been for years the richest citizen of the United States. He is as careful of his vast property as if he were not worth a hundred dollars; and to-day, in his seventy-sixth year, he takes more note of a trifling expenditure than a clerk whose annual salary is not much beyond his hourly income.

Every one knows how John Jacob Astor, at the age of twenty, left his village home in Baden, so poor that he walked to the nearest seaport, with a small bundle, containing all his worldly goods; spent his last penny for a passage in the steerage; sailed for New-York and would have arrived here with nothing but youth and health, had he not sold on the voyage half a dozen flutes given him by his brother in London. For the flutes he received twelve dollars, and having made the acquaintance of a furrier on board the ship, and talked with him about the trade, he invested his small capital, on debarking, in furs. From that small beginning he steadily and rapidly rose, until he founded the American Fur Company, sent his ships to every sea, and died worth $50,000,000.

But few know how William, the son, has, during the twenty years since his father's death, devoted himself constantly to swell the fortune, whose income is more than any one man should have. He has little life outside of his mortgages and investments, and at an age when most good citizens are sleeping quietly in their graves, indifferent to securities or titles, he is hard at work in his back office closing every crevice through which a dollar might slip.

Many persons wonder why men of great fortune continue to labor, instead of resting and enjoying themselves, and attribute it to mere love of gain. They do not remember that long habit becomes second nature; that such men find rest in constant occupation, and that the enjoyment prescribed for them would be the severest punishment that could be inflicted.

For more than fifty years William B. Astor has been a daily worker at his desk. Sentence him to idleness to-morrow, and before the Christmas chimes were rung from Trinity, the family lot in Greenwood would have another occupant.

Astor was born in a small brick house, built by his father, and occupied as a fur store, but long since torn down, at the corner of Broadway and Vesey—the site of the present Astor House. He has seen wonderful changes in the City and the World. When he was a babe New-York had a population of not more than thirty thousand souls; our Revolution had just ended; George Washington was still alive; Thomas Jefferson was President of the United States; Bonaparte was unknown; Frederic the Great had very recently died; the French Revolution was thrilling the time with horror; Vesey street was in the country; Bowling Green the centre of trade; Wall street and its vicinity the quarter for fashionable residences, and the Republic itself a handful of feeble States that were still suffering from the struggle that had given them their independence.

Astor was carefully educated by his father, and after leaving college, traveled in Europe, where, it is said, he spent less than a quarter of what his parent had allowed him. After his return he went into business with John Jacob, and became more watchful of his interests and his money than the old man himself, who was never accused of any extraordinary carelessness in that respect. Though presumptive heir to a great estate he lost no opportunity to look out for himself, and, at his father's decease, was individually worth

$6,000,000. He is declared, by those who ought to know, to be less liberal than his father—no spendthrift by any means—and a man of less kindly feeling and less generous sympathy. He is reported to be very charitable on occasions; but he rarely gives to those who solicit charity, and his brusque refusal of the constant petitioners for assistance of all kinds through a series of years has earned for him the reputation of extreme closeness, if not penuriousness. To common beggars and seekers for subscriptions he turns a deaf ear, and the fact is now so well known that he escapes much of the annoyance to which accessible rich men are perpetually subjected. He makes it a rule, I have been told, never to give anything during the hours of business, and always to investigate any and every case earnestly brought to his notice. If he finds it worthy, he is reasonably liberal, but privately so, having no ambition to gain a reputation that would prove troublesome, not to say expensive.

I have no reason to doubt this; indeed I am inclined to believe it; for many persons give from their vanity, while others who are silently charitable pass for the very opposite in public opinion.

Still Astor cannot be regarded as a liberal man, considering his immense wealth and the superabundant opportunities it gives him for doing good in his native city, where the Greeks are ever at his own door. Of course he has a perfect right to do as he chooses with his own. He knows that, too, and follows his humor.

The public is very exacting of the wealthy, who are roundly abused when they decline to open their purses as it directs. They are so besieged and badgered with applicants and applications, so imposed on and cajoled, that it is not strange they grow callous. Even Astor and Stewart, if they responded to all the calls upon them for aid, would be beggared in a twelvemonth. But there is so little probability of their responding that it is not needful to expend any sympathy in anticipation.

Astor's office is in Prince street near Broadway, a one-story brick, with heavy shutters, reminding you of a village bank. The office has two rooms, and he occupies the rear one, very plainly, even meagerly, furnished, which he enters punctually every morning at ten o'clock, rarely leaving his desk before four in the afternoon. He is not shut away as Stewart is. His back can be seen by any one entering the office, and any one can step in and see his face also, if he be so minded. To those who pay him a visit he is so chary of words as to seem impolite.

He usually waits to be addressed, but if he is not, he turns a cold face upon the visitor, and says, "Your business, sir."

If it be an application for charity, in nine cases out of ten he cuts off the story before it is half told, with "I can do nothing for you, sir," and resumes his work.

If it is an application for reduction of rent or for the sale of property, he generally answers "No, sir," and relapses into silence, from which it is difficult to arouse him.

If he is annoyed by further speech, he says curtly: "I am busy: I have no time to talk;" and there the interview ends. Few persons feel encouraged to stay in his presence, which to strangers, is no more inviting than the Morgue at midnight, or a tombstone on a Winter's day.

Astor has none of his father's liking for trade. He deals altogether in real estate and in leases of property owned by Trinity Church. He has a wonderful memory. He can tell every square foot of property he owns, the exact date at which each lease expires, and the amount due on it to a penny. He very rarely sells any of his property; but he is buying constantly, and will be to his dying day, though it cannot be many years before he will be obliged to exchange all his valuable sites and acres for a three-by-seven lot in a corner of Long Island. He scarcely ever improves any of his real estate. He buys it for an advance, and lets it go only when he thinks it has reached its maximum rate.

Astor lives at No. 32 Lafayette place, in a handsome though somewhat old-fashioned, brick house, adjoining the Astor Library. His residence was built for and given to him by his father. Most fashionable and wealthy people have moved up town, but he is conservative, averse to change, and will breathe his last under that roof. He is temperate in all things, and has always taken excellent care of his health. He likes a good dinner however, and a bottle of wine, and sits long at table. His is not a very sociable or gregarious nature, but he gives elaborate dinner parties, and often has company at his house. As an entertainer few surpass him. On a social occasion his plate is the most massive, his viands the costliest, and his wines the richest to be found in New-York.

He is very fond of walking, going from his home to his office and back almost invariably on foot. He is a tall man, fully six feet, of heavy frame, large and rather coarse features, small eyes, cold and sluggish-looking, much more German than American, nothing distinguished or noticeable about him, whom no one would suppose as old as he is by at least fifteen years. He has a strong constitution and is in vigorous health, and may see his hundredth birthday. He has two sons, John Jacob and William B. Astor, Jr., both of whom are as close applicants to business as their father, and several daughters, all married to wealthy gentlemen. Mrs. Astor who is the daughter of General Armstrong, James Madison's Secretary of War, is a woman of culture and accomplishments, and lends grace and dignity to her husband's hospitality.

William B. Astor's wealth cannot be accurately determined. He does not know himself; but it is probably $65,000,000, or $70,000,000, perhaps $80,000,000 or $90,000,000. It increases largely every year by reason of the advance in property, and may nearly double in value before his death. His income is greatly disproportioned to his fortune, because he owns such a large amount of unproductive real estate. He has much property that even his sons know nothing of, and, like his father, seems unwilling to have any one understand the immensity of his riches. It is said he is very anxious to live to see how many of his investments will turn out; but at seventy-six that rare pleasure can not be much longer enjoyed.

CHAPTER XXXVI.

THE CONCERT-SALOONS.

Concert-saloons, with pretty "waiter-girl" attachments, which have of late years become so discreditably popular in the various cities of the Union, had their origin and earliest impetus here. They are particularly adapted to the large, loose, fluctuating, cosmopolitan life of New-York, and represent in a strikingly unfavorable light some of the worst elements in the great commercial and social centre of the Republic.

During the present year, the concert-saloons have perceptibly diminished in the City, though there are yet many more than any one would suppose the idle and profligate among the million and a half of people in this vicinity would or could support. It is but a few years since the first concert-saloons were opened in Broadway and the Bowery, and they at once found patrons innumerable. Their illuminated transparencies, their tawdry display, their jangling music, their painted and bedizened wantons—such is public taste—made them immediate pecuniary successes. Their bad example was contagious. They sprang up, immoral mushroons, all over town; and, in less than twelve months from the time the first one showed its hydra head, four or five hundred of the establishments assisted to corrupt the most frequented quarters of the Metropolis.

Their number has been as high as six hundred, and they have given degraded and degrading employment to three or four thousand young women.

Since the passage of the Excise Law, many of the concert-saloons have closed; but a large number remain open, pretending to sell nothing but "temperance drinks,"—thereby escaping the clause that forbids the granting of license to dispose of spirituous or malt liquors. Even this assumed restriction is one of the moral spasms with which New-York is periodically visited, and which usually react for the worse. It has no other effect than to draw the curtain before evils that will not be repressed, and to add to other vices the compulsory one of hypocrisy.

The patrons of concert-saloons are mainly strangers, —country people, as it is the fashion here to call all persons living outside of New-York,—though not a few of our resident citizens contribute to their support in more ways than one. One would suppose that the customers of the saloons were very young men, mere boys, whose follies and foibles are to be leniently regarded on account of their immaturity and inexperience. It is not so, however. Men of middle and old age are often found among the regular attendants, and the most devoted admirers of the unchaste nymphs who pour libations to Venus and Bacchus from the same satyr-shaped chalice.

Men from every grade of life visit the concert-saloons: many from curiosity, and more from a relish of what they find there. The laborer and mechanic, the salesman and accountant, the bank-clerk and merchant, all meet in the subterranean dens, and guzzle in secret lager-beer and poisonous liquors, and philander with the libidinous Hebes with a zest that is surprising.

The concert-saloons differ in their size and appointments, as much as they do in the appearance of the attendants and the character of the *habitués*. Some of them, like the Louvre and Oriental, are handsomely fitted up and furnished, and have a certain kind of order and decorum. The waiter-girls are gaudily attired, and have some pretensions to comeliness and propriety of conduct. The masculine visitors are of the best species of patrons of such places—generally sober, well-dressed, and tolerably well-behaved. The first-class saloons are in Broadway, albeit many of them in that great thoroughfare are of a very degraded kind; but the worst are in William street, Chatham street and the Bowery.

The latter description discard the form of decency to a great extent. The men swear and talk obscenely in loud voices; drink to excess; leer, and roar, and stagger, and bestow rude caresses on the women, and are thrust violently into the street when they have lost their senses and spent their money. The women are coarse and sensual in form and feature, lascivious in conduct, rude and harsh of speech, degraded in feeling, outcast in society. The proprietors are generally besotted ruffians, doomed to die in a drunken fit or a drunken brawl,—fellows conceived in sin, reared in iniquity, and predestined to the penitentiaries.

The concert-soloons do little, and expect to do little, during the day. At night is their harvest; and all the poetry of the night is needed to relieve the excessive prose of such haunts and habits. When the gas flares, and the tinsel glitters, and the paint hides, and the chemical decoctions sensualize and stupefy, vice is robbed of half its grossness, and delicacy and reason of all their instincts.

Soon after the great stores of Broadway are closed and bolted; when down-town is partially deserted; when New-York has dined, and is determining how to pass the evening most pleasantly, the concert-saloons reveal their fascinations for the idle and unwary. Then the transparencies blaze, and large black and red letters inform promenaders and loungers where fine musical entertainments may be had gratis; where the prettiest waiter-girls in the City may be seen; where the greatest and cheapest pleasure may be enjoyed.

Up from basements that have been quiet and unobserved all day long come the sound of boisterous music, and the noise of many voices, too loud for gayety and too discordant for sobriety. If you have nothing to do—for leisure is the parent of mischief—or if you are a stranger, you feel an idle curiosity to look into the underground abode; and you do, probably.

You descend the steps, and are in a vast hall filled with small tables, at which men and women are seated, chattering like monkeys and drinking like doves. On one side of the room is a bar, behind which half a dozen or more bar-keepers are filling the orders of the waiter-girls with careless celerity. On a raised platform at the lower end of the hall is a group of musicians, playing vociferously out of tune, and fortifying their wasted powers with frequent fluids.

Throughout the place is a rattling of glasses, a chaos of voices, a cloud of tobacco smoke, an odor of bad beer, a discord of instruments, with a sense of heat, impurity and debauchery, that repels and shocks you at first.

If this do not drive you out at once, you gradually become accustomed to it. One of the waiter-girls—what bitter irony it is to call most of them "pretty!"—approaches, and proffers her services. She tells you that so good-looking and nice a gentleman ought not to be alone, or go without a drink; informs you she will take something with you, and keep you company.

Without more words, she brings from the bar a glass of beer or liquor, and places herself at your side; asks you if you like women; invites you to visit her when she is at home; perhaps grants you permission to escort her from the saloon—though, if she do this, you may conclude you have a verdant and rustic air, and do not seem a bit like a New-Yorker.

If the experience be new, you may wish to see what will come of it all. You drink the contents of the glass before you, and call for a cigar. Then you have another drink, and another, and another. The nepenthe that the wife of Thone gave to Jove-born Helena seems in the glass. Everything is metamorphosed as if you had been reading Ovid. The scene of repulsion is replaced by one of attraction, almost of fascination.

The music is no longer strident and odious. The tones of your attendant Circe change. They appear soft, and low, and sweet; and her once harsh face grows lovely in the glamour before your eyes. The tawdry hall becomes a place of enchantment. You wonder you did not visit long before such a palace of delights. You call for more liquor. You sing; you dance; you are happy. You whisper tenderly to the nymph at your side, as if she were Urania and you Strephon, in the midst of a new Arcadia. Then objects and sounds grow confused. There is a floating, swimming motion before your eyes, a feeling of irresistible drowsiness and languor, and soon complete oblivion.

Your consciousness is restored; and there is a violent pain in your head, and a burning heat in your throat. You have no idea where you are, or what has passed, or how much time has sped since you lost your reason and your senses. You may lie in the station-house, or in your own room, or in a strange one, of which I will not tell, because I know you would not like to tell yourself.

When you rise, and look about you, you find you have no money. Your foolish experience has cost you something; but you have learned your lesson cheaply if you will only profit by it. You are repentant, as punished men always are; and you walk confusedly into the street, if you happen to be at liberty, with all your future compassed by a bottle of Seltzer water.

At some of the saloons—the very lowest—customers are systematically robbed, and beaten if they resist. But generally, at such places, their drink is drugged, and they are non-combative victims. At the best of the saloons, you are defrauded of your change, unless you be on the alert, and every effort is made by the waiter-girls to render you intemperate in passion as well as thirst. You cannot go often to the best conducted music-halls without a diminution of your self-esteem which makes temptation strong and seduction easy.

The waiter-girls are more to be pitied than despised. They are frequently drawn to this vocation by lack of employment, and the impossibility of obtaining it elsewhere. They come mostly from the country, and are often virtuous when they enter the saloons. But they cannot continue so. The strongest of our sex, and the purest of theirs cannot resist temptation and circumstance beyond a certain point. And how can they, with nothing to restrain and everything to compel them?

Yet the waiter-girls have virtues, if not the (considered) cardinal one. Strange anomaly to those who do not understand what a mixture of good and evil human nature is, waiter-girls not seldom support aged mothers, and educate younger brothers and sisters, by the wages of sin and the saloons.

They have aspirations, doubtless, for a better life,—for a higher sphere. But the World frowns, and Society rejects them. They could not do otherwise if they would. So they must wait until the grave makes all things even by making all things forgotten.

CHAPTER XXXVII.

CORNELIUS VANDERBILT.

MEN like Stewart, Astor and Vanderbilt, who either make or manage great fortunes, are little inclined to sentiment, and, therefore, rarely popular. Such men are doers, not sayers, and speech attracts more than conduct. They are so practical of necessity, so absorbed in their own affairs, that they have little time or sympathy to give to the great mass that does not in any way affect their interests.

Cornelius Vanderbilt is a man of power, unquestionably. Many fear, but few love him; nor has his course been such as to endear him to any very large number of people. Through nearly half a century he has employed his extraordinary energy, tact and managing force to the advancement of his own pecuniary interests, never slacking exertion or sparing toil in the accumulation of a colossal fortune, whose income he cannot and will not use.

Cornelius Vanderbilt is, as his name indicates, a descendant of the early Dutch settlers, and inherits from them the industry and thrift that have been largely instrumental in securing him his superabundant riches. He is altogether a self-made man, his origin being humble and his education neglected. He was born in 1794, on Staten Island, his father being a farmer, who tilled a lot of ground for the purpose of supplying the New-York market—an undertaking in which he thrived. The elder Vanderbilt, in carrying his products to the City, began to take passengers who had no boats of their own, and in due season became a regular ferryman. His perriauger made one round trip a day, and he prospered more by it than by his farming.

To the ferry between the island and New-York, Cornelius succeeded at the age of sixteen, having shown such a marked and unconquerable dislike of books and the restraints of school, that his parents despaired of his education. He was ignorant of the common rudiments, and was unable to determine, in his twentieth year, whether his name should be spelled with a W or a V. He had an instinct, however, for arithmetic and calculation, and knew what a dollar stood for as well as any boy in the country. He was soon the owner of a perriauger himself, and developed a remarkable capacity to make money, which has grown with his growth and strengthened with his strength. He proved himself an excellent judge of human nature, too, so far as trades and bargains were concerned, and beyond that he cared nothing for it. In his eighteenth year he was the owner of one of the largest perriaugers about New-York, and during the war of 1812 he was active in furnishing, at night, the forts near the City with supplies. He was resolute and courageous, rarely failing, it is said, to keep his given word, or to execute any commission, however hazardous, he had agreed to perform.

In his nineteenth year he married Sophia Johnson

—his wife died very recently—of Port Richmond, Staten island, and removed a few months after to this City.

At the age of twenty-three he had saved $10,000, considered a handsome sum in those days, but which he regarded merely as a basis for future operations. Perceiving the great advantage that must result to commerce from steam power, which had been recently applied to navigation, he entered the service of Thomas Gibbons, a wealthy New-York capitalist, then engaged in transporting passengers between here and Philadelphia. He remained with Gibbons twelve years, and manifested such shrewdness and energy—successfully evading the act of the Legislature forbidding any vessel to enter the waters of the State without license, on the pain of forfeiture—that the capitalist was unwilling to dispense with his invaluable assistance. Vanderbilt wished to be his own master again, especially as he had obtained a practical knowledge of steam navigation, which he was confident he could turn to most profitable account. For the next twenty-five years he did little else than build steamboats and steamships, and always succeeded by having better and faster and cheaper lines than his competitors. The accommodation of the public was always made subservient to the interest of Vanderbilt, and always will be; for he makes no secret of the fact that he is his own—I will not say only—best friend.

In 1850 he established a rival line of steamships to California, by way of Nicaragua; sold it out to advantage three years afterwards, to the Transit Company, and became the president of the company in 1856.

In 1855 he went to Europe with his family, in his

own steamship, the North Star—the first fitted with a beam engine that ever crossed the Atlantic—and attracted much attention by the novelty of the expedition. After his return he built a number of ocean steamers to run between New-York and Liverpool, having received a contract to carry the mails between the two countries. One of the vessels, the Vanderbilt, made the fastest time ever made, and, during the War, he presented it—it cost $800,000—to the Government as an addition to the navy. The act was officially recognized by Congress, and is very noticeable as something the "Commodore" was not expected to do. He has been in the habit of supervising all the work he orders, even to the minutest details, and never accepting anything that does not suit him. He has built and owned more than a hundred vessels, and not one of them has been lost by accident, it is said, which may be the reason of his constant unwillingness to insure his property.

For the past few years Vanderbilt has turned his attention to railways, and has shown himself as admirable a manager on land as on water. He obtained possession of the Harlem in 1864, and from a merely fancy stock, paying no dividends, it has been made very profitable. He gained control of the Hudson River and of the New-York Central also, and has for months been striving to get hold of the Erie. No doubt it would be for the interest of the stockholders that he should; but the public, who have no reason to like him, are opposed to his monopolizing all the railways leading out of the City, which is evidently his ambition. He will be master of the Erie ere long, though, and his numerous enemies can console themselves with the utterance of the Congressman who thanked God that men couldn't live more than a hundred years; that if they could, such fellows as Vanderbilt would own the whole World. Before another twelve months he will, probably, control railway lines representing an invested capital of $100,000,000.

No one knows how much Vanderbilt is worth, but his fortune is probably not less than $12,000,000 to $15,000,000, some rating it as high as $20,000,000. He is the railway king of America, and the great power of Wall street. Among the shrewd he is the shrewdest; among the bears, the most bearish; among the bulls, the most bullish. He always plays to win, and he is so accurate a judge of men, so clear-sighted, so fertile of resource, so skillful an organizer of combinations, and the wielder of such an immense capital, that failure is next to impossible. A man of great nerve and determination, entirely self-confident and self-sufficient, with half a century of training in the school of financial selfishness, able to draw his check at any moment for millions, he is a foe even Wall street stands in awe of.

Vanderbilt has an office in Fourth Street, and conducts his immense business as easily as if it embraced only a few hundreds. He goes to Wall street every day, but his work is usually done in four or five hours. He is a passionate lover of horses, has half a dozen of the fastest trotters in the country in his stables, and would give $25,000 to $50,000 any time for any of the famous animals he has long coveted. The way to the Commodore's heart lies through the stable, and two or three of his favorites have reached it by that road.

Every pleasant afternoon he can be seen driving in the Park, and he enjoys it as a youth with his first horse might. He is a good liver; but is too discreet, too careful of his health to become the victim of the larder or the wine cellar. He enjoys a woodcock or Spanish mackerel, a *paté de foie gras* or saddle of venison, a rare old bottle of Burgundy or Veuve Clicquot; but he has never suffered from the dyspepsia or the gout. He is hale, hearty, and, though nearly an octogenarian, younger than many men with half his years, so ruddy, erect and vigorous that few would believe him beyond the prime of life.

He has a strong, expressive face, and his clear complexion, aquiline nose, strong frame and clear-cut stature of six feet, entitle him to the reputation of a handsome old man. He certainly enjoys himself. His life is divided between railways, horses and whist, of which last he is a devotee, playing almost every evening with a zest that never tires. Talleyrand said to a young man who did not know whist, "Alas! my friend, what an unhappy old age is before you!" Vanderbilt has provided against that, and when his partner returns his lead, and isn't afraid of trumps, his evenings are blessed.

Seventy-four, and worth millions, Cornelius Vanderbilt, at least, has a large family to leave them to, and when the thin gentleman who is supposed to ride on a pale horse, calls upon him, he will ask what time the steed can make, and go along satisfied if he can do a mile inside of Dexter's best.

CHAPTER XXXVIII.

BROADWAY.

Broadway is New-York intensified,—the reflex of the Republic,—hustling, feverish, crowded, ever changing.

Broadway is hardly surpassed by any street in the World. It is cosmoramic and cosmopolitan. In its vast throng, individuality is lost, and the race only is remembered. All nations, all conditions, all phases of life are represented there. Like nature, it never cloys; for it is always varying, always new.

A walk through Broadway is like a voyage round the Globe; and to the student of humanity it is interesting every day and every hour of the seasons. For years I have floated up and down its regular tides, and yet it is fresh to-day as it was in early childhood. Its gaudiness and frippery no longer attract, but its human interest grows and expands.

No thoroughfare in the country so completely represents its wealth, its enterprise, its fluctuations, and its progress. Broadway is always being built, but it is never finished. The structures that were deemed stately and magnificent a few years ago are constantly disappearing, and new and more splendid ones are rising in their places.

Wood has yielded to brick, brick to stone, and stone

to marble. Before the next decade has passed, Broadway is likely to glitter in continuous marble from the Battery to Madison Square; and, ere the century is ended, it promises to be the most splendid street, architecturally, on either side of the Atlantic.

The rent of one of its ordinary stores is a princely income, and its cost exhausts a liberal fortune. Poverty is rigorously excluded from its imposing confines, and pecuniary success alone is recognized by its stately piles. Trade must of necessity thrive there. If it be crippled never so little, rude Prosperity crowds it into humbler quarters. "Come not here," say its showy structures, "if you have not money; for only lengthy purses can buy you welcome!"

Whatever is purchasable can be had in Broadway. Virtue and honesty may be bought there like tropical fruits and diamond bracelets. All the markets of the Earth coutribute to its supplies, and its goods are furnished from every port whence vessels sail.

You need never go out of Broadway for the obtainment of every luxury and the indulgence of every pleasure. Stay there contentedly, and Paris, and London, and Berlin, and Florence will come to you. The wares and products of Europe and of Asia are within your daily promenade. Open your purse, and all your desires shall be gratified.

Lucullus, and Sardanapalus, and Apicius might have delighted every sense with the last refinements of voluptuousness between Canal and Twenty-sixth street, and found new joys as fast as the old were sated. Banquets as rich as theirs, music as sweetly seductive, women as fair and frail, would come at their pecuniary bidding, in this as in the centuries long past.

Vice wears a fair mask at every corner, and Art smiles in a thousand bewitching forms. Hotels, and playhouses, and bazaars, and music-halls, and bagnios, and gambling hells are radiantly mingled together; and any of them will give what you seek, and more sometimes.

Be it India shawls or Italian singers; Mechlin laces, or mementoes of the Orient; Persian silks, or poems that every age makes newly immortal; lore of the ancients, or love-adventures; flowers of the tropics, or fleeces from Thibet,—anything rare, or ripe, or dangerous, or dainty,—each and all are within your reach, if you can pay the price morally and materially.

But to the philosopher, no less than the pleasure-seeker, Broadway has its charms; for he can find there stimulant for thought and food for feeling. He can meet at every turn his brothers from other climes, his sisters in other spheres. Their blood has flown in such divergent streams that he knows his kindred not. Yet, if he tarried with them long, he would see how they are related.

How the ranks and antagonisms of life jostle each other on that crowded pave! Saints and sinners, mendicants and millionaires, priests and poets, courtesans and chiffoniers, burglars and bootblacks, move side by side in the multiform throng. They touch at the elbows, with all the World between them. They breathe the same breath, and yet they are entire strangers.

The same bodies and the same souls, something lies between them they shall never cross, unless fickle Fortune makes them golden equals. But in this broad, free air there is hope for all.

They may change positions in a few years. The

lowly strive to climb, and the lofty are like to fall. Let the kaleidoscope of destiny turn, and the same elements assume new and shining forms; and still they are only bits of gaudy glass.

You and I, reader, can see all our friends, if we are so fortunate as to have them, and our acquaintances of other days in Broadway.

The men we met up the Nile, and climbed Mont Blanc with, and dined opposite at the *Trois Frères* and gossiped about at the bull-fight in Madrid, will bow at the corner of Houston or Warren street. Or, if they do not, they will come by and by.

The dark-eyed gipsy who won such rolls of coin at Hombourg; the olive-cheeked beauty we captivated with our slender Italian at Rome; the fair and *spirituelle* American to whom we made love on the deck of the vessel that sailed so dreamily down the Danube under the star-studded sky,—they will pass us, if we wait and walk often in Broadway.

With how many companions have I strolled and ridden through Broadway during the past twenty years! As a child, I remember being borne along by the hand, when Canal street was up town, and Union Square the terminus of the promenade. Those companions, like the buildings of the street, have disappeared in the grave or in the spaces of the Globe, and were forgotten until some incident or association brought them to memory again.

Every day one meets those he saw last on the other side of the ocean or existence, or under circumstances directly opposed to the present time or place.

A walk through Broadway revives recollection; makes life flow backward for the hour; lifts the curtain from scenes of the past; recreates feelings often pleasant, oftener painful,—all ghosts of the dead years that shimmer through our darkened memory.

Come with me, you who have traveled and seen the World at strange angles, and had loves, and hates, and ambitions, and expectations; and Broadway will show you how hollow they all are; how experience repeats itself, and the divinest passions pall and pale.

In the midst of this bustle, and fret, and hurry, Poetry gleams out fitfully, and Philosophy looks steadily with calm, sad eyes.

There dashes by in the handsome carriage the woman who vowed she worshiped you once, though she was another's; who called you her lord, her master, and her king; and all whose peace, she declared, lay in the little words, "I love you!" Perhaps you believed it then. But she and you mutually forgot. Circumstance strangled sentiment, and Destiny passion. And now she knows not your face; and what then seemed to you tragedy proves a droll comedy after all.

You are wiser in the present. You have concluded that what we call Love is merely sweet cordial. It intoxicates for the time, and we see not things as they are. But soberness returns, and the purple phantasy vanishes, and Love proves to be a dream, which has its attractions, though we are aware it is only a dream.

That face looks familiar as it goes by. Reflection tells you it belongs to your nearest friend, of a few years ago. You and he quarreled about a trifle—perhaps a pretty face, perhaps over a warm argument. You wonder you could have liked him ever. He is hard and selfish whom you believed the soul of generosity and chivalry. But so it always proves when separation mars idealization.

Who would suppose that large, ruddy creature, the mother of half a dozen children, was the sentimental school-girl whose blue eyes you kissed, and whose golden hair you caressed, in the New-England town, or in the sunny South, ten or fifteen years ago? You are not conscious of it. But it is so. The inexorable facts of life have hidden her identity, and changed her inwardly and outwardly.

The well-to-do person who pushes past was your companion-in-arms during our great War. The last time you saw him, he was bleeding in the hospital-tent, amid the roar of the fierce battle. You left him dying as you thought, and hurried to the front line. Since then you have not met him, and now he is a successful merchant in Murray street.

What a badge of prosperity wears he who steps into his *coupé* and drives off with the air of a nabob. You remember you lent him, in Chicago or New-Orleans, the means to buy his breakfast at the convention some years before the civil struggle. Since that period he has made a million in Wall street, and is director in one of the largest of the Broadway banks.

In the next block you encounter a haggard, poverty-stricken man, whom you knew in the South as a planter that reckoned his estate by hundreds of thousands. Fortune went ill with him, and he lives now by the charity of a few, and lives hard, Heaven knows, though he has given away what would make him rich again.

Brawny and muscular is the man with the dark eyes and coal black hair across the way. He was a black-leg and prize-fighter ten years since. He is now a blackleg and a companion of bulls and bears, and a member of Congress, who is not wholly out of place in

PARK BANK, BROADWAY.

Washington either; for far worse men than he have been there,—are there at this moment, the more's the pity.

But who is not in Broadway? All who are not dead are, or have been, or will be. And the dead may be, too, in another form. Stay there, and the World will come round to you in its own season.

Expect the Emperor of the French, and the Czar of Russia, and the Pope, and the Sultan; for Broadway draws the streams of the World into its strong currents more and more every year.

CHAPTER XXXIX.

THE THIEVES.

CRIME has a strange fascination for the best of us; and a deep interest in its details belongs to human nature. After fairy tales and wonder-books little people are drawn to the horrors of vice as babes to the maternal bosom. And children of a larger growth rarely lose their taste for the terrible save through the purification of discipline and culture. The "Pirate's Own Book" and the confessions of murderers the precocious boy soon loses his relish for; but even in mature years he finds highly-seasoned food for his mind in the career of burglars and the adventures of assassins.

This is not singular either; for every phase of humanity concerns us, though unconsciously, as a possible experience of our own. If we are broad and philosophic, we read of shuddering vices as something we escaped by favor of circumstance. If we are narrow and commonplace, we find satisfaction in the thought that others are so much worse than we, forgetful that organization and surroundings determine fate.

But, however interesting crime may be, criminals are not, unless set in illusion and encircled with romance. Stripped of the raiment with which fancy invests them, they are like the tinseled kings of the stage when the curtain has fallen upon their mimic sway. They are personally and mentally what they are morally—common characters without the smallest poetic pegs to hang idealization on.

Jerry O'Brien may glimmer for a moment like a hero, as he stands young and sober, penitent and calm on the scaffold. Bob Lefferts may seem daring and desperate as he appears in a flash print leaping with a dark lantern from one roof to another while policemen follow the burglar with flashing pistols. But examination proves them to be vulgar villains, whose manners are quite as repulsive as their morals.

Robbers and thieves have long been made the creations of romance by men of genius as well as by common scribblers pandering to vitiated tastes. Schiller made Charles de Moor a model of romantic scoundrelism, and Walter Scott painted the cattle-thieves and coarse freebooters of the Highlands as magnificent fellows devoted to a sacred cause. So the poor brains of writers for the New-York weeklies strive to invest the thieves of the Metropolis with high redeeming virtues, and partially succeed with such readers as know nothing of the plundering class. They are petty and sorry rogues, however, when you see them as they are, and won't admit of sentimental or sympathetic treatment.

The professional thieves of the Metropolis, independent of those in the City Hall, number 6,000 or 7,000. They are rapidly increasing, and are said to be nearly double what they were fifteen years ago. Their calling is as distinct, their business as systematic, as that of their more honest neighbors. They form a part of our great centre of civilization, and perhaps regard themselves as essential to its continuance. No doubt they perform certain functions which result indirectly to the advantage of the community, though their immediate effect can hardly be considered beneficial.

The thieves of New-York are of various kinds, though they may be divided into five classes, each of which is separate from the other, and demands the exercise of particular capacities or qualities. The classes are burglars, hotel-robbers, shop-lifters, pickpockets, and sneak-thieves. They never interfere or associate with each other, and the lines of demarkation are as firmly drawn between them as between lawyers, physicians, and merchants.

Burglars are at the head of the profession; are looked up to and admired as congressmen by ward politicians, or full-fledged authors by novices in composition. They have necessarily more brain and nerve than common pillagers, and they believe that for eminent success they must be born to their vocation as poets and orators are. Pure American burglars are scarce, but, when found, are shrewder and more dangerous and reckless than those of foreign birth.

Most of the tribe are English, with a considerable intermixture of Irish and Germans. Now and then you discover a Scotchman, Frenchman, or Spaniard among them, but very seldom; for those nationalities show little genius for the peculiar calling. They are rarely if ever men of education,—few of them can write indeed,—but they are constitutionally cunning and bold, with all their animal instincts strongly developed. They closely resemble prize-fighters in character and habit, and occasionally sink to the grade of fistic champions by force of circumstances. They are usually indolent, and operate only at considerable intervals;

prudence as well as temperament requiring that their labors should be succeeded by long intermissions. After varied experience, however, they attain a love of adventure and danger that sometimes prompts them to misdeeds when necessities do not. One or two burglaries a month satisfy their avarice and ambition; and, if they are well rewarded in an enterprise, they often lie idle for a whole season.

Burglars proceed cautiously and systematically always; doing their work by prescribed degrees and after a thorough maturing of their plans. They first select a house or store into which they intend to break; watch it generally for several days, perhaps weeks, to determine the habits of its inmates,—when they come and go, how many there are, where they secrete their valuables, what precautions against thieves are adopted or omitted, and aught else needful to be learned.

The robber always has a confederate, sometimes two or more; the confederate keeping vigil to give due warnings of the approach of danger, or to draw attention away from his chief while the crime is accomplished or escape secured.

False keys are largely employed by the burglar, who manages to obtain an impression of the key-hole in wax when unobserved, and so supplies himself with the means of ingress.

The key procured, and the habits of the inmates and the construction of the building having been ascertained,—this branch of the art is technically called "planting,—the burglar and his confederate, thoroughly armed, either to terrify others or defend themselves, and provided with gunpowder, dark-lantern, jimmy and outsider, go to the place selected, and proceed to business.

When everything is quiet—about 2 or 3 o'clock in the morning is the time generally selected, as persons sleep most soundly then—the confederate takes his stand outside, while the burglar applies the key; uses his jimmy, if necessary, to pry off bolts; and enters, carefully closing the door after him. He knows where he is going, and exactly what he seeks. If a safe is to be entered, he accomplishes his purpose; abstracts the contents, and departs noiselessly in his soft slippers provided for the occasion. If a silver closet is to be ransacked, he has a bag with him; carries off his plunder, rejoins his confederate, and they go cautiously to their abode or an appointed rendezvous. In the event of a surprise by policemen, the confederate gives an understood signal, commonly a peculiar whistle, and the insider escapes as best he can. If the occupants of a dwelling are awakened, the burglar, too closely followed, will often attempt to frighten his pursuer, and sometimes take life to avoid arrest. Generally, however, it is his interest to hurt no one, and he will abstain from the use of weapons while it is possible to get away. Many robbers are cowardly when confronted; but others are courageous and even desperate, and will not long hesitate between shooting and escaping.

The first-class burglar universally prefers stores or warehouses to dwellings, for the former offer greater inducement, and can be entered with less peril. Private houses are most likely to be entered in the Summer, when families are absent from the City, and robberies in that quarter are mainly confined to the out-of-town season.

Hotel robbers, as their name implies, frequent hotels, generally boarding at them, and passing for strangers. They dress well; have quiet manners; assume to have business with various firms, the location of whose stores they inquire at the office; go out and come in at stated hours; read and write spurious letters, and play the country merchant like the trained artists that they are. The members of this class are generally educated, partially at least, and bear nothing suspicious about them.

They are ever on the alert, and soon learn what boarders are worth stealing from. When the occupants of certain rooms are out, they slip in with false keys, and possess themselves of such valuables and garments as they can lay hands on. They remove the screws of bolts, and leave the bolts in their places by means of putty or wax, so that they can obtain entrance after the guest or guests have retired for the night. Nearly every public house in town has some of these thieves among its boarders; and yet the special detectives employed by landlords do not know the scoundrels. The rogues operate very adroitly, and generally so securely that years elapse before they are found out. They do not stay long in one house, or in one town, but make tours of the large cities, remaining long enough away from New York to recruit any unhealthiness of reputation. Once detected, their usefulness to themselves is seriously impaired, as they are marked characters ever afterward, and expelled the moment they enter a public house, unless they are very carefully disguised. Even if suspected they fare badly; for to be suspected is nearly as bad as to be proved guilty.

The hotel-thieves are the "gentlemanly" thieves *par excellence*, and are more likely to impose upon the community than any others. They are apt to begin by genteel swindling, and end as forgers. I have known them to be men of quite respectable family and considerable culture, who, from living beyond their means and borrowing money recklessly, so lost all credit and self-respect that they were finally compelled to steal to sustain their extravagance.

Shop-lifters are composed of both sexes, the women being quite as numerous as the men. They confine their depredations entirely to stores, and adopt many ingenious devices to plunder. They are compelled to resort to new shifts, as the old ones are discovered after a brief while. They have confederates generally, that the attention of merchants may be engaged while the purloining takes place. They steal from the front of stores—the Bowery is a favorite field of operations—while their associates are examining goods inside. They acquire special skill, and can pick up a ring or a bracelet, a pair of shoes, a piece of silk or lace, and conceal it before the very eyes of a clerk, in a manner that would do credit to a professional necromancer.

Sometimes they have capacious bags into which they sweep articles when the salesman's back is turned; then purchase a trifle and depart. Both sexes wear sleeves that favor concealment, and have a knack of hiding things about their persons that only long practice could have perfected. They frequently purchase a box of goods, conceal it somewhere and carry it off, leaving another much like it, prepared beforehand, in its place; say they will return and pay for it, and get off undiscovered. Children are trained to the art, and prosper in it, because, from their tender age, they are not suspected. Little boys and girls of nine and ten, and even six and seven, are taught to steal by their parents, and do it so well as to prove that certain kinds of genius are hereditary.

Pickpockets seldom enter upon their profession until they have been educated, by learned professors, to the needful sleight of hand and delicacy of manipulation. There are places in the Fourth, Sixth and Eighteenth wards where schools like those of Fagin, and disciples like the Artful Dodger may be found. Pickpockets are well, but modestly, attired, and ply their trade at the places of amusement, in Broadway, in the stages and street-cars, at fires and the ferries, where there is a crowd, with its attendant jostle and confusion. Their dexterity is marvelous. If the opportunity be favorable, they can get your watch and pocket-book every day in the week; and yet each time you will wonder how they did it.

Recently some of them have become ticket-speculators in front of the theaters, where they have admirable facilities for robbery, and avail themselves thereof to the utmost.

A favorite plan of theirs is to excite, or assume to excite, a disturbance of some kind, and under the apparent endeavor to extricate themselves from the crowd, to reap a digital harvest. Not infrequently they charge an honest man with taking their pocket-book, and, during the temporary excitement, steal his, and make off with it.

New-York is the best place in the World for pocket-picking, in consequence of the carelessness of the people, their haste, and habit of carrying considerable sums of money upon their persons. Traveled gentry of light-fingered proclivities testify they can do better in the Metropolis than anywhere else.

Sneak-thieves have no regular method. They get their name from sneaking into entry ways and shops and hotel rooms, carrying off hats, boots, coats and small articles generally. Sometimes they make a bolder flight; sneak into bank-vaults, and steal bonds and securities; but this is more properly the business of ingenious robbers who make their calling a study and an art.

The sneaks are a most contemptible class, and are despised by all others whose profession it is to steal. They have a hang-dog look, and cannot meet the gaze of a passerby. Without courage, skill or tact, they are stragglers from the army of common scoundrels; robbing children, old women, and drunken men. They are the fellows who sell brass watches to country people; play the ball-game and the little joker; plunder poor emigrants at the Battery; pass the night with wretched courtesans, and steal their clothes in the morning.

They run so few risks; are so timid and unambitious that they are not very often arrested, and when they are, are merely sent to Blackwell's island for a few months, and released to continue their small villainies.

"Cheating luck never thrives" is a homely proverb, but true. Nor does stealing, either. Few of any of the hundreds of thieves that infest the City ever accumulate anything. They are all prodigal, wasteful, dissipated—gamblers, debauchees, lechers; work harder and suffer more to be dishonest than they need to be honest and prosper.

But, like all the rest of us, their destiny is determined for them by circumstances, and they move in the direction their organization propels them. If they are thieves, they are in good company; for tens of thousands of more fortunate New-Yorkers steal with, but not like them.

Their conscience need not trouble them sorely—nor does it, I suspect, for those we call the worst are prone to justify their conduct to themselves—because they can walk down the fashionable avenues and the business streets, point to the brown-stone and marble palaces and say, "Here are our brothers in misdoing; but they rob more freely and securely, and we are punished for all!"

CHAPTER XL.

SUNDAY IN THE METROPOLIS.

THE difference between Sunday and what is known as week days is more distinctively marked in the Metropolis than in any American city outside of New England. Paris and Palmyra are hardly more unlike than New-York on Sunday and New-York on other days.

The mighty machine with all its wheels, and cranks, and levers, and cylinders, stops on Saturday night like a clock that has run down, and does not move again until Monday morning. Broadway and Wall street, the Bowery and Nassau street, Fifth avenue and Twenty-third street, lose their characteristic features on Sunday, and hundreds of thousands of persons and things suddenly and mysteriously disappear during a space of twenty four hours. New-York, so noisy, so feverish, so gay, so bewildering on six days of the week, waxes quiet and sober on the seventh. The wild week's spree of Manhattan ends with the midnight of Saturday, and is followed by repose, if not reflection.

Strangers who dote on the great City for its excitements and sensations abhor its Sabbaths, and depart if possible before its desolation comes. The hotels, crowded to suffocation, begin to empty on Friday, and by Saturday night look as deserted as if the plague had stricken them. Gotham is the embodiment of dullness to all but native Metropolitans on Sunday. No theaters, no opera, no races, no libraries, no ever-changing Broadway, no teeming piers, no turbulent Wall street—what can the mere sojourner find for his profit or amusement? He is caught by a run-out tide, and he may hoist signals of distress, never so many; but he is little likely to be relieved until Monday's returning tide takes him off again.

Time was, before the Excise Law, when strangers consoled themselves for lack of externals by inward administerings. They fled to bar-rooms for cocktail comfort and brandy smash satisfaction. They got drunk in self-defense. Sunday was specially distinguished for its inebriates. Bar-keepers divided their labors with policemen. The station-houses were full, and head-aches, nausea and repentances were the inseparable accompanient of Monday morning. All that is changed now. Drinking saloons are closed to the multitude. They who are stranded in the Metropolis on Sunday must keep sober as their surroundings; cultivate philanthropy; be patient until the little world along the Hudson revolves again.

Sunday in New-York may not be a day of worship, but it is a day of rest. Everything rests but the street-cars, and druggists, and journalists. Their toil is Sisyphian; the wheel to which they are bound Ixionic. Broadway is locked and barred and bolted, all the way from Bowling Green to its upper terminus. Exchange place is silent as the tomb of the Ptolemies. Broadway is hushed as Herculaneum and Pompeii. The Stock Exchange and the Gold Room, those temporary asylums for financial maniacs, glare like the dead in marble stillness. The hundreds of seething operators and speculators have dispersed as if nature had read the riot act to them. The bears have lain down somewhere with the lambs of peace; and the bulls have wrapped their horns with the folds of domestic felicity.

The City Hall has forgot its cunning; and councilmen and aldermen steal not until the morrow. The Fourth and Sixth wards attempt a feeble show of decency; wash half their face, and see some of the filth they live in. Dover, and Oak, and Cherry streets draw their sooty children from the reeking gutter, and greet the soft sunshine with new rags of fetid finery.

The fires of the thousands of subterranean boilers go out down town, and the powerful engines sleep on their oily pillows. Only in the neighborhood of Printing-House square do keen-eyed men telegraph thought to the World with the click, click of their falling type, and bend over paper-heaped desks, and feed fires, and make steam that starts the thunder of giant presses that rumbles throughout the Globe.

And yet New-York is neither devout nor prayerful. It believes more in Sunday than the Sabbath. It ceases from labor rather than from sin. It obeys nature, not theology. It is not contrite, but its hands are tired. The churches do not draw to their sanctuaries one in twenty of the rest-takers Many have no faith in them. And those who have cannot afford the luxury of divine service any more than that of an opera box. One costs nearly as much as the other, and the latter is to many more attractive. The worldling reasons thus:

" Why should any man feel obliged to weary himself with tedious sermons monotonously delivered when he can remain at home and rest comfortably? It is no more a duty to go to church than to Europe; and he who goes merely from sense of duty would better remain away. To be inspired with new and good resolutions, to be truer, juster, purer, more charitable— that is what we should seek. Wherever we become so is the best place for us, whether at the altar or the theater, whether in the kneeling congregation or in the solitude of our own chamber."

Our three or four hundred churches would not begin to hold the million that sheathes its claws of toil on Sunday. They who are benefited by churches find them, I suppose, in spite of repellent sextons and frigid worshipers whose eyes say: "Come not here! You may be holy, but you are not well-dressed." But the many seek religion in rest, in communion with their families, in pleasant books, in the fresh air of the sea, in the visits of their friends, in the sweet consciousness of belonging for one day to themselves. Those things sing and preach to them better and more effectively than paid choirs and doctrinal clergymen. If to labor is to pray, rest is the answer to the prayer; and we all need leisure and freedom even to be good.

But for Sunday few of our mechanics or merchants would become well acquainted with their families. When they step from the tread-mill in the evening they are too worn and tired for full appreciation of their homes. Tasks that cannot wait, engagements that must be met drag them away from hasty breakfasts and unfinished sentences to the workshop over the river or down-town. They know nothing can be done on Sunday. So they free their minds as well as their hands from the week-day slavery, and give their heart and soul fourteen or fifteen hours out of the hundred and sixty-eight.

Monroe the banker, who has talked, thought and dreamed of nothing but stocks, finds on Sunday he has some interest in his wife's happiness; that affection pays dividends larger than New-York Central, or Chicago and Rock Island. He discovers that a true woman wants something more than money, and that the most liberal purchases at Stewart's and Tiffany's will not quite fill her heart.

Bigelow, the great dry goods jobber, ceases to figure for the Fall trade, and, taking his blue-eyed baby in his arms, becomes indifferent to the decline in woolens or the price of sheetings for all time to come.

The ambitious young book-keeper who has worked half the night for a month past, hoping to have an interest in the house some day, remembers on Sunday evening he has not for months seen that gentle girl who took such angelic care of her sick father until he died. "By Jove, she'd make a capital wife for some man," he thinks. "Why not for me? I'm not vain; but I can't help believing she likes me. When I took her hand the first time in the little parlor, it certainly trembled, and so did her voice. Strange; I had nearly forgotten that. I'll go, and see her at once. My prospects are good; I'll propose. Benedict was right. The World must be peopled."

The salesman on West Broadway who is compelled to keep his little family out of town for economy, and live in the City himself on account of the hours he is occupied, rejoins the loved ones Saturday evening, and

Sunday reopens the gates of his domestic Eden shut all the week to its master and its lord. When his dear young wife runs to meet him at the gate with the baby in her arms, does he not bless Sunday, and Heaven that gave him such a treasure, with the "prettiest and smartest child in the world," in one and the same breath?

During the warm months excursions are abundant here on Sunday; and, were it not for the frequent rowdyism that attends them, they would be unalloyed pleasure to the poor. Even as they are, they are most desirable; for they give new health and life to the laborer and mechanic, whose hard labors shut them up in New-York as if it were a besieged city.

Boats leave for almost every point on Sunday, to the East and North rivers, up the sound, down the bay. Staten island, Coney island, delightful spots on Long Island, groves, green hills, cool valleys, the seaside—are all within easy reach. The charge is small. For a dollar or two one can have a quiet day beyond brick walls and burning heat.

It is pleasant to see the crowd of bronzed and muscular men with their wives and children thronging to the piers on Sunday, and steaming off in quest of recreation and repose. They are not handsome nor elegant, nor entirely polite; but they are honest and industrious and human; and their happiness reflects itself upon every soul that is in sympathy with its fellows. If their life is hard, and their circumstances narrow, they can enjoy themselves more easily than those whose lot is above theirs. They are far happier than the more fortunate would suppose. Trifles give them satisfaction, and the atoms in their little sunbeams dance to pleasant tunes.

The City never appears so well or so contented as on Sunday, which is the whitest day in the seven. It is the waking from the restoring sleep after the long delirium, the return to consciousness after the muttering fever. The look of anxiety and restlessness peculiar to American faces in great cities is gone. Something like the old child-like color comes back to them in gratitude for the Sabbath. New-York grows young again on that day; for its cares and concerns are set aside. The fierce storm of Broadway has lulled. You can see its pavement clear and clean from Morris street to Grace church. Along its sidewalks are no hurrying feet. The lumbering stages have departed—would they were all at the bottom of the East river!—there is no blockading, even at Fulton or Courtlandt street. No body of desperate pedestrians are charging upon the Astor House or St. Paul's, or endeavoring to surround the City Hall Park, and cut it off from the main army marching to Whitehall. Park Row and Nassau street, after 11 o'clock, are innocent of yelling newsboys, who would have driven Frederic Fairlie, Esq., to immediate dissolution, and before whom Astrea over the way seems nervous through her marble robes.

The parks (all this when the weather is pleasant of course,) are filled with men, women and children. They sit on the benches babbling of their small concerns, quite as important to them as our greater ones, or stroll or play in the walks, giving out the unmistakable sounds that never come from heavy hearts. I wish there were more Sundays in the week. We should be better for them. New-York seems like Paris on Sunday in its contentedness; but we are still far behind that city in our capacity for quiet pleasure and innocent recreation. In Paris Sunday is enjoyed rationally by the people at large, and if you have spent the Sabbath there, you may remember that you thought the city seemed less wicked then than on any other day of the week; for it suggested outward and inward peace.

We have not yet dared to open the theaters and amusement-places for those who wish to go. We have musical entertainments like those of any other evening, and call them Sunday concerts.

There must be something very wicked in music not christened "sacred," or in any recreation entirely innocent and even desirable on week-days, if it be indulged in on Sunday. But unilluminated heathen cannot see the difference the day makes. Heretics and sinners are inclined to believe that what is lawful and rational on Monday must be lawful and rational on Wednesday, or Saturday, or Sunday. But their opinions are not entitled to serious consideration, certainly not to much respect. When they are converted, they may be listened to; albeit, while they stumble in the darkness, and declare they are not afraid of pits, the orthodox lantern must not be hung out for their accommodation.

Our churches and religious societies do much good. They might do more if they were broader, and did not insist on every one seeing with their eyes and speaking with their tongue. But the secular and spiritual-minded are agreed upon the beneficence of Sunday. It is a beautiful and peaceful, a wholesome and a healing day, whether the church-bells or the symphonies of Beethoven, or the verse of Shakspeare, or the laugh of gladness—they are all religious—welcome them in.

Sunday "knits up the raveled sleeve of care," and lays the aching head upon pillows of down. It touches the fevered brow with the cool hand of sympathy, and baptizes with delicious moisture the lips that have grown dry and hot through the week's work. Sunday is a blessed and a blessing thing; and before its fair Aurora the shadows of six days of weariness fade into light.

CHAPTER XLI.

THURLOW WEED.

WITH the single exception of William Cullen Bryant, Thurlow Weed is the oldest editor in New-York, having been born in Cairo, in Greene County, of this State, November 15, 1797. Widely known and highly influential as he is and has been as a journalist, his connection with a metropolitan newspaper is very recent.

Weed has had quite a varied career, having been a cabin boy, a wood-chopper, a printer, a soldier, a politician and a journalist, faithfully serving and long working, which last should redeem any sins, physical or spiritual, he may have committed. After "running" on the Hudson during his tenth and part of his eleventh year, he entered a printing office in the village of Catskill in the peculiar capacity of "devil." In his thirteenth year he went to Cincinnatus, Cortlandt county, then on the frontier, and for some time led a primitive backwoods life. At the age of fourteen he returned to the art typographical, working at the case in several newspaper offices.

He volunteered in the War of 1812, serving as private; subsequently established a paper for himself, and was the editor and assistant editor of some twelve country journals. He was violently opposed to Masonry, about which there was so much excitement in this State in 1826 and '27, and was twice elected to the lower house of the State Legislature. While there he so distinguished himself as a party manager, though he seldom spoke, that he was regarded as a marvelously proper man to oppose the body of Democrats known as the Albany Regency. He contributed very largely to the election of De Witt Clinton, and in 1830 removed to the capital, where he became the responsible editor of the *Evening Journal*, which immediately rose to a power in the State.

Since that time, a period of nearly fifty years, Weed has been constantly in politics, and a prominent figure in public life. He has never, save his brief service in the Legislature, held public office, though he might have had any position, from Vice-President and member of the Cabinet to that of Governor or State Senator. And yet he has been more a maker of politicians than any man in the country, and justly deserves the name of the political Warwick. In politics he literally lives, and moves, and has his being. Little has ever been done by his party—he has always been a Whig and Republican—without his counsel and co-operation. He attends every session of the State Legislature and National Congress, and is styled the greatest wire-puller and lobbyist in the Union. He seems to have more offices in his gift than the President of the United States, and the Custom House of this City appears for many years to have been more under his control than if he had been the Collector of the port. To obtain the favor of Weed is to secure office, and his smile and frown have been for five and thirty years the delight and terror of all place-seekers along the Hudson.

It used to be said that no man could be sent to the

Legislature whom Weed could not win over to his side if he deemed it worth the while. Assemblymen and State Senators bitterly and ferociously opposed to Weed, went to Albany—elected by his most violent enemies—and before they had been there three months they would undergo a revolution, coming to the conclusion that the great political manager was one of the most mis-represented men in the Republic. He understands human nature thoroughly; has admirable tact and profound insight into character. He flatters the vain; supports the weak; softens the bold; encourages the timid; sympathizes with the strong, and leads men by seeming to follow them; molds and controls them through their interest and self-love. Hundreds of instances might be given of his adroit dealing with stubborn spirits, whom, in most cases, he has brought over to his will. Let one suffice.

A very contumacious fellow was sent to the Assembly who hated Weed, and who had often declared he would make an expedition to the Bottomless Pit before he would vote for anything Weed advocated, and that he took no one's opinion but his own. It happened that T. W. wanted the man's vote, so he introduced himself one morning, saying: "I have often heard of you. I know you don't like me, and I respect your candor. I always esteem an open enemy. You are one of the few men who are self-reliant, have wills of their own, and won't be influenced by others. I like that, too; I recognize in you a kindred spirit. We won't and can't agree, but that is no reason we should quarrel. Drop in and see me. I enjoy original men. You see I know you. If you won't be influenced by me, perhaps I can learn something from you."

In less than a week the resolute Assemblyman was carefully under the dominion of Weed, and believed the eminent manager had actually taken his counsel.

The great Whig triumvirate of Seward, Weed and Greeley, had things pretty much their own way in this State until the last-mentioned member of the company, believing he had been very unfairly treated by his partners, dissolved the firm, and has since been their most persistent and uncompromising foe.

Greeley seems to hate Weed as if he were a brother-in-law, and loses his temper whenever he refers to him, bursting out into such phrases as "the old villain lies, and knows he lies," with a spontaneous virulence that does more honor to his love of vigorous Saxon than his regard for courtesy.

Since T. W. became the editor of the *Commercial Advertiser*, he and H. G., before Weed went abroad, had controversies almost weekly; and whatever may be the respective merits of the argument, the advantage of manners is in favor of Weed. He seems to be calm and gentle compared to the *Tribune* chief, who raves like a very drab when contending against the veteran of the *Advertiser*. The initials T. W. and H. G. appear so supremely inharmonious that it is fair to suppose their owners must have been born under adverse planets. Those who pretend to know, say Weed enjoys "stirring up" his adversary very much as a showman does the lions, for the sake of hearing them roar.

More than a year ago Weed purchased an interest in the *Commercial Advertiser;* finding that he could not be satisfied outside of a newspaper office. I remember, twelve or fourteen years ago he took leave of the public in the Albany *Evening Journal*, closing with the remark that he was mindful of Gil Blas' advice to the Archbishop of Granada. But he has not failed in power as the vain prelate did, and he has no need yet of a critical valet to inform him of his decay. The *Advertiser* has much improved since Weed took charge of it, and is far better than the many who never see it suppose. He is one of the few leader-writers who understand that leaders compared to other parts of a journal are of small consequence, as they are not generally read.

Weed, now in his 71st year, shows signs of age and failing health, but is ambitious and resolute as ever. He devotes only two or three hours a day to his paper, having purchased an interest in it more for the purpose of having a vehicle of expression than with any view of adding to his fortune. His true throne was at Room No. 11, in the Astor House (he has just gone to the Fifth Avenue Hotel) where he held a perpetual levee, and where, on an average, fully one hundred men called daily, most of them on political errands. The ins were to be found there no less than the outs with every grade of public officer, from United-States Senator to deputy keeper of the Custom House coal-cellar, seeking interviews between the hours of 12 and 3 o'clock.

Thurlow Weed does not look at all like the man one would fancy him. Instead of a person of presence and high-bred air, he is a tall, thin, stooping man, carelessly dressed, with shambling gait, hurrying about as if he had a note to pay in fifteen minutes, and wanted to borrow the money of the first stranger he encountered. He gives one no impression of magnetism; and yet he must be a singularly magnetic man to wield so great an influence and exercise such unlimited control over his fellows. He seems to want nothing for himself, but to spend his life obtaining place for others. His manners are very pleasant. He is extremely kind-hearted and charitable in every way, never rude or inconsiderate, making friends of all who are near him, and doing hundreds of good deeds of which no one hears, and he never speaks. His ambition is power; but he seems to use his power mainly for others. His intimates are greatly attached to him, and say he is a much abused and thoroughly upright man,—political and crafty in politics, but honorable and chivalrous wherever his word is given, or his faith is plighted.

He married early, and had three daughters; has long been a widower, and lives with his youngest, a maiden lady of most estimable character, who has preserved all the records of his life. Of these her kind father promises to make an interesting volume when his gray-haired youth is over, and he retires from active and engrossing duties. He will never fulfil his promise. He is too busy for such a task. He will never have leisure to die, though Death will not be talked over or put off even by Thurlow Weed, the great tongue-wagger to some purpose. He is rich, his fortune having been set down at $2,000,000 to $3,000,000. He may not be worth more than $1,000,000; for he is said to have lost largely of late years. But, whatever the amount of his fortune, it is certain that he has been very careless in its collection. If his mind had been concerned about money-getting he might have been as wealthy as Vanderbilt; for he has had opportunities to make millions, and, so far as is known, has surrendered them all to gratify his love of power.

He talks of retiring from tne *Advertiser*, of giving up work, of living in the country; but he won't, or can't, I suspect. He has lately returned from Europe, and his health is still infirm. He has lived all his life amid the turmoil and strife of caucuses and political chambers. Near the bustle of Wall street and in the roar of Broadway it is fit he should close the busy days, which, with all their ambitions and contests, have left the gray-haired Warwick alive to every form of suffering, and tender as the finest of women to the heart that needs help or healing whenever its need is made known.

CHAPTER XLII.

BLEECKER STREET

No street in the Metropolis has changed more than Bleecker, especially west of Broadway. Twenty-five years ago it was the abode of wealth and fashion; and the then grand mansions stand conspicuously in the thoroughfare, with a semblance of departed greatness, and an acknowledgment of surrendered splendor. The high stoops before which private carriages stopped, and emptied loads of feminine fragrance; the broad halls and airy drawing-rooms that were trodden by dainty feet, and filled with soft voices and voluptuous music, are profaned to-day by more common uses. The old family mansions are restaurants or private boarding-houses, barrooms or groceries, peculiar physicians' offices or midwives' headquarters.

The day when Broadway above Bleecker was the quarter of the mode, has long passed, and the neighborhood of the latter street has become a synonym for singularity, if not mystery. The reputation of Bleecker street is not positively bad, as that of Greene and Mercer and Houston street is bad; but it is questionable and just a little suspicious. It is like that of a woman who is much gossiped about. No one knows anything concerning it; no one says anything direct; no one makes accusation. But everybody has an opinion in private, and the presumption is against it.

The denizens of Bleecker street are in the shadow. If the broad sunlight streamed in upon them, something morally unpleasant might be discovered. It more resembles some of the streets in Paris than any other in New-York. It is the haunt of ultra Bohemians of both sexes. In the French Capital it would be termed the Rue des Maitresses, and the name would not be inapt. Much of the atmosphere of the Latin Quarter breathes through the thoroughfare, and its poverty is frescoed with the colors of art.

No street is more thoroughly cosmopolitan, more philosophic, more romantic. It is the Great City in miniature. Its photograph would be a copy of the features of the Metropolis, many of which we are prone to keep hidden from the public view. A walk through it any day, from Eighth avenue to the Bowery, will convey to an observer and man of the world, much of its hidden meaning. He will see strange characters and strange places that he does not notice elsewhere. A certain free and easy air will strike him as pervading the houses and shops and people. A peculiar air fills and surrounds them. They are decorous enough, but insouciant and independent. What they conceal they conceal from an art sense, not from ethical motives. They tell you nothing. You may conjecture what you may, and draw inferences to the end of time, and Bleecker street will smile coldly; shrug its shoulders, and say: "Perhaps;" "As you will;" "I confess nothing; I deny nothing;" "Hold your own opinion, but keep it to yourself!"

You will meet there the neatly, but not studiously-dressed woman, with dark eyes and mouth so freshly and moistly red that it will suggest carmine more than health. She is pretty, but has a self-consciousness and assurance which barely escape boldness, and intimate hardness somewhere. She meets your gaze steadily, as if she relished and were accustomed to admiration. Her glance expresses, "I know I am comely, if that is what you mean. If you are fond of me, say so; such declarations I have heard often. Don't be afraid. We women are not the coy creatures you think us. We adore boldness, for boldness wins."

Don't you recognize her? She is the popular actress whom many of the critics praise far beyond her deserts, because their personal liking for her has biased them. No man can coldly judge a woman at night, when he expects the next morning to be at her feet.

She is a combination of Becky Sharp and Blanche Amory. She has had a score of lovers; has several at this moment. Yet she makes each believe himself the only one. She dupes them charmingly; for she is an artist and a sentimentalist. She is naturally affectionate and tender, and has power to delude herself as well as her nearest friends.

She remains on the stage because the stage lends her a bewitching something that does not belong to her. She knows men are selfish and sensual; that desire and vanity bind and hold them more than aught else. She is generous, but not improvident. She is aware the day will come when her charms will fade, and her seductive arts will lose their potency. She is providing for that day, and the Winter will not come with an ungathered harvest.

When her lovers desert her, and the World frowns, she will quit the City; remove to a distant town; change her name; become a widow; turn devout like Peg Woffington; do acts of charity; die esteemed and beloved, perhaps a wife and mother, perhaps a spinster, full of saintly virtues.

The young fellow who calls a carriage and steps into it, redolent of perfume, fresh from the bath and the barber's, you have seen often in Broad street. He is a stock-broker, shrewd, energetic, rather unscrupulous. Men cannot deceive him, but women can, without trouble. He has just come from his mistress' chamber, in that hotel kept on the European plan. He believes she is his, sense and soul; and he lavishes money upon her, which she gives to others of her favored friends.

Not sixty minutes since he quitted her; and yet the man she really loves, mean, and despicable, and vulgar as he is, is with her, and kissing away her protector's kisses. Vanity blinds the victim. He is infatuated, too, and would hardly trust his own senses if they contradicted his conviction. Hack-drivers and Houston street panders point him out, and call him a "flat" as he goes by; but he swears she is so loyal nothing can alienate her from him. If conscious what common creatures he supplied with the means of living, he would be wounded to the core. He will make the discovery some time, and then be clamorous concerning woman's frailty. Because a wanton is not faithful to a fool, he will vow the whole sex is false.

How many men are either too blindly confiding or morbidly skeptical! They rarely learn the exact truth, that between extremes **Nature** and **Truth** walk hand-in-hand.

The ballet girl trips happily along. She is in the receipt of a regular salary from Niblo's, and she has just awakened to the absorbing passion of her life. She is yet unstained, though she has for four years been employed at the theaters. She has been assailed times without number; but she has never loved till now, and she was strong, therefore, against temptation. Her heart now pleads against her, and she cannot resist its pleadings long.

Four weeks ago—how well she remembers the evening—she observed a handsome gentleman at the stage door; and since then his face has been looking into hers in dreams by night and dreams by day. The second evening he was introduced to her; and ever since he has accompanied her to her lodgings, and kissed her at parting. Each time he has lingered longer and longer, and before another month he will not go till morning.

This morning she is up two hours earlier than usual and off to Broadway without breakfast, hoping to see him before she goes to rehearsal. She does see him in a carriage, near Canal street, with a proud-looking lady, who may be his wife; but he does not see her; at least he does not appear to. When they meet, she mentions the circumstance, and he, with a confused manner, tells her the lady is his sister. He is afraid to acknowledge it is his wife, for he has declared himself a bachelor.

Six months hence there will be a sudden death in the stuccoed building where furnished apartments are rented, and the morning papers will chronicle the distressing suicide of Ada Allen, a ballet girl at Niblo's. The deceased, they will say, was beautiful and well educated, but for some time past she had been suffering from low spirits, caused, it is thought, by an unfortunate love affair. The Coroner's inquest was in accordance with the above facts.

Mr. Myrtle, junior partner of the well-known Church street firm, reads the item at his breakfast table, and spills his coffee and his face undergoes a change.

"Are you ill, my dear?" asks Mrs. Myrtle.

"O, no; I saw the failure of a house that owed us largely. I think I would better hurry down town and write to the West about it."

And the seducer and deserter hurries into the street, and for fifteen minutes feels like a villain. He loved Ada all he was capable of loving—far more than he loves his spouse. But he couldn't remain with her; for some of his mercantile friends were talking of his mistress on 'Change, and he is a member of a church, and can't be scandalized by such stories, which are the worse for being true.

The young fellow who looks darkly out upon the fair day, and whom the fresh breeze does not inspire with hope, is a child of genius and of melancholy. He has cause for despondency; for he has never had encouragement. He is an artist, and the picture he has been painting for three years is finished at last, and no one pays the smallest attention to it. The subject is singular, the coloring peculiar, the treatment original. Hence criticism will be unfavorable; and he has no money to bring his work into notice. At this moment he has not money enough for a slender breakfast, but he has for two cocktails, and he buys them at the first bar-room. He walks gloomily over to the East river, and saunters along the pilers, and wonders what will become of him. "If the worst come to the worst," he thinks, "I can jump off, and that will be the end. Ambition, poverty, neglect can't trouble me in the grave. The river will be the remedy when all else fails. But I won't fail, by ——. I'll struggle on. The World shall recognize me. I'll keep on. While there is life, there is hope."

The resolution, inspired by his double drink, saves him. He never desponds after that, and he is ultimately born to fame and fortune. Let no one denounce cocktails. They have some virtues to offset their many vices; they preserve as well as destroy, though they slay hundreds where they save a single soul.

Bleecker street is the place of rendezvous for countless illegitimate lovers. Husbands meet other men's wives; wives meet other women's husbands. And young people who love too little or too much for wedlock find consolation in each other's company in that peculiar quarter. Bleecker street asks no questions. Every man and woman who are together it supposes have a right to be together by a higher, if not enacted law. Privacy can always be had for a price, and many wives are unwedded there.

The couples who disappear, or are seen in Bleecker street are presumed to be mutually fond. No one makes comment on their relation, but few are there who do not suspect its character. The first thought of many an intrigue has arisen from a vision in that neighborhood. But those who detect others are themselves detected, and guilt can keep its own secret.

Many representatives of art of some kind repair to Bleecker street for the cheapness of its accommodations as well as for the freedom of its life. Poor scribblers and scholars, painters and engravers, actors and poets may be found in its lodgings. Some fare sumptuously on second floors; have wine and dainties and servants But most dwell in rear rooms and garrets, and lead that careless and reckless, but rather gay career for which the artist tribe is famous. They enter their apartments at all hours save those that are early, often in care of companions less tipsy than they, and often in charge of policemen who claim to appreciate the ornamental above the useful class.

The rented apartments are scenes of wild carnival at times. When their occupants have a "streak of luck," they invite boon companions of both sexes; and cards, and chat, and song, and sentiment make wassail through the night, and the dawn finds dissipation running into riot.

"I lodge in Bleecker street" is a biography in brief. If he who says it be poor, the reason is apparent. If he be prosperous, his morality is questioned at once. And yet Bleecker street is respectable enough, if one have no insight into character and conditions. Indeed, the thoroughfare is so delicately unique you can hardly make any positive statement in regard to it. Many very staid and amiable and conventional people inhabit it; but it is so much a favorite with those who are a law and a religion to themselves that it has gained a reputation for irregularity because of non conformity.

Whatever Bleecker street is or is not, it is extremely broad. That will not be denied. The freedom there of every sort is absolute; and if you seek to be independent of opinion, above scandal, preserved from criticism, become a dweller in its confines. You can do, or refrain from doing, what you like. You can come home at sunrise roaring out bacchanalian songs. You can have half-a-dozen dubious relations. You can appear half disrobed at noonday, you can set public opinion and private prejudice at defiance. You can keep a trombone, and play on it at two o'clock in the morning. You can select a dozen bass singers, and order them to execute the "Bay of Biscay, O!" to the inspiration of whisky punch, from midnight to early breakfast time, and not a soul will complain.

Every lodger in Bleecker street gives and takes. They believe in the largest possible liberty to each individual. If Mr. Jones disturbs Mr. Smith to-night, Mr. Smith will endeavor to drive Mr. Jones distracted the night following. But he won't. The residents of Bleecker street are not to be distracted. If they are annoyed, they will either bear it philosophically, or go somewhere else until the annoyance is over. They rudely imitate the Platonic republic; and if they fail of their ideal, they strive to endure the actual with the best grace and in the best spirit that their own temperaments and the gods will permit.

CHAPTER XLIII.

NASSAU STREET.

THERE could be no mirror of Manhattan that did not present the image of Nassau street—one of the most peculiar and striking thoroughfares in New-York. Only ten blocks long, it probably contains more varieties of architecture, business and character than any street of its extent in America. Beginning with the Treasury and a banking-house, it ends with the *Tribune* and Tammany hall—though the latter is rapidly undergoing the process of ultimate extinction.

Crooked, contracted, unclean, with high houses and low houses, marble palaces and dingy frames, it reminds one more of a street in an old Continental town than of a popular thoroughfare in the new Republic. But there the resemblance ends; for in no European city—unless in London, perhaps—could such a strange stream of humanity be flowing and overflowing for ten or twelve hours of every day in the week.

Nassau street is New-York in miniature even more than Broadway. Its contrasts are more observable, and its mottled life is more intense. By a singular blunder, explicable only by the fact that it was made in Gotham, one of the smallest and most inconvenient streets in the City has been appropriated to the transaction of an immense business, to which the same space in Canal street would hardly be adequate.

Think of the Post-office, where nearly a million of letters are mailed and received every twenty-four hours, a number of the largest banking-houses, four or five of the leading newspapers, one or two hotels, a dozen auction rooms, and hundreds of places of constant ingress and egress, in an irregular, ill-paved lane, less than half a mile long; and exercise your skepticism touching the wisdom of the three wise men of Gotham who put to sea in a bowl! My own impression is, that their notion of sufficient space, as shown in their nautical expedition, was reflected in Nassau street, in whose unfitness to do what it is called upon to perform I am persuaded that trio had some hand. The truth is, however, Nassau street is not so much to blame as is the City for outgrowing it, and turning the brain of the begrimed little quarter with sights and sounds it never expected, in its early years, either to hear or see. The great Metropolis has, like the hungry sea, gone roaring up the arid wastes of the northern part of the island, and left Nassau street whirling in its eddies, hopelessly and helplessly.

One gets but little impression of what Nassau street really is by passing through it, even if he go from end to end a dozen times between breakfast and dinner. Its unseen life is more curious than that which surges over its sidewalks. It has more back-offices, and upper stories and creaking stairways, and cobwebby corners, and dingy crannies, and undreamed of lofts, and out-of-the-way places generally, than could be found in all of Dickens's novels.

Buildings have grown bronzed and gray in the

street, and no mortal save the occupants is conscious who inhabits them. Indeed, the persons on the first floor are as ignorant of those on the second, and those on the second of those on the third, as they are of the appearance of the lackeys in Buckingham palace.

Down at the street-door one may read a bewildering number of signs assuming to direct him to B. F. Betts, counselor at Law; George Bishop, publisher; Henry Wisch, fruit-seller; Stephen Craig, artist; J. P. Ludlow, dealer in French engravings; Myron Burt, stock-broker; A. B. Weibel, gold-beater; Julius Wilson, manufacturer of jewelry; A. Alexander Wissop, agent literary bureau; Thomas Markworth, translator of foreign languages; W. W. Young, Boarding-house broker; George Bridges Brown, matrimonial agent, and forty other persons and places no one has ever thought about or suspected the existence of.

You begin to have a realizing sense of what the Egyptian and Cretan labyrinths might have been, if you undertake to find any one in the upper stories of Nassau street. You wonder why felons for whom great rewards have been offered do not seek sanctuary there. If Wilkes Booth had only changed his name and taken an office anywhere between Spruce and Liberty streets, he would have been forever safe. What is the State of Virginia to Nassau street as a hiding place!

Men there have become bent with years, hollow-eyed and wrinkled, going in and out of mysterious passages, leading—who knows whither? And yet no one is aware of their occupation, or cares either. They seem not to care themselves. They appear born to come into and go out of Nassau street all their lives long, with no destiny beyond.

The being and calling of our fellows are concealed from us as the animalculæ in whatever we eat, or touch, or breathe. In the vast workshops of cities we hear the din and see the smoke; but we never stop to think what the busy creatures busy themselves about.

I have often penetrated the lofty darknesses of Nassau street, and returned to the lower light with surprised remembrances. I have witnessed strange sights there that I cannot describe; beheld strange things I may not name. Curious needs has this planet of ours, and extraordinary are the demands it makes upon the rarest ingenuity of vice.

Young and old men toiled in rear rooms and garrets over tasks that taxed the senses and the brain. Women did offices of trust because their labor could be had cheaper, and children ran hither and thither oiling the wheels within wheels that connect Nassau street with the machinery of the outer world.

No where else in New-York are as many persons in business crowded together. In a single building are professions enough to fit out a good-sized town. No corner into which a cat could crawl is unoccupied. Every square inch of ground and floor is used to the best advantage. The rooms grow smaller and reach higher with each succeeding year. A large part of New-York seems resolved to wedge itself into the miscellaneously crowded quarter; and the building-fronts glare with signs, until all the painters appear to have set up their specimens there for the admiration and confusion of passers-by.

Such a hodge-podge of occupations, such an ollapodrida of interests, such a salmagundi of people was there ever before within such confines? Persons may keep out of Broadway; but they can't out of Nassau street. Due concern, or desire, or obligation will lead or drive you there every week or two, however isolated or humble your life may be.

It is a strong whirlpool of bankers and newsboys, of journalists and beggars, of government officials and boot-blacks, of public men and private nobodies, of policemen and pretty women, of capitalists and bar-keepers, of auctioneers and thieves, of shoulder-hitters and courtesans, of poets and rag-gatherers, of artists and all sorts of people. And then all nationalities are represented; for the Post-office draws foreigners of every tongue to look for letters. So your ear is greeted with Italian, and German, and Spanish, and Dutch, and French, and Portuguese, and even Arabic, Turkish, Greek and Chinese drop their strange syllables like pebbles into the seething sea.

Everybody is in haste when he enters Nassau street; for no one goes there without business, and no one wishes to stay there after he has completed it. It has no tide like Broadway. People hurry up and down the side-walk and in the street, from one side to the other, apparently without any clear perception of what they are doing or where they are going. Not so, however. There are few idlers or loungers in Nassau street. They who fill it have a clear purpose. They are in earnest, have motive and their cue, and are shrewdly adapting means to ends.

There each man is emphatically for himself, and indifferent to his neighbors. No one considers himself bound by the common laws of politeness. No one explains or apologizes for mistakes or indecencies. They are inevitable to the street which, by reason of its narrowness and inconvenience, bears all the responsibility. If you don't want your hat knocked off, or your boots trodden on, or your coat torn, or your nose thumped, or your eyes put out, don't go to Nassau street. They indulge in those pleasantries there in self-defense. Hats, and boots, and garments, and noses, and eyes have their natural rights, no doubt, but you must seek other localities to have them respected.

Patience under affront and injury is the reigning and necessary virtue of Nassau street.

I have seen sensitive and impetuous gentlemen who, in the Avenue, would have knocked the fellow down that looked displeasure, submit, without a murmur, to be hurled against a lamp-post until their spine cracked, in Nassau street. I have noticed delicate dandies, with lavender kids, violets in button-hole, breathing dainty odors, upset by an ash-cart, and smile serenely in the gutter. I have known nervous capitalists to have their pockets picked, without ever turning to look at the rogue who robbed them. They cared nothing about it. And if they did, the operation in which they were engaged was too important to permit attention to trifles, or even serious affairs involving delay.

Men who want to borrow millions; who wish to mail a letter clandestinely to their mistress; who have an article for the *Tribune* or *Post* on the national debt, designed to electrify the Republic; who are looking for a cheap cake of soap, or a cool glass of beer, or are in quest of luncheon, or about to consult their lawyer, or sell a picture, or search for a black-letter volume, all rush to Nassau street. They can get anything there, from a splashed pair of trowsers to half the five-twenty loan, from a cutaneous disease to a seat in Congress.

In consequence of the extreme narrowness of the streets, peddlers and hawkers of cheap wares are permitted to occupy stands on the sidewalks, and crowd pedestrians off. Stationers abound there, and so placard their goods that you are induced to believe you can write all your days, be they as many as Methuselah's, for fifty cents in the currency of the treasury. Viands of every kind are advertised liberally, alongside of bulletins of the newspaper offices, informing you of attempts on the life of the Pope and Victoria, and another revolution in Mexico.

Newsboys play hide-and-seek between your legs while you are endeavoring to grasp the hand of your friend, (just returned from Japan,) separated from you by a box of books thrown from a truck the moment you said "How are you, old boy?" Your companion offers you a cigar he will guarantee to be imported; and, while you are taking your first connoisseur-like whiff, it is dashed into the face of an elderly man in a white coat, (one of the greatest sharpers in Wall street, by the by,) who looks benignly at the sparks, and ventures the opinion that it is a warm day.

A malignant urchin in the form of a boot-black, puts a "shine" upon your white pantaloons as you are wedged into a corner, and coolly asks for fifteen cents for "doin' it extray, boss."

One of the features of Nassau street is its old bookstores, where more curious and antique volumes can be unearthed than in all the rest of the country. Their proprietors look as if they were specially intended for the business, being usually old, snuff-taking, seedy, abstracted creatures, with soiled fingers, and spectacles balanced on the extremities of their nose. They occupy dingy quarters, and have a passion for rummaging among worm-eaten, dogs-eared, large-typed tomes when they have no customers. Those customers are often like themselves—bibliomaniacs, who talk erudition to the shop-keepers until they forget what they wanted.

Not a few of the proprietors of the stores are modern-looking, well-dressed men, who appear literary, but wide-awake and genial—nothing of the Dominie Sampson about them. They are of the progressive school—men who live in the present as well as the past—who think and write, as well as read and quote.

No single article can do justice to Nassau street; it is so diversified, and unique, and heterogeneously-homogeneous.

Imagine a hundred thousand people going to the Post-office and coming away; twenty thousand hurrying to the vast banking quarter that bounds the street on the south; the busy crowd having business with the daily press; the concourse that is hungry and thirsty, and hastening to luncheon and drinks; the multitude who seek legal counsel, who need boots and shoes, books and papers, pictures and pocket-knives, anything and everything, indeed, between love and liquor, literature and lager—and you will have some faint notion of the immense gathering between Frankfort and Wall streets.

Nassau street has material enough for half a dozen volumes, if it were written up thoroughly; and Eugene

Sue, (were he alive,) and Dickens, and Wilkie Collins, could find better matter for plots there than they have ever wrought. How many startling cases at law, how many mysterious investments, how many dramatic characters, how many profound intrigues, how many heroes and heroines full of laughter and tears, would they reveal!

But the writer, who is too indolent to soar, and too weary to examine, is kinder than those geniuses. He makes the outlines, and leaves the rest to the imagination.

CHAPTER XLIV.

THE HOTELS.

Hotel life as it exists in this country is unknown in Europe, and foreigners have no idea of its extent and peculiarities.

In Great Britain and on the Continent, hotels are, for the most part, small and quiet, and much more home-like than in the United-States. Only strangers and travelers occupy them, and a few days or weeks includes their longest stay. No one thinks of remaining in them permanently, least of all with a wife and family; while, in our cities, a hotel is the only home that thousands of our citizens know or care to have.

Americans, although they fancy themselves such, are not a domestic people, those residing in cities and towns at least. They are strongly attached to their country, but not to their own firesides, or to fixed localities usually made sacred by associations.

Wherever an American is to be for twenty-four hours, there is his home. He is a kind of civilized Bedouin, who carries his home in his trunk, the law and the constitution in his revolver, and his religion in his disposition to do as he pleases.

Americans like to talk of home—to honor it in prose and verse; but it is rather a sentimental idea with them than a living reality. They resemble their countryman Payne, author of "Home, Sweet Home." The man whose song will always touch the heart and moisten the eye never had a home; was a wanderer all his years, and died at last in a foreign land.

The American is at home on the back of a camel in the midst of an Arabian desert; smoking his pipe on the summit of the Himalayas; swinging in the branches of the bamboo in India, or whistling "Yankee Doodle" among the ruins of the Coliseum.

In New-York, hotel life has breadth, and variety, and uniqueness that it has no where else. It is a peculiar form of existence, and its characters vary like the leaves of Autumn.

There cannot be less than seven or eight hundred hotels, all told, in the Metropolis, though fifty or sixty would include those that are very well known. Twenty-five or thirty of them are considered in every respect first-class and fashionable; that is, their patrons are generally well-dressed, and able and willing to pay extravagant prices. Nearly every prominent house has its special customers and characteristics, and furnishes a field for the study of a different phase of human nature.

A popular fallacy of the day is, that one must go to the country for comfort. The truth is, that whatever is good or dainty, or desirable there, of a material kind, is brought to the city. The country is stripped to supply the great centers. The farmers and gardeners cannot afford to consume their own products when the towns will pay so liberally for the gratification of the senses.

Probably no such luxury can be found anywhere as at a New-York hotel, if you have the means and disposition to pay for it. You can get almost anything the vegetable or animal kingdom contains. Take your seat at the table; fee the waiter; call for whatever the Earth bears, and in less than five minutes it will be before you. All climes will ripen, all vessels come freighted for you from every sea.

Many of our hotels have national reputations; and, at least once a year, American life from all the other cities streams through their corridors, chambers, and ordinaries.

At a New-York hotel, you are likely to meet acquaintances you have not seen for ten or twelve years; the friend that helped you out of that unpleasant difficulty at San Francisco; the odd-looking personage who lighted his cigar from yours at the base of the Matterhorn; the blonde beauty who flirted with you for a month in Vienna, and disappeared mysteriously from the steamer on the Danube.

The Astor House is probably the best known, the most historic hotel in the Republic; and, strange to say, though 35 years old, it still fully retains its reputation as a first-class house. Twenty years ago, the Astor monopolized nearly all good hotel-keeping in the country, and to visit New-York meant to go there of necessity. Col. Charles A. Stetson, still the ornamental landlord, though his sons are the proprietors, took it a few months after its opening. He says he used to shake his carpets in Chambers street, and was glad to obtain full boarders at three dollars a week.

All the distinguished men in the country, from Henry Clay and Daniel Webster down to Gen. Grant and Secretary Seward, have been guests of the Astor. Stetson is full of reminiscences and anecdotes of famous politicians and statesmen, living and dead, and could compile an interesting volume of his experiences and recollections. He is a capital talker, and would have made a most popular stump-speaker,—a vocation for which he was eminently fitted, and which, for his reputation's sake, he ought to have embraced.

The Astor has always been, and is still, the headquarters for politicians, which may be partially accounted for by the fact that Stetson feels a lively interest in politics, and that Thurlow Weed was for thirty years a boarder in the house. Meetings and caucuses, especially of the Republicans, are held there constantly, and Weed gave audiences from the first of January to the thirty-first of December.

Many old-fashioned people usually stay at the Astor, —those who have been "putting up" there for the last quarter of a century, and could not be induced to sojourn anywhere else.

A score or more of wealthy bachelors, from thirty to seventy, are generally permanent guests of the Astor, which seems, too, to be a favorite with journalists at home and abroad, and of many varieties of the literary class.

The St. Nicholas is an extremely popular caravansera. Every one goes there; and in its spacious halls and dining-rooms you can encounter the representatives of every State. Western people have a preference for the St. Nicholas, and southerners used to have; but they have lately gone further up Broadway. Fast persons affect it a good deal; and you are likely to encounter more pinchbeck material there than at any other house on the great thoroughfare.

The hotel is elaborately furnished, but too much

given to show and something nearly resembling tawdriness. After the late dinner, before the places of amusement are open, the halls, and saloon, and reading-room of the St. Nicholas resemble a human bee-hive, and the sidewalk in front of the building is so crowded with loungers that it is difficult to pass.

No hotel in town does a larger or more profitable business; and it has already made fortunes for half a dozen different proprietors. When it was first opened, fifteen or sixteen years ago, it was all the rage; but new houses were built, and the City grew and expanded, and the tide rushed by it to Fourteenth street and Madison square.

The Metropolitan is the resort of Californians and people from the new States and Territories, of men engaged in mining and mining interests, in quartz-crushers and Pacific railways. The patrons of the Metropolitan are peculiar and individual-looking; are remarkable for bronzed complexions, the consumption of tobacco, nervous energy of manner, and liberal display of jewelry. They give you the impression of men who have made and lost fortunes; who have had strange experiences and desperate adventures; who would spend the last ten dollars they had in the world for a bottle of wine, play poker with you at a thousand dollars ante, or fight a duel with you in the dark for the sake of the sensation.

Such are the people most conspicuous about the hotel, in the office, on the steps and in the smoking-room; but a great many quiet people from the country and the large cities fare sumptuously and spend prodigally at the corner of Broadway and Prince street.

The New-York, particularly since the War, has been

the staying-place of southerners and those who sympathize with them,—indeed, of the traveling Democracy generally, whether for or against the rebels, from every point of the compass. Hiram Cranston, the proprietor, has long been a noted Democratic politician, and is personally known to and popular with the prominent members of his party.

The New-York is a sort of offset to the Astor, and Cranston to Stetson; and its reputation is such that the politics of a man who registers his name at that house almost ceases to be a matter of doubt.

The hotel is one of the best kept in the City, and attracts many persons, independent of politics, by the excellency of its table and the comfort of its internal arrangements.

The Fifth Avenue is, par eminence, *the* great fashionable hotel of New-York, and is the haunt and home of stock operators and gold speculators, where they may be found after dinner, when the Mammon temples in Broad street have shut their doors. New-England and the residents of this State go there a great deal; and of late, Chicago, Cincinnati and the other Western cities have sought refuge at that shimmering shrine. Among the great hotels on the American plan, the Fifth Avenue is the mode; and consequently interspersed with really elegant people, one encounters there some absurd specimens of parvenuism.

Ill-breeding never appears so ill as when it is heavily gilded; and the well-fed guests of the Fifth Avenue are often amused, and then disgusted, with the pretentious commonalty they cannot escape.

The corridors of that hotel swarm like those of the St. Nicholas; but no one down stairs ever talks about anything but the closing rate of gold, and the next contest in Erie. The last bulletins are always on the walls; and dozens of men are constantly scanning them, and wondering what turn the market will take to-morrow.

On the second floor, the scene is different; for there the other sex hold sway, and the men, weary of talking-business, ascend to the handsome, brilliantly-lighted parlors, and chat and flirt with the women they may chance to recognize. The gentle fair are elaborately attired, look their fairest, and act their sweetest,—frequently failing of interest by their excessive effort to be engaging,—while their gallants seem delighted, and tell their fashionable charmers everything but the truth.

The hours from 8 to 11 and 12 o'clock are devoted to gossip, gallantry and gayety; and no other hotel in the country, outside of the watering-places, presents such a field for fashionable flirtation as the Fifth Avenue after dinner.

The Brevoort, corner of Fifth avenue and Clinton place, is on the European plan, and one of the quietest and most expensive hotels in the City. Foreigners generally go there, though a number of families make their home within its comfortable walls. It is a small house, but makes as much pretension to style and elegance as almost any hotel in town. The names of ministers from abroad, consuls and diplomats are generally found on its register, and persons of title are very common among its patrons.

The Barcelona, in Great Jones street, is no more. It was a Spanish hotel, and exclusively patronized by the Cubans and Spanish who visit us. English was rarely spoken in the house, which had Spanish clerks, chamber-maids and waiters, and staying there reminded you of your travels in Arragon and Andalusia. If you did not understand the language of Calderon and Cervantes, and relish oil and olives, you were wise to keep away from the Barcelona.

The Barcelona is now the Maltby. It is patronized by Americans, and is on the European plan.

The fashionable European houses, are the St. James, Everett, Hoffman, St. Denis, Grammercy-Park, Clarendon, and a dozen others which have no distinctive features. They are well kept and patronized; and they who live there think their particular hotel the best in New-York.

The Grammercy-Park, Union-Place, Clarendon, Spingler and Westminster are little resorted to by the miscellaneous public, but have their own class of patrons, many of whom are private families.

The second-class houses are far more numerous than the first-class, and among them French's, Lovejoy's, the Merchants', Western and Courtlandt-street, are the most frequented. They are said to be comfortable; though the class of persons you meet there are not apt to be as cultivated and agreeable as at the Broadway houses. You must pay something for your company as well as your accommodations; and most persons in this country are willing to do so, if they have the money, or can borrow it.

New-York generally is a very expensive place, but you can live cheaply if you are willing to go where your fastidiousness is not consulted, and cleanliness is not ranked second to godliness. Thousands of persons keep up a certain respectability of appearance here on a slender income; but they suffer more from their false pride than they would be willing to in a worthier cause.

If many a trusting Don Cleofas would take hold of Asmodeus' cloak, follow him in his flight to the steeple of Grace Church, and gaze at the unroofed hotels, he would have his faith shattered and his peace poisoned. He would see that countless men who wore the bays of belief concealed beneath them what loved and trusted women had put there.

Hotel life is agreeable and desirable for masculine celibates; but he is unwise who takes his wife and family there for a permanent home. How many women can trace their first infidelity to the necessarily demoralizing influences of public houses,—to loneliness, leisure, need of society, interesting companions, abundance of opportunity, and potent temptation!

There is a happy medium between ever-jealous husbands and secure simpletons. Master Ford was made ridiculous by his suspicions; but I am afraid Falstaff's story was not fully told.

Women have too much natural craving for mental excitements, too much fondness for sensational experiences. They are a thousand times better and purer and less selfish than men. But their nearest friends and protectors have no right to expose their light garments to the fire, and wonder they are scorched.

Love and knowledge are the best guardians of every woman's purity and peace; but we should all remember there are crimes made venial by the occasion, and temptations that nature cannot master nor forbear.

CHAPTER XLV.

WILLIAM CULLEN BRYANT.

WILLIAM CULLEN BRYANT is the Nestor of the Metropolitan press, and one of the best known men in the country. His name is familiar to all Europe as a poet, *littérateur* and journalist, and well it may be, for he is one of the best types of the editorial profession in the New World.

William Cullen Bryant's name is almost a household word throughout the land. Yet such is the indifference and absorbing nature of New-York life that when he walks up Broadway, as he often does, not one person out of five thousand who pass would recognize him. Say, however, "There goes Bryant," and almost every one would turn to gaze in the direction indicated. No reputation secures to a man in New-York what Horace considered the assurance of fame: To be pointed out as you go by, and hear 'That is he!' Giants of celebrity, monsters of notoriety may pace from Bowling Green to Madison Square, and no quick whisper, no pointing finger, no hurried comment wounds their sensibility or flatters their self-love.

Bryant, born November 3, 1794, in Cummington, Hampshire county, Massachusetts, is the son of Peter Bryant, a physician of the place, a man of fine literary and artistic tastes, who taught the boy to love poetry in his earliest years. The affection existing between William and his father was of very ardent even romantic character, as is shown in some of the first verses the poet wrote. Like Cowley, Milton and Pope, Bryant wooed the muses as soon as many boys learn to read. He might well say, with the author of the "Essay on Man":

"While yet a child, nor yet unkown to fame,
I lisped in numbers, for the numbers came."

In his tenth year he wrote verses, and in his fifteenth published them. They were so very clever that few persons would believe they were his. They could not be convinced such extraordinary productions were the work of a boy of his age, and a rigid examination was necessary to satisfy the skeptical. In precocity he closely resembled Chatterton; writing "Thanatopsis," considered his best poem, and by many critics at home and abroad, the best of American poems—in his nineteenth year. "Thanatopsis" remained in MS. for three or four years, and was printed in the *North American Review*, in 1817, when it gained at once a wide reputation, and has grown so popular since that many of its polished lines have been worn threadbare by quotation.

Bryant in his thirtieth year, I think, removed to New-York, and in 1826 connected himself with the *Evening Post*, with which he has remained ever since. For a number of years he was a very hardworking journalist, writing the leading articles, especially on political subjects, during two whole decades. The *Post*, in those days, was Federal, but Bryant, always Democratic (in the true sense of the term) in his views and sympathies, did much to make the paper reflect his opinions. Under his administration it grew to be a Democratic journal, continuing such until the question of slavery entering into politics gave birth to the Republican party, of which Bryant became a firm but independent supporter.

During the past twelve or fifteen years, many of which he has spent abroad, he has rested somewhat from his labors. Now-a-days he rarely writes an editorial, leaving the management of the *Post* to Charles Nordhoff and Augustus Maverick; but indulges his journalistic habit by writing on minor topics, with a pertness and vigor not to be expected of a man more than forty years in the editorial harness.

His literary life is too familiar to speak of at any length. In addition to a book of poems published thirty years ago, which was warmly praised by the British reviews, he printed a volume, in 1849, entitled "Letters of a Traveller," made up of his correspondence to the *Post.* Although a journalist and accustomed to daily writing, he is not fond of literary composition, seldom attempting it unless there is something he particularly wants to say. Poetry, with him, is not only a labor of love but a love of labor. He composes with the greatest difficulty, owing to an extreme fastidiousness that refuses to be satisfied. Like Pope and Campbell, he is always anxious to alter and revise, and is ever finding what he conceives to be happier words of expression. It is said he wrote "Thanatopsis" a hundred times, and that he now has a copy of the poem with various changes from the published form. It is often asked why he does not write more; but those who know him wonder not at his infrequent accomplishment of verse. Poetry is a mental agony with him. He takes as much pains and toils over his lines as Jean Jacques did over his prose, or Tennyson over his verse. He has almost invariably declined to furnish poems for college commencements, public occasions and national festivals; his talent not being of the ready or spontaneous sort. The sole instance I know of his departing from the established rule of his life was when he furnished two short poems to the *Ledger*, for which Robert Bonner paid him the extraordinary sum of $3,000. He has none of the *curiosa felicitas* that distinguishes many literary men, particularly those who have been bred to journalism, or who have long followed it as a profession.

I know a score of clever fellows in the vicinity of Printing-House square who would write a drama, half a dozen pieces of verse, a story, two or three columns of paragraphs, and a score of letters to the country press while Bryant was inditing a short poem. I am bound to say, however, his work would better bear critical examination than theirs.

His travels have been quite extensive. He has been abroad five or six times, having visited every part of the continent, Egypt, Syria, Judea, and other portions of the East. Like a true journalist he has always corresponded with the *Post*, making there a record of his impressions of the people and places he has visited. His letters are unusually interesting, as they would naturally be, coming from a man of such refined and cultivated tastes. He is thoroughly acquainted with art, a passionate lover of nature, a poet in his life no less than in his written word. He enjoys travel and nature more than almost anything else, and finds, like the melancholy Jacques, sermons in stones, books in the running brooks, and good in everything. He has been and is the intimate friend of a number of the best artists at home and abroad, and has all the artistic feeling and sympathy of the plastic tribe.

His domestic tastes are remarkable for such a wanderer. In 1845 he purchased a beautiful piece of property on Long Island, near Roslyn, and has ever since been cultivating it with the greatest care. It is an idyllic poem in nature. His charming home is literally embowered in roses, sheltered in the midst of the most luxuriant plants of every variety. He spends much of his time with his flowers, and while he walks among and watches them with a floral affection, his youth seems restored, and his years sparkling backward in the morning sunshine. He is a widower now; but all his life long he has been devoted to his family —he has two daughters—and a model of all that is lovable in the relation of husband and father. Of late years he passes much of his time in his old homestead, making visits to the *Post* office only once or twice a week, and then remaining but a short time.

Personally, Bryant looks like one of the ancient patriarchs. His hair and beard, which he wears long, are of silvery white and of silken softness, and he might well sit for a model of Calchas. Though his face is deeply wrinkled, he is erect, lithe and vigorous as a man of thirty and, in his seventy-fourth year, is probably the best preserved New-Yorker in the neighborhood of Manhattan.

Men usually die here of old age before they are forty, but Bryant is an exception to those who surround him. Few young men can walk so far, take so much exercise, or do so much work as he can to-day;

and he attributes his extraordinary strength to the abstemiousness of his life and his passion for nature, which has caused him to pass much of his time in the open air. He is inclined to be shy, albeit he enjoys congenial society, and has spent many happy days with Washington Irving, Fitz-Greene Halleck, William Leggett, James K. Paulding and other noble fellows and *beaux esprits* whom he has survived. He is a most entertaining talker, and it is a rare treat to listen to his reminiscences of the distinguished dead and the historic spots he has known so well. He is a fine specimen of the American gentleman of the past generation; and yet he is so hale and hearty there is good reason to believe he may brighten the next generation with his silvery hairs.

CHAPTER XLVI.

THE MARKETS.

The domestic markets of New-York are the best, and the market-houses the worst, in the country. The two are 'antipodes. They remind one of delicate and delicious viands served on broken and unwashed dishes and soiled table-cloths. Who can enter any one of our dozen market-houses, see their profusion and excellence and variety of supply, and contrast them with their surrounding dinginess and squalor, without a feeling of disappointment approaching disgust? There is hardly an exception. Fulton and Washington markets reflect all the rest. Jefferson is little better than Catharine, Union than Clinton, Franklin than Centre; but Tompkins is deserving of consideration.

It is well known that no people under the sun have so many material comforts as Americans. As a nation, we are luxurious, self-indulgent, extravagant. We are the modern Assyrians. We will have what money will purchase, come what may. No true son of the Republic believes he shall ever suffer from deprivation; for he has faith enough in himself and his country to think all the necessaries and many of the superfluities of life will be always furnished. The poorest American often fares better than the richest of the ancients. The salaried clerk and the retail tradesman sit at tables that would have shamed those of Caligula and Cleopatra. The barbaric splendor is less, but the material comfort is more. We melt no pearls in vinegar; but we melt our incomes in dainty superabundance.

In our mode of subsistence there is a wonderful equality. The salesman with fifteen hundred a year has the same bill of fare as his employer worth half a million under the hammer.

Foreigners are surprised at the profusion of our markets, and still more at the number of people who purchase at them. What in Europe only a certain class would buy seems here to be within the means of all. Within the purse would be the apter expression; for its contents are the measure of our wants.

Market-going is unpleasant and prosaic. It is the soberness and seriousness of marriage after the romance and illusion of passion; the standing behind the scenes after the close of the beguiling play; the entering the kitchen before the arrangement of the feast.

I have had much experience as a market-goer; and, the more I go, the less I like it. There may be those who relish kissing an eternal farewell to delightful dreams, leaping from their cosy beds at early dawn, and trudging off to a confusion of buyers and sellers, to the inspection and purchase of roasts and birds, of sirloins and side-pieces, of carrots and cauliflowers, of lettuce and lobsters. But I am not of them.

I infinitely prefer total ignorance of the price of marketing, the place of its sale, and the mode of its preparation. I like to go to breakfast or dinner at my entire leisure; look at the bill; call for what I want; pay for it; and think no more about it.

To be independent of the rate of provisions is to enjoy a freeman's privilege; to hear no quotations of the substantials of existence is a blessed immunity. Ye who think otherwise, consign yourselves to a private boarding-house, and be taught the sagacity of my opinion by bitter experience.

I have known men who refrained from matrimony because it brought among its lesser woes the woe of market-going. They fancied they could bring themselves to endure the great sacrifices and responsibilities it imposed; but the prosaic littleness of bartering with butchers and hucksters was beyond their bearing. Unlike many men, they were unwilling their wives should go to market, and they were right. If the larder must be supplied by household devotion, and the servants be incompetent, as they usually are for such service, the melancholy duty obviously belongs to the proper head of the family. Women always endure the greater burthens of wedlock. They wear petticoats, and bear children. Let their husbands go to market.

Let us, you and me, reader, go to market,—ideally I mean,—and see how they do such things in the Metropolis.

Washington and Fulton markets are the best known and most frequented; but they are all alike, and one will answer for all. We can visit any, and see whatever is to be seen. Call it by the name you prefer. Here it is, and well attended, though the sun has not yet risen.

There is little order or regularity in the stalls. The

buildings are old, rickety, uncleanly, patched and added to until they seem like old garments made older and more unsightly by excess of bad mending.

We cannot help thinking of the model market-houses of Philadelphia,—so clean, so spacious, so airy, and so sweet. The City of Brotherly Love may be an overgrown village; but its market-houses are what they should be, and its municipal government won't steal more than fifty cents on the dollar. Would we could say the same of Gotham!

But, if the houses are poor and paltry, their contents are rich and superabundant. Nothing is lacking to gratify the palate,—to delight the most jaded appetite. The best beef, mutton, veal and lamb the country affords are displayed upon the stalls. Those roasts and steaks, those hind-quarters, those cutlets, those breasts with luscious sweetbreads, would make an Englishman hungry as he rose from the table. Those delicate bits, so suggestive of soups, would moisten the mouth of a Frenchman. Those piles of rich and juicy meats would render an Irishman jubilant over the memory of his determination to emigrate to a land where potatoes were not the chief article of food.

What an exhibition of shell-fish, too! Crabs, and lobsters, and oysters in pyramids, yet dripping with sea-water, and the memories of their ocean-bowers fresh about them. And vegetables, of every kind, and fruits, foreign and domestic, from the largest to the smallest, from the rarest to the commonest, from the melon to the strawberry, from the pine apple to the plum. Fish from the river and mountain stream, from the sea and the lake. Fowls and game of all varieties, from barnyard and marsh, forest and prairie.

WASHINGTON MARKET.

everything that can appeal to and gratify the epicurean sense.

We think of the consolatory reflection of the newly landed Milesian, that no man can starve where provisions are so plenty, when we walk through the markets and see the overwhelming contributions.

Everything is exceedingly high, considering the quantity; but, in a great centre like this, there are so many mouths to be fed, so many consumers, and so few producers, it is not strange prices are at the top of the scale.

People complain of quotations, and declare they can't live. But they do, and keep buying the best the market affords; for what it affords they can, or do, at least. It is easy to show on paper and by figures, how people can't live if the necessities of existence go much higher. But the necessities steadily advance, and the bills of mortality do not increase. Nature and requirement have a way of answering the question, How shall I live? that is mysterious, but quite satisfactory.

Rates decline with the hours. You can buy at 9 thirty per cent. less than you could at 5, but not so excellently; for the market is now stripped of its choicest and best. The ordinary rule is reversed in market-going. They who are prosperous are the earliest customers, and the poor are the latest. It is the fashion of the fashionable to purchase when the sun is low and the price is high. They send their stewards, housekeepers and caterers before the humble in circumstances dare invade the sanctity of elevated figures.

At this timely hour, we see the caterers of the great

hotels among the first visitors. They are on the alert for the choicest beef, the fattest mutton, the freshest cutlets, the earliest fruits and vegetables; for the reputation and patronage of their houses depend upon the excellence of their table. The Fifth Avenue, St. Nicholas, Brevoort, Metropolitan, Astor, Hoffman, St. James, and all the others are represented; and the indefatigable steward of Delmonico is never behind.

Butchers and gardeners have orders in advance to keep such and such things for the hotels and restaurants; but those establishments deem it necessary to have an artist on the spot. The rivalry is too sharp to admit of implicit faith in promises, and market-people are vulgarly venal often.

They who purchase for the denizens of Fifth avenue and other fashionable quarters, are stirring betimes. They select without regard to price, and are, therefore, most desirable customers. It is not always so, however. Some of the wealthiest New-Yorkers are economical to niggardness in their dealings; chaffer and cheapen for half an hour; go from stall to stand; and lose more time in the endeavor to save a few pennies, than would serve, if rightly employed, to earn dollars. Several of our millionaires are notorious at Jefferson and Fulton markets. They will not even trust their servants, and buy such provender as is usually sold to keepers of cheap boarding-houses in East Broadway. The same persons will spend prodigally for their vanity; but for their private table, unless there be invited guests, they are sparing of food.

The colored servants (always good, but expensive market-goers) of gambling-houses and bagnios, are among the generous patrons, and they are the most monetarily reckless of all. They do not use their own means, and their employers stint them not. The quality of their purchases, not the quantity of their outlay, is impressed upon them; and they little care for complaint on that score.

The late customers, as I have said, are the penurious or the poor. They go when prices have fallen; when the best articles have disappeared; when prospects of bargains have brightened. The middle classes, so far as circumstances are concerned, attend at medium hours. The really indigent tarry from obligation, and the parsimonious from election.

After 7 or 8 o'clock, the delicacies and desirables are not to be had. Then eggs are suspicious; butter potent; vegetables wilted; meats irresponsible; fish uncertain; fruits deceptive.

The moral tone of dealers lowers with the advance of morning. A butcher who is undoubtedly honest at sunrise, will cheat you without hesitation at 10 o'clock. The vegetable woman who would keep all the commandments before 6, would break almost any of them for money after 9.

The latest and hardest customer is the cheap boarding-house keeper. She (for that is her sex generally) is resolved on buying much for little ; and the quantity of leather steaks, highly perfumed butter, limed eggs, green fruit and unsavory vegetables she carries off, awakens sympathy with her boarders, and uneasiness respecting their digestion. She is fond of saying she knows what's what; but I don't believe her patrons do. If they are so endowed, they must regard ignorance as bliss.

Occasional visitors are the infatuated strangers who

consider markets among the lions of the Metropolis. We all like to know how our neighbors live—it is a subtle as well as interesting problem—and the curious strangers seem to understand the question in a material light. They wander from one end of the market-house to the other; ask prices; handle meats and vegetables; criticise them; make inquiries of every kind; wonder and speculate; and return to their hotels with a better appetite for breakfast, because they believe they have done their duty.

Other visitors are the young women who appear leaning heavily on masculine arms, looking fond and happy and enthusiastic. They never release their escorts for a moment. They pout and blush, and glance significantly out of the corners of their bright eyes. They must be in love with their companions, or they wouldn't act so.

They are. They are new-made wives. Harry or Julius gets up like a true gallant, and goes to market, begging Lucy or Harriet to lie still and sleep until he returns. But she won't do anything of the sort. How could she sleep in the absence of her darling husband? So she accompanies him, and, when they return, she either prepares or superintends his breakfast, and they sit down like two doves to their morning meal.

In a few weeks a change comes over the spirit of their dream. The young wife doesn't go any more. She lies in bed; sleeps like a dormouse, and is cross when awakened even with a kiss. At the end of six months, Harry or Julius holds down the pillow, and she is compelled to provide for the household.

Fulton market is famous for its oysters, and Dorlan

is *the* oyster man of all others. For twenty years he has been here, and his shell-fish are the best on the Planet. It is strange the saloons there are patronized so liberally by a class you would never expect to find at such an uninteresting place. But it is the fashion to go to Fulton market, and that fact, more than the excellence of what you get, preserves the extraordinary custom. The people you meet at Delmonico's, you see at Dorlan's—men of wealth, and women of society; fastidious scholars, and authors of renown.

Into those plain and noisy saloons go models of elegance and extremes of mode—the money king of Wall, the great importers of Beaver, the famous shipping merchants of South street, the belles of Madison avenue, and the staid clergymen of Brooklyn. Vanderbilt, Drew, Belmont, Stewart, Bellows and Vinton, Beecher, Greeley, Tyng, John Morissey, Mrs. Stanton, Fanny Fern, the venerable Gulian C. Verplanck, Moses H. Grinnell—every body, high, low and in middle station, are patrons of the market.

If you wish to see one of the peculiar phases of New-York life, go to Dorlan's at lunch time, and observe, amid its clatter and confusion, what fair and expensively attired women, what distinguished and gifted men, you will meet there. About those little tables, over those delicious oysters, what strange stories have been told, what heart-histories revealed, what secrets of the soul poured into sympathetic ears! Fulton market has a history in itself, and Dorlan is its central and commanding figure.

The evening markets are almost entirely democratic. They have no grades, no visitors at different periods. The humble and common-place patronize them generally; the wealthy seldom. They are the resort of blacklegs and courtesans, often, who make assignations there, and leer, and wink, and act indecently when they dare. Such markets are a confusion of bad manners, and high voices, and familiar dealers, and vulgar customers, and over-dressed people.

We won't go there, reader. We'll leave those who like such places to go in our stead. We'll be exclusive, and touch hands, and part here until to-morrow. Aye, to-morrow; for to-morrow never comes.

CHAPTER XLVII.

THE POST-OFFICE.

The New-York post-office is characteristic of the City—an indirect way of saying it is as bad as it well can be. Governmental slowness, added to municipal carelessness, makes blundering unavoidable and failure magnificent.

In no other place than the Metropolis could the general post-office have been kept in an old church, a narrow and crowded street, and an out-of-the-way locality, for a whole generation. Something more than stupidity is required for that; something more than indifference to the public interest; and that something more, which is dishonesty, turns to fruit on every bush on the island of Manhattan. The people have complained and clamored year after year. Everybody knew and said the post-office was a nuisance. But nuisances are cherished and perpetuated here, as Broadway, the police system, the City Hall, the street-cars, the unbridged rivers, the unventilated theaters for instance; and the post-office, having been universally declared a nuisance, was by divine right entitled to remain such. Whenever removal has been determined on; whenever the citizens were likely to be advantaged, long purses were opened, and before the glitter of coin the prospect of change was lost. But the World moves.

We now have reason to hope that we shall have a new post-office during the century; and we are resigned to continued annoyance out of consideration for our posterity.

What a human bee-hive is the old Dutch Church in Nassau street, bounded by Liberty and Cedar! An entire stranger would think that the big and broad church to which so many anti-creedists belong. All the lower part of town runs in and through it, and overflows with the rising tide that pours out at its swarming door-ways. Not all the churches in the City have so many worshipers, such earnest, devout, regular attendants. Interest preaches in that pulpit, and human nature goes to hear the preacher; for he charms with the dreariest themes and the shrillest voice. His is the universal religion that requires no teaching, understood alike in the temples of Boodha and Brahma, of Jupiter and Jehovah. When he opens his lips to shriek or thunder, every ear is stretched, and every breast leaps to listen.

That popular church is the general post-office, which has fourteen stations or branches in different quarters of the town; employs nearly five hundred clerks and managers, about three hundred outside attachés, and does more business than any other three offices in the country. It has about six thousand boxes, and yields to the Government, above all expenses, a million and a half of dollars per year,—an income that is regularly increasing. All the other offices of the United-States about pay their expenses; the department depending for its sole profit upon New-York.

Nearly one million of letters are delivered every week, and over fifty millions every year; while a hundred tons of mail matter pass through the office each twenty-four hours. In 1854 the amount was about eighteen tons, showing an increase of more than five hundred per cent. in thirteen years. Of money orders thirteen or fourteen thousand dollars are sent, and about sixty thousand cashed per week. Of stamps eight thousand dollars are sold per day, or more than two million six hundred thousand per annum. The registering department does business enough for an ordinary office, from seven to fifteen millions worth of bonds being registered on steamer days.

Forty-five or fifty regular mails leave, and about the same number are received every day. Twenty-five mail steamers sail from here every week; all of them carrying heavy mails, especially those for foreign ports.

From these facts and figures some idea may be obtained of the immense business at the New-York office, and the need of intelligence, system and fidelity in every department. It is useless to say they are not to be found; nor will they be while the post-office is merely part of the political machinery of the Republic. The department has been but a partial success here from the beginning, and grave doubts are entertained of its ever being what it should until it is placed in the hands of private parties who can be held responsible, as express companies are, for failures or losses.

One of the great defects of our country is its postal system. Mails are as uncertain as to-morrow's sky, (give me credit for not making the time-honored pun,) and to rely on them is like putting your trust in silver mines. The City mails here are particularly deranged. You can send a letter to Boston, or Albany, or Chicago, with a tolerable certainty of its reaching its destination some time. But if you mail a missive from your office in Pine or William street to your friend in Grammercy park, or Lexington avenue, or direct a note to your cousin round the corner, the chances of its ever being heard from are slight. The time usually occupied *in transitu* between "down" and "up town" is 24 hours to 24 days; and men have been known to visit Europe and return before a city letter at a mile's distance could reach them. Such are the blessings of a republican postal system.

The American people, being the most intelligent, are naturally the greatest letter-writers on the Globe. It is often an event in the old World to get or read a letter. But here children indite epistles, and every cross-roads has its post-office. The man who has not received a letter has not been discovered, though, if he exists, he lives in the interior of Arkansas or the Eastern part of Louisiana.

If you take your stand at the corner of Liberty and Nassau streets any day between the hours of 9 and 6, you will imagine half of the planet has fallen in love with the other half, and is telling the loved half of the fact every minute. Stand firmly, hold to something, or you will be swept off your feet as you are by the under-current at Long Branch, by the tide of swift passers-by. Hundreds of people of every sort hurry by into the vestibule; hurry out, and disappear. Some seek letters; some are mailing them. Some want stamps; some want information; but all have urgent business, and hasten and fret as if they had bought a through ticket for Heaven, and they had hardly time for the last train.

Within you observe the long lines of men and boys with money in their hands, earnest-faced, yet patient, waiting for their turn at the stamp-windows. At one window any number of stamps can be had; at the other sums of one dollar and upwards only. The links of the chain fall off at the head and increase at the tail. For hours it is about the same length. But as the hands on the large clock at the end of the Cedar street hall creep round toward 5 o'clock, the throng becomes a mere group.

To the north of the Nassau street entrance are boxes labeled "City," "Eastern States," "Western States and territories," "Northern States and Canada," "Southern States," and into those, letters are thrust so rapidly that the apertures are almost choked at times. What a deluge of envelopes of every hue to every point of the compass? What can they all contain? What can all those people find to write about? How industrious Americans are! What a mania they have for wasting pen, ink and paper! Have they an interest in paper mills or stationers' establishments that they thus throw themselves into expression?

The boxes are constantly thumped and the clerks thrust out their hands full of matter, and dart to another number, and empty that, and fly to a third, and deliver to the messengers who receive and depart without end. What hosts of correspondence from all over the habitable Globe! Advice from India, quotations from St. Petersburg, questions from Constantinople, warnings from Frankfort, remittances from Vienna, information from Berlin, orders from Smyrna, gossip and love messages from Paris, friendship reaffirmed from London; business intelligence and sympathy from every clime and zone. This is indeed civilization, enlightenment, when every man in any part of the World can communicate with his fellows on the other side of the planet, across deserts and seas, in lands the belief in whose existence is only a matter of faith.

There are the general delivery and the window for advertised letters. They are besieged all day long. No one who is quite indifferent calls for letters; but the clerks are enough so to make up for the interest of the outsiders.

Post-office clerks are models of unconcern if not rudeness, all the country over. In that particular they are in advance of all other government employés, of bank officers, of railway underlings. I have often believed they were born only to have their noses pulled; and it is a great pity they so often miss their destiny. It is wonderful how such dull fellows can be so ingeniously offensive. All the capacity they have is directed to disobligation. The study of their lives seems to be to offend. If Caligula's destructive wish had referred merely to the class I have named, he would have been a true philanthropist. I would vote for him to-day for dictator of New-York.

"Letter for Wm. B. Haskins!" The clerk runs over a pile of letters much as professors of legerdemain do a pack of cards, and throws them back without reply. Time was when they would hurl "nothing" at your head as they would a missile at an enemy; but that is considered needless politeness now. Perhaps the question is repeated quietly more than once; and the clerk, by way of reply, insults the questioner. It was a wise precaution to make postal windows small, if the prevention of clerks' heads from much merited punching were deemed desirable. Few persons who inquire for letters would be so treated if the insolent behind the partition understood that insult would meet with punishment

What becomes of all the advertised letters? Nearly half that are asked for are either gone or never found.

Is it that names are too much alike, or that clerks are too lazy to look for them? I have frequently applied for such letters at the New-York Post-office, and never yet obtained one. Perhaps it is thought enough to advertise without delivering them.

The general delivery is a study, and a sad one. They who call there usually have needs of the purse or needs of the heart. They are for the most part strangers or in adversity or misfortune of some kind. No one, unless a clerk, could have failed to notice the anxious or pale faces that go to the window day after day, and the expression of disappointment and pain that follows the turning of the back, the shaking of the head. The weary waiting, the hoping against hope, the clinging to the straw of belief in the sea of improbability are pictured in the eyes and features of many of the callers for letters that never come. Every disappointment is an added pain, a new weight laid upon the throbbing breast. The familiar faces cease to come at last. Where have they gone? Perhaps they might be recognized at the morgue.

But they who get letters often open them with wild pulses and trembling fingers. Did you ever watch the faces of those whose eyes devour letters just received? If you be a skilled physiognomist, you can learn the contents by the reflections above them. There is wealth; here satisfaction; there is hope;

here despair; there is love; here hate; there is saintliness; here sin. What may not a letter convey? What potent influences, what great changes, what spiritual revolutions may it not bring? Letters that make no outward alterations cause inward transformations beyond imagining. The great World goes on with imperceptible variation; but our world, yours and mine, which is all the world we care for, may be shattered any hour, and the fragments not worth the keeping.

How indifferently the clerks in the office rake and toss and tumble and pack the thousands and thousands of letters away! Every one of them has a history or a poem for some one, a wound or balm, a weal or woe, a rose or thorn. But they are all thrown in a heap, like the just and the unjust, the pure and coarse, in the plan of creation. They are all bound and tied together and jested and sworn over, and carried to the station or steamer, and nobody cares.

Still, in all that multitude and confusion and chaos of letters, no two are alike. Each can be distinguished from its fellow, as can the individuals of the crowd on Broadway. The observer, he who has seen life, can guess at their contents; can almost find out the business from the love-letters; those of the wife from those of the mistress; can determine that this is sentimental, and that practical; this cheerful, that despondent; this sweet and that bitter; for analogies run through the Universe, and earnest study will enable us to read them.

The stations are for the accommodation of persons in all quarters of the City. They are as different in appearance and their habitués as the locality in which they are established. At some of the stations the letters are nearly all neat, even dainty. The people who call are well dressed, and have style. At others, the missives are addressed in coarse and sprawling hands, and their receivers uncultivated and common-place, if not vulgar. The stations are the favorites of intriguers of both sexes, and are frequently made rendezvous for interdicted communication and illicit pleasures.

Occasionally some unsophisticated citizen complains of such things through the newspapers, but New-York cares not for them. It is too busy to attempt to regulate the lives of persons to whom it is indifferent.

Like Paris, it says, " Enjoy yourselves as you like, if you can do it at your own expense. Your morals are yours. It is quite as much as I can do to look after my own."

CHAPTER XLVIII.

THE GAMINS.

NEW-YORK is as remarkable for her gamins as Paris is for hers. They are more peculiar, too, and more varied in their order. The strange little creatures who flaunt their rags and make grimaces in the face of the Hudson, are no imitators of those who gibe at Humanity and Fortune along the Seine. They are entirely original. They have not even heard, the most of them, of their tattered brothers over the sea, and would wage fierce war with them, should those ever find their way into Broadway or Park Row. No doubt they would be victorious over the foreigners; for our gamins have a species of savage energy and desperate determination, with a sturdiness and muscular power, that would be apt to triumph where hard blows are given.

Their antecedents are the opposite of favorable. They are almost always of foreign parentage, generally Celtic, sometimes German; born in wretched tenement houses, their earliest memories those of drunken and brutal parents, of harsh treatment, of errands to the corner grocery for liquor, of rags and filth, of poverty and vice. The gentle and kindly influences that surround and mold other children are unknown to them.

They are social barbarians. They have no conception of what "home," in its true sense, means. Beauty and Love are almost taken out of their lives. They hear no music; they see no flowers, unless they catch the strain of the street-musicians, or the vision of the bouquet-baskets when they wander into Broadway.

All existence to them is a struggle of squalor with sin, of passion and ignorance with hard materialism and the established order of things. Almost as soon as they can walk, they are thrust into the street to beg or steal, or contribute in some manner to their parents' miserable support; though it frequently happens that they never know their parents, and are outcasts from their earliest consciousness.

Abused and beaten by those who should be their natural protectors, they soon abandon their "homes," and seek their own fortune. Strictly speaking, they have neither childhood nor boyhood. They pass from neglected infancy, almost by a bound, to an immature and unnatural manhood, compelled by a sense of self-protection to a rugged and semi-savage independence. Long before their teens, they are fighting against want and fate, like shaggy veterans, and grappling with circumstances that would appal men who might be their fathers.

Their number can hardly be ascertained. It is steadily on the increase, and might to-day be counted by tens of hundreds. The gamin is to be seen anywhere and everywhere, in any part of the island, at any hour of the day or night. There is no mistaking him. If you did not observe closely, you might imagine the little fellow who wanted to carry your valise at the Courtlandt street ferry, or black your boots in

Fulton street, or sell you the *Evening News* in the Third avenue car, the same identical urchin. He has much the same expression of face, much the same voice and manner. His clothes have the same disregard of fit or wholeness, the same fantastic tatters and ridiculous disproportion to his figure.

Go where you will, you find him looking shrewdly from under his unkempt locks and fragmentary cap; standing in his great and broken boots, which he has either found in an ash-heap or purchased at a second-hand shop in the Bowery; proffering his services in some manner, if you indicate any need of them; or if you don't, staring at you half-curiously, half-critically, and evidently seeing your every grotesque or peculiar point.

Their favorite callings are boot-blacking and newspaper-selling, for which they have an original genius. Often they do both, and carry parcels and valises besides; but generally a boot-black refuses to dishonor his profession by any fugitive occupation, and a newsboy deems it undignified to embark in less exalted enterprises. They are very industrious up to a certain point; and after they have reached that, they become indifferent to compensation.

Almost every gamin begins the day with an exact idea of how much his requirements are, and until he obtains the sum needful, he is supremely energetic and active. His wants are few, and more likely to be luxuries than necessities. Tobacco, beer, the *Police Gazette* and *Herald*, an oyster stew, coffee and cakes, a pit or gallery ticket to the Bowery or Tony Pastor's, include his common needs.

Of course he has hardly a vestige of a shirt, and if

"FIVE FOR TEN CENTS!"

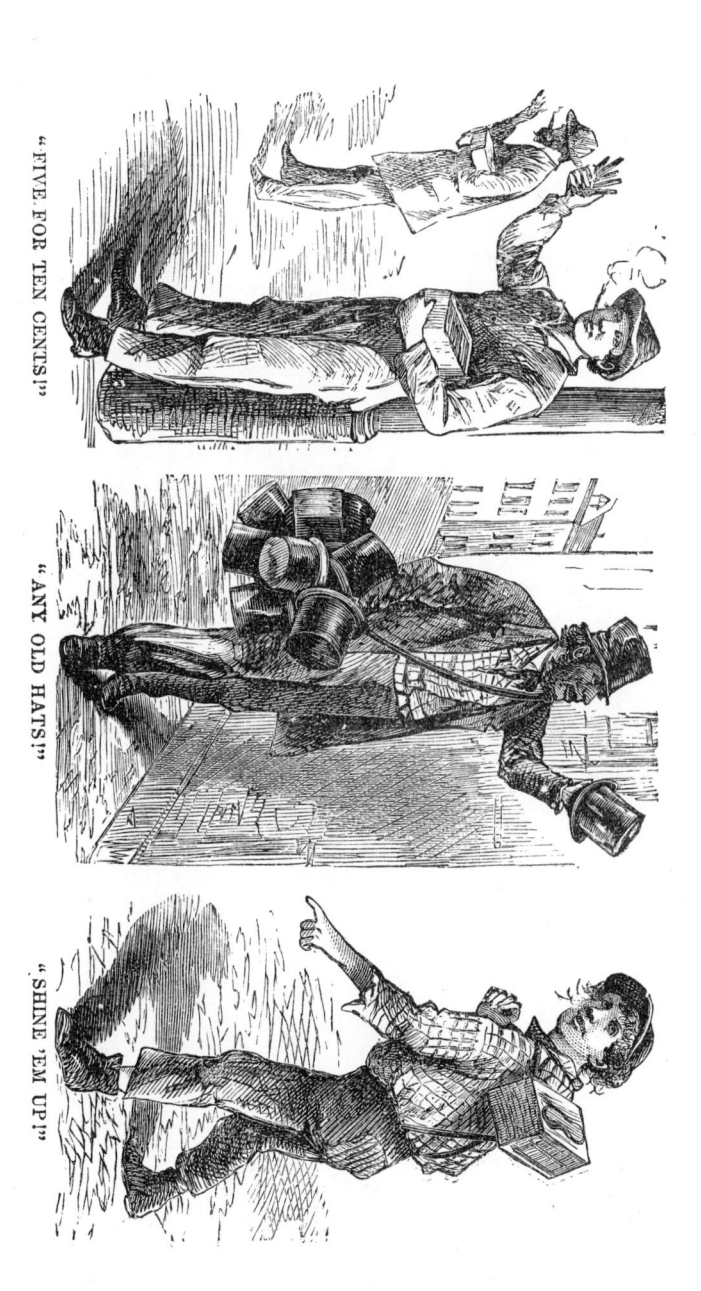

"ANY OLD HATS!"

"SHINE 'EM UP!"

the weather be moderate, no shoes—at least none to speak of—not a garment he could not leap out of, or which a hard wind would not blow to pieces. "But confound it," he thinks; "what does a boy want of them things?" He can get them any time. He can pick them up if he is abroad early enough; and he is no sluggard.

With all his rags and carelessness of appearances, he is luxurious in some of his tastes. He'll buy early fruit when it is nearly worth its weight in silver, and possess flash literature whatever its price. His dinner, even in Chatham or Nassau street, frequently costs him a dollar, and he'd gladly pay two dollars for it, if his appetite craved more. He is generous, too, at times, and gives to boys just "starting in business," enough to "set them going." He flings coppers at beggars as dukes would, and buys clothes, which he would not buy for himself, for his companions, when the Winter sets in.

One marked peculiarity of the gamin is his perseverance, and a certain kind of independence. He solicits you sufficiently to inform you of what you ought to have; and, if you reject his aid, he turns away from you with an air of mingled pity and contempt. He appeals to you eloquently on the subject of your boots; bestows a critical and condemnatory glance on their unpolished condition, and offers, in a careless way, to "shine 'em up, boss, for five cents," if you seem to hesitate. Should you take him at his offer, he will try hard to get twice as much for his job, by declaring "that's a ten-cent shine," and informing you that the other boys will whip him, if he works below the price.

He does not flatter you. He does not tell you your feet are small, or your boots neat, or your pantaloons handsome, or that you are a nice gentleman, as menials so often do. On the contrary, he vows your boots are big and dirty; intimates that it must have been a long time since they were "polished up," and that you're not what you pretend to be, if you do not give him an extra five cents.

He is quick to discover intentions. Before you have quite made up your mind about having your boots blacked, he is down on his knees, with your feet on his box, brushing away until the perspiration starts from his unwashed forehead. If he be a leading artist in his profession, and have an acknowledged reputation, he will have observers and imitators among his companions. Several of them will group themselves around him, on their knees, on the sidewalk, and watch the process closely. They are novices, probably, and taking lessons. When the master boot-black has blown his last breath upon the leather, and struck the toe with his brush to signify completion, cries of "bully, old fel," are heard from the circle of admirers.

If you want a good polish, you must watch the boy or he'll shirk his duty. He'll forget to touch the heels, and neglect the toes, unless he chance to be giving instructions to his less experienced comrades. Having secured you, he considers his price secured, and the sooner he can get the job done, the better he is pleased. If you complain, he'll do it faithfully, but give you to understand all the while, he has earned more than he receives.

The newsboy is not uncommonly a graduate from street-begging, bundle-carrying and boot-blacking, and usually considers himself in the front rank of his fellows. He is much more intelligent, often more unscrupulous than they; begins to have decided opinions and theories of life, with hopes, ambitions, expectations. He has learned a great deal by his constant reading of the papers, and can astonish you by the variety of his information. He has acquired facility, if not correctness of expression, and gives council, at times, to those on a lower round of the ladder.

Believing the newspaper the great educator, he is resolved every one shall read it. He offers inducements through his imagination, when you are averse to buying; looks into your face and conjectures your calling or character. If you impress him as a merchant, he informs you of a sudden movement in dry goods, an advance in gold, a decline in imports, of which you have never heard.

If you are pale or pensive or abstracted, he fancies you literary, and speaks of some new poem, very new to you and the rest of the World,—or cries out "Serious illness of Carlyle," "Accident to Emerson," "Important about Dickens." Manifesting no interest, he concludes you an invalid, and changes his key. Then you learn something about "valuable remedies for consumption, debility and dyspepsia," "new discovery in medicine," or "blessing to the sick."

If serious and solemn and unhappy, he regards you as a clergyman, and " Great spread of the Gospel," "Noble work among the missionaries," " Revival of religion in the country," are the phrases he is voluble upon.

Should you wear a bland and meaningless and hollow smile, and move your right arm as if you intended to offer it to every passer-by, he will clamor concerning "Reconstruction in the South," "inexplicable conduct of the Radicals," "New movement among the Democracy," presuming you are a politician.

He will probably take you in some of those verbal nets; and before you have glanced over the paper, and had an opportunity to discover his deception, he will have disappeared in the crowd. He does not resort to such shifts unless he has had ill success in his sales, or the paper is devoid of any intelligence of an exciting character. He is a profound believer in the newspapers, for they have brought him all he knows; and perhaps he deems any trick which will make you read them, beneficial in the main, even if you are disappointed in certain particulars.

A common ground for the gamins is the old Bowery theater, and of late Tony Pastor's opera-house, as it is termed. The gamins are excessively fond of amusements such as the Bowery furnishes—sensational dramas founded upon robbery, seduction, elopement and desperate encounters; tragedies in which ranting, blue-fire, bloody villains and horrid murders form the chief features. They don't affect any thing humorous on the stage unless it be in the shape of burnt cork or comic songs. They would hiss the most sparkling comedy brilliantly performed from the boards; decide "Much Ado about Nothing" a bore, and Congreve's liveliest sallies stupid. They delight in horrors, and banquet upon moral monstrosities.

Of all histrionic heroes Richard the Third, as Shakspeare caricatured him, is their favorite; though if Gloster play his part as he ought, they'll bellow at him in indignation. He must writhe and roar and grimace, and strike fire with his sword, if he expects their applause. All fencing scenes they enjoy amazingly, and all struggles on the stage, from one side to the other, up and down, to spasmodic orchestra, and ricochetting on the principal violin are apples to their eye.

They are exacting and critical, and if the performance does not please them; if there be any abatement of the murderous or sulphurous element; if the trapdoors fail, or the demons don't appear in crimson throughout, they resent the defect at once, and cry out against the decline of the drama. They are the standards for the manager; and what they approve he knows will be successful. They are to him what the professional wits were in Queen Anne's time. Without them he is hopeless. But when they applaud, he bids defiance to Wallack's and the latest Broadway sensation.

How and where does the gamin live? is a natural question. He can hardly answer, for he does not fully know himself. He is sure of the past, confident of the present, indifferent to the future. He exists in harmony with his nature, which is unnatural enough; does not apologize, nor indulge in make-believe nor sham of any kind. He neither regrets nor repents. He is on the exact plane of common things; seeking for himself, asking no favor, plucking the very beard of fortune, and grinning at destiny.

He begins very bad, and often ends worse. But sometimes he is developed into something higher and better. His very errors and sins make him wise in his own interest. Intelligence more than moral teaching shows him that honesty is policy, and rectitude advantage. He begins with reading the *Police Gazette* and *Clipper;* passes to the *Ledger* and *Herald;* and rises at last to the *Tribune* and *Nation.*

He blackens himself with a kind of whiteness. The polish of his boots is gradually transferred to his manners and understanding. He finds others feel an interest in him, and that gives him an interest in himself. Benevolent persons and societies strive to benefit him; to take care of his earnings; to instruct him in the value of pecuniary independence. As he accumulates a little money he grows less reckless, and by degrees discovers himself somewhat conservative. He finds he can do good; that he has influence, and bears responsibility.

The ill-fortune of his companions who have turned to different paths is a warning and an example. He perceives that beer and tobacco and dishonesty lead to the Tombs and Blackwell's island, and they to Sing Sing and the gallows. He has a small capital before he is out of his teens. He changes his calling; becomes a porter or mechanic; studies in his leisure hours, and having been tried in the fiery furnace, is not likely to be scorched by common flame. At five and twenty he is married, and probably has a patch of ground he can call his own; enters upon a new life, and thanks his stars that he escaped unhurt from the dangers of the old.

Such information, improvement and advancement are rare, however. The gamin would be more than mortal if he could, save in exceptional cases, rise above his surroundings; drag his garments through the mire year after year, and not be soiled. Thrust upon the World while a child, with no sense of right or justice, remembering only a drunken father and a virago mother, cruelty at home and abuse in the street, is it not natural he should take sides with the mean, the vicious and the strong? All his best influences, his affections, his instincts to good are crushed out; and he falls into the habits of the little tyrants and ruffians who fight their way to the hardest livelihood.

A bar-room becomes his highest ambition; a prize-fighter his hero. As he grows older, he patronizes one and consorts with the other. Vile habits fasten themselves upon him, and the poor little wretch whom sympathy would have transformed, and kindness preserved creeps up through poisonous atmospheres into a pimp or blackleg, a thief or ruffian, a burglar or a murderer.

The school is too strict, the ordeal too severe. Society casts him out. The law exacts penalty, but does not restrain him; and when the unfortunate gamin, who had never home or friends or education or counsel, commits crime and is punished, the very society that would not receive or help him, lifts its soft hands in horror, and declares with modulated utterance that the times are degenerate, and that the way of the transgressor is hard.

CHAPTER XLIX.

THE DEMI-MONDE.

Woman's chastity is so delicate a subject that not only all discussion of, but any allusion to it, is tabooed in society. The mere mention of sexual passion sounds the alarm for all the proprieties, and he who proposed to consider it in any mixed company would be deemed either a mad philosopher or a social savage.

The relation of the sexes is the problem of the age more than any other that demands solution, and lies nearest the hearts of the present generation. Every one feels there is something wrong in the existing condition of things; but either the fear of making bad worse, or the unwillingness to change what law and custom have sanctioned, prevents any general attempt at reform. The evils of lewdness are widespread and monstrous; but marriage also has its evils, and who will deny that a certain moral prostitution is sometimes common to both?

The only purity is in passion spiritualized by sympathy and sanctified by affection. Neither tradition nor ceremonies can make any relation virtuous where love and harmony are not; nor can conventionality and prejudice prevent Nature from obeying her instincts and obtaining her rights.

We all deplore the effects of illicit relations; but few find a voice to denounce the unchastity of discordant wedlock, which has more sins of impurity to answer for than the World dares name. The woman who gives herself unreservedly where love has gone before is stained indelibly, while she who lives a wedded leman, and wrongs and degrades herself and Nature by every fresh bestowal, walks in seeming saintliness with society's approval on her unblushing brow.

But poor woman, why should man, the author of your wrongs and woes, condemn you? You are not immaculate, but you are angelic compared to him. If you are weak, it is a lovable weakness. If you are wicked he has taught you wickedness. You are ever suffering for sins that are not your own; and he should remember he was placed here for your protection, not your persecution. When you are feeble, it is his duty to hold you up, not drag you down. When you are tempted, it is his obligation to make you strong. When you despair, he should give you hope, and make the dark future kindle with the radiance of his love.

Yet not many think, and very few act so. Men for the most part seem to consider woman a proper object of attack wherever found; that the contest is equal, and victory glorious by whatever means obtained. They have even come to believe, so false have been their teachings, that she despises the neglecter of any opportunity to do her wrong, and only crowns him with love who is ungenerous enough to betray her.

No wonder that woman complains that she is misunderstood; for men explain her mysteries by their own sensuality and selfishness, and with their false key unlock new chambers of unhappiness in the house of her heart.

The sin, man is constantly committing against her is almost the only one he will not forgive. He wrongs her, and calls her wronging a wrong upon himself. He demands that she shall keep what he is ever urging her to part with; and what she yields as the highest expression of her love he declares the evidence of her dishonor.

Poor woman, I say again, how shall she distinguish between her friends and foes? They both treat her alike. They both deceive and betray her. They both stab her with a kiss, and desert her at last for the very thing for which they sought her first.

It is estimated by those who ought to know that there are in New-York about ten thousand women who live directly and solely upon the wages of prostitution,—professional courtesans in a word,—independent of twice as many more who lead unchaste lives, but preserve an outside show of respectability. Like other evils, this is steadily increasing; the increase being entirely out of proportion to the growth of population. The War, by throwing many out of employment, by removing their natural protectors, and increasing temptation in various ways, added largely to the list, and Peace has not yet caused any favorable reaction.

The great majority of these unfortunates are Americans, and were originally residents of the country. As a class they are very comely, and I have heard strangers say they were among the prettiest women in New-York. With very rare exceptions they are uneducated, and have little knowledge of the World outside of the narrow and vicious sphere in which they move. Their history is very uniform, and that of one would answer for that of another. Their agreeableness of person is their first danger without, and their knowledge of its existence their companion danger within. In their rural homes they are either seduced by men and their own vanity, or, with ideas and feelings above their station and surroundings, they come to the City for expansion, and soon find their undoing. Many, however, are very pure and honest at home, and seek New-York for employment. Failing to obtain occupation, or losing it after a certain time, they are thrown into the way of temptations or necessities they cannot resist. Having taken the initial false step, all other steps downward are easy; and, before the poor creatures are fully aware of it, they are following a course it is almost impossible to retrace.

The remorse and misery which abandoned women are popularly supposed to experience are much overrated. They are not happy any more than saints would be on this planet, nor contented, for their lives are wholly unnatural; but they are ignorant and insensible, and seldom have a pleasant past to compare with their reckless present. We all accept what we deem inevitable, and in some way excuse, if we do not justify, our own errors to ourselves.

The unfortunate cyprian, while in good health and materially comfortable, considers her career an accomplished fact, and lives, as all her sex do more or less, in the dissipation of the hour. She has a good appetite, if not what casuists style a clear conscience, good digestion and good capacity for sleep; and, with such physical blessings, spiritual troubles rest lightly on her. When sickness or adversity comes, she loses all her strength and cheerfulness; grows superstitious and desperate without the support that fatalism yields. Then she flies to the excitement of liquor or the oblivion of suicide. The draught of brandy sinks her lower; the draught of poison gives her rest.

Prostitution like everything else, has its degrees, its upper, and lower, and middle class, with miscellaneous varieties.

The highest grade is composed of women who are young and desirable, and prosperous so far as their immediate wants are concerned. They live in the best houses and pay the largest prices for their board; are the sought rather than the seekers; air their finery in Broadway and the Park; are often the mistresses of blacklegs and other members of the "sporting" fraternity, and exercise a certain influence in the community. They never drink to excess, or use tobacco or obscene language in company. They lay some claim to taste as well as decency; can frequently thrum a little on the piano or guitar, read and write, and talk in a stereotyped way very tolerable English. They learn something from the plays they see, and the novels they read, and the men of culture they often encounter and have relations to. They know how to appear well for a certain time, and are able to palm themselves off upon the uninitiated as fine ladies and fascinating vestals.

The second class are the women who abide in inferior places; whose life is more fluctuating than that of their luckier sisters; who seek patrons when patrons do not seek them; who get intoxicated occasionally;

make spectacles of themselves in the streets, and are carried to the station-house. They are the elaborately dressed women you meet on Broadway after dark, and whose names you see in the police news as offenders against the public peace. Very often they have been in the upper grade, but have declined to the second, and will in due season fall even lower. Their position shifts like sand, and the shadow of sudden death is always above their head.

The third class are those that pace the street day and night in search of victims, whom they debauch and rob if they can. They have a room or rooms in some Greene or Mercer street establishment, to which they introduce their customers, and after their reception go in quest of more. Such characters are arrested every once in a while for theft, and sent to Blackwell's island or the Tombs. They make no pretense of decency; have no regard for person. They drink like ward politicians, and are nearly as dishonest. They swear like sailors, and fight like tigers when angry. They have usually lost their youth and beauty; become careless of appearances, and indifferent to their fate. The hospital to-day; the prison to-morrow; the deadly potion or the dark river the day after.

A fourth or fifth class might be added—the wretched females (all the woman seems to have gone out of them) who haunt the Water street dance-houses and the dens of Cherry street. They live on mere animal excitements and liquid fire; are ribald and profane,—the very harpies of their kind.

The better class of courtesans pay so much per week to the proprietresses of the houses of ill-fame,—from $25 to $50 according to the accommodations—

and depend upon their arts or charms, or both, to defray their expenses. A certain sum they must have, or the hard-hearted "landlady" will seize their baggage for debt, and drive them into the street. They are almost always lavish and improvident, saving nothing in the event of sickness or adversity, and are therefore liable to suffer for the want of food or shelter at any time. Some mysterious Providence seems to watch over them, though, as over everything else, and enables them to live year after year without crisis or calamity.

And yet they rarely live long. Who ever saw an aged courtesan? They slip off the Planet mysteriously, or are lost in the hubbub of the World before years come upon them. After a certain period they are disqualified from success in their vocation by reason of the failure of their charms. What they do then no one knows. Vast numbers die from disease engendered by their unnatural lives; and suicide is as natural to them as summer complaint to infants.

Courtesans rarely become quite as depraved as men who have surrendered all regard for the World's opinion. They often preserve such virtues as generosity, pity, charity, tenderness, and devotion, to their dying day. Even their outlawry and the brand of infamy society has fixed upon them do not drive the woman wholly out of their being. In emergencies they show beautiful traits of character and noble qualities which would reflect honor upon the noblest ladies of the land. They prove that a woman may have almost every virtue but one, as their more fortunate sisters sometimes do that a woman may possess no virtue but one.

What is most remarkable in courtesans of every grade is their inextinguishable affection for some one of the opposite sex. However unworthy, however mean, selfish, and brutal the man, they will fix their best love upon him; make sacrifices for him; give him worship; cleave to him through all wrong-doing and adversity.

A thousand times deceived, they trust the thousand-and-first time still. Their hearts trampled upon like dust, their souls wrung to agony, they yet have power to love and idealize the object of their love. They reveal that woman's whole instinct is to loyalty, to one affection, to one absorbing devotion; that her natural disposition is to purity; and that, broken and ruined as the fair temple may be, there is an inner and a secret fane on which the word Woman is graven with the point of a diamond in letters of gold.

CHAPTER L.

THE CLUBS.

NEW-YORK has more clubs than all the other cities of the Union combined. Their number is steadily increasing, and is likely, before many years, to be as large as that of Paris or London.

Clubs are the late fruit of a high civilization—the outgrowth of leisure, luxury and cultivated unrestraint. In new and small towns they are impossible. In old and large cities they are needful, because they answer to a positive want in an excessively conventional and surfeited community. They have their origin in certain superfluity of means, and a kind of inverted satisfaction. They are anti-matrimonial and anti-domestic, and present the paradox of a longing for society and a tendency to isolation.

Every club is a blow against marriage, a protest against domesticity; offering, as it does, the surroundings and comforts of a home without women or the ties of family. Clubs increase in an inverse ratio with matrimony, and each new member is an encouragement to celibacy.

There must be more than a hundred regular organized clubs of all kinds here, though comparatively few of them are well known, and have expensive and luxurious establishments in which to keep up their state.

The Metropolis has boat clubs, cricket clubs, chess clubs, yacht clubs, ball clubs, billiard clubs, press clubs, as well as art, literary, and merely social clubs. In fact, almost every game, and pleasure, and circle of artists and literary men, has its nucleus and focus in the form of a club, and club life of some sort is growing more and more in favor and fashion.

The social clubs are, however, the fashionable and famous ones, because of the wealth and character of their members, and the luxury and elegance of the mansions they occupy. The best known and most pretentious of these are the Century club, No. 109 East Fifteenth street; Union League club, corner Madison avenue and Twenty-sixth street; New-York club, No. 2 East Fifteenth street; Union club, corner Twenty-first street and Fifth avenue; Manhattan club, corner Fifteenth street and Fifth avenue; Travelers' club, No. 222 Fifth Avenue; Eclectic club, corner Twenty-sixth street and Fifth Avenue; City club, No. 31 East Seventeenth street; the Harmonie club, Forty-second street, near Fifth Avenue; Allemania, No. 18 East Sixteenth street; American Jockey club; Olympic club, No. 16 Union Place; and New-York Yacht club, club house at Hoboken. The Athenæum club was long a favorite club, but dissolved some months ago.

These clubs, as will be observed, are in the most fashionable quarter, and the houses they occupy are among the handsomest and costliest in the City. Many of them were private dwellings, but required little alteration for the new purpose to which they were converted. The rent of the club-houses is from $8,000 to $20,000 a year; they are furnished in the richest and most elegant manner, and kept up in princely style. The initiation fee and annual dues vary from $50 to $150 for the former, and $50 to $100 for the latter.

The club-houses are little more than hotels on the European plan, where one pays for what he gets. The members have no rooms, but often take their meals at the club; while others attend the regular meetings only, and pay their regular dues. Others, again, do not go there once a year.

The members vary from 300 to 800, half of whom are usually absentees in one form or other. They include almost every class. Merchants, clergymen, lawyers, physicians, authors, journalists, artists, bankers are eligible, and may be elected if formally proposed and regularly balloted for.

In most of the clubs, one negative vote in ten is sufficient for a "blackball" or defeat of the candidate, so that it is well for persons of delicate pride and sensibility to learn beforehand, through friends who are members, what will be their chances of election.

In the London clubs, lodgings are furnished to those who desire them; but the Union League is the only club here where members can have rooms for the night. Other club-houses will soon imitate the Union League, it is thought, and the Metropolis of America will become in that respect like the metropolis of Great Britain. The charge for meals is high, usually; but they are excellently served, and dining at one's club is quite the mode. The ordinary expense of belonging to a club is light, as the privileges of the house in no instance cost more than $100 a year.

The Century club, originally a sketch club, is the oldest here, having been established fully thirty years ago. It is considered the most aristocratic and exclusive in the City, and the most difficult, therefore, of *entreé*. Many months of notification of desire to become a member must be given, that the character and claims of the candidate may be duly and fully considered. Designed originally for a strictly literary and artistic association, it has departed from its first intention, and is now open to any gentleman—any one so regarded, at least—whom the members may approve.

William Cullen Bryant is president, and A. R. Macdonough secretary. Among its members are Bierstadt, McEntee, Gifford, Gignoux and Cropsey, the artists; Bayard Taylor, George Wm. Curtis, Parke Goodwin and William Allen Butler, *littérateurs;* Rev. Dr. Bellows and Dr. Osgood, clergymen; Edwin Booth and Lester Wallack, actors; John Jacob Astor, Alexander T. Stewart and August Belmont, millionaires. Many other of the prominent merchants, artists and authors belong to the Century, which has the reputation of having "blackballed" more candidates than all the other clubs in town.

The Union League and Manhattan are political clubs —the former republican and the latter democratic— the most prominent members of the two parties belonging to the social organizations. Augustus Schell is president, and Manton Marble secretary of the Manhattan; of the Union League, John Jay is president, and J. L. Ward secretary.

The Manhattan was begun in opposition to the Union League. John Van Buren and Dean Richmond were leading members of the Manhattan; and August Belmont, Fernando Wood, Manton Marble of the *World*, Erastus and James Brooks of the *Express*, and John

T. Hoffman are at present active members. Horace Greeley, Wm. E. Dodge, Charles A. Dana, Marshall O. Roberts, and other well known politicians and journalists are among the Union Leaguers. Programmes and platforms are arranged in these clubs, and the course of either party has been time and again dictated from Madison and Fifth avenue.

The Travelers', W. B. Duncan, president, F. W. J. Hurst, treasurer, was primarily intended for the encouragement and entertainment of distinguished travelers, and Bayard Taylor, George William Curtis, and Herman Melville, and other wandering New-Yorkers, are honorary members. Most foreigners who have seen the World are invited there on their arrival in the City, and frequently lecture before the club. The Travelers', however, like most of the clubs, has tended more and more to a social form, and is now little else than a mere social organization.

The Athenæum was one of the oldest and most popular of the City clubs. Literature and art gave it its rise, and membership was at first confined to persons of those guilds. After two or three years' existence, it was deemed wise to include men of other callings; and it was placed on a footing with the rest. More journalists belonged to the Athenæum than to any other club; and its quarterly receptions, when several hundred guests were invited, were very pleasant occasions. The evenings were spent convivially and conversationally, and as clever a set of fellows, both in the European and American sense, were there brought together, as can be found anywhere in Manhattan. Mismanagement and reckless extravagance brought the popular club to an untimely end.

The New-York, H. H. Ward, president, J. F. Ruggles, secretary; Union, Moses H. Grinnell, president, J. Grenville Kane, secretary; City, C. L. Tiffany, president, S. Crocker, secretary, and Eclectic clubs, Henry J. Scudder, president, A. G. Montgomery, Jr., secretary, are entirely private and social; and membership is mainly confined to men of fortune, who live on their incomes, and are not engaged in active pursuits of any kind. The New-York, Union and Eclectic have splendid club-houses, and everything in and about them is in the most expensive style. Few, if any, persons known to fame belong to those organizations, which hold wealth and fashion above character and culture.

The members figure conspicuously in the Park drives and in Fifth avenue Germans, at Saratoga-hops and morning service in Grace Church, at the Academy and late Delmonico suppers. They wear the sleekest of silk hats, the shortest of sack-coats, the most elegant of pantaloons, and the daintiest of gloves that are visible of an afternoon promenade in Broadway.

They lounge their lives away luxuriously, if not profitably, and have clerical falsehoods drawled over their silver-mounted coffins before they are deposited in family vaults at Greenwood and fashionably forgotten.

The American Jockey Club, August Belmont president, John B. Irving secretary, were to occupy the handsome club house of the Union League, but abandoned their intent when it was completed. The members have a pleasant house near the Jerome Park, Fordham, where they often go; but they have no particular place of rendezvous in town.

The Harmonie, M. Siegman president, Leopold Cahn secretary, is a Hebrew club. The members are wealthy, and have a fine house most elegantly furnished. The Allemania is a German club composed mainly of importers and retired merchants. The Yacht club, H. G. Stebbins commodore, Hamilton Morton secretary, exhibits itself upon the water more than upon land, and is famous for its fine marine performances.

The *Herald* has a club composed of members who are or have been connected with the paper, and meet at a dinner once a year. The *Tribune* has or had a club which included a number of literary men and women of distinction,—among them Horace Greeley, George William Curtis, Bayard Taylor, George Ripley, Edmund Clarence Stedman, Alice and Phœbe Carey, Lucia Gilbert Calhoun, Kate Field, and others. It has not met for a long while, and is in a sleep so profound as to be an excellent counterfeit of death.

The Press club formed a year ago will flourish, it is to be hoped, though no one can determine if the representatives of the different dailies will co-operate with each other in perpetuating such an organization.

The New-York journalists are often very narrow and envious. They are lacking in *esprit de corps* and generosity of feeling for each other. The smallest jealousies characterize many of the order of Metropolitan scribes, so much so that all attempts thus far to create a catholic and fraternal feeling among them have been signal failures.

A new bachelors' club, it is said, has recently been formed in the City, and the members, already numbering several hundreds, have rented a handsome house in Lexington avenue. Celibacy is required for eligibility.

and no one is admitted who is not 25 years old. The members, so reports run, are young men of good family, and fashionable, for the most part, and have entered the organization more to protest against wedlock than from any inadequacy of means to support wives. Some of them have incomes of $20,000 to $40,000; and that sum, with care and economy, will provide, in Manhattan, for a woman who has no social ambition and no fondness for parade. They are not bachelors, I fear, in any true sense; but they have elected to live with the moral freedom which marks Paris and the continental cities generally. Bachelorhood is apt to be pleasant to men until fifty, at least; but, after that, they lose much of their passion for adventure; women grow less fond of them; their days of sentimental experiences are on the wane; they wax conservative, and begin to want some feminine creature who wildly worships them, and longs to be enslaved by her own affections. The instinct of tyrant man asserts itself, and it is usually obeyed.

Quite a passion seems to have manifested itself in the City for feminine organizations,—more than half a dozen having been formed, if rumors may be believed, within as many months. From every one of them men are rigorously excluded; and, it is said, this is a kind of womanly revenge for the establishment of wholly masculine clubs. An effort has been made in the petticoat fraternities, by some of the sentimental members, to admit the lords of creation; but the sterner sisters have frowned down the incipient weakness,—declaring that the life of their peculiar organizations depended upon rigid adherence to the rule.

The proceedings of the feminine clubs are kept as

secret as they can be, considering the nature of their composition. From floating gossip, I have learned something of their character.

The Sorosis, or Blue Stocking Club, as it has been called, is composed chiefly of literary women and feminine artists. It was formed last Spring, and has been the subject of interminable comment in the City, and particularly in the country press. Some of its members are Alice and Phœbe Carey, Kate Field, Lucia Gilbert Calhoun, Octavia Walton Levert, Mary E. Dodge, Sarah F. Ames, Jennie C. Croley, and Mary Clemmer Ames. The Sorosis has no special purpose beyond enjoyment and the formation of a nucleus for women of liberal mind and cultivated taste. The members meet every month at a luncheon at the upper Delmonico's, and have a pleasant time. They have once accepted the invitation of the Press Club, between which and their own there seems a strong bond of affinity. They are agreeable and accomplished women, and their unpretending organization is deserving of commendation.

Another one of the clubs consists of women who are spiritualists, but don't want to be known as such. Many of them are mediums; but, fearful of ridicule, they meet in strict privacy. They claim that the spirits of their friends and of distinguished persons communicate more freely with women, fully in sympathy with the supersensual doctrines, than they would if men, naturally hard and skeptical, were present. Not a few of the spiritual sisters belong to fashionable society, and some of them are known in literature. All of them assume to have advanced much higher, and to have more thorough acquaintance with affairs in the other world, than any of the common spiritualists.

Their *séances* are said to be very interesting. They who attend them are reported to "take on" alarmingly at times,—talking, laughing, and weeping with the dear departed as they would were the spirits in the flesh.

Still another club is composed of woman's rights women who seek to avoid publicity. They are not so ultra as the Cady and Anthony school, having no desire to vote; but they demand the same rights in property, society, and morals, that men have. The majority of them are married, and confide to one another the secrets of their households. Their woes are relieved by sympathy, and they find much comfort, as women always do, in pouring out their inner lives to each other. They give counsel to one another, and they believe they receive vast benefit from the association. The married say, too, that the perfect freedom they have in the club renders them more loyal and secure. The organization prevents them from temptation, and from confiding in some man beside their husband, which they are right in considering the first and most perilous step a wife can take.

A fourth club is made up of young women, belonging to the same "set," who have banded together for the purpose of making eligible matches, and to find out whether the men who pay them marked attention are really in love with them. By such means, they are apt to detect deceivers and mere flirts, many of whom are said to have been surprised at the sudden repulses received from girls they had fancied desperately enamored.

Emma informs Mary what Charles has said; and Bessie tells Nellie what Augustus has vowed by the light of her eyes. So, when Charles or Augustus comes to repeat his gallant speeches to a second or third fair one, he is confounded by the revelation of his own perfidy.

No one can doubt this is an excellent society, and ought to be styled the "Unwedded Woman's Heart-protecting Association."

A fifth club is composed of maids, wives and widows, who meet at such times as a committee may appoint. Their object is, I understand, merely to have a "good time;" and they have one with chatting, music, wine, and the discussion of the virtues and vices of their masculine intimates. I should suppose that would be the most entertaining of any of the clubs, and that any Peeping Tom might be paid for his curiosity. I hear the applications for membership to that society are much more numerous than to any other. Women are such ardent lovers and pursuers of pleasure that a "good time," with them, must mean something. I opine a fit motto for them would be Pope's familiar couplet:

> Some men to pleasure, some to business take;
> But every woman is at heart a rake.

The sixth class is composed of actresses of an inferior grade, including a number of ballet-girls, and very much resembles a benevolent society. The members pay so much into the treasury every month; and when any one of them is out of a situation, she is assisted to obtain a new one, or receives a certain sum for her support. Several of the leading actresses have solicited the privilege of becoming honorary members, and have been very liberal in their donations. Every theater in the City is represented; and the Dramatic club may do much good.

The seventh club consists of the class known as "unfortunate women." They seem to recognize prostitution as unavoidable in the present condition of society. They make no effort toward reform, but aim to help with money those who are sick, indigent or aged. They say they have befriended a great many of their fallen sisters, having, in numerous instances, preserved them from self-destruction. Singular and one-sided as this charity is, it is far better than none, and may lead to means of prevention among the most wretched class of beings over whom the heavens bend.

Club-life is not materially different from life at the Brevoort, or Hoffman, or St. James', except that it is more private and exclusive, and passed outside of the society of women, who are not admitted to the club-house in any other capacity than as domestics.

Women are inclined to say, if not to think, that clubs are the dullest and dreariest places in creation, because they are excluded from them. But candor compels me to say, although I do not wish to violate the sanctity of the confessional, that club-houses are quite as pleasant as many houses which pretend to include paradise within their limits. They are quiet, well ordered, properly managed, and bountifully supplied; and what more could a reasonable man ask?

The members lounge, read, smoke, talk, play billiards, cards and chess. They have the leading papers and magazines, domestic and foreign; and, on the whole, enjoy themselves very tolerably. Some of the members are at the club twelve or fourteen hours out of the twenty-four, while others do not go there once a week. There are as many married as single members, and the former are often the most regular frequenters; while those who have pleasant homes and affectionate wives are rare visitors. When a home is happy, the club loses much of its attractiveness.

I fancy a feminine reader interjecting something about woman's bright smiles and sweet sympathy, the prattle of little children, and the music of their tiny feet. That is a very pleasant picture; but it has its disagreeable reverse.

Women weep as well as smile, and indulge in tantrums as well as sympathies; and children's lungs and limbs are not always exercised as poetry and parents would have them. So men without any particular inclination to domesticity, live very calmly and contentedly at clubs.

"What do you men do? How do you amuse yourselves without us?" asks Ida, the inquisitive, of a club member.

And he answers:

"We do well enough. We find amusement, interest, instruction—call it what you may—looking at life through the windows; in reading, smoking, dining with a few agreeable fellows; hearing the gossip of Society, without making part of it; lounging the days and nights away serenely, undisturbed by flirtations, and unhaunted by visions of sentimental scenes that may be postponed, but cannot be avoided."

"But what do the husbands and fathers mean by staying away from their wives and children in that manner?"

"It has been so long since I was a Benedick and a paterfamilies that I cannot remember. But I presume the charming family gets along quite as comfortably without the member of the club as he without them; and I am bound to say he seems beyond the need of consolation as he watches his smoke-wreaths with a merry twinkle in his eye, and with a certain air of indulging in an interdicted and, therefore, delicious pleasure."

"But I think it is abominable for men to act that way; and I wouldn't marry a man who belonged to a club," declares Inez with temper, which she considers the sweet sympathy of the sex.

A cynic replies:

"Adhere to that, my dear child, and the membership of clubs will increase accordingly."

"Now you are hateful. That's the effect of belonging to a club. I guess many of the members of your club would be only too glad to have me for a wife."

Perhaps they would. There are a good many muffs in the concern."

"Now, I——I——"

"By Jove! I've raised a scene," continues the cynic; the woman's weeping. What shall I do? While the tears flow I'll light my cigar, and think whether I had better kiss the pretty simpleton or run away."

CHAPTER LI.

THE BEGGARS

THE common remark of foreigners visiting the United States that there are so few beggars in this country, will soon cease to be true if all the American cities develop public mendicancy like New-York.

The Metropolis, I suspect, has as many professional beggars as all the other cities of the Republic combined, and the number seems steadily and rapidly increasing. With very rare exceptions, however, the eleemosynary tribe is composed of foreigners, who, devoid both of the pride and energy of the Americans, take to the pitiable calling very kindly, even if they have not followed it before leaving home.

The number of beggars varies here with years, seasons and business. When times are dull, the tribe increases, and when they are active it increases also, for then more strangers are in town and the field of operations is larger. In the Spring and Summer it is more convenient and comfortable to be abroad, and the warm sunshine acts upon mendicants as it does upon flowers and women,—bringing them out in profusion. During a period of commercial depression, alms-seekers augment perceptibly, many of them, no doubt, being forced to solicit charity by stern necessity, and others expecting to profit by the sympathy created through the Press in behalf of the suffering poor. Each year, however, owing to the vast immigration and the tendency of foreigners to settle in cities, the list of beggars swells. Twenty years ago beggars were comparatively rare, and even ten years since, there was hardly one where five may be counted now.

The number of professional mendicants in New-York is estimated at five or six thousand, with several thousand amateurs and persons of both sexes who embrace the vocation when the harvest promises an abundant yield.

The varieties for the most part are four—cripples and the sick, children, impostors, and pretenders — the third class being the largest and most characteristic, including many of the most curious specimens, and requiring ability and enterprise above the others.

STREET BEGGAR.

The notorious beggars of New-York, who had become familiar to the public through a series of years, have disappeared since the War—at least most of them. The half dozen old blind men who were seen in Broadway every fair day as regularly as Trinity clock sounded, the ancient hag in the vicinity of Fulton ferry, the armless Frenchman near Hanover square, the hideous humpback in Canal street, the shriveled witch and legless skeleton· in the Bowery, have retired either from life or business. The Mackerelville dwarf, the noseless Pole, the crippled Italian who pretended to have fought through all the Napoleonic wars, the wooden-limbed sailor who sang ballads in Water street and swore roundly that he was with Perry on the lakes, and even the gray-haired fury that frightened the frowsy children in the Sixth ward, have stepped into the poor-house or the grave.

But another order of beggars is waxing visible,—beggars of larger scope and higher aspirations, more ambitious and enterprising, more daring, original and fruitful of resources, more reflective of the country and the time. Every ship that reaches Castle Garden is importing them, and the day may not be remote when we shall rival London in hordes of alms-seekers.

Of all the cities of the world, New York is the best for beggars to thrive in; for Americans are more careless of money and more charitable than any people under the sun, and Gotham gives, unquestioning, with open hand.

The fame of Manhattan has doubtless gone abroad, and every nation will send her beggars to us in increased numbers. They are unpleasant additions; but there is room for them all, and credulity and alms for every mother's son and daughter who makes a wry face, and puts forth an empty hand.

As it is, beggars penetrate every quarter and corner of the town. You dare not leave your front door open, lest they enter your library or private chamber with a face that would curdle milk. They steal into every hotel drawing-room, in spite of porters and servants, and show you their lacerated forms. They come between you and your friends in Broadway whom you have not seen since boyhood, and thrust their sickening rags into your very face. They are under your feet while you listen to the sentimental confidences of Dora or Drusalinda, and pluck your gloved hand from Althea's graceful arm as you offer to assist her to her carriage in Irving place.

The first class meet with the quickest sympathy and receive the readiest assistance ; for no man of feeling can see a blind, or maimed or diseased person without a touch of pity and a prompting to charity. Everybody knows there is ample provision in the public institutions for such, and that they would be a great deal better off there than exposing themselves to sun and storm, to painful attitudes and excruciating grimaces, for artistic and pecuniary effect. But, to the credit of humanity be it said, our pity for suffering and our desire to relieve it are so great we can hardly help giving a trifle on principle ; though it often happens that, for the sake of freeing ourselves from annoyance or the contemplation of pain, we bestow unwilling alms.

The sick and crippled are attended, of course, by some one who does the talking and describes the woe. And this companion of misfortune is either a relative of the afflicted or an employé who receives a proportion of the receipts for his services.

The most unpleasant thing connected with this class is, that the cripple or his agent insists upon proving to you ocularly that there is no deceit or imposition in the case. To that end, shriveled limbs, unsightly stumps, ghastly wounds, and festering sores are revealed before you can take your money from your purse or get out of sight. When you are on your way to dinner, or to visit your beloved, or have composed in your mind the last stanza of the new poem that has given you such trouble, it is not agreeable to be confronted by some loathsome vision. You would have paid liberally to have been saved such an exhibition, and do pay promptly to be favored with as little of it as possible.

Beyond question, this revelation of hideousness is a trick of the trade; the wretched mendicants know that sensibility will convert itself into charity rather than be shocked. They have discovered that preparations for exhibition have a quickening effect on purse-strings and a certain carelessness respecting change. I have more than once observed grim smiles of satisfaction on pallid and repulsive faces when such words as "Here's something; for Heaven's sake don't show it to me!" have reached their ears.

Begging one would suppose the hardest of lives, particularly for the halt or the invalid, and yet, such is the singularity of temperament, persons without health, or strength, or perfect limbs, will endure day after day what no one of vigorous constitution would for the income of Astor or Stewart. How they live through it all is beyond solution. But they do, and apparently are not harmed by it. Year after year they sit in the broiling sun, or under the descending storm, with a sublime patience worthy the admiration of the gods. Begging is their destiny, and they seem so superior to the laws governing the rest of mankind that I am convinced beggars are the only immortals.

The second class are usually the healthiest and cheerfulest children in the City. They are rosy, but dirty; robust but ragged; and enjoy begging as they do sweetmeats. Many of them are sent by their parents into the streets to ply their vocation, but more are engaged in it on their own account. They are generally amusing, and some of their efforts at deception are very droll. They are too young and natural to be artistic, and consequently they blunder not a little.

As you come round the corner of Fourteenth street from Broadway you see several of them playing and laughing merrily; but the moment they espy you they go apart, assume a most woe-begone expression of countenance, advance to you with outstretched hands, muttering, "Please help a poor boy whose father's dead and mother's twelve small children,"—all in one word. They follow you the length of half the block sometimes if they see a penny in your eye, reluctant to surrender hope. But if you go on without regarding them, they turn away, and laugh and play again until the next stranger appears.

The juvenile vagabonds are frequently beaten at night by their unnatural parents if they bring home no money. But the children so soon learn to cheat and lie, and steal, as to prevent such punishment. If they have one good day, they save over a part of their receipts for a bad one. If they get too little they steal something and sell it. And, after a certain amount of experience, learning their own efficiency, they run away from their parents and set up for themselves, until they find their way to the Tombs or Blackwell's island.

Not a few of the children are pale and haggard, and sad-eyed, reminding you of Smike, Oliver Twist, or Little Nell, with the promise of better things in them. With education and training, they would be intelligent and worthy men and women. Their little eyes look appealingly at you, and mayhap you try to do something for them. But, unless you take them from their surroundings, they become necessarily corrupt, and sink below the reach of reform. Poisoned air and poisoned example are too potent, and they graduate at last into barkeepers, and burglars, and ward-politicians.

The impostors might be termed the intellectual class, for they require invention, expedients, originality and tact. They, more than any of the others, are born to their calling, and are artists after a certain fashion. Like their fellows they pay a very high price for the smallest success; but they enter into and prosecute their profession with enthusiasm, and rejoice over the cleverness with which they cheat the public. They have much of the dramatic element in them, playing parts often more skillfully than the actors in Broadway.

They represent blind men one day, cripples the next, wounded soldiers the third, robbed immigrants the fourth, southern Union refugees the fifth, discharged laborers the sixth, and victims of a railway accident the seventh. They make up admirably; hide one eye, conceal an arm or leg, create a cicatrice, simulate a sore, counterfeit an agony, imitate a grief, in a manner that would yield them histrionic laurels.

They are jolly fellows in their way. They usually spend freely at night what they have earned by day. They drink, gamble, lay wagers on dog and cock fights, and are splendidly improvident, on a small scale; for have they not genius that can be converted into postal currency or national banknotes at twenty-four hours notice?

A large portion of these are the men and women who have led similar lives in Europe, and who have come to America induced by the accounts they have heard of its excellence as a field for their peculiar talents. They are the borrowers of children and babies, the offerers of certificates of worthiness, of discharge papers from the army, of letters of recommendation from "well-known citizens"; and every other conceivable fraud of person, manner and document. They probably get more money than any other class, as is natural enough, for properly directed and intelligent effort always has an advantage over desultory labors.

In spite of their disguise, they stand in a little awe of New-Yorkers, and prefer to practice their arts on strangers and people from the country, being much surer of appreciation and recognition from that quarter. Like most persons of originality and individuality, they have strange episodes and crises in their lives, and usually die dramatically by knife or revolver, *delirium tremens* or suicide. They hate quiet existences, as Harry Percy did, and, like the fiery Scot, have a penchant for breathing their last with their boots on.

The fourth class are they who make an assumption of giving an equivalent for charity. They carry about or have with them detestable cigars that would not have smoked in the great New-York fire, cheap ballads, papers of pointless pins, withered bouquets, unreadable books, and the like, accompanied with mumbled utterances concerning extreme poverty or peculiar misfortune. Often they have dyspeptic bagpipes, or broken fiddles, or consumptive accordeons, which any person of sound hearing is willing to pay to stop. As no one ever takes any of their merchandise, their stock, however small, will last for a season.

This class congregates mostly about the City Hall park, where last year an irrepressible fiddler, who never knew a note, was paid a certain sum by the newspapers to go elsewhere, and where a veteran bagpiper is now receiving proposals to the same effect. The pretenders also infest Broadway as far as Union Square, and show an unwelcome fondness for Fourteenth street, Fifth, Lexington and Madison avenues.

Oh well, let them obey their instincts. They are human, though unfortunate. They are annoying and irritating, but they have a hard lot, and perhaps deserve more than they get for their trouble in asking. Ninety-nine out of every hundred are impostors or professionals; but the one before you may be the exception and really suffering. What you give will not harm you, and may serve him much. It is better to be deceived all your life than once to withhold from the truly needy.

When you have come to such conclusion, and act upon it, you will probably find by the first experiment that you have been deceived.

The other day an old woman, having a few apples and a little candy to sell, was set upon in Broadway by a drunken sailor who knocked her down and hurled her humble wares into the gutter. The ruffian got away; but the crowd pitying her, made up a little purse for her. A curious reporter followed her to the Bowery; and there the scene was re-enacted exactly and completely. It was repeated a third and fourth time, and the performance was always creditably given. The fellow who played the drunken sailor was the woman's husband, and the two made money by their original performance.

The Beggars.

The fortunes of mendicants are usually the creations of journalists and letter-writers. Few beggars die with any considerable sums of money, for they either squander it, even after long hoarding, or it is stolen by their own class. They adhere, most of them, with a strange perseverance and perversity, to their calling. Begging must have a species of infatuation, like burglary, war, the stage, and journalism. The New-York mendicants usually live in noisome cellars and garrets, in the Fourth, Sixth and Eighteenth wards; live in a wretched manner, that Crabbe would have delighted to describe; live away from sunlight and pure air; live worse than the swine until all the sweetness of nature is crowded out of their ill-conditioned souls, and they find the only peace possible to them in the grave, most charitable of all alms-givers to the wretched and forsaken.

MACKERELVILLE TURN-OUT.

CHAPTER LII.

STREET-RAILWAYS.

New-York is much better shaped for a cucumber than a city. It is so long and slender that people who abide here pass a large part of their lives in getting up and down town. Take the hours in which they are so engaged out of their existence, and they would not know what to do with themselves. Such a change would be like extending their day to forty-eight hours. But getting up and down town, like everything else, has its uses. It helps to kill time, (why shouldn't we kill, when we can, what kills all of us at last?) and that was one of the original purposes of the Metropolis. In that, New-York has been a complete success. A man, and of necessity a woman, can employ more hours here with less profit, than in any city of the World, Paris perhaps excepted. It is always noon in New-York, and before you think of the hour again it is midnight. So one can get through with his life very readily while wondering how he has wasted it.

To prevent Gothamites from being surprised at their own funerals while going to and from business, with the unimportant consideration of making large fortunes by swindling and incommoding the public, street railways were established. They were, doubtless, designed by Providence to show mortals the wickedness of human ways, and to plant thorns amid the roses of their pleasure. But for the railways man might long to linger forever in Manhattan. Compelled to patronize them, however, day after day, he sees this World is hollow, and aspires to another where the railways are not. Thus (it is the Pantheistic belief that partial evil is universal good) the railways have theologic virtues and enforce upon the human family the benison of wretchedness after the most approved orthodox fashion.

What sybarites and epicureans might we not become, without the trials and sufferings resulting from the railways! Through them literally and metaphorically the iron enters the soul. Beauty and bouquets, love and happiness may await us up town. But remembrance of the means of getting there spiritualizes the senses, abates all transports of the blood. It is the skeleton at the feast, the hair shirt against the bounding heart, the sword of Damocles above the luxurious board.

The Rubicon of the rails divides us from our hopes and anticipations, and when we have passed it, affliction has tempered us to moderate joys. The rails are as the purgatory through which we must wander before ascending to the blessings of paradise.

It is a common error to suppose our street-railways were made for New-York. New-York was made for them. The island was formed by nature expressly for their construction, as a glance at the City map will instantly show. Without them people might get home too soon, and the weekly bills of mortality would be too small. Without them human patience and strength, fortitude and agility, would be less valued because less needed. New-York would be the very city of delights—a Sodom and Gomorrah perhaps—would undergo a revolution of agreeableness, but for the iron bonds that bind us to a cruel doom and the inexorable destiny of riding on the cars.

This City is for its sins accursed with at least twenty street-railways in the worst possible condition, running wherever one does not want to go, through the most repulsive quarters. They make money beyond all proportion to their investment; the public patronizing them liberally because the roads cheat passengers regularly, and are opposed on principle to granting any accommodation. The roads have no rights (those of rendering their customers as uncomfortable as possible are of course natural and inalienable) that vehicles are bound to respect; and every vehicle that can interfere with the progress of a car has won the favor of fortune. The commerce of the Metropolis is opposed to the railways, and does everything in its power to increase their odiousness. Every possible box and bale, every truck and truckman that can be used to obstruct the roads is brought into requisition.

Wagons bearing huge stones and ponderous machinery lie in wait for cars, and break down across the track. Brick piles tumble at the precise hour one selects to go up town, and cover the rails with impassable débris. Even trees blow down, and old women are seized with fits, and fall directly across the iron-bound way. External, no less than human nature, seems in league against the roads; and yet the passengers alone are the sufferers. Everybody and everything declare the railways nuisances, yet they endure and continue in the face of all opposition, and before the serious discountenance of the deities themselves.

The railways are all close corporations. The managers and stockholders always deny their profits. They secretly divide 15, 20 and 25 per cent., and beg for new privileges to sustain themselves. They declare they are merely anxious to accommodate the public, and the only man who ever was accommodated by them died the next moment from the unexpectedness of the sensation.

The more money the roads make, the meaner they get. The larger their dividend, the greater their curtailment of the starvation-salaries of the drivers and conductors. They complain that their employés rob them. Why should they not? The owners plunder the public; why deny to their servants the same privilege? If ever men were justified in stealing, the drivers and conductors are. Indeed, I am not sure it is not a virtue, when they are paid forty or fifty dollars a month, by those whose income is half as much an hour.

If the employés would only steal the roads and the right of way at the same time, they would be public benefactors. We should honor them with crowns, and guarantee them against the prosecution of directors.

The wonderful creature who renders street-railways impossible shall have a monument in Union Square higher than Washington's, and be represented on two horses. What is the father of his country compared to the mother of reform? The former was childless. The offspring of the latter will be blessed and unnumbered.

Extinguish the street-railways, root and branch, and

steam-cars, the greatest need of the Metropolis, will supply their place.

The traveler in the cars has a career of his own. The experience is peculiar as a life in Japan. One learns cynicism and feels suffocation in daily rides, so-called for courtesy, through the sinuosities and odors of the filthiest streets. There is no monotony, some romance, much danger and more disgust in the cars.

Certain preparations are desirable, however, for the performance. The regular passenger should lose his sense of smell; have the capacity to shut himself up like a patent umbrella; be able to hang on a platform by the lids of his eyes; hold drunken men and fat women on his lap, eight or nine at a time, without dissatisfaction or inconvenience; put weeping and screaming children in his waistcoat pocket, and deliver them promptly when wanted; keep his temper and his portmonnaie; be skilled as a pugilist and a crack-shot with a revolver. Those are the essentials for anything like resignation in the cars. The *desiderata* are beyond enumeration. But the best thing for a man or woman to do, who deems himself or herself compelled to ride on the cars, is to take some other conveyance.

A volume might be written on the drolleries and adventures of the railway victims. He who has ridden on the cars for a few years, and outlived it, is as interesting as a man who has been through the War, or thrice married, or half his life a prisoner with the Indians. He bears a charmed life. He could jump over Niagara without disarranging his hair; or walk up to the bridal altar without trembling. He could do anything. He could read the morning papers without falling asleep.

He has had all sorts of diseases, from the *acuta scabies* to typhus fever. He has been run over in every part of his body. He has been robbed of his valuables so often that conductors believe him a monomaniac on the subject of pocket-picking. He has been beaten and cut and shot almost everywhere between his head and heels by pleasant gentlemen who insisted upon confounding his watch with theirs, and who held it as a cardinal article of faith that any one that insisted on keeping his own property deserved killing for the first offence, and to be a City Alderman for the second.

The discomforts and perils of car-journeying can hardly be over-estimated. That our people will undertake it merely proves the national recklessness. Prudent persons leave their purses and watches in the safe deposit company, and carry bowie-knives and derringers before venturing from Barclay to Forty-second street. I am often lost in admiration at the feats of postering and corporal convolution I witness on the cars, and wonder why people will pay to see the Arabs and Japanese, when they can for nothing have much more of that exhibition than they want.

Think of a corpulent fellow balancing himself on a young woman's toes, and stealing his neighbor's breast-pin without changing his position! Imagine a slender little chap holding himself over the end of the car by thrusting his head between the conductor's legs, and gamins in the street pulling his boots off, unknown to him, while the car goes round the corner! Fancy a baby sleeping on the summit of a drunken man's hat which is waltzing over the top of the vehicle! Picture a clown making a boot-jack of a pretty seamstress' bonnet while his back is endeavoring in vain to accommodate itself to the digestion of that timid clerical-looking person, who is dozing from exhaustion, and dreaming his stomach has been made the foundation of the new post-office, already complete. Could the gymnasts of the other hemisphere do anything like that?

How true it is that we never appreciate what lies before us! The marvels of street-railways impress us not. Neither their tragedy nor their comedy touches us. We have no idea what we endure, or what we escape, when we ride up or down town. We breathe an atmosphere of poison, and do not die. We travel with thieves and ruffians and murderers, and feel no alarm. We seize men by the beard or nose, and hang there, our feet resting only on vicious atmosphere, until we reach Harlem or Yorkville; and they never murmur; for they can't surrender the luxuries of the cars.

Who says the days of miracles have passed?

Our street-railways are still tolerated; and New-York yet remains outside of a lunatic asylum—perhaps because it is a paradise of fools.

CHAPTER LIII.

THE PAWNBROKERS.

Love of money is the root of all evil, according to the Scriptures; but in these modern days, want of money is nearly as prolific of ill. In great cities where almost everything must be bought, poverty is at least one parent of sin. The prosperous are rarely tempted; have little excuse for crime. But to those whom indigence presses, the way to wickedness is all down hill.

In vast commercial centers, sin is only another name, usually, for ignorance or suffering. Where ease and culture are, the ghastliness of crime is rarely seen. But material necessity drives men headlong, and urges them to perdition or to woe.

These truths are constantly exemplified at the pawnbrokers' offices, the sombre half-way houses between wretchedness and death. The pawnbroker's shop should be under the shadow of the Morgue, for the distance between them is often shudderingly short. Pawnbrokers' offices are plague spots upon the fair forms of cities. They show deep-seated if not incurable disease. They are the symbols of suffering, the representatives of misfortune and of want. They cannot exist in entirely healthful atmospheres. Like certain noxious plants, they feed on the poisons of the air.

Pawnbrokers' offices are bad signs for cities. Where they are most, the places are worst. The locality that favors them is sickly and stricken with grief. Dirt, and over-crowding, and rum-selling, and prostitution, and wretchedness in every form, are fit neighbors for pawnbrokers' shops; for among, and out of, such surroundings, the three golden balls gleam dismally.

Our best quarters reveal no pawnbrokers. They are banished from the light of content and of comfort. They creep out of Broadway even, away from the pleasant breathing-places, into the regions where the air is foul, and the houses look dark.

The east side of the town abounds in them. Chatham street and the Bowery are devoted to them. There are several hundreds, probably, in the whole City. They grow with its growth of poverty, and strengthen with its strength of misfortune. They may not impress others as they do me. But I never pass them on the fairest day, that the sun does not seem a little obscured, and the freshest breeze touching them has the sense of taint.

Pawnbrokers are born; they are rarely made. Like corporations, they have no souls. They subsist on adversity as vultures on carrion. They are of ill omen, and riot in ruin. They are of one race, generally, and look like cruel brothers, banded together in the cause of avarice against humanity.

The phrenologists are fond of giving typical heads, calling them the thinker, the observer, the bully, the fool. Why don't they give the pawnbroker? He is distinctive. He is a human type of inhumanity. You would know him among a thousand men. His eye is keen, but cold and pitiless. His complexion is unwholesome. His atmosphere repels you. His beak is prominent and sharp. His movements are stealthy. His air is treacherous. When he passes, if you are sensitive, you shudder without seeing him, and instinctively feel for your pocket-book. No doubt he has a heart somewhere, could you but find it; but it is not in his business. When he enters his shop, he shuts up the troublesome organ, locks it, and hangs the key out of reach.

"Come hither, ye that are needy," he says, "and if ye have aught, it shall be taken from you."

I presume he reasons himself into a certain stern justice of his calling. Perhaps he says to himself: "I am hard; but the World is hard also. I am pitiless, but destiny is pitiless. I must live. I am against my kind; but my kind is against me. Am I not wise to steel myself against my fellows, who would cheat me if they could?"

The pawnbroker offends not the law—the law that legislators make. Neither does the smooth destroyer of human happiness, the quiet treader upon tender hearts. Alas, that the deepest crimes are those the law cannot reach!

Pawnbrokers' offices are different in seeming, though their dealings are all alike. They show the close connection between moral and material purity. They are generally dismal and unclean. They are musty, and savor of foulness. Dust and grime are upon them. They reek with unwelcome odors. But sometimes they affect cheerfulness and pleasantness. They put flowers on their counters, and birds against their walls.

But they are the wreaths on tombs. The flowers have little fragrance; the birds will hardly sing. Nature has her own secrets, and she cannot deceive.

Look into yonder shop! A fleet of all wares seems to have stranded within its walls. What old jewelry and old clothes establishments have emptied themselves there! What glitter, and gewgaws, and rubbish! What odds and ends of civilized forms are these! Has the Nile of creation overflowed, and left these *débris* upon its banks? One wonders so small a place can hold such variety. Here are watches of every pattern and value, from the elegant and modern chronometer, to the queer, old-fashioned time-piece George the First might have carried; from the dainty, enameled trinket that may very naturally have forgotten to reckon time in some sweet woman's bosom, to the pewter monster created to deceive. Here are diamonds, and rubies, and pearls, and emeralds in gold forms, that our great-grandmothers wore, and in gold fresh and bright as from Broadway cases.

Weapons of divers sorts are in the place, as if the broker had gone with a search-warrant for arms, over all the World. Guns, and pistols, and knives, and swords, and daggers. Curiously wrought, some of them; such as I seem to have seen in Sicily, Smyrna, India and Arabia. A Colt's revolver lies against a Revolutionary musket. A Spanish stiletto supports itself upon an American bowie-knife. A delicate poniard hangs from the same nail with a Scotch broadsword.

What a heap of clothing, too! The remnant of Life's masquerade might have ended here. The last revelers must have been frightened, slipped out of their costumes, and fled. The fashions of centuries seem represented. Gowns that the duchess of Portsmouth might have worn for profligate Charles' admiration, or Maintenon asked Louis to approve, or Agnes Sorrel put on to find new favor with her royal lover. That resembles the dress the handsome English woman danced in that memorable evening at Brighton, and ran away in, perhaps, the next morning, with her lover, her husband's best friend. This delicate, but now soiled pearl-colored silk, I imagine I waltzed with last season, at the Academy, in a space five feet square. But I dare say I am at fault. My imagination deceives me as it did about the wearer. She was a darling while I flattered her; but a devil when I told her the truth.

We wear the invisible cap, you know. You and I will stand aside, reader, and see who patronizes the broker. Our Hebrew friend is engaged in filing a gold coin, and won't perceive us, so intent is he upon his little fraud.

No grief in this showy, coarse woman's face as she enters. She is gaily and expensively attired. She is painted like a new sign-board, and redolent of musk. Her voice is unpleasant, and her syntax blunders.

"What'll you lend me on this 'ere? (She offers a large gold miniature, with a sad, feminine face that looks older from trouble than years.) You see it's purty."

"Vell, madam, ve can't shell dese tings.. Osher beeble's picshers ishn't vorsh much vid us. Only goot for ole golt, dat ish all, madam, I pledges you mine vort of honor. I geeve you fife tollars—dash ish more dan it ish vorsh, I shvear."

"O well, take it along. I don't want it. It makes me feel onpleasant whenever I look at it."

She delivers the miniature, receives the money, and trips out.

"Dat ish a goot bargain," chuckles Mr. Abrahams. "I knows dem kind of vimmen. Dey'll take anyshing. I can git twenty-five dollars for dis any time I vant. I hope I ave more cushtomers like her."

The miniature has a history, as almost everything else has in a pawnbroker's collection. It belonged to a poor seamstress who came to the City from New-Jersey, and with whom fortune went ill. She was thrown out of employment; was almost starving; was driven to prostitution. For two years she led a life she hourly revolted at. She fell sick of brain fever. Before a week was over, the proprietress of the house in which she sold herself—the coarse woman that has just departed—demanded payment of the girl's board.— Money the girl had not, nor a friend in the whole City. The hard woman searched her trunk; found the miniature of the poor child's mother, and seized it for debt. Edith pleaded hard for that; but she pleaded to marble. Forsaken, wretched, desperate, consumed with fever, mad with sufferings of body and mind, she went out that very night; begged money enough to buy laudanum, and was found dead in the morning. Old as the story is, it were blessing if age could rob it of its horror.

This sleek-looking person puffs his cigar calmly as he draws a fine watch and chain from his pocket, and lays them silently on the counter. "Feefty dollar," hesitatingly utters Mr. Abrahams.

"O you be d——d! Give me a hundred, and you shall have it."

"Vell, I'll shust tell you, Misther Munroe. Dis vatch——"

"O dry up, you old Jew! Give me the money or the watch!"

"You'se a sharp shentleman;" and the Israelite tries to laugh, as he hands over a hundred dollar note.

"Sharp, you old scoundrel? The watch is worth three times this. I'll redeem it to-morrow. But I had a bad run at faro last night. Better luck to-night."

Soliloquizing he departs.

The watch belonged to a merchant in West Broadway. His son has been gambling lately; and his father refusing to give him money, the young scapegrace carries off the paternal chronometer; places it before the hungry tiger, and the tiger devours it at a mouthful.

A low, square forehead thrusts itself into the doorway. A bad eye darts into the shop, and then up the street and down and across. Then a heavy form with a light step advances warily.

"Somethin' han'some this mornin' Abrahams. Good for sore eyes, old cully."

"Come dish way," and the broker beckons the brutal-looking man into a little room in the rear.

A conversation in a low tone; and in a few moments the cautious animal creeps out; again darts his eye up and down and across the street, and hurriedly disappears.

The broker returns to the shop, his eyes dancing over a pair of bracelets that kindle in the light. In his gladness he knocks down a musket in the corner. He starts in terror; conceals his treasure, and tries to look bland and innocent, which makes him seem twice a villain.

The bracelets were stolen two nights before by the burglar who brought them there, from a house in Twenty-third street, where the inmates sleep sound, and leave their keys in the doors.

Mr. Abrahams has a number of such customers, but he does not keep what they leave with him in pledge; for he fears the police may be looking for the stolen wares, and knows that they will never be redeemed.

Pale and sad is she who comes so timidly in. She looks the picture of pity. Any lineament of her face would melt any heart but a pawnbroker's. Lamartine would write a poem to it; and an unsentimental American would give it five dollars. She trembles, and is so nervous she cannot speak while she draws from her bosom a little gold cross and chain. She turns partially, and kisses them ere she delivers them to his unholy hands. She puts her delicate hand to her slender chest, and coughs hollowly. Her lips move, but no audible sound escapes.

"Vas ish it, mish? I cannot hear you."

She summons courage and strength, and says, "My mother is dying, sir. We have no money in the house. I can't even buy medicine for her. Give me something for the little cross. But keep it, please. It is very precious to me. I'll redeem it when my poor mother is dead; for then I can work again."

Tears choke her, and, putting her head in her hands, she sobs bitterly.

"Your mutter is dyin'; oh, yes; mutters die like everybody elsh. But is it sholid gold, mish? I give two tollars."

"Two dollars?" and the weeping girl looks up. "It cost $30."

"But den you see prishes has gone up so dese tings isn't worsh so much as dey vas. Two tollar is de full value. Nopoddy would geeve more."

"I thought you would give me at least $10. But I must take what I can get. Do not detain me, please. There's nobody but a little girl who lives down stairs with mother."

"Dere ish two tollar. I would not geeve so mooch. But we musht be sharitable to de poor. De Hebrews always ish."

The girl was gone without hearing this richly-deserved eulogium upon the remnant of the Lost Tribes.

Such are but a few of the scenes that daily occur at the pawnbroker's. He is patronized by gamblers, courtesans, adventuresses, thieves, and men-about-town. If they were his only customers, it would be well. But the honest poor, the suffering needy, the unfortunate, the outcast, the miserable waifs floating between despair and suicide, are taken in his cruel net. They all pay tribute to his avarice. Every fresh call makes them wretcheder and more dependent. The small "advances" they get are wrung out of their blood and being. Each loan is a new fetter and another stab. The pawnbroker covers them—with a shroud—and helps them—to a pauper's grave. They never reach him until friends and fortune have deserted them. When they knock at his door hope has almost gone out of their heart. The three balls represent poverty, misery, abandonment. When their shadow has fallen often upon the needy it is rarely lifted.

The shade of the pawnbroker's shop is baleful as

that of the fabled Upas. Content quits the borrower at the threshold, and adversity and woe bring him back. Dissipation and idleness frequently lead to it; but they who are victims of one or the other, are not less to be pitied because their temperament binds them to their courses. Struggle as we may, organization and circumstance are the genii that control our lives.

Every pledge has its secret history. A tender and tearful idyl is hidden in that necklace; a strange romance is locked up in this casket; a tragedy of life and love is in the well-worn cashmere shawl. The pistol ticketed 415 made a death that startled the community. The musket in the corner killed Albert Sidney Johnson at Shiloh. The carbine wreathed with cobwebs made the fatal wound of Stonewall Jackson, and blew perhaps a whole year out of the War. The locket with the golden hair nestling in it like a sunbeam might tell a tale so sad that to hear it would be to weep. The cameo pin was worn on a pagan bosom that stilled its pangs of passion with poisoned wine. The garnet ring was worn by one of whom the World has heard. It passed from him to a leman's finger, and now burns for the unforgotten shame of a deserted wife and a base intrigue.

The prose and poetry, the sin and suffering, the romance and reality, the comedy and tragedy of life are strangely blended at the pawnbroker's; and he who could unravel all the strange facts from the heterogeneous mass could give new plots to new Cinthios, and **wonderful narratives for Bocaccios yet unconceived.**

CHAPTER LIV.

CHILDREN'S AID SOCIETY.

WHAT is at present known as the Children's Aid Society is one of the most valuable and deserving among the many charities of the Metropolis.

A prominent feature of the society is the newsboys' lodging-house, for many years in Fulton street, near Nassau, but recently removed to 49 and 51 Park place. The house was established in 1854, by the Rev. Charles L. Brace, who had been pained to observe the little vagabonds sleeping in boxes, stairways, and coalholes, in the vicinity of the newspaper offices. He called the subject to the attention of a number of benevolent persons; and the first means to defray the expenses of the enterprise were raised in the Rev. Theodore Cuyler's church. The earliest difficulty in the way was to obtain a place for the newsboys, who were not then any more than they are now, a very inviting class to those whose sympathies are wholly of an æsthetic character. Various localities were found; but no one would have the soiled and sinful urchins on his premises.

At last, Moses Y. Beach, of the old *Sun*, offered the loft of his building for the purpose, and said the boys should be kept there if every tenant left. The quarters were not pleasant by any means. They were festooned with cobwebs and frescoed with dirt; but soap and water, whitewash and paint, soon rendered them habitable, and even respectable.

Accommodations for 75 or 80 lodgers were prepared; notice given in the daily papers, and the leaders of the boys informed of the fact. For a short time the superintendent had considerable trouble with some of the little wanderers; but discipline and order were soon secured. The boys could not understand what all this care for them meant. They were naturally suspicious; thought it was a prelude and disguise to some kind of house of refuge: they even termed it a Sunday school trap; but they were so kindly treated and given so much freedom, that they finally concluded the intention was to benefit them.

Gambling and useless spending of money were the most grievous faults of the lodgers. Some of them earned $4 or $5, and others only 75 cents to $1 a day; but all their earnings, whether great or small, went for the theater, cards, dice, betting and lottery tickets; while they remained ragged and needy as ever. To counteract such follies, checkers, backgammon, and dominoes were introduced with excellent effect; and a bank was also established.

The bank is a table with a drawer, divided into separate compartments, with a slit in the lid,—each compartment being numbered and reserved for a different depositor. Into the little boxes the boys put their money; and at the end of a month, it is returned to them, to do what they choose with it. They are generally surprised to find how much they have saved, and either buy clothes or place their money in a regular savings bank. The custom cures most of them of extravagance. They are paid five per cent. interest per month, and premiums are given to the lads who save the most. They save $200 to $250 a year, independent of what they deposit and invest for their own benefit.

The present house is a vast improvement o n theold one. It is a handsome building; three floors are used; and the rent is $4,500 per annum. It has large, airy dormitories, bath-rooms, gymnasium, school-room, and chapel,—$8,000 or $10,000 having been expended in fitting up the building. The directors hope soon to erect a house of their own in the Bowery; and probably they will have the necessary means before another year.

The house now has accommodations for 260 boys. They pay five cents for their bed and five cents for their meals,—a small payment rendering them independent, and exercising a good influence that would not exist if they were treated as paupers. If the little fellows have no means, they are provided with food and shelter just the same, and make payment when they can. Those who are able rarely fail to meet their obligations; and the training they receive inspires them with a sense of honesty and honor.

Since the establishment of the house, over 300,000 lodgings have been supplied to homeless boys; and it is estimated that 40,000 different lads have been the recipients of the charity. The lodgers have contributed nearly $3,000 a year to the support of the institution, and the receipts from that source are constantly and steadily increasing.

The house is not a home, as many suppose. It is the special design of the directors that it shall not be. If it were, the lodgers would lose their self-reliance and ambition.

Emigration is one of the peculiar and best features of the house. The lodgers are sent to the country, and there provided with homes. They are shipped in companies, and at very considerable expense, to all parts of the country, but mostly to the West. A single company, which varies from 15 to 100, sometimes costs $1,000. During the past year, 1,381 boys emigrated; and 473 girls, 38 men, and 51 women, from other charitable institutions in the City,—making a total of 1,943. The expenditure of this house for the year was $9,916.31, deducting $3,177.69 paid by the boys.

The effect of the society is shown in the decrease of street-vagrants and wanderers from 40,000 in former years to 15,000 to 20,000 at present. Of the whole number for the year, 147 were restored to their friends.

The Girls' Lodging-house, No. 205 Canal street, is not designed for the fallen or for mature women, but for young persons exclusively who have not been tempted into the one sin society is so loth to forgive in the other sex, and so prompt to pardon, as if a glory, in ours. The superintendent's orders are not to admit girls over 18, unless in cases of emergency or evident suffering. The house has been sorely in need of funds; but what means it has had it has expended judiciously. It is economically and plainly conducted; but it is an improvement on what the poor girls have been accustomed to. During eight and a half months, nearly 1,000 girls were lodged. During the past year, 1,079 were lodged, and 10,216 lodgings given, of which 3,400 were paid; 29,761 meals furnished, and 6,805 paid. Of the number, 158 girls obtained situations; 19 found employment; 44 returned to friends; 49

went to other institutions; 50 went West, and one to Europe.

The receipts during the year were $1,380.36, and the expenditures three times as much. Many of the inmates are girls from the country, who come to the City with the hope of improving their condition, or tempted by what they conceive to be its attractions. Some are driven from their homes by the unhappiness they experience there, and others by a spirit of desperation.

Girls who go there without money can pay for their board by work. They perform the household duties, and some of them learn to sew excellently. The discipline is very light, and little is required. They can leave the house when they like; but few, unless they run away, depart until they have procured good situations. They have pleasant social gatherings and evening parties, when they talk, read, and have quiet games. It not unfrequently happens that girls who have been betrayed into unchastity are reformed at the house. When quite young, repentant, and anxious to lead a better life, much success has been had with them.

The Refuge for Homeless Children, corner of Eighth avenue and Twenty-fourth street, is another lodging-house for boys. This charity is maintained at very small cost, the rent being more than met by sub-letting. The net cost of last year, with an average of 65 boys to feed and lodge at night, was only $1,075 to the public. The total expenses for that time was $5,141.68. Eight hundred and ninety-seven were received, of whom 11 were sent West; 18 obtained situations; 36 were restored to friends; 85 sent to friends; 9 to other institutions. The number of lodgings furnished was

23,933, of which but 933 were free. The meals supplied were 39,401, and 3,655 of them free.

Another boys' lodging-house, for the benefit of the homeless boys of the Eleventh ward, is doing a good work. It furnished during the past year 11,583 lodgings, and 12,810 meals, at the usual price, 5 cents each, and collected $1,175.54. It lodged during the year 635 boys.

Other lodging-houses are open for homeless boys, in First avenue, and at Corlear's Hook; and twenty industrial schools, with four night schools and four free reading-rooms, are included in the Aid Society. The schools have 47 teachers, and the children in attendance, nearly all of them little girls, numbered in the aggregate last year almost 6,000. The average attendance was more than 2,000. One school, No 110 Centre street, exclusively for Italian children, contains about 200. Another, solely for Germans, No 272 Second street, has some 400 in attendance. Still another for colored children, No. 185 Spring street, has nearly 100. A new school, lodging-house and free reading-room, opened last year, at No. 327 Rivington street, has some ninety children, and the lodging-house nightly shelters, on an average, eighty homeless boys. Some of the best women of the City voluntarily and gladly devote themselves to the industrial schools. They feed the hungry, clothe the naked, and enlighten the ignorant. Many of the little outcasts are unfit to be seen until they are supplied with garments.

The expenses of the Aid Society last year were about $115,000, and for fifteen years $510,243.35. The number of children who have emigrated was 207 in 1854, and last year 1,943,—a steady increase each year, and swelling in the whole fifteen years to 14,879, nearly nine-tenths of whom may be said to have been literally saved.

The inner history of the Society would read like a romance, and prove conclusively the extent and solidity of its benefits. Dozens of men and women, now well educated, in prosperous circumstances and honored members of society, were not many years since, little outcasts and wanderers, and would have come to a bad end but for the protecting arms of the Aid Society.

In 1856, a boy of sixteen lost his parents through excessive intemperance, and, thrown upon the street, he began to sell newspapers for a livelihood. He was intelligent, energetic and persevering; but he had inherited a love for liquor that he could not resist. He squandered his money; was a drunkard in a few months, and would have died in the gutter but for the influence of the Society. Some of the benevolent persons belonging to that organization saw him one night when he entered the lodging-house intoxicated; cared for him kindly, and the next morning, when he was sober, talked to him earnestly and tenderly, painting what would be his future unless he reformed. He said he could not stop drinking; that he had tried in vain. They urged him to abstain for a week, at the end of that time, to make it a fortnight, and then a month.

The experiment was entirely successful. He did not drink a drop of spirituous liquor for six months, and has not from that day to this. He was placed in a large mercantile establishment as a messenger. He was quick-witted, trustworthy, truthful, industrious.

He lost no opportunity of learning. He attended the night-schools, and at the end of the second year was made assistant book-keeper. He was again advanced and his salary fixed at $2,500. An opportunity for a good business interest occurred in the West, and the senior member of the New-York firm lent him the money to put into the concern. He became a partner; is there now; happily married; worth $30,000, with years of usefulness before him. His example is one of many.

Religious exercises and instructions are given in all the houses and schools. An effort is made to prevent the boys from continuing long as newspaper-sellers, boot-blacks, rag-pickers, messengers, or peddlers, as the continuance of such callings is found to be pernicious. A good home in the country is the best place for the children; and the Aid Society is doing such a noble and excellent work in that way, as few persons who have not examined into its system and operations can believe. All who visit the institutions approve and applaud the charity, which, it is to be hoped, will be enlarged and perfected more and more as the City grows and the years go on.

CHAPTER LV.

JAMES GORDON BENNETT.

JAMES GORDON BENNETT, the journalist, is known on both sides of the Atlantic; James Gordon Bennett, the man, is hardly known outside of the *Herald* office. Indeed, persons who have been employed in that establishment for years have never set eyes on its famous editor and proprietor. All his power, reputation and influence exist in and through the *Herald*. In it, he is every thing; out of it, nothing.

Probably the history of journalism in this or any other country does not show another instance of such complete absorption by, and identification with, a newspaper as that of Bennett and the *Herald*. To the *Herald* he has devoted most of his mature life—his best, and ripest, and richest years. All that he is and has been he has poured, with mental and physical prodigality, into the great newspaper which bears his name, and has yielded him a vast fortune for his purpose and his pains.

Bennett was born of Catholic parents, in 1797, in Banffshire, Scotland, and remained at school there until he was fourteen or fifteen. He was then sent to a Catholic academy at Aberdeen, with the view of taking sacerdotal orders; but after staying there for two or three years, during which time he devoted himself assiduously to his books, he became dissatisfied, and resolved to surrender all priestly aspirations. His parents, said to be wealthy and influential, had set their hearts upon his leading a clerical life, and were so much opposed to his abandoning it that a rupture ensued between them and their boy, and he quitted his native land forever.

Young Bennett, in 1819, with a companion of about his own age, embarked on a vessel coming to America, and arriving at Halifax, without money or friends, took to teaching for a livelihood. He did not succeed to his satisfaction, and in a few months went to Portland, Me., and then to Boston, where he found employment as a proof-reader in Wells & Lily's publishing house. At that time he was much addicted to solitary rambles and the exercise of his imagination. He wrote a number of poems of rather a cynical, semi-sentimental kind, suggested by his lonely walks in and about the metropolis of New-England.

In 1822 he came to New-York and engaged himself to some of the daily and weekly papers as a reporter and general writer. But wearying of his journalistic connections, he went to Charleston, S. C., where he was employed by the *Courier* as a translator of French and Spanish, occasionally contributing sketches and poems to the paper. In his early years he was singularly restless, though very industrious and of remarkable versatility in composition. After a year or two he returned to New-York, where he undertook to set up a commercial school, but either failed or abandoned his design. He next turned his attention to political economy, and delivered a series of lectures on the subject, in the vestry of the Old Dutch Church, in Ann Street.

About this time he began to entertain the idea of

adopting journalism as a profession, having come to the conclusion that it was his vocation. In 1825 he made his first effort as a proprietor, in the *Sunday Courier;* but not succeeding he became a reporter and writer for its columns. He left the paper, however, in a few months, began the *National Advocate,* a Democratic journal, and opposed the tariff and the system of banking. In 1827 he became a warm advocate of Martin Van Buren, at that time in Congress, and, on the decease of the *Advocate* he associated himself with M. M. Noah in the editorial management of the *Enquirer,* then in the Tammany Hall interest. The year following he went to Washington as correspondent of the paper, and, after serving faithfully and zealously in that capacity for about twelve months, he became the associate editor of the *Courier and Enquirer,* the two journals having been merged in one. Remaining two or three years in that capacity, he quarreled with James Watson Webb, the leading editor, went out of the concern, and issued the *Daily Globe.* The new paper lived exactly one month and expired. It did not require much capital to conduct a paper thirty-five years ago, even in the Metropolis, but the funds required for such enterprises were very difficult to raise.

Bennett, then in his thirty-fifth year, had been connected with at least a dozen papers, in different capacities, and had been any thing but prosperous. Those who knew him declared he had mistaken his calling; that while he had decided ability and energy, he lacked tact and managing power. He, however, retained his faith in himself, and was wont to say he had never got started right. He continually talked about having a paper of his own some day, which he felt sure would be a great success. It is quite likely he had become somewhat discouraged by his failures here, for he went to Philadelphia at the latter part of 1832, raised money enough to purchase the *Pennsylvanian*, and assumed editorial charge of it. That city was not large enough for him, and he still believed New-York to be the best place for him to fix the lever with which he hoped to move the American world.

Consequently, after two years' residence on the Delaware, he came back to the Hudson, and in 1835 issued the first number of the *Herald*.

Bennett had very little money—only a few hundred dollars, it is said, when he set up his last newspaper in the basement of a building in Ann Street, not far from where the present marble structure rears its costly head. His editorial desk was a board on two barrels, and on that he wrote untiringly, for the first few weeks doing all the editorial work himself, filling the little sheet with verses, aromatic gossip, pungent paragraphs, city sketches, and such light and varied matter as the public always like to read.

Whatever the character of the contents of the *Herald* in those days, Bennett knew what the mass of people relished, and he catered to them zealously. The paper was a pecuniary success from the beginning. In a few weeks he was enabled to employ assistance, making a feature of city news and local events, in which he had no rivalry, the dailies being heavy, and prosy to the last degree. The *Commercial Advertiser*, *Evening Post* and *Journal of Commerce* were alive then, but they seemed scarcely conscious of the fact, and did nothing to dispute the more modern and novel field the *Herald* had opened.

The great fire in this City, soon after the birth of the new paper, gave Bennett ample opportunity to show his enterprise, and he embraced it vigorously. The following morning the little daily contained a full account of the "destructive conflagration," as the reporters would call it, with all the incidents and accidents given in a vivid and picturesque style. That was really, as the *Herald* is so fond of stating, a new era in journalism; and from that day to this, merely as a newspaper, it has probably had no equal anywhere.

Bennett the man is Bennett the journalist. He has breathed his individuality and all his idiosyncrasies into it. Not many persons believe in the *Herald*. Its influence is limited among cultivated people; and yet hardly any one denies its tact and enterprise. Bennett makes no pretension, privately, to molding public opinion: he follows it. He is inconsistent, because it is his interest; for his avowed object has been from the first to give the news and make money. Principle he has not, because he believes in no one. He has no convictions, and does not think any one has them. Nothing, in his view, deserves serious treatment. All men and all pursuits are shams. One thing is no better than another, and we are all selfish to the core when found out.

He understands the philosophy of journalism; that a newspaper is entirely a thing of to-day; that few readers care for the issue of yesterday or to-morrow, which are as if they had never been. Therefore he issues every number of the *Herald* as if there had been none before, and would be none after it. He believes with Emerson that "Consistency is the hobgoblin of little minds," and acts accordingly.

Privately, Bennett is a very honest and strictly moral

man. He owes no one, and so far as I can learn, never did owe a dollar; paying his debts having always been with him the first of obligations. He was never other than industrious and abstemious, and is said to be very charitable without the least ostentation. Ever since his marriage, which was, I think, in 1837, he has been a pattern of domesticity; is extremely devoted to his wife, a highly accomplished woman, and his two children, James Gordon, Jr., the manager of the *Herald*, and a daughter Lily, a promising girl of sixteen. He has a very handsome house at Washington Heights, and a fine private residence in Fifth Avenue. His income from the *Herald* is fully $300,000 per annum, and his fortune is estimated at $3,000,000 or $4,000,000, every penny of which he has made by his journal. He is, and has always been, the opposite of gregarious. He never went into society, and the sole instance I can remember of his presence at any festival or public occasion, was at the Sir Morton Peto dinner at Delmonico's in the Autumn of 1865. Then he seemed quite lost and ill at ease. He did not appear to know any one, nor any one to know him.

When sought, he is affable enough, but talks little, and has no relish for society of any kind.

Personally, he is over six feet in height, but is now bent with age. He is rather slight, his eye gray, his hair white, and worn rather long, with a strange, half cynical, half comical expression, which makes his countenance difficult to read. He still speaks with a strong Scotch accent, which is very marked when he is irritated, and his irritation has increased with his years. His intellect is clear and vigorous, and his acquirements numerous. He writes nothing in these days; but in his working period he wrote rapidly, nervously, and gracefully on almost any subject; the skepticism, cynicism, and raillery of his temperament, always cropping out.

Of late years Bennett has shown signs of declining health. He takes excellent care of himself, however, going to bed every night at nine o'clock. He visits the *Herald* only two or three times a week, but is still in every respect its editor, and feels as much interest in it as when he toiled to establish it.

There is little need for his visiting the office often; for he can direct the establishment by telegraph, a wire communicating with it from Washington Heights. Whenever any event of consequence occurs his opinion is obtained in regard to its treatment for the next day's paper, the name of the required writer being frequently given by him. All the City and leading country dailies are taken to his house every morning. He reads them; marks the articles that strike his attention; makes suggestions as to the editorials; sees proofs often, in fact; supervises the *Herald* very much as he used to when he wrote on the head of a barrel in the Ann Street cellar.

Bennett scarcely ever goes off the island; seldom comes to his elegant town-house in the Avenue. He is methodical, abstemious, industrious, isolated. He rises at five; never calls on anybody, but receives courteously and hospitably all who visit him. Mrs. Bennett and her daughter are in Europe, where they spend half their time, and J. G. B., Jr., is fond of rambling, and wedded to his yacht.

Lonely old man is he; but he has attained his sole ambition—he has made the *Herald* a great newspaper—and in the midst of its reputation James Gordon Bennett, the man, is hardly known, rarely esteemed, never loved.

Bennett has few friends—he does not want them, I suspect—no hopes and no ambitions outside of the *Herald*. He can not live much longer; but while he does, he will be its autocrat and master mind; and his last hours will doubtless be comforted with the thought that James Gordon Bennett was to the very last the editor and proprietor of the New-York *Herald*.

CHAPTER LVI.

THE CHINESE EMBASSY IN NEW YORK.

THIS chapter shall be devoted to a very liberal translation of a letter written by Ghin Sling, one of the Chinese embassy, while here, to his friend, Nho Gho, an estimable citizen of Foo Chow, and which has appeared in the *Yah-ki-li-yo Link-kins-ko* (the morning bulletin) of that city. The impression and opinions of the intelligent and observant Celestial are of interest as showing how many things in the Metropolis appear to the unbiased eyes of a person whose experiences and sympathies have been so widely different from our own. His letter reads as follows:—

Beloved and serene Nho-Gho, Friend of my Soul and Idol of my Heart: I am filled with amazement in this new and wonderful country. I admire it very much; but I can't at all comprehend it. This City, which they tell me is larger than Peking, and Canton, and Shanghai combined, delights and surprises me more and more as I get acquainted with it. I can't resist the temptation of telling you something about New-York, or Gotham, or Manhattan, or the Empire-City, or New-Amsterdam, or Swindletown (it has all these names); for it is a puzzle more ingenious than the ones we used to amuse ourselves with when we were at the imperial university at Souchong.

When we first went to the hotel,—it is named after some clergyman,—I ordered a stewed puppy for supper; but the landlord (they call him such because he isn't a lord and hasn't any land) told me that he was out of puppies; but that there was one in the room next to his which barked all night, and that I was welcome to it. He said I must catch it myself, as it was the custom of the country for gentlemen of distinction to hunt their own game.

He advised me to stand in front of the door of the room, and whistle for a few minutes. I could not whistle,—though all the Americans whistle,—so I sang the song of our native land, " Hi, Hi, yah-che-ning," at the top of my voice.

The door opened in a moment, and a lady with a singular costume, cut low in the neck and short at the bottom, hanging loose and entirely plain (I had never seen any such before, but I have learned since that it is a full evening dress), made her appearance, holding a little white woolly dog by a blue ribbon, and crying, " Burglars, burglars."

I said, " Beautiful lady (she wasn't beautiful at all; but, unless you call all the women beautiful, you are a brute), ' Burglars is not my name. I am Ghin-Sling, of the Embassy."

"Oh, I have often heard of you," she answered. "You're an old friend of my husband. He is very fond of you; but I hate you."

I did not like to dispute what she said; for men who contradict women are considered monsters here. I thought I'd merely get the dog. I therefore seized the blue ribbon, and pulled the little animal along the hall, his loud yelps much increasing my appetite. Alas, the lady made more noise than the dog. She cried "Murder, fire, thieves"; and in a minute the hall was full of persons, many of them servants, who seized me by the pigtail, and asked me where I was going, and what I was about.

I said I was about stopped.

The lady declared I had stolen her poodle (what a queer name that, for a dog!) and tried to break into her chamber.

At this I was dumfounded, or found dumb, I don't know which, and, with open eyes and mouth, stood helpless in the hands of my enemies.

I recovered my voice at last, and explained that the landlord had told me to take the puppy, and have it cooked.

A burly fellow said he'd cook my goose for me. I replied I didn't want a goose, but a puppy.

The landlord was called, and I appealed to him. He ordered the man to let go of me, and said he didn't mean I should carry off the lady's dog; that he intended it as a jest. "It's strange, my friend," he added, "that you can't take a jest."

"He can't take any thing but poodles," said the lady sharply from behind the door where she had retreated because she was too much dressed, I suppose, to receive common company.

The dog was restored to her, and the landlord asked me down stairs to try an "eye-opener." I went down to what they style the bar, because it is so easy to get into it, and tried the eye-opener, which was something very hot in a tumbler.

I liked it, for it made me feel as if I were light as a feather, and a mandarin with three pig-tails. I repeated the remedy a number of times, and got lighter and lighter. I danced the chop-stick dance, and quoted Confucius, which, I was told, sounded like a speech in Congress.

I found, however, the eye-opener, like every thing else here, is misnamed; for my eyes grew so heavy that I couldn't keep them open. I made an effort to embrace the landlord, and fell through the window-glass. I didn't remember any thing more until I woke up with what I thought to be live coals in my mouth, and a feeling as if the yelping puppy had gotten into my brain.

I didn't want any more eye-opener.

My experience at the hotel induced me to go away from it immediately after breakfast. I ordered fried rats. They were strange rats I ate. They had wool on them; but I suppose they are different in America from the rats in China.

I hardly knew where to go. So I took a City directory, and concluded to visit the different places of interest in town. I looked for the Morgue, and, following the directions of the book, I went up one street and down another; retraced my steps; crossed forty or fifty back yards; fell into a number of cellars; was attacked by dogs because I wanted to take some of them to the hotel for dinner. I was really sea-sick; but, determined to be guided by the book, I walked into the river.

This created an excitement on the dock, and a stalwart fellow pulled me out by the pig-tail. I was asked my name. I gave it, when the crowd laughed; some declaring I had taken too much water in my gin-sling, and others, that I had taken too much gin-sling in my water. I was a very singular spectacle when I was pulled out. I had an opportunity to judge; for an enterprising photographer of Broadway copied me in water-colors before I had been in the river two seconds. He sent me one of his pictures, which I inclose to you.

He asked me to forward him a portrait of the Emperor of China in return, and an autograph letter recommending his establishment. I did so the next day, and I have since learned he exhibits my letter as the original manuscript of the editor of the *Tribune*, an excellent but peculiar gentleman, who keeps a private secretary to decipher his articles for him after they are written, and to inform him when he gets hungry.

I tried to find Central Park by the directory, and got into the Communipaw slaughter-house; to reach Greenwood, said to be the most lively place about New-York, and found myself in a beer-brewery. They tell me there is a good deal of beer in both localities. After that I lost faith in the directory, and, rambling about by my own instincts, I got along better.

I had heard much of the Chinese in Vesey street,—I presume it is a misprint for Tea-see street,—and, longing to meet some of my countrymen who had been here a great while, I went there.

I soon discovered a Chinaman, with a long cue, in our native costume. I addressed him in our own celestial tongue.

He replied: "Arrah, now, ye spalpeen, what wud yez be afther? Yer' no Chanymon. Git out wid ye, or I'll split the ear of ye, by the mim'ry of St. Pathrick."

I could not understand such Chinese as that, and concluded that he must have forgotten his own language, he'd been so long in America.

I determined to buy some of the tea, and I did. I drank it the same evening; but didn't recognize it as tea. It's a new kind, raised mostly in New-Jersey, a country the Americans talk of annexing to the United States if they can buy it of Camden & Amboy, two gentlemen who own the entire region, and compel people to pay a tax for traveling through it.

I was rather hungry by this time. I walked up Broadway, the principal street, where thousands of persons perform extraordinary and perilous tricks, such as leaping on stages, running under horses' feet, and clambering over the heads of carmen. They do it for amusement; not charging any thing for the exhibition. The police arrest men there often for getting in the way of wagons, and fine them, when they have their legs broken, for obstructing the progress of commerce.

When I came opposite a large house where many men were eating, I entered and sat down. I was opposite a famous juggler, who performed wonderful feats of knife-swallowing, and seemed entirely indifferent to the admiration he excited. A boy came to me and asked me what I wanted. Having had unpleasant experience in puppies and rats, I asked for crackers. "Chinese crackers?" he inquired.

"Yes, if you have them."

"Will you have them light?"

"Certainly, the lighter the better."

In a few minutes he returned with a plate full of the little red paper pop-guns we make in our country; and, before I could remonstrate with him, he lighted them, saying:—"Look here, old Celestial, this is one of the matches made in Heaven!"

The crackers went off in fine style, and I did likewise. Before I had gotten far, a boy from the eating-house ran after me, and pulling my cue (why in the name of Josh does every one try to take the cue from me?), inquired: "Buy these? Buy these? Good, good; bow, wow, wow!" So speaking, he held up a long line of sausages, and again made the bow, wow, wow sound.

I told him I spoke English. Then he remarked: "Dog in all of these. I know—we make 'em ourselves. Don't use any thing but dog. Get dogs in the Pound, every Summer; make great many sausages out of 'em. Genuine dog-sausages. Buy 'em, old fel?"

I declined, and the boy left me, with the remark that I was an old pudding-head, which no doubt was complimentary, as it signified something to eat, and that I was a man of desert.

While I continued walking up Broadway, there were several alarms of fire, and I saw two or three stores burn up—they say "up" when they mean "down," in this strange country—in splendid style. I asked where the roast pig was; but was informed they didn't roast pigs that way here.

I met a gentleman looking on like myself, and I expressed my surprise at so many fires.

"The reason," said he, "is the dullness of trade, which makes buildings so inflammable, they catch fire when there isn't a spark near them."

I said I couldn't comprehend how the state of commerce could make houses spontaneously combustible. He replied that the insurance companies were in my predicament; that they couldn't tell either, though they had given a deal of attention to the subject. He said the best way to insure a house against fire was not to insure it at all; that uninsured buildings, for some mysterious reason, wouldn't burn.

As I walked on, I noticed a number of signs above underground places, about "pretty waiter-girls." I thought I'd like to see them. So I went down into one of the saloons, as they are called. The girls carried waiters, but not prettiness. Indeed, they were excessively homely, several of them having painted their noses red, and their eyes black and blue, which didn't improve their appearance. Two of them came up to me, and sat down in my lap, declaring I was a "hunky old boy," which I didn't understand. Several placards stated that no intoxicating liquors were sold; and I was surprised to see men drink a few glasses of soda-water, and go out reeling like sailors in a storm. I believe the soda-water in New-York is very strong. The "pretty waiter-girls" were very kind to me. They played with my pig-tail, and induced me to "treat." They urged me to treat again, and I retreated.

When I got out, I missed my purse, and I suppose the good girls took it to remember me by. One of them had wished to borrow my watch to take medicine by, she said; but I refused to let her have it. I missed that, too. She had helped herself to it, no doubt.

Dear girl, what a delicate proof of her devotion! What charming surprises this country has for me!

I had become very tired by this time. I stepped out of Broadway, where I had difficulty in getting along, and where everybody seemed to have only a few moments left to do something very important. I had noticed several men who hurried by me as if they were walking for the championship of America,—a patriotic obligation here,—and, when I had proceeded a little farther, I perceived them lounging on the hotel steps, yawning from weariness.

A street car passed me, and I was about to get on, but the car was crowded inside and out, a dozen men holding on by their hands.

"Come on, Johnny," cried the conductor; "plenty of room for you;" and he reached out, and catching me by the cue tied me to the platform. I was dragged for several blocks. When he asked for my fare, I said I had not ridden, but he swore I had had a preferred seat; that it was the custom to charge double for dragging a man in that fashion; but that if any one made a row, he could pay single fare and walk.

I went inside then, as a hundred or two had got ten off. I hadn't been there but a few minutes when two brutal-looking fellows (I imagine they contradicted women, and called them homely) sprang upon the car; shook hands with the driver and conductor, and began to take the passengers' watches and pocket-books. When they demanded mine, I said I had lost them. "Oh, yes," they replied, "you've been on another car. Here, Bob," said one to the other, "give this chap a pass." So "Bob" gave me this slip of stiff paper, on which was printed: "Let the bearer alone. We've been through him. All right. Bummer & Co."

The two fellows remained on the car, and in a short time began taking the coats of the passengers. Not liking that, I got off, and walked to the hotel.

I was very tired, and ordering a plate of rice and a chop-stick, which was a mutton chop when it came, I ate it, and went to my room.

I lay down and reflected on the beautiful freedom of the country. In what other land would strange men and women help themselves to your watch and purse; pull your pig-tail; and explode crackers in your face?

O, blessed America, I have never appreciated you half enough! And, so thinking, I turned over and fell asleep.

Adoringly and eternally yours,

GHIN-SLING.

Here ends Ghin-Sling's letter, of which I have endeavored to give the true spirit, and whose openness and candor no one can help admiring.

CHAPTER LVII.

JENKINSISM IN THE METROPOLIS.

The race of Jenkinses is numerous, enterprising, and gifted. Jenkins, the original, and his numerous imitators, have of late performed many extraordinary feats in the way of florid description and picturesque detail. Weddings are their delight. They revel in weddings; exhaust metaphor, the dictionary, and patience. I have secured for this volume a Jenkins, one who will do honor to his tribe. He comes to me highly recommended. He can acquit himself more creditably at a dinner, by reason of his excellent appetite, and can use more words with fewer ideas, than almost any of his profession. He has just assisted at a hymeneal union (I employ his expression) in the City, and sends me his account, which I print with small variation from his eloquent MS. Thus it reads :—

For months past the most elegant and *recherché* society of the gilded and perfumed Rosemary square has been in a condition of the genteelest excitement over the announcement of the engagement of Miss Sophronia Clarissa Lovelace, youngest daughter of Peter Lovelace, Esq., an accomplished artist in hides and leather, and brother of the distinguished William Lovelace, Esq., third vice-president of the Boyletown Base Ball club, and R. Simpson Wiggins, Esq., a gentlemen of means and culture, who at one time presided over the destinies of a tape establishment in Sixth avenue, and won for himself fame and fortune by selling short measure with a grace and urbanity that will long be remembered.

Hundreds of beautiful creatures who had vainly sighed for R. Simpson Wiggins were distressed and made desolate when they heard the news; so painful to them, so delightful to Sophronia Clarissa. They forbore to take tea for an hour and a half, and threw out dark hints of joining the Sorosis. They yielded, however, to the inevitable, and made congratulatory visits to the fiancée. They found her beauty changed sadly; but they kissed her, calling her "dear," with cherry lips.

The months of fluttering were quieted when the high wedding came off in the church of Saint Hymen, which had been newly painted for the occasion, and which seemed to smile from its richly stained windows upon the lovely couple who were to be made one, unless incompatibility of temperament, or unwillingness of the bridegroom to disgorge the spondulicks (a modish phrase for paying bills), interfered with their domesticity.

The scene was imposing and touching to the last degree. It moved the elder Lovelace to transports of delight; and he clutched his pocket-book as if he thought that instrument of his power would henceforth be in less demand.

A dozen milliners and mantua-makers, who stood on the outer rim of the brilliant assembly, smiled blandly on the bride, and glowered on the bridegroom as though they meditated revenge upon his swollen purse.

A score of bridesmaids, wearing trains that were longer and moved slower than those of the Camden and

Amboy company, and bearing a sunflower above their charmingly *retroussé* noses (the noses were of the newest pattern, and brought over by the last French steamer), lent dazzling radiance to the beatitudes of the occasion, and promised to keep Lent with as much religious rigor as though they had been umbrellas. Their hair was splendid, having cost $500 apiece, and every mother's daughter claimed she wore the identical tresses severed from the head of Marie Antoinette on the eve of her execution. The bridesmaids were as accomplished as beautiful. They spoke French so excellently that no native of Paris could understand them; were magnificent croquet players, and deeply versed in the literature of Madame Demorest's magazine.

As to the bride, how shall we describe her? She looked like Venus on the half-shell, or Juno before beginning a row with Jupiter, or Hebe with the (hic)cup of nectar drained by the immortal gods. Heaven was in her eye; and in her hand a handkerchief trimmed with lace, wrought in the looms of Hoboken at $50 an inch, and which the gallant and chivalrous Wiggins was wont to declare over his Rudesheimer he paid $50.75 an inch for.

The exaggeration must be forgiven to Wiggins, in consideration of the enthusiasm of love and his fondness for base-ball, which we have heretofore neglected to mention, and which was largely instrumental in bringing to the elder Lovelace's mind his fitness to become a son-in-law.

Miss Lovelace wore a dress of satin damask persiflage, with trimmings of Bourdaloue *baisezmabouche,* looped up with purple *paté de foie gras* of petroleum wells in miniature. Her gaiters were of white bourgeois silk, coming above the classic ankle, and lined with perfumed *ailes de papillon* from Astrachan. She also wore an overskirt of demi point and demnition-foinc Mantalini lace, while her imperial veil, covering her from her chignon to the Castilian arch of her alabaster foot, was a fragment of the original vale of tears, usually donned somewhat later in life. Her gloves were embroidered on the back with the monogram of her family, S. H. A. M.; each glove having four fingers and one thumb, and ingeniously arranged with a large hole at the end to facilitate the ingress and egress of her fairy-like hand, which is asserted to be so good that it will beat four aces in the elegant pastime of draw-poker.

The lady's robe was also trimmed with sprigs of mint, specially ordered by the bridegroom, that during their bridal tour he might, in the event of reaching an uncivilized place, make juleps from his wife's toilette. About her snowy neck hung a strand of diamonds, dug from the mines of Chatham street, and so remarkable that three balls were given in their honor when they last changed hands.

Miss Lovelace was finally attired in a pair of blue eyes, bordered with a delicate crimson, and a mouth of so genuine a carmine that the color had been actually known to rub off. Before the ceremony, she fainted three times, but was restored through sympathy with the bridegroom, who went out to " see a man," and returned looking as if he had found him.

Mr. Wiggins was the embodiment of imperial splendor. He had traveled. He had sailed up and down the Dead Sea until some of his intimates called him a dead beat, —a flattering epithet he modestly rejected. He had been in the interior of Africa, and had traveled under the guidance of some of the natives farther into New-Jersey than any civilized person had ever before penetrated. He had explored the sources of the Nile, the Hackensack, and Schiedam Schnapps. He was a man of nerve and a gymnast. He had wrestled with the decanter; and had been thrown again and again; but he had always returned to the charge, though it was often as high as fifty cents.

Mr. Wiggins's cosmopolitan experiences had taught him to disregard the conventional forms of dress. On the occasion, he discarded black, except a black eye, which he had contracted the night before, in endeavoring to investigate too closely the kind of wood of which a policeman's mace was made. He had on a green coat (bottle green), with copper buttons, a scarlet vest, blending beautifully with his complexion, and pants of profound azure, assimilating with his next morning moods. He wore a hollyhock in his button-hole, and his nose was arrayed in deep purple.

Asked by the Rev. Dr. Bumfoozle if he would accept Sophronia for his wedded wife, Mr. Wiggins exclaimed, in very musical tones, "You bet;" and invited the clergyman out to drink. When the couple were pronounced man and lady, the organ pealed, which shocked the sensitive bride, who could not bear tones, to such a degree, that she said, "Take me to my ma."

The tune was changed at once, and Offenbach's "O, landlord, fill the flowing bowl!" substituted. That so exhilarated Mr. Wiggins, that he showed his appreciation of the music by having a first-class attack of delirium tremens, which the elegant company applauded to the echo.

The bride said, "Dear Wig, do it again! It's really

splendid, you shake beautifully, and when you cry out, 'Look at the snakes in my boots!' I forget for the moment you have on pumps." Mr. Wiggins declined to respond to the *encore*, but offered to read one of Tupper's poems instead, which was not accepted. The organ then performed a *pot-pourri* from Belladonna, while the chief vocalist of the choir sang a solo—so low no one could hear it—and Herr Limberger, a relative of the Bier family, performed an obligato on the bass drum.

An affidavit was now made that the ceremony was over. The bridegroom danced a clog dance, and having gone to see several more men, he was carried home on a shutter,—a paper prepared for the Historical Society being read over his prostrate form, with such happy effect that he had only two more attacks of del. trem. *en route* to the bride's father's palatial residence.

Among the distinguished guests present we noticed Darius Alexander Jones, Esq., who led the German last winter—off the dock, and had to pay his funeral expenses. P. Berwick Dexter, Esq., known to the scientific world as having assisted in making most of the artesian wells in the country, and recently engaged in conducting the operations of the Hoosac tunnel. His ancestors died at Potter's Field, and he is a direct descendant of the ancient augurs.

Col. Charles Augustus Wishawashy, who was one of the first gentlemen that ever led a little dog with a ribbon down the Avenue, and who can distinguish guipure lace from Valenciennes with his eyes shut and his coat off.

Hon. Paul Jeunechien, who has received the endearing name of "puppy" from his fashionable lady friends, and who has the smallest foot, considering the size of the boot he wears, of any bézique player in Poodle Place.

Dr. George Lancet, whose fondness for horses induced him to abandon the lucrative profession of borrowing money when no one would loan him any more, and turn his time and talent to the diseases of equine quadrupeds. In the choicest circles he is familiarly known as "Old Vet;" but is in no manner related to the contributor of the *Times*.

After the wedding, a reception was given at the mansion of the bride's father. During the evening, a number of the gentlemen ate Sweitzer cheese for the championship of America, and closed the hospitalities of the delightful occasion by sleeping in the station-house. The affair was one that will long be remembered by the persons who furnished the feast and can't collect their bills, and by the courteous policemen who assisted at the dénouement.

Here Jenkins's account ends. What could be more magnificent?

CHAPTER LVIII.

FASHIONABLE WEDDINGS.

The great social sensation of this City is a wedding. Beyond that, fashion does not look, and society has no ambition. In fashionable circles a daughter is merely something to get married. From the moment of her birth until her name is changed, her mother and feminine friends give most of their serious thought to her establishment in life, which means the securing of a husband whose income is large, and whose allowance will be prodigal. A rich and liberal husband is the one thing needful, the sole object desirable. Having him, all is had, and the future loses its significance.

Marriage means much in all cities; but in New-York it means every thing. A stranger can form no idea of the overwhelming importance attached to wedlock in the Metropolis,—not to the fitness or sympathy of the life-contracting parties, but to the forms and ceremonies of the occasion, the bridesmaids, the surroundings, the trousseau, the presents, the gilded *entourage*.

In society, no one asks, "Is he good-hearted? Is he chivalrous? Is he intellectual? Is she fine? Is she cultivated?" Those are foolish, not to say impertinent, questions.

The essential things to know are: Has she style? To what set does she belong? What are her diamonds worth? What time can his horse make? What club is he a member of? How much money is he worth? These questions having been answered satisfactorily, the sacrifice can proceed.

New-York has its wedding-season as it has its racing-season, its yachting-season, its picnic-season. The wedding-season is usually from the latter part of October to the close of May, the warm months being deemed unfavorable for modish nuptials. Love is declared to be impatient; but love has so little to do with most of our fashionable weddings, that there is no need of haste.

Such weddings are really what the French would call marriages of convenience, though they are found in most cases to be the very opposite. They are entered upon with all the deliberation with which the demonstration of a theorem is accompanied. They are cold-blooded calculations, determinations for vulgar display, meretricious shows from beginning to end. There is slender opportunity or desire for election in them. They are often brought about by others, on whom the responsibility of the inharmonious and unhappy unions ought to rest; managed, directed, and accomplished by and through ambitious mothers and their thoroughly disciplined daughters.

Men, who are presumed to be the seekers and the determiners of their matrimonial destiny, are seldom consulted. They are drawn into a flirtation, which continues so long that, before they are aware of their danger, they find themselves engaged to Margaret or Matilda, who was the last woman they thought of taking for a wife. They are in no peril, unless any are wealthy or believed to be so.

The proverb says, The traveler with an empty purse laughs at robbers. So here the man of society without income is safe in the hands of match-makers. For him no traps are laid; no schemes are formed. He enjoys the reputation of a not-marrying man, for the reason that in his set no one wants to marry him. He is a fortunate fellow. He sees the spectacle without paying for it; shares the pleasure, and escapes the pain.

Women of a certain age tend to match-making; and, when they have daughters, match-making becomes a religious duty. When mamma's eldest girl has quitted school, and formally "come out"—an event usually celebrated by a party, to which all eligible young men are invited—the first thing is to provide her with a husband. The claims of the men entitled to consideration by reason of their incomes are discussed by mamma and such other feminine friends as have daughters to marry, or as have shown proficiency in disposing of them to the highest bidder. If the requisite knowledge be lacking to determine a choice, inquiry is made of competent authorities, and the needed information is at last obtained.

The means or expectations of the half-dozen prospective Benedicts having become known with sufficient accuracy, a programme is arranged for their entertainment. Margaret or Matilda is thrown in their way, and enjoined to render herself agreeable to any of the selected victims. She must humor them; be coy or bold; melting or insensible; romantic or reasonable,— as any one of them demands.

She must be certain to ascertain the particular vanity of the predestined husbands, and flatter that to the fullest.

If Charles fancies himself handsome, he must be adroitly told of his beauty every day.

If William prides himself upon his clothes, his taste in dress must be commended, and his extravagance caressingly censured.

If Robert have an ambition to be thought profligate, mamma must lecture him on his wicked ways, but so tenderly that he will feel that bad morals are attractive; while the daughter must deplore the fact that women all love rakes, and will to the end of time.

If Joseph plumes himself on his business talent, his views must be shared and his sagacity applauded.

If George has a passion for horses, all his opinions about the turf and blooded stock must be listened to with patience.

Margaret or Matilda experiments upon each of the sex; and he who reveals most susceptibility is marked and doomed. One after another is dropped as he shows resistance or unmanageableness. He who is resolved upon is surrounded, attacked on every side, and at last compelled, from his desperate condition, to surrender. He may look woeful over his defeat; but while he is wondering at his novel situation, mamma sweeps in and congratulates him upon his acceptance, and the rare good fortune which he is too dazed to appreciate as he ought. The happy day is fixed. The invitations are given to the wedding on Gimbrede's latest style of cards; and for many weeks Margaret or Matilda's friends, especially the bridesmaids, are all in a flutter about what they shall wear, and how they shall look—the poles of anxiety in a fashionable woman's being. Before the wedding, every effort is made to get paragraphs into one of the gossiping journals, reading, "A charming Fifth avenue belle is soon to be led to the altar by a prominent member of the stock board;" or, "The approaching marriage of a Twenty-third street beauty, who was greatly admired in Paris last season, is creating a sensation in fashionable circles."

The wedding takes place in a fashionable church, at noon—that is the appointed hour—and, the fact having been advertised in all the papers that will print it, a vast crowd is assembled to see the carriages with liveried servants drive up and deliver their human freight of perfumed satin and orange-flowers, black broadcloth and white kids, rare diamonds and elaborate hair-dressing, upon the carpeted way leading to the altar.

The service is imposing so far as clothes can make it; but it is soon over, and the wedded pair, with all their showy attendants, go back to the carriages, amid congratulations that seem funereal, and return to the bride's father's house. There the guests are bidden; delicate and rich food is eaten; costly wine drank; commonplace observations exchanged; criticisms passed upon the bride and bridegroom; presents given (it often happens that they are hired, and merely exhibited in the drawing-room); and every thing done that can be to render the occasion expensive and vulgarly pretentious. All persons are bound to say the bride looks beautiful and interesting, and that the bridegroom conducts himself admirably, very much as if he had been leading a forlorn hope to battle.

After the proper amount of inanity, and compliment, and dissipation, the affair is over, and the couple go off traveling, as if they had done something they were ashamed of, and wanted to hide themselves until their confusion had passed.

FASHIONABLE WEDDINGS.

The day after the wedding, the gossiping journals give long and fulsome descriptions of "the event in fashionable society;" state what all the women wore; declare that they all looked lovely, and were perfectly fascinating; closing with a minute description of their wardrobe which no one but a mantua-maker can understand.

This is the end of Mr. and Mrs. Fleetfast. No one cares for them any longer. Even the council of mammas congratulates itself upon having made another match, and turns to new fields of commercial enterprise. When the wedded couple have passed their honeymoon—sometimes before—Mr. Fleetfast returns to his billiards, his old and his former rapid companions; stays out until three or four in the morning; comes home with a limber right-leg and a peculiar tone in his voice. Mrs. Fleetfast is anxious and pale for awhile, and her eyes look red and swollen at breakfast. But she soon learns from mamma that all men of the world act like her husband, and that there is no need of a heart-break over what is to be expected. So the delicate little lady puts on rouge; studies the art of flirtation; and soon learns it so well that her acquaintances believe she does not care a fig about Mr. Fleetfast's irregularities.

How many Mr. and Mrs. Fleetfasts there are in New-York to-day, and will be any day in the future!

To a fashionable wedding three things are essential—Delmonico's, cash, and Isaac H. Brown. The last is the far-famed sexton of Grace Church, who for twenty or thirty years has been an authority in society, and claims to know the antecedents of all the families in the City that have any pretense to gentility. How the fat old gabbler ever contrived to make himself a power in fashionable circles is past finding out; but that he has done so there is no doubt. He is deemed indispensable on all grand occasions, and the invitations are always intrusted to him. He revels in weddings, and is a necessary evil to the whole tribe of Jenkinses. He believes no lady of the town can be properly and modishly disposed of without his assistance, and he is officious, and self-important, and garrulous enough to please an army of silly women. To Brown, Grace Church is merely an architectural appendage in which he airs his flesh on Sunday, and punishes his spirit on week-days.

He has presided at thousands of weddings, and has lived to see many of them result as unhappily as the bitterest cynic could desire. If he would unfold his observations, he would tell sad stories of diamond weddings that proved nothing but paste; of sparkling eyes, and lips with soft music on them, which lost their luster through care, and waxed pale through wretchedness untold.

Fashionable weddings are growing more fashionable, and meretricious every year in New-York. They are mockeries of love, satires on marriage, insults to nature. They who make them assume a responsibility that is dreadful, and pay the penalty violated sympathies, and false vows, and starved souls sooner or later exact from all that give hands without the consecration of hearts.

CHAPTER LIX.

CITY MISSIONS.

ALADDIN'S palace in the place of a muck-heap could hardly be a greater change than the Five Points Mission on the site of the Old Brewery, for many years the purple plague-spot that revealed the fatal moral pestilence of the Sixth Ward.

The Five Points is bad enough now, Heaven knows, but compared to what it was twenty years ago, when Murderer's Alley and Cow Bay were shuddering horrors, and when subterranean passages communicated between pits of debauchery and dens of crime, it is an abode of purity and peace.

The Mission is a plain brick building in Park street, near Baxter, the front part of which is rented to tenants. It contradicts all its surroundings; looks as if it had gotten there by mistake, or would look so, if it were not kept in countenance by its sober, comfortable companion, the House of Industry, over the way. It has one or two offices, several school-rooms, and a chapel, all plain, but scrupulously clean.

The Mission was the pioneer of reform in that repulsive locality, having been established in 1850. It is under the direction of the Methodists, but the services there, though doctrinal, are not sectarian. Rev. L. M. Pease was the founder of the Mission, which was at first deemed a quixotic enterprise, and indeed it seemed such; for philanthropists and reformers had surrendered all hope of introducing light into that benighted region. In a few months an astounding change was apparent, and such beneficial results were wrought as the most sanguine had not anticipated. The noble effort blossomed with good fruit, and richly repaid those who had made it. After two years the reverend superintendent retired, and founded the House of Industry. Since then both have continued to flourish, and produced the most beneficial results.

The Mission is simply a school. The children there have parents usually—in that respect they are different from those of the House of Industry and the Boys' and Girls' Lodging House—and seem on the whole more intelligent and of a finer organization than in most of the charitable institutions in the City. The Mission has eight or ten teachers, all women, paid regular salaries by the Board of Education, and five or six hundred pupils on an average, who, during the Winter, are increased to eight hundred. The institution, like most of the municipal charities, is supported wholly by voluntary contributions. Rev. J. N. Shaffer is the superintendent, and gives his entire time to its management. As usual, all the children are of foreign parentage, Irish predominating, and Germans next. Every Tuesday evening and Sunday, interesting religious exercises are held in the chapel. A large infant school is taught in the Mission, and is one of its most attractive features. Every day visitors go there, and rarely depart without seeing and feeling the necessity and advantage of such a charity.

The House of Industry is fifteen years old, and has long been under the superintendence of S. B.

Halliday. It is a plain building, much like the Mission; has an office, school-rooms, dormitories, a chapel, washing rooms, and whatever is needful for the purpose. About two hundred children are generally in the House, though the number is greater in cold weather. During the past year 1,075 children were admitted; 512 were sent to situations; 179 returned to parents; 58 sent to other institutions; 275 left voluntarily; 17 expelled for misconduct; 19 ran away, and 5 died. The average attendance was 413, which is larger than during any previous year. The teachers are nine in number, and very energetic and conscientious in the discharge of their duty. The Sunday-school has twenty teachers, with an average attendance of 350 pupils. The religious progress has not been so great as is desirable, but still it is encouraging. The number of meals given during the year was 385,502. It often happens that two or three hundred men and women apply daily for food, and are given an inexpensive but substantial dinner, which does not cost more than four cents for each person.

Many thousand garments are made and repaired every year, and some ten thousand articles of clothing are given to the children and out-door poor. The shoe-shop is excellently managed, hundreds of shoes being made wearable from old ones that seem entirely worthless. The nursery usually contains twenty to twenty-five little ones, from eighteen months to six years of age. The difference between the children when they are first received and after they have been there a short time is remarkable. They are converted from squalid, ragged, pallid little wretches to clean, well-clad, wholesome creatures. Gradually their old, sad, hard look wears away. The light begins to dawn in their faces, as if from redeemed souls.

The expenses of the House were, for the year, $32,114.94, and the donations $33,568.27.

The Howard Mission, or Home for Little Wanderers, is at No. 40 New Bowery. Over the gateway that leads to the institution is the name of the Mission, and under it are the words, "Homes for the homeless, and bread for the hungry."

The Mission is under the direction of Rev. W. C. Van Meter; has large and well-ventilated school-rooms and chapels, and is excellently conducted. It is regularly incorporated; not sectarian; never turns a child from its doors, and is entirely sustained by voluntary contributions, receiving no aid from the Legislature, City, or School Fund. In six years it received 7,581 children, and the number taught, fed and clothed during a month is about 500. The day school is from 9 to 2, and the several exercises from $1\frac{1}{2}$ to 2 o'clock. Prayer meetings are held every Tuesday evening, and regular devotional exercises on Sunday.

The Howard Mission is one of the best of our charities, and is an object of curiosity and interest to many strangers and citizens. The little wanderers are very kindly and even tenderly treated, and no one who visits them often can fail to be concerned in their development—physical, mental, and moral. They are very sensitive to kindness, and show, as all animated nature does, that love is the best teacher and the truest religion.

The history of each one of the children is known by the teachers, and if published would show the source of most of our social evils. The little creatures are suffer-

ROOM IN HOWARD MISSION.

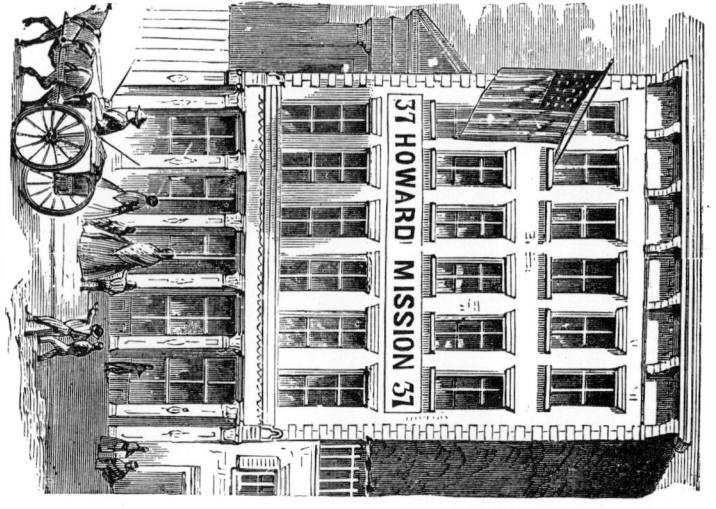

HOWARD MISSION.

ing for the sins of their ancestors, and the chief sin is intemperance. From intemperance come nearly all the others—idleness, dishonesty, incontinence, selfishness, and brutality, and with them theft, violence, murder, and every other species of crime. Hardly one of the little wanderers and outcasts that has not, or had not, drunken parents. Generally the father is dissipated; often both the father and mother.

I have heard the antecedents of the children related. One had a father and a mother who probably inherited their thirst for liquor from their parents. The father died of delirium tremens; the mother fell from the window of a tenement and broke her neck. A second was found nearly naked in the street, where it had been left to die of exposure. A third had a father who murdered his wife, and was executed for the crime. A fourth was rescued from the flames of a building fired by a drunken maniac. A fifth was left an orphan by the death of its mother from typhus, and the suicide of its father while mad with delirium tremens. A sixth has parents, but they are always on Blackwell's Island or at Sing Sing, and have no more care or thought of their wretched offspring than if they had never been born. A seventh has a decrepit mother in the hospital, and had a father who was shot in a Water street brawl.

Everywhere the same story is told. The trail of the rum shop is over them all. No wonder persons, conscientious and philanthropic, favor compulsory measures for the abolition of intemperance. It is the crying curse, the besetting sin of this and every other land. Destroy intemperance, and the World would be more than half reformed.

CHAPTER LX.

THE TOMBS

EVERYBODY in the Metropolis has seen the Tombs, as the City Prison is always called here, but few have been inside of its gloomy walls; nor would they like to be, if they knew what wretches and wretchedness it contained.

The Tombs occupies one square, or block, bounded on the east and west by Centre and Elm, and north and south by Leonard and Franklin streets. It was built about thirty years ago, of gray granite, in the Egyptian style of architecture, at a cost of $250,000; and it is safe to say no such amount of money was ever expended for a more dolorous purpose. Its gloomy semblance gave it the name it still bears, and will bear while one block of the dingy stone stands upon another.

When the prison was built, it was considered a remarkable structure,—which, indeed, it is; and, for years, it was the architectural wonder of the east side of the town. The vicinity of the Tombs has little to boast of now in the way either of cleanliness or beauty; but, at the time of its erection, squalor and sin reigned supreme thereabout, and the prison might well be considered the tomb of purity, order, peace, and law.

The gray, begrimed building one sees in passing

through the streets is merely the walls of the prison, inclosing a quadrangle full of narrow, ill-ventilated, dismal cells, arranged in rows one above another, and reached by iron steps and galleries. There are three different departments in the Tombs,—one for boys, another for men, and a third for women; and the three classes are kept carefully apart. They are all miserable enough, Heaven knows! and no sympathetic person who goes there can withhold his pity from them, however hard, or vicious, or degraded they may be.

The Tombs is a prison of detention, for the most part; persons being confined there for trial, and sentenced to Blackwell's Island or Sing Sing when convicted. The prisoners are locked up in their cells during the night and much of the day, but are permitted to take exercise, and go through the farce of getting "fresh air," in the galleries at certain hours. "Fresh air," indeed! The atmosphere of the Tombs is as vicious materially as it is morally. It is foul, even poisonous, and enough to breed a pestilence. The Board of Health long ago declared the prison a nuisance, and all who visit it think it should be abated, as such. But the voice of justice and reform is seldom obeyed in large cities, where selfishness is the end and corruption is the rule.

The inmates vary in number with the season and the condition of business. When the weather is cold and trade is stagnant, there are more than during the warm months and periods of activity; showing that crime is the result of temptation and necessity. Usually, the Tombs has about 400 inmates, three-quarters of whom are men. Most of them are hardened and degraded creatures, who have been there, at the Island, and in the penitentiary, again and again. They have lost all sense of shame; for they feel they are outcasts; that no one cares for them; that no one will help them to reform. They come into contact only with their own fallen kind, and with policemen who are as callous in their way as the prisoners are in theirs.

If we could but look into the hearts of criminals, could fathom the mysteries of vice, would we not find that the divorce of the erring from human charity, their despair of human forgiveness and love, was the cause of most of their so-called sins?

Not a few of the prisoners are slight offenders, novices in vice,—men who have become intoxicated, perhaps for the first time, and who awake from a mad delirium to mortification and bitter repentance in the ghastly cells of the Tombs.

Men of influence, and wealth, and position, have been there more than once, particularly strangers, who come to the City to see its sights, and, after drinking and dissipating, have been borne down by the fiery draughts they had swallowed. Printers and reporters, I am sorry to say, are occasionally found at the Tombs, ending a spree there most gloomily, when they set out for a night of gayety and pleasure.

The Tombs has a history, and a very sad one. It has seen tragedies whose horrors thrilled through the land, and were repeated with pale lips for many months, and are now remembered only as dim traditions. Men have spent terrible days and nights there, with death, for which they were wholly unprepared, staring them in the face from the gallows' beam. What ghostly visions of murdered victims have trooped through those cells! What agony and terror have wrung their souls!

Men have destroyed themselves within those pitiless walls; and eternal farewells have been taken from friends, and wives, and mistresses, who loved none the less for the great crimes that had extinguished the sympathy of outraged society.

Col. Monroe Edwards, the famous forger,—scarcely remembered by this generation,—occupied one of the cells. Cancemi, the assassin; Mrs. Burdell-Cunningham; Baker, the murderer of "Bill" Poole,—were there. And Colt, who slew Adams the printer, and afterward stabbed himself to the heart, was found stiff and stark on the very morning named for his execution. The story of the mysterious murder—the sending of the box containing the body to New Orleans, its discovery, the arrest, the exciting trial, the effort of influential friends to save him, the romantic attachment of his mistress, and then the final cheating of the gallows— was long remembered, with all the wild rumors of his escape by the substitution of another body for his, and his living in prosperity in Europe.

One might write a volume of the tragedies of the Tombs, and to-day they would be almost as fresh as when they first startled the City and the country at large.

The gallows has stood a score of times within the walls of the Tombs, and the timbers of which it is composed are carefully laid by, to be put up whenever the shuddering spectacle of judicial murder shall again be presented. Who, that has heard the hollow echoes of gallows-making, on some sepulchral morning before sunrise, will ever forget the awful sound? What morbid curiosity is always felt by the depraved to witness executions! How all the house-tops in the gloomy square have been blackened, and will be blackened once more when some trembling wretch is swung off into eternity!

The courts held in the Tombs are the police court, presided over by Justice Dowling, an officer worthy of the revolting place; and the special sessions, where petty offenses in the eyes of the law are tried, and humanity held up to merciless judgment.

The atmosphere of police courts is always sickening, and that of the Tombs unusually so. I feel contaminated whenever I enter Dowling's tribunal. Every thing seems so hard, so vulgar, so pitiless, that I long for the sunshine of Broadway, the fresh breeze of the parks, as if I had been deprived of them for months. The police strike me as unpleasantly as the criminals; for familiarity has made them callous, and they laugh and jeer at degradation which is revolting, and at misery which is too deep for tears.

The tragedies of the wretched creatures that have fallen into their hands, are broad farces to them. The judge sentences the culprits as he would call off a list of articles at an auction. The officers of the law give evidence under oath as they relate a coarse story at headquarters. Crime is a matter of course—punishment an inevitable duty. All wickedness and infamy belong to the daily routine, and are neither to be censured nor deplored.

Oh, the pain and shame of the police court! It is a tribunal without dignity, and a sentence without sympathy. It seems to rob justice of all beauty by its coarseness, and to strike humanity into the dust with a brutal hand. It has its uses, I suppose, but they are the uses of adversity deprived of aspiration, and cut off from the hope of improvement.

I have gone into the Tombs and talked with the prisoners, and I have known others to do so. If you are gentle and sympathetic, they respect you at once; and no wonder, for they have no reason to look for kindness, from their past experience. But even they will show the better side that every mortal has, if you will persevere, and prove to them you are their friend. Charity not only covers a multitude of sins; it turns them back to the source of good intentions, and enables us to judge as we would be judged.

The men are not so pitiable as the boys and women; for these might be reformed by proper treatment. But, in the atmosphere of the Tombs, reformation seems impossible. The grim, hard stone of the building appears to mock every effort to change; its dreary echoes to laugh at every sigh, or moan, or prayer.

The Tombs! It is well named. Who so christened it, was wiser and bitterer than he knew. In it are swallowed up the best purposes and resolves; and its ponderous architecture crushes any remaining instinct to good.

When I pass it under the lightness of noon, I feel a shadow in my way; and even the purity of the moon seems stained when its beams fall upon such hideous ugliness.

Sunday, at the Tombs, is the grand gala day of transgression and judgment. On that day the police court presents a more revolting spectacle than on any other day of the week; for the crowd is greater, and the offenses are more repulsive. Saturday has long been known as the drunkards' night; for then that vast class of people in great cities who live from hand to mouth,—from the rum-shop to the poor-house, it might be stated—

who seek relaxation from exhausting toil in degrading dissipation,—give loose to their passions, and fall into the clutches of the police.

Often a hundred and more cases of drunkenness, rowdyism, fighting, and wife-beating, are disposed of on Sunday morning by Justice Dowling, at the rate of one or two per minute. The blackened and bloodshot eyes, bloody and bloated faces, ragged and quivering forms, repulsive features, mis-shapen by generations of wrongdoing, will haunt you long after your visit to the court.

Religious exercises are held there, too. Religion in such a place is like peace in Pandemonium. The exercises are a ghastly satire on the spirit of Christianity; for, while the form is observed, the soul of humanity is crushed. The Sisters of Charity—truly such at all times—have charge of the boys and women, and, by their earnestness, lend a little halo to the place; but the Protestant worship, progressing amid the trials, and intermingling with clamor and coarseness, seems to deepen the shadow of the ever-shadowed Tombs.

CHAPTER LXI.

THE MIDNIGHT MISSION.

Society seems from its organization to have taught that all sins are pardonable in men, and that all errors but one may be forgiven in women. Inhuman and baneful as this belief has been, it has been practically held, and has, generation after generation, removed fallen women from the possibility of reform.

Whatever else this age may be, it is certainly an age of humanity, and for it was fitly reserved the dealing with the great social problem in a thoroughly human way. The great reformatory movement for women, most justly styled unfortunate, was originated by Mrs. Emma Sheppard, of Frome, England, who began her great and good work in 1855. She first visited her erring sisters in what was known as the "black ward" of the work-house; afterward in the penitentiaries of Bath, Cleves and Pentonville, and labored constantly and conscientiously for the reclamation of those whom society had cast out, and even the Church would not receive.

Four years she devoted to the excellent work with excellent results, and then had the courage to open her own home to the shelter and protection of the poor pariahs. Her undertaking produced good fruit, and in the winter of 1860 the "midnight meeting movement" was begun. It was soon extended to other cities of Great Britain, and to this country and City in 1867.

The founders of the Midnight Mission here were ten in number, seven men and three women, representing commerce, medicine, and the pulpit, and had their first regular meeting on the first of February, in rooms at the corner of Twelfth street and Broadway. Public opinion, always slow and rarely enlightened, was opposed to the movement, and some of the churches were bitter in their hostility, repeating the old cant that such a charity would do more harm than good; that it was not practicable, and that sympathy with lewdness would increase it by making it attractive.

Money was wanting, too; but the members of the Mission were so resolute, so active, that the work advanced in spite of drawbacks, and steadily gained the confidence of the community. At the end of the first year the members were quadrupled, and the rooms in Broadway were found too small. The Mission removed to a large dwelling, No. 23 Amity street, where it still remains. The new house is plain, but very neat and comfortable, and under the direction of a kind and entirely sympathetic woman.

Two nights of every week—Thursday and Friday— are devoted to the cause which is advertised by printed cards that read :—

"The Committee of the Midnight Mission will be happy to see you at tea at 10 o'clock on any Friday evening at 23 Amity street, between Greene and Mercer. Rooms open every day, from 2 to 4 P. M., for private conversation and friendly advice."

The cards are distributed among the unfortunate women wherever found, in the street, at the dance-houses, at the bagnios. On the nights named men of years, benevolence, and high social standing, go out into the highways and byways of the City, and gently but earnestly invite the poor wanderers to the Mission. They are not often rebuffed, for the quick instincts of the women reveals to them at once that the good men are really their friends. They do not tire of their undertaking. No ill temper, no insult repels them. They are always gentle, tender, entreating, and prove that to the expression of genuine sympathy the sternest nature yields.

The evening receptions are on Friday. The noble women who belong to the Mission prepare simple refreshments, and receive the unfortunates who come voluntarily, or whom the members find in their search. The poor girls are usually very shy and timid at first, but they soon gain confidence from the loving kindness of the ladies of the committee. They are encouraged to unburden their breasts, to tell their sad stories, and to enter upon a new path of life. After refreshments come devotional exercises, which close with a hymn and prayer, in which all are urged to take part. No one, whatever his religious opinions, can attend the receptions without being touched by what he sees and hears there. He can not fail to perceive the work is good, and that such a work is blessed indeed.

The unfortunates who visit the Mission are from sixteen to twenty-five years of age, and the number is divided about equally between foreigners and Americans. Many of them are pretty, but few are educated.

The greater part of the Americans are from the country, having fallen victims to the temptations and wickedness of the great City.

Nearly all make the same sad confession. They have sinned from love—strange paradox!—having been betrayed by the man they trusted, and having taken one false step, they could not retrace it. Once fallen, the brand of shame was fixed upon their brow, and they were sent forth to the avoidance and the scorn of the World. Many of them are afraid to return to their relatives or friends after their seduction, and many are spurned as loathsome creatures by those who, in the crisis of their lives, should stand between them and their fighting souls. Having placed their foot upon the plowshare, they can hardly escape the terrible ordeal. The way of their downward course is deftly paved. They steadily descend, as by a winding staircase, and every year, and month, and week, and day, they look back to less loathsome heights they never can regain.

"God help us!" they may well say; for Man abandons them to their remorseless fate. The houses of prostitution are regularly graded. No sooner does one expel them than another takes them up. They are in a great moral maelstrom. In vain they struggle: in vain they stretch forth their pleading hands. Round, round, down, down they go until they are swallowed up in death, and not even Heaven seems to hear their despairing cry.

Nearly every one of the poor girls says she had lost all hope; that she had no faith in the sympathy or pity of her kind; that the humanity of the Mission surprises and bewilders her.

When we remember that there are twenty to twenty-five thousand courtesans in New-York, the capacity for good there is in such an organization as the Midnight Mission can easily be perceived. If they fail to reform, it is because they don't know how. They stumble in the thick darkness, and beg in vain for the smallest glimmer of light.

The severe censors who declare that fallen women can't and won't be lifted up should attend the receptions of the Mission. During the exercises many a poor girl lives her sad life over again; becomes an innocent child once more; and as the hymns and prayers bring back to her memory the days of happiness and home, her lip trembles; her eye moistens; and all her soul bursts out at last in an agony of sacred and repentant tears. Not long since one of the poor outcasts, who went to the Mission merely from curiosity, was so overcome by the sympathy expressed for her that in the midst of a hymn she broke down completely. "What a load is lifted from my bosom!" she sobbed out. "My heart feels so light. It seems as if I could go up. I haven't been so happy since I was at home. I'm so happy I wish I could die now. You're all so good to me. I didn't believe any one could be but my dear mother. She is dead, and I've often been glad, for she loved me so, and I didn't want her to know what a bad girl I was. But now I wish she was alive to see that I've changed, and won't do wrong any more."

The repentant girl kept her word. She remained at the Mission for some weeks and obtained a situation through the Committee; studied hard, and, being naturally intelligent, is now teaching a village school in New-England; is a church member; often writes to the good women here; says she is happy all the day long, and shall ever be grateful to them for preserving her from utter ruin.

Such an example, were it single, should encourage the good work, and strengthen the hands and hearts of those engaged in the enterprise. But the example is one of many, and proves that the women who have been driven to prostitution can be returned to purity, be made useful, noble, Christian.

The report of the first year shows that during the twelve months past eight hundred women attended the Friday evening receptions; that of the number seventy-seven were induced to remain (the Mission is now fitted up for a temporary home), and that forty-eight of the seventy-seven have thoroughly reformed. Of those who remained in the Mission fourteen have found virtuous homes; seven have been returned to their friends; eight placed in charitable institutions; nine have been lost sight of; twenty-two have gone back to their old life of shame, and seventeen were in the Mission House at the close of the year.

The expense of the Mission, supported from voluntary contributions, was $50,000 during the year—about $200 for each woman saved. Surely, salvation is cheap at so small a price. The Mission has no Utopian ideas; has no hope of destroying prostitution, or working a general reform among the unfortunate. It directs all its efforts toward individuals; opens the way of return to those who have wandered; is the means of showing to the miserable class that there are good souls in the World who will take them by the hand and assist them to live virtuous lives.

The women who visit the Mission are always invited to stay. Some remain over night only; others for days and weeks. Besides assisting in household duties, they are provided with sewing, and receive half the proceeds. Six hours of the day are occupied in reading, talking, and in innocent recreation, of which music forms a part.

Many of the Magdalens are very intelligent, and fitted for useful positions in life. Though the Mission is intended only as a temporary asylum, no one of the inmates is ever asked to depart. On the contrary, all are encouraged to remain as long as they like.

The charity is most noble, and very effective withal. While the Mission continues it will be a beacon-light to those who deem themselves lost. It will be a bridge connecting virtue with unchastity, over which those who wish can pass from darkness to light, from wretchedness and sin to peace and purity. It is doing what He did who sat beside the fallen woman at the well of Samaria, and talked to her lovingly and forgivingly of her duty and her destiny.

CHAPTER LXII.

THE ASSOCIATION FOR THE POOR.

ONE of the wisest, best-managed, and most practical charities in the City is the Association for Improving the Condition of the Poor, of which James Brown, the eminent banker, is President, and Robert B. Minturn, the late distinguished merchant, was Treasurer. Its other officers, its advisory committees and visitors, are among our best citizens, who have for years been laboring for the purpose that the name of the organization indicates.

The Association was organized in 1843, and incorporated in 1848, and each year has made it more useful, and increased the field of its operations. Every person who becomes an annual subscriber, a member of an advisory committee, or visitor, shall be a member of the Society, which is under the control of a Board of Managers. Nine members constitute a quorum at any of the meetings, which are held regularly every month —July and August excepted—or specially whenever deemed necessary. The City is divided into twenty-two districts, each ward forming a district, and the districts are divided into sections. Each district has an advisory committee, consisting of five members, and each section a visitor.

The rules for the government of the Association are as follows:—

To regard each applicant for relief as entitled to charity, until a careful examination proves the contrary.

To give relief only after a personal investigation of each case, by visitation and inquiry.

To relieve no one except through the Visitor of the Section in which the applicant lives.

To give necessary articles, and only what is immediately necessary.

To give only in small quantities, and in proportion to immediate need; and of coarser quality than might be procured by labor, except in cases of sickness.

To give assistance at the right moment; not to prolong it beyond the duration of the necessity which calls for it; but to extend, restrict, and modify relief according to that necessity.

To require of each beneficiary abstinence from intoxicating liquors as a drink; of such as have young children of a proper age, that they may be kept at school, unless unavoidable circumstances prevent it; and to apprentice those of suitable years to some trade, or send them to service. The design being to make the poor a party to their own improvement and elevation, the willful violation or disregard of these rules shall debar them from further relief.

To give no relief to recent immigrants having claims on the Commissioners of Emigration, except, in urgent cases, for two or three days, or until that Department can be informed of such cases, when the responsibility of this Association toward them shall cease.

To give no aid to persons who, from infirmity, imbecility, old age, or any other cause, are likely to continue unable to earn their own support, and consequently to be permanently dependent, except in extreme cases for two or three days, or until they can be referred to the Commissioners of Charity.

To discontinue relief to all who manifest a disposition to depend on alms, rather than their own exertions, for support, and whose further maintenance would be incompatible with their good and the objects of the Institution.

The late census shows that the population of the City consists of forty-one nationalities, representing every quarter of the Globe, and embracing, necessarily, corresponding varieties of race, language, color, habits, temperament, moral character, religions, political proclivities, and occupations. The following is a classification of the inhabitants according to their nativity, as gathered from the census of 1865 :—

American born	407,314 or 56.85	per cent.
From Ireland	161,334 or 22.21	"
From German States	107,267 or 14.77	"
From England	19,699 or 2.71	"
From other foreign countries	30,772 or 3.46	"
Total	726,386	100

The foregoing figures show the aggregate of the foreign-born in the City to be 319,074, or 43 15-100 per cent. of the population. The statement is accepted, though difficult of reconciliation with probability or fact; for, as early as 1855, the ratio of the foreign-born was 51 19-100 per cent., and, as 1,342,965 immigrants landed at this port during the ensuing decennial period, it appears questionable that their number, meanwhile, should have decreased in this City more than 8 per cent. Again, according to the census of 1865, the native voters were 51,500, and the naturalized, or foreign-born voters, 77,475, thus giving the latter, though numerically 8 per cent. less than the former, 50 per cent. more voters. As most of the poor here are foreigners, it may be well to state that the native-born, who comprise rather more than half the inhabitants, give about twenty-three per cent. of the City indigence; the foreign-born, including those aided by the Commissioners of Emigration, amount to seventy-seven per cent., which is nearly four imported paupers for one American. Of the 68,873 persons arrested for offenses against person and property, for the year ending October 31st, 1865, 45,837 were foreigners; and of these 32,867 were Irish, and but 23,036—white and black, all told—were natives. Of the whole number arrested, 13,576 could neither read nor write. Many of the native-born paupers and criminals are the offspring of foreigners, who were themselves paupers and criminals. Hence much of our indigenous pauperism and crime is immediately traceable to foreign parentage.

Twenty-five years of experience have tested the efficacy of the system adopted by the Association in benefiting the poor. Thousands of our wealthy and generous families have found that the cessation of miscellaneous almsgiving at their doors and elsewhere, and the substitution therefor of the present charity, has not only been more effective, but has materially reduced able-bodied vagrancy. The members of the society feel assured that their plan is the true one, and believe that by general co-operation professional mendicancy could soon be suppressed. The number of members is steadily increasing, and is now over twenty-seven hundred.

The visitors go to every tenement and place of poverty in their particular section, make personal investigation of the cases of destitution, and report them to the

Association. In no ordinary case is money given, for when it is, it is liable to be expended for liquor. The Association distributes nothing but food and fuel, and that often finds its way to the corner grocery. Tickets are used for the purpose. Any member hearing of a case of destitution fills the ticket as follows :—

Mr. JOHN JONES, *Visitor, No.* 48 *Stuyvesant street:*
  Please visit Patrick Murphy, No. 93 James street.
            JOSEPH SMITH,
          Member N. Y. Association
       For improving the Condition of the Poor.
Residence, 56 Fifteenth street.

If Mr. Jones finds Patrick Murphy deserving, Murphy gets a ticket like this, to the grocer, specifying by list No. 1 or No. 2 the articles needed :—

Mr. GEORGE JENKINS, 44 *Eighteenth street:*
  Please let Patrick Murphy have the value of $1, of list No. 1.
            JOHN JONES, *Visitor.*
October 14, 1868.

List number one represents food for persons in health, number two represents food for persons in sickness. The number is written in ink so that it can not be readily altered. In this manner the prospect of being imposed upon is lessened.

A statement of the labors of the Association shows that in 1844 there were 244 visitors, 10,082 visits were made, 1,560 families and 6,240 persons were relieved; $10,522 were received and $8,704 disbursed. Last year there were 339 visitors, who made 22,509 visits; 5,141 families and 19,097 persons were relieved; $57,837 were received and $59,058 disbursed.

The Association has rooms at No. 39 Bible House,

CITY MISSIONARY.

and from this, as a radiating center, the visitors go forth upon their mission of charity and mercy. The labor of the good and humane persons who compose the Society is constant, indefatigable and beyond all praise.

The members are among the best people in the City. Fine men and delicate women, in the prosecution of benevolence go through the filthiest streets and into the most noisome dens; do every thing in their power to feed the hungry and clothe the naked, and ask no reward but the precious consciousness of benefiting their kind; thus proving themselves Christians whatever their creed.

CHAPTER LXIII.

THE WORKING WOMEN'S HOME.

The high price of living in New-York has borne so heavily upon the poor that it has crowded them into tenement houses, and compelled them to subsist in the most unnatural manner. The numerous women, who rarely earn more than about half the wages of men, even when they do men's work, are, and always have been, oppressed by the high prices they have been compelled to pay.

Any and every boarding-house keeper is prejudiced against women; would much rather have men at the same rate; and does his or her best to avoid taking them. One woman is more burdensome, they say, than half a dozen men; for she is so much in the house, and gives so much more trouble than the other sex. Unprotected young women are exposed to dangers and temptations in the tenement houses, and yet they have no other place to go.

To obviate this difficulty, and to provide comfortable and healthful quarters for them, the Working Women's Home was established in this City about a year ago. The idea was borrowed, I believe, from the model lodging-houses of Great Britain, which have been of great benefit to the laboring classes, and have become popular and been reformatory wherever they have been opened.

The Working Women's Home.

The Home, No. 45 Elizabeth street, near Canal, is a large six-story building, formerly a superior tenement house, erected originally by several benevolent New-Yorkers for colored families. For some reason, the colored people got crowded out, and persons of the usual miscellaneous character obtained possession. The philanthropic citizens who had the enterprise in charge, thinking the location favorable, and knowing the superior character of the building, bought it for $100,000, and expended $50,000 more to put it in order. They opened it as soon as the necessary repairs were made; the house having been cleansed from top to bottom, painted, and properly furnished.

Three months were required to advertise the object of the Home, which was for a long while supposed to be a charitable institution. When its character was made known, it received, in a few weeks, about 100 boarders. The number increased, and has been increasing slowly but steadily ever since. At present it has 245 boarders —many more than it has had at any previous time,— and before the Winter is over it will probably have not far from 500, for whom there are ample accommodations.

As you enter the house, you find yourself in a large office, presided over by a young woman, who receives the money, attends to the register, and performs the duties of a clerk in a hotel. She is always at her post; is polite and attentive, and might give valuable lessons to men in the same position. Adjoining the office is a large parlor and reading-room, divided into three compartments, in the first of which the boarders are privileged to receive their friends of either sex; while the others are of a more private character. The reading-room has files of the daily papers, with a well-selected but small library, and the parlor contains a piano and melodeon. The boarders have music; talk, dance, and enjoy themselves until 10 in the evening, when they retire. Adjoining the parlor is the dining-room and laundry, and in the basement is the kitchen, bakery, and bath-rooms. On the second floor are sleeping apartments, and also on the third, fourth, fifth, and sixth, the apartments opening into a broad and airy hall. The halls have such names as Cooper hall, Aspinwall and Astor gallery, being christened after the donors of the establishment. The beds are ranged side by side, and, separated by white curtains, are models of neatness and sweetness. Every thing about the house breathes the air of order, cleanliness, and comfort, and is decidedly attractive. The washing is well done, the cooking excellent, and the tables look inviting. While every thing is plain, it is substantial and satisfactory. On the south side of the building is a promenade, where the boarders walk and take the air when the weather is pleasant.

When the Home was first opened, the charge for board and washing was $3.25 a week, but since then $1.25 has been fixed as the rate for lodging and washing, payable in advance, the meals being paid for when they are had. The $1.25 per week entitles the boarders to all the privileges of the house, and the meals, received on the European plan, cost them from $1.75 to $3.25 additional. They live very well, though the price of their meals does not average 20 cents each.

No restrictions are placed upon the boarders. They are admitted until 11 o'clock at night. If they come after that hour, they are still let in, but 25 cents extra is charged for the trouble of rising and unlocking the door. This is an objectionable regulation that should be changed. To guard against improper persons, references as to character are required in all cases. The trustees, including some of our best citizens, desire to make it a well-regulated Christian home; but they do not attempt to interfere with the opinions or liberty of the boarders. Prayers are made every evening, and those desirous of assisting at the devotional exercises can do so, or absent themselves if they choose. Applications for board can be made at any time. It is not customary to take women for less time than a week; but the rule is often violated when there is urgent reason. Sometimes women go there late at night, and, having neither reference nor money, are directed to the House of Industry or St. Barnabas. The money is insisted upon, to preserve the dignity and self-respect of the boarders, who would not remain if they considered themselves objects of charity.

The greater portion of the women are foreigners, but many of them Americans. They are generally between 18 and 35. No restriction is made about their age, beyond the fact that they must not be children, or feeble or infirm from years. Any neat, healthy, capable woman of good character is admissible as a boarder. Many of the boarders are not only intelligent, but well educated. Bookfolders, hoop-skirt-makers, cloak-makers, artists, students, teachers, and printers are among the number. They rise when they please, and go to their duties; returning as they like. They can remain in the house if so disposed. Indeed, there seem to be no more restraints upon them than there would be at any well-regulated hotel. The parlors are always open, and the library is always accessible, so they who choose can spend all the time there. At the hour for going to bed, ten o'clock, the lights are put out, and the boarders retire.

Though the boarders at the Home are more numerous than they have been—there are forty-four more now than there were on the first of last month—there are not nearly so many as there should be.

The idea that the Home may be considered a kind of charity, which is so abhorrent to the American mind, has prevented many persons from going there, particularly those of native birth. Some abuses, too, have either crept into the institution, or are believed to have done so,—and the effect is the same. The Home has been avoided, without good reason, and the objections urged against it, even if well-grounded, might easily be removed.

There ought to be dozens of such homes in New-York, and there will be, no doubt, in a few years. Compared to tenement houses, they are a blessing, and offer inducements apart from economy that few working women can afford to dispense with.

During the year, the receipts have paid the current expenses, and next year will yield, probably, a small interest on the investment.

The principal obstacle to its complete success is its fancied charitable character. But it is no more a charity than the Fifth Avenue or Metropolitan hotel is a charity. Its boarders pay all that is asked of them. No obligation is imposed, no favor conferred. Persons there, are, and should feel, as independent as in their own household. The trustees and incorporators, among whom are many of our best citizens, are anxious to have the Home filled, and are gratified when it is well patronized. Most of the boarders are young women. Not a few of them have been married, and are still; but their husbands are dissipated, and squander their wives' earnings. Consequently the wives have come to the Home as to a kind of asylum, and live there practically divorced until their husbands die or reform. The Home has not been patronized by the class one would expect—the poorest; but by those who are in comparatively comfortable circumstances.

Some of the boarders earn $10 to $12, and even $15 to $16 a week, though the majority have no more than $6 to $7. They can live for almost half of that, which enables them to save $100 or so during the year.

The institution is excellent, and in a great centre like New-York, very necessary. It will be imitated, no doubt, in other cities, and certainly deserves to be.

CHAPTER LXIV.

THE MILITARY.

The Metropolis delights in the military, and might aptly sing the popular song from Offenbach's opera, now so much in vogue. The parades of its different regiments the City enjoys like a fresh-hearted child. Whenever they turn out the streets are crowded, and busy Broadway and the fashionable avenues stand and stare with admiring eyes. Constant displays never seem to tire the Gothamites, whose appetite for shows and spectacles can not be sated.

Manhattan, from the earliest time, has had a military force for its protection, and it needs such protection to-day more than it ever did before. Its military organizations have always been numerous and effective, and very creditable specimens of citizen-soldiery. They have shown themselves worthy of trust and praise in time of need, and are really essential to the City's security and well-being. They have been styled holiday-soldiery, and carpet-knights, and taunted with the epithets; but when good service was wanted the ridiculed regiments rendered it promptly and courageously.

In all great cities the military are, if an evil, a necessary evil. But for military aid New-York would have suffered incalculably in times past. The times when it prevented or suppressed riot and bloodshed are memorable, and many of them of recent date. When the abolition mob raged here, long ago, the City soldiery prevented the houses and stores of many residents from being torn down. During the great fire of 1835, which destroyed the entire business portion of the town, the military came out after the firemen had been exhausted, volunteered their services, and worked day and night until the flames were subdued. The flour riots that followed in the Spring would have ended very disastrously if the soldiers had not awed the mob into quietude, and frightened them into dispersion.

When Mayor Clark, in 1837, was elected, the banks had concluded to suspend specie payments, and fearing that the movement would cause a riot, he called out the military. They took their position before Trinity church, planted cannon there, and pointed them down Wall street. Those iron monitors kept the peace. The precaution was wise; for the suspension caused great excitement, which would have burst into fury and destruction but for the armed preparation.

The famous Astor-Place opera-house riots, in the spring of 1849, were caused by the adherents of Forrest, who resolved to mob Macready, then playing there, because, as they alleged, the English tragedian had created prejudice against the American when he was in London. Some of the most notorious rowdies in the Metropolis were in the mob, and while the tumult was at its height the Seventh regiment was ordered out. It was then, as now, composed of young men of standing and education, and was called in derision the "kid-glove" and "dandy" regiment. The roughs did not suppose the luxurious Seventh would be of any service, and shouted defiance when it was ordered to fire. It did fire, however, and wounded several persons, and showed such determination and courage that it put down the mob.

When the present Metropolitan police were created by the legislature, during Fernando Wood's first term of mayoralty, and he, at the head of the City police, refused to acknowledge their authority, there was as fine a prospect for municipal war as there ever has been in the City. Wood was in the City Hall; the Park was full of his police, armed with revolvers and clubs; and he had sworn he would not permit the warrant that had been issued for his arrest to be served upon him. The Metropolitan police were under the command of Simeon Draper, and it was that body which was particularly offensive to Wood. While there was every probability of a hostile collision, the Seventh regiment, on its way to Boston, marched down Broadway, and General Sanford, who had charge of the militia, halted them, and ordered them to serve the warrant. The City police insisted it was their right and duty; but the General, believing that such an attempt would cause bloodshed, demanded that the military should perform the service. They did. An officer entered the Park and the City Hall, and served the writ upon Fernando Wood, who had declared again and again that he would not surrender alive. The presence of the soldiers either overawed him, or caused him to change his opinion; for he made no resistance, no further menaces. The serious complication was quieted without trouble; but if it had been left to the two bodies of police, no doubt hundreds of lives would have been lost.

A few years ago the state militia was converted into the National State Guard, which is the best organization we have yet had. The regiments in the City are called the First division, and include the following: First, Second, Third, Fourth, Fifth, Sixth, Seventh, Eighth, Ninth, Eleventh, Twelfth, Twenty-second, Thirty-seventh, Fifty-fifth, Sixty-ninth, Seventy-first, Seventy-ninth, Ninety-sixth, First Artillery, Washington Gray Cavalry, First Cavalry, Second Cavalry. They are well equipped, well drilled, and well armed, and have a true soldierly pride in their organization. Of the different regiments and battalions few are complete.

The crack regiments are the Seventh, Ninth, Twenty-second, and Fifty-seventh, of which the Seventh is, of course, the most renowned, if not the best.

The whole division numbers about 13,000 men, who are of a superior order. They include various nationalities, and many of the members have seen and made part of numerous well-fought fields. When the War broke out, they proved that they were not soldiers in time of peace only, by volunteering promptly, and marching to Washington almost in a body.

The city sent 100,000 men to the field, though, of course, a large proportion of those enlisted were from other cities and towns—part of the throng of strangers who find their way here by a natural law. Of the entire number enlisted, 9,000 were killed and wounded, and 37,000 served as officers during the rebellion.

When any of the four crack regiments turn out, particularly the Seventh, men, women, and children turn out likewise, and stand by the hour on the corners which it is known they will pass. It is singular, this curiosity, this fondness for sight-seeing of New-Yorkers, who, in many things, are so *blasé;* yet, in others, so excitable.

Waving plumes, gold lace, flashing bayonets, swells of

music, seem to have strong magnetic power for the populace. Not infrequently the lines of stages are drawn off, and the whole tide of vehicular travel interrupted, that the pompous parade may be seen to advantage. The chief defect of the Metropolis is, that it has but one good thoroughfare,—Broadway,—and for that reason any public demonstration here is much more of a nuisance than of an attraction. But our citizens forget all inconveniences when their eye is appealed to and their love of display gratified.

Considering the immense number of scoundrels and desperadoes here, New-York needs a stronger body than her two thousand police to prevent the terrible riots that might any moment be directed against property and life. We have had instances, again and again, of the dangerous element in the midst of us. We know how formidable and ferocious it is, though it hides from the sunshine, and many deem it non-existent because invisible. We can detect, at any time, if we will go out of our accustomed paths, the dens of the desperate men who have neither conscience nor heart; who would rob for pleasure; burn for malignity; murder for excitement. There are thousands and tens of thousands of such wretches within musket-shot of the fashionable promenades and business quarters, and I can not help but think that their knowledge that the transmission of a message over the wires would bring 13,000 disciplined, determined, experienced men to confront them with deadly weapons, exercises a wholesome restraint.

That is a small army, and would be more than a match for ten times the number of villains and criminals with no higher courage than brutal strength and desire for plunder and rapine give. I fancy nervous people who have property, parents who have fair daughters, fine men who have lovely wives, rest more calmly over this volcano because they remember that the means of extinguishing its fierce fires, should they burst forth, are near at hand.

The military have an honorable record in New-York, and are indispensable to its security. They are not costly, for each regiment receives but $500 a year from the City for its armory; all their other expenses being met by the members themselves. They keep up the soldierly spirit, and preserve a wholesome feeling of rivalry among the different corps. They do a deal of good in various ways, and like sentinels in camp make it safe for virtue, and wealth, and beauty to sleep while the enemy is near.

Broadway can not exist without its sensations. I was recalling the other day the many and different ones it had had; and it occurred to me that the grandest of all was the departure of the Seventh regiment for the War, in the Spring of 1861.

Broadway was never so thronged before. Every window, every square foot of space, every doorway, was crowded. The Seventh, composed of the élite and culture of the town, marched from Eighth street to Cortlandt; marched, it was believed, to martyrdom; but marched unflinchingly, determinedly, heroically to meet their doom for their dear country's welfare.

It was two days after the killing of the Massachusetts soldiers in Baltimore, when the entire North was in a state of doubt and anxiety about the issues of the Rebellion.

Such a greeting as the regiment received. A storm of handkerchiefs, a deep, earnest, prolonged cheer, and the tens of thousands of men and women standing there with wet eyes, and unuttered prayers upon their lips. The scene was more trying to the gallant soldiers than any shock of battle could have been. They were like marble; moved like machines; looked not to the right or the left, lest the eager face of a loved friend might, with its intense sympathy, stir emotions that could not be controlled. They went on; and before, and behind, and around them, the deep expression of admiration, sympathy, and love, roared like a boisterous and melancholy sea.

There were fine natures, generous souls, chivalrous spirits, marching stoutly, as it was thought, to death, through the spotless gates of honor.

There Theodore Winthrop, the knightly gentleman and fearless soldier, walked beside his howitzer, no more to return alive, but to come home dead upon the gun, all draped in crape and wrapped with the banner of stars, the Nation mourning him as heroes are ever mourned.

Sad, eventful day, it will never be forgotten. It was one of the first great impulses, the deep agonies of the vast struggle which made ambition virtue and courage patriotism.

Broadway had never seen its like; has never since; will never see it again. Those who witnessed it bear it in mind as an inspiration and an era of painful joy. The mighty City felt the going of the Seventh regiment to its heart's core. The event has never been described as it ought to have been. It thrilled through the land. It gave the country five hundred thousand soldiers; it was the beginning of the War, the nerver of the struggle, the guarantee of victory.

CHAPTER LXV.

THE FIRE DEPARTMENT.

The abandonment of the old system of the Volunteer Fire Department, and the adoption of the present Paid Department in New-York has been a very efficient cause of diminished lawlessness and ruffianism in the City.

Rowdyism never received two such severe blows as the establishment of the Metropolitan Police and the Paid Fire Department gave it, and it will never recover from them. The old police system encouraged ruffianism and disorder, by insuring to ruffians and criminals immunity from punishment, and the engine houses furnished them shelter and rallying points for additional outrages. The engine houses were indeed the abiding places and recruiting offices for the worst class of our population.

The old police were the aiders and abettors—often the friends and companions—of the fire-boy roughs; and between the two, rowdyism had an organization and a system that made it a power in the municipal government most formidable for evil.

For years before the City Police and the Volunteer Department were abolished, every intelligent person saw that they were the most serious impediments we had to contend with in the establishment of public peace and private security. All the clamor against them, all the earnest effort to get rid of them, were of no avail until the desperate condition of affairs in the City transferred the appointment of the police to the State, in 1857.

The conflict on the 9th of June of that year, for the possession of the Street Commissioner's office, when Fernando Wood, as Mayor, refused to surrender the keys, and the Governor ordered his arrest, is still fresh in the minds of the public. The Mayor resisted, and the old police under him sided against the Metropolitans, causing a fierce fight on the steps of the City Hall, in which many were wounded.

On the evening of July 4th the trouble, which seemed to have been settled, broke out anew, and caused what is known as the Dead Rabbit Riot. The Dead Rabbits—loafers and roughs, thieves and convicts, belonging to the Five Points—were on the side of the old police, and attacked the Metropolitan patrolmen in the Bowery. The Bowery Boys, then a notorious organization of fighting men, supported the police, and a series of riots ensued in the Sixth Ward; the women of that locality hurling bricks, stones, and other missiles, from the houses, upon the heads of the Metropolitans. The military were called out, and suppressed the riots, but not before twelve persons had been killed and more than two hundred wounded.

The Dead Rabbits were actually dead after that; but the Bowery Boys lingered on until the adoption of the Paid Fire Department, four years ago, which put a quietus upon the Boys, and removed almost every trace of their noxious existence.

The reformation of the engine houses had the same

The Fire Department.

effect on the rowdies who frequented them, that the breaking of pots of earth has upon the plants they contain. The roughs lost their rendezvous, their asylums, and they disappeared as an organization. New-York still has rowdies in excess, but they are less numerous and far less dangerous than ever before; and the Paid Fire Department is the new boundary between past disorder and present improvement.

The Metropolitan Fire Department is under the control of a Board of Commissioners, five in number, who have their office in Firemen's Hall, 127 and 129 Mercer street, where all the affairs of the Department are transacted. The Department has one Chief Engineer, at a salary of $4,500; one Assistant Engineer, at $2,500; ten District Engineers, each at $1,800; forty-five Foremen of Companies, each at $1,300; thirty Assistant Foremen, each at $1,000; thirty-two Engineers of Steamers, each at $1,200; four hundred and one privates, each at $1,000; five hundred and nineteen men in all.

The engine houses, sixty-three in number, have been materially altered and improved since the abandonment of the old system. The volunteer firemen had done much damage to the houses, and in many cases had claimed, carried off, and stolen private property. The buildings were erected by the City at great cost, many of them having been elegantly decorated by private contributions; and since they have been repaired they are very comfortable and handsome. The paid firemen feel a pride in them, and instead of lounging about the doorways, carousing and fighting, and often insulting passers-by, as their predecessors did, they occupy well-furnished sitting rooms while awaiting duty.

The number of hand-engines is nine, of steam-engines in active service thirty-four, and in reserve eight. The hose carriages and hook and ladder companies are respectively fifteen and eight. The second class steamers have been found the best for general and efficient service, and cost about $4,000 apiece.

The cost of the Paid Fire Department the past year was nearly $900,000, while that of the volunteer system during its last year was less than $600,000, though it must be remembered that about $700,000 of the former expense was for the pay of the force. Whatever the increase in expenditure, there is no doubt the Paid Department is much more serviceable and effective in extinguishing and preventing fires than was the Volunteer.

On an alarm of fire an average of one-sixth of the entire force goes to the place designated, and if the alarm be repeated the number is increased to one-third. The time required for harnessing the horses and leaving the engine house is twenty-five seconds.

The present force is under almost military discipline, and furnishes a marked contrast to the volunteers. A few years ago a fire in New-York was a revolution, caused much more clamor and excitement than a change of Government in Mexico or the South American Republics. When the alarm was sounded the town was turned upside down. A wild mob rushed through the streets with the engines, bellowing through their trumpets, hallooing at the top of their voices to the terror and danger of all quiet citizens. A fire then was little less than a riot. It furnished excitement to the idle, and an opportunity for the dishonest. Dwellings and stores, near the fire, were often broken open and plundered under pretense of saving property. Anybody could act as a fireman. There was no order, no restriction, no responsibility.

With the new system every thing is different. Order and discipline take the place of numbers. The police exclude all persons not members of the force, and each man does his own work. Robberies at fires, once the rule, have now become a rare exception. As an instance, not long ago, during a fire near Tiffany & Co.'s great jewelry establishment, in Broadway, the firemen had access to every part of the building. They could have stolen and concealed small articles of great value without any fear of detection, and yet nothing whatever was taken, a fact that the firm gratefully acknowledged at the time. The members of the force, as a class, are sober, intelligent, and exemplary citizens, as unlike their predecessors as it is easy to imagine.

The whole number of fires during the past year was 873, incurring losses of $5,711,000, being $717,736 less than the loss of the year previous. It is believed that the number of fires will steadily decrease as the department is improved and perfected. New-York has long been famous for fires, and many foreigners religiously believe there is no hour of the twenty-four that some building is not burning down here. No wonder they thought so once. We have made a reformation, however, and before many years a fire will be as unusual in New-York as it is in London.

Many of the fires are incendiary; but such increased vigilance has been instituted that they must grow rarer and rarer. It has long been observed that the dullness of trade in the City acts like a combustible, and that well-insured stocks of goods when not in active demand are in the greatest peril of being burned. This phenomenon has never been satisfactorily explained, though there are doubters of human integrity who claim to account for it by natural causes.

The fire-alarm telegraph has greatly improved in its working, but would be still more effective if the Relay & Bell magnet, with the Morse key, were introduced into the engine houses, so that alarms could be sent out for other stations than their own. The expense attending the purchase of the best apparatus would be so large that the Commissioners have refrained from obtaining it. The fire stations of the City are about 500, and are indicated by the striking of the bells in the towers according to the numbers. Thus, 323 is the corner of Twenty-sixth street and Eighth avenue. Ten strokes give the general alarm; then follow three strokes in quick succession; a pause; two more strokes; a pause, and three strokes, which, by consulting a little pamphlet distributed throughout the City, shows almost the exact location of the fire.

All the fires, with important particulars, are telegraphed to police head-quarters in Mulberry street, where the reporters of the daily papers obtain their information without going to the spot, which, in a city like New-York, would often occupy more time than could be spared between the occurrence of the fire and the hour of publication.

The bell-towers in different parts of the town are furnished with excellent bells, that can be heard to a great distance. The bells at the Post-office, City Hall, Union and Jefferson Markets, are among the most famous and resonant; three of them are new, and well sustain the reputation of the old.

The condition of the firemen, morally and physically,

is very good. They keep their uniforms, their apparatus, and their horses exceedingly neat; showing much of the care and pride about person and property that regular soldiers feel. It used to be said that men who were hired would not be found to discharge the duties like volunteers; but the experiment has proved exactly the opposite.

The Commissioners have constant applications for situations, and whenever vacancies occur, there are at least ten candidates for each vacancy. The spirit of rivalry which once resulted in violent quarrels, fights, and riots, now reveals itself in a spirit of generous emulation, that redounds to the general advantage and efficacy of the Department.

The fire insurance companies, more deeply interested than any other portion of the community, bear witness to the great superiority of the new system over the old. Improvements are being made steadily, and, though New-York is still behind other and smaller cities in its Fire Department, it is likely that in a few years it will be equal to any of them.

No one living out of the Metropolis can realize what a great relief and advance the Paid Department is. Instead of being a nuisance and a nest of rowdyism and vice, it is a protection, an insurer of the public peace, and a municipal benefaction.

CHAPTER LXVI.

RACING AND FAST HORSES.

The Metropolis has "developed" in nothing more rapidly than in the quality of its horses. The last ten or twelve years have made a revolution in horse-flesh. Men now drive, and have an enthusiasm about blooded stock, who, until recently, had no interest in the turf, or any thing belonging to it. They were satisfied to jog along behind slow and sober steeds, until, catching the fetlock fever, they subscribed to *The Spirit of the Times*, and spent thousands of dollars in making additions to their stables.

America has been imitating England, the North following the South, in making the turf one of the pleasures proper and honorable to the class of gentlemen. The time when men owning and delighting in horses were contemptuously spoken of as "jockeys," no longer exists. No man of the world, who has liberal means and aspires to fashion, considers his establishment complete without a well-supplied stable. Our first men of business, and even members and dignitaries of the church, possess and enjoy handsome roadsters, and discuss their "time" and "bottom" over the dinner-table, in the counting-room, and in ecclesiastical portals.

The opening of the Central Park, with its fine drives, has, more than any thing else, given a new interest to fast horses and fine stables. The Park is a magnificent place to exhibit horses, and men buy them for the privilege of displaying their good points and high spirit there. Any pleasant afternoon you can see in the Park the change it has wrought upon persons who like to move rapidly on wheels.

The race-courses of New-York have, until recently, been on Long Island. The Centreville has fallen into disuse; but the Fashion, Union, and Long Island tracks are still the scenes of spirited contests between trotters. They are not so popular as they once were; for they are out of the way, and the roads leading to them not desirable. Ten or fifteen years ago, the most remarkable contests were on those tracks, both by running and trotting horses. Eclipse and Sir Henry had their great struggle; Fashion made her famous running time; Gray Eagle and Wagner awoke wild enthusiasm; Lady Suffolk, Flora Temple, George M. Patchen, Dexter, Gen. Butler, Whalebone, Lantern, Mountain Boy, and other celebrated trotters have shown their best speed on the Long Island courses. Of late, only trotters have gone upon those tracks, which though very good, decrease each season in public favor.

The Jerome Park, the newest and finest course in the country, at Fordham, Westchester county, is now devoted to running races exclusively. It is named after Leonard W. Jerome, the well-known turfman and Wall street operator, who gave the land for the purpose. The Jerome Park is managed and controlled by the members of the American Jockey Club,—citizens of fortune and education, of high social position, and prominent in business circles. Their intention has been to make the turf respectable; to render racing a refined and dignified recreation among gentlemen, and to remove from it all unfairness and trickery. This has been accomplished, and the races at Jerome Park resemble the Derby in England, and the Longchamps in France. The best class of people, of both sexes, attend, and the grand display is well worth witnessing.

The men and women dress for the Jerome Park, though in different style, as they do for the opera or an evening reception. They are brave and gallant; look their prettiest, and behave their best. You see there the Broadway merchant and Beaver street importer, the Broad street broker and exchange place banker, the Nassau street journalist and Fifth avenue dandy, the club-lounger and Tenth street artist, the belle of Madison avenue and the leader of Twenty-third street fashion, the majestic entertainer of Fifth avenue and the charming coquette of Stuyvesant square. Silks and laces, velvets and jewels, plumes and perfumes, flowers and brocades, ravishing beauties and chivalrous cavaliers, are there in profusion. The Park is an excellent place to witness the fashion, and wealth, and culture of the City; and the races there often become secondary, as an attraction, to the brilliant crowd in attendance.

Another show-place for fine trotters is Peter Dubois's track, near McComb's dam, where, on any fair afternoon, most of the fine horses owned by private gentlemen can be seen. Many a friendly contest is had there; and speed is reached, not unfrequently, that surprises the drivers themselves. Dubois's is growing more and more into favor, and several hundreds of thousands of dollars' worth of blooded stock is visible there in a few hours, during the pleasant Spring and Autumn months.

Harlem lane is still another field for the display of fine stock. General Grant was invited there when he visited New-York, after the close of the Rebellion, and was delighted with the splendid turn-outs that dashed before and around him, doing honor to the occasion. It is an excellent trotting-ground, and has a wide reputation with lovers of the turf.

Samuel N. Pike, of opera-house fame, is soon to lay out a splendid race-course, on the New-Jersey flats. He has a very liberal way of doing things, and will, no doubt, give New-York something to be proud of.

Among the many gentlemen who own blooded and expensive horses, Robert Bonner, of *The Ledger,* is the most conspicuous. In his stables are Dexter (the fastest trotter in the World—his best time being $2:17\frac{1}{2}$), the Auburn horse, Young Pocahontas, Peerless, Lady Palmer, Lantern, and Flatbush Maid. Bonner, though willing to spend any sum for a good horse, is conscientiously opposed to racing, and will not consent to any contest for money, under any circumstances. He will not sell horses, either. He gave $25,000 or $30,000 for Dexter, and would not part with him for twice the amount. The value of his blooded stock is not less than $100,000 to $150,000. He has an ambition to own the fastest trotters in America; and, no doubt, if some horse were to do a mile inside of Dexter's best, Bonner would pay $100,000 for him. He has been urged again and again to trot Dexter against some other fleet animal, but his invariable reply is, that $2:17\frac{1}{2}$ must be beaten before the proposition is even entertainable. The only way he will bet is to put up a certain amount on his horse's capacity to trot a mile within a certain time. If he don't, Bonner will give the amount named to a charitable purpose.

The famous journalist seems to have almost as much interest in horses as in *The Ledger*. He is what might be called, if there were any such word, an equinarian. He takes the same care of his beloved steeds that a parent does of a favorite child. He studies their comfort in every way, and his handsome stables are models of horse-homes. Every day he visits his elegant stalls; examines his fleet property; fondles and talks to it in the tenderest manner. They know him thoroughly, and will, no doubt, in time, be induced to write for *The Ledger*. Almost every afternoon he drives in the Park or Harlem lane, on Dubois's track, or to High Bridge, in a double team; and his splendid turn-out always attracts attention on the road.

Cornelius Vanderbilt, after Bonner, is probably the greatest horse-fancier in Manhattan. He has long been anxious to buy Dexter and some other of the journalist's blooded stock; but he can't, with all his millions. The Commodore owns a dozen fine horses; but his best and fastest are Mountain Boy, Post Boy, and Mountain Girl, which could not be purchased at less than fabulous figures, as Vanderbilt, like *The Ledger* proprietor, is a buyer, not a seller.

William Turnbull, a prosperous merchant, is a prominent turf-man and lover of horses. He has extensive and costly stables; and, among other crack trotters, boasts of Commodore Vanderbilt, Lew Pettee, and Willie Schepper.

William Simmons, the wealthy broker, shows off his two fast trotters, George Wilkes and Honest Allen, in the Park drives and along the Bloomingdale road (now Broadway), when the weather is favorable, and has several roadsters beside.

Daniel L. Pettee, the South street iron merchant, has Ella Sherwood. Gardiner G. Howland, the well-known merchant, owns and drives Lady Irving and mate. George B. Allen, the Broad street broker; Edward Matthews, Jerome B. Fellows, Lester Wallack, E. T. Simmons, and many others, have fine trotters in their stables.

Among the owners of running horses are August Belmont, the banker; William R. Travers, the William street broker; John Hunter, M. H. Sanford, Leonard W. Jerome, Francis and Lewis Morris, James S. Watson, Paul Forbes, and others. They all have fine stables, in which numerous thorough-bred roadsters may be found, faring almost as daintily as the celebrated stallion that Caligula made consul.

The number of superb horses that are owned and driven here, though they may not be called fast in sporting circles, is very large. It is not uncommon for men of business and retired merchants to have stables that have cost from $10,000 to $50,000, and not a few have expended $100,000 on horse-flesh alone.

Fast stock and betting are like cause and effect. Owners of good horses always have faith enough in them to back their performances with money; and, consequently, laying wagers on races is becoming more and more a custom and a fashion. Whenever a contest is to take place over the Union, Fashion, or Long Island courses, or at the Jerome Park, pools are advertised and sold at some well-known place, like Lafayette Hall, or the Astor House, or some club, or rendezvous of the sporting fraternity.

Pool selling is managed in this way: The man who sells the pools asks those present how much is betted on the choice of, say four horses,—Dexter, Mountain Boy, Lantern, and Bruno. A bets $1,000, and takes Dexter; B bets $300, and takes Mountain Boy; C bets $150, and takes Lantern; D bets $50, and takes Bruno. Of course, Dexter is the favorite; but the smaller amounts laid on the other horses are thought to make the chances about even. The pool is $1,500, and the better on the winning horse gets the whole amount.

Pool-selling usually draws a crowd, when the race is an interesting one. All sorts of people attend it,—turfmen of fashion, blacklegs, loafers, merchants, and pickpockets. Betting and racing make strange companions, and establish a bond of sympathy between persons of the most different calling and character.

Men who experience a passion for horses are often more affected by it than by any other passion. It seems to absorb them. They turn to the subject on all occasions, and their conversation is interlarded with phrases borrowed from the stable. Horses are a source of profound pleasure to many of our citizens, as is evident to one who drives out to the Park or Harlem lane, Dubois's track, or High Bridge. He will see, at any of those places, splendid turn-outs, from the single horse in a light buggy to the pretentious four-in-hand. Long strides, crimson nostrils, sleek coats, whirling wheels, admiring faces, tightened reins, clouds of dust, with a general rapidity of life and a great enthusiasm for the road, will be strikingly apparent. Our fashionable turf-men would be wretched without their daily drive. It is meat and drink for them. Every year it grows more a necessity of their daily life, and is now the brightest segment in their round of pleasure.

CHAPTER LXVII.

GIFT ENTERPRISES AND SWINDLES.

CITIES take the nonsense out of a man, it has been said. They do more: they take his purse whenever they have a chance; and the longer it is, the more apt he is to lose it. New-York, particularly, is armed against unsophisticated strangers, and offers the services of its sons to relieve them of the last dollar they have at the earliest moment, and with the most imperturbable audacity.

William Sharp stands in Broadway and the Bowery, in Chatham and West street, waiting for his good friend, John Greenhorn; takes John to his bosom, and robs John according to the code of metropolitan morals.

Hundreds of persons in this City live year after year by plundering those whose homes are in the country. Frequently they have an opportunity to swindle the rustics in town; but so many of the latter fail to visit Manhattan that it behooves Sharp to communicate with John upon his native heath.

To do this effectually Gift Enterprises, as they are called, have been established. They extend throughout the country; all credulous men, women and children are made parties to the liberal scheme. The Enterprises are managed thus: the principal office is located in New-York, with branches in Boston, Philadelphia, Baltimore, Chicago, and all the principal cities. The managers call themselves Boggs, Simpkins & Co., or Thompson, Jones & Smith, take an office in some prominent quarter—Broadway is their favorite—and advertise in all the country papers that they are to have a grand concert at Irving, Tammany, or Apollo Hall, when a drawing of handsome prizes will take place. A list of the prizes then follows, and is of a very tempting character. Gold watches, diamond pins, pearl bracelets, melodeons, pianos, emerald rings, horses and carriages, are offered, with the statement that the prizes will, if required, be exchanged for money.

The managers of the concert get hold of directories of various cities, country newspapers, letter lists, subscription lists to newspapers, and obtain from them thousands of names. To those names, all over the country, they direct neatly lithographed circulars, setting forth the advantages in glowing terms of the proposed concert and drawing. It is expressly stated that any one taking a set of tickets, fifteen in number, will be guaranteed a prize worth at least $100, on condition that the person receiving the prize will show it to his or her friends, and inform them how and where he or she got it.

The tickets are $1 each; but, as a special inducement, it is declared that a set will be sent for $10, if the tickets are distributed. By such means the cupidity of credulous people is appealed to. They fancy they will have a handsome reward for their pains. They make an effort to merit the prize, and usually dispose of the entire set of tickets. They inclose $10 to Boggs, Simpkins & Co., dream of what they will secure, very much as children dream of hung-up stockings on Christmas eve, and never hear any thing more of their money or the concert.

Possibly they come to town, and try to find out something about the firm. They call at the office. It is handsomely furnished; but Boggs can't be found, nor Simpkins, nor the Co. Each one of the firm has gone somewhere. They may call again and again; but it will always be with the same result. The truth is there is no such person as Boggs or Simpkins. The managers are fictitious; have a nominal existence only to swindle.

If the question is laid before the police nothing can be done. The ticket admits the holder to a concert when it takes place; but the date is never given. The managers have a right to charge what they choose to an entertainment, and to offer any prizes they see fit. These Gift Enterprises have been so often exposed of late that they don't meet with such success as they used to. But still there are persons verdant enough to be imposed upon, and will be, no doubt, for many years.

The managers of such swindles often claim to have drawings; giving as prizes, watches, rings, and bracelets, valued at such and such a rate. If the victims have received a watch for $200, worth $10 or $15, and seek redress, the swindlers say *they* valued it at $200; but the worth of it is quite another thing; and so evade the law again.

A very common mode of operation is for a fictitious firm to inclose a lithographed note to some one, whose name they have obtained in the manner already described, stating that he has drawn a prize valued at $200; that the rules of the company require payment of five or ten per cent. upon all prizes drawn; that, therefore, on receipt of $5 or $10, the prize, usually a gold watch, will be sent by express.

The person into whose hands the note falls knows he has never bought a ticket, but presumes he has been mistaken for somebody else. His covetousness is appealed to. He is tempted into dishonesty. He becomes a party to the fraud; incloses the sum demanded, and of course that is the end of the matter. He is naturally ashamed to confess his weakness, and the swindlers in turn profit by his cupidity.

Still another trick is to send a circular to one of the greenhorns in the country, inclosing a ten-cent note postal currency (genuine), informing him that if he wants one hundred of the notes for a dollar, he can get them by inclosing the amount. The packets are from $10 to $100. The swindler says the currency will do for betting or making a show, but does not mention any thing about passing it as counterfeit money. Greenhorn sees the postal currency looks well, and after investigation learns that it is good. He immediately jumps at the idea of getting ten dollars for one dollar, and writes with inclosure. It is needless to say he never receives an answer to his letter, and does not deserve to.

Drawings for money are advertised, prizes $5, $10, $50, and $100, up to $500 and $1,000. A confidential circular is sent, and the recipient is told if he will aid the managers in making their lottery known, that he shall have a prize of $100. Numerous tickets and circulars are forwarded for his distribution. Whether he does any thing with them or not he pretends to, and writes the firm to that effect. The swindlers return answer that they have set aside $100 for his services; inquire if he will have the money remitted by a draft or in Treasury notes; and add incidentally that five per cent., according to the inflexible rule of the firm, is always charged for such advances.

The unsophisticated fellow sends $5, and loses it instead of getting $95 for nothing, as he fondly imagined.

These scoundrels have still another device. They send a packet of tickets for a lottery to anybody whose name they have procured, requesting that he will return the money for them by mail. Of course no man is foolish enough to do that. The tickets are returned, left in the Post-office, or destroyed with some indignation.

In two or three weeks another circular is mailed to the effect that no doubt the person addressed had remitted the money, but that, owing to postal detention or failure, it had not been received. The lottery dealers inform him one of the tickets has drawn a prize, and that it will be forwarded as soon as the percentage, five per cent., is sent to the address. The prize named is generally $100 or $200. Verdant hastens to mail $5 or $10, and the firm is silent forever after as the grave,

Sham jewelry establishments and one dollar stores are the abode of swindlers. Every thing sold there is manufactured for the purpose. It is not what it appears; and those who patronize the concerns are wheedled out of their money always. They are sold fine silver and gold watches that prove pewter and brass; and yet, by a quibble or some kind of adroitness, no hold is given to the law.

Mock auctions, though not so common as they used to be, are still carried on in Broadway, the Bowery, Canal street, and Third avenue. The buyers who are in the stores are all in league with the auctioneers. They bid up the goods, praise them, declare them great bargains; offer to give greenhorn twice what he pays if he will call at their place of business; and he fancies they are strangers, and honest like himself. The auctioneer exhibits one article; greenhorn buys it, and before he gets it, it is exchanged for something else.

A good gold watch is offered, and knocked down for $20, though it is evidently worth five times the amount. The watch handed over to the countryman is pure brass, its value $2 or $3. If he attempts to get his money back, he is outsworn by a dozen audacious fellows, who protest before high Heaven that he never paid more than $2 for the watch. They threaten him too, and if he is not a man of nerve, they intimidate him. Generally he deems himself lucky to escape with an unbroken crown, and is in no mood for searching after the money he has been defrauded of.

New-York must have several hundreds of these gift enterprises and swindling establishments. No one is responsible for them. No actual legal guilt can be fixed upon them. The police have broken them up time after time; but they arise in another place. They seem perfectly irrepressible. They will continue while some men are dishonest and others are credulous; and in such a city as New-York it is not likely they will ever cease to exist. It is wonderful in this day of general education and universal newspaper circulation, that so many persons can be defrauded by such shallow tricks as those that have been described.

One of the most extraordinary frauds since the War was that of the Gettysburg Asylum, which was to be a home for invalid and crippled soldiers of the Union cause. The managers had actually obtained a charter from Pennsylvania in consideration of $10,000, and several Northern Generals were induced to lend their names to the scheme. Magnificent prizes were offered, a brown-stone mansion in Fifth avenue, a farm, a lot of splendid diamonds, $100,000 in Treasury notes, and rosewood pianos among the rest. Their complete value, according to the advertisements, was $700,000, and they were to be distributed among 1,200,000 ticket-holders at $1 apiece.

The papers were full of the lottery; a small ship used to be drawn up and down Broadway, distributing circulars; every effort was made to call attention to the swindle. About one million tickets were sold, when it was discovered that the managers of the enterprise were notorious lottery dealers in Baltimore.

Pennsylvania withdrew its charter, and the Generals their names. The scheme began to look fraudulent, but the advertisements were kept up; a concert was given at Irving Hall; the crowd in attendance was assured all the promises would be redeemed. A fortnight after, the whole thing fell to pieces.

The public lost a million, and to this day not a single ticket has been worth the paper it was printed on.

For all who feel tempted to invest money in lotteries and prize concerts, it would be well to remember that any man who proposes to give more than dollar for dollar in any way is a designing scoundrel seeking for a victim.

CHAPTER LXVIII.

THE WICKEDEST WOMAN IN THE CITY.

The wickedest woman in New York, according to the popular verdict, is no doubt Madame Restell, the famous or infamous " female physician and professor of midwifery," as she is styled in her advertisements and in the City Directory.

Some sixteen or seventeen years ago she was arrested and tried for abortion; and the death of a young woman, who had been put under the Madame's treatment to conceal a story of sin and shame, was laid at the midwife's door.

Restell lived in Chambers street then, and was comparatively obscure. Her trial created intense excitement all over the country. The newspapers teemed with its details, and editorials upon editorials were written, reflecting severely and eloquently upon the crime with which she was charged. Enough evidence was offered to prove her guilty, not only of the particular offense, but of numerous other offenses equally heinous.

There seemed to be no escape for her. The penitentiary stared her in the face, and if the law and justice had been administered, she would have been sent to Sing Sing for the remainder of her natural life. But she was tried in New-York, where law is one thing and justice another; where he who has the most money, or the political influence to bear upon the judge, is sure to gain his case. The Madame had liberal means, acquired by her calling, and consequently she escaped. She bought witnesses, judges, juries, it is alleged, and was duly acquitted. It was stated at the time that she purchased "justice" to the extent of $100,000, and that she considered it one of the best investments she had ever made. It certainly was, if preservation from life-long imprisonment has a value in money.

That trial of Madame Restell was a superb advertisement of her business. It made her known everywhere, and has probably been the means of adding to her fortune twice the sum she expended.

Some years after the trial she removed up town—it was considered very far up then—having purchased a lot in the Fifth avenue, corner Fifty-second street, and erected a large and comfortable brown-stone front there. She is said to have made the purchase through an agent, as the owner of the real estate would have declined to sell her the property on account of her profession and unenviable notoriety.

The fashionable thoroughfare was more and more occupied with elegant mansions. Real estate advanced in price, and as the tide of society went toward the Park, many and munificent were the offers to the midwife to dispose of her property. She was pressed to take five times the amount she paid, but she would not. She said she had bought the place for a home, and that she intended to end her days there. No importunity, no display of bank checks or bank notes could change her resolution.

There she remains, in her tall, tawdry-looking house to this day. The lots at the side of her dwelling can not be sold, even though houses built on them would be too far from hers to catch contamination. They have been offered, it is said, at one-quarter of what those on the next block have brought, but there are no takers. Lawsuits have been threatened against Restell to dispossess her; but she has no dread of law. She declares she is a regular physician, and as much entitled to practice her profession as Dr. Carnochan or Dr. Dixon. Those who are anxious to get rid of her, remember her triumph long ago, and feel that she is too rich to be prosecuted with any hope of success on the Island of Manhattan.

Restell is so notorious that she is more talked of and written about than even Greeley or Stewart. She is a godsend to correspondents of the country press, and they tell such tales of her as are related of Messalina, Sabina Pompeia, and other notably wicked women of antiquity, in the interdicted books that have come down to us.

She does precisely what might be expected from her calling, and, to those acquainted with her, makes no secret of it. She claims, say those who pretend to know her, to have done a great deal of good by preventing the errors of persons of position from coming to light; to have saved many good but unfortunate women from ruin and self-destruction; to have increased the sum of human happiness rather than to have diminished it. Her logic is peculiar, and the investigation of her premises would open a series of moral questions that are too delicate for public discussion. She declares she has possession of too many secrets of fashionable families ever to be disturbed in her home; that she is a power in the Great City, and that if she wished she could open rich and fragrant closets, and show skeletons whose existence no one suspects.

How much of her statements is true, and how much mere menace and gasconade, only she and her patrons know. There is good reason to believe, however, that a woman who has spent thirty years in a luxurious and licentious city like this, and followed her calling perseveringly, must have knowledge that would better be hidden from those who would keep their faith in human nature.

Restell advertises her medicines, her offices, her hours, and her peculiar practice, in the daily newspapers, as do dozens of the same profession. Everybody is aware of her business and her location. She can not be accused of walking in darkness, or shrouding herself in mystery.

She is reported to be immensely wealthy, but no doubt her wealth is exaggerated. She has a husband—a genuine husband, they say—to whom she was married years ago, and a daughter who is herself a wife. He is a Russian named Lohman, and is her financier. She is English, and was once a bar-maid in a London gin-shop. She came here at eighteen; made the acquaintance of a physician; obtained a smattering of medicine, and conceived the notion of adopting the calling she has since so successfully followed. Before she entered upon her present profession she was for some time a clairvoyant physician and fortune-teller, and by that trickery got a start in life. It is said she has much knowledge and skill, which she might easily have after twenty-five years of such a specialty.

Once she was handsome, I understand; but now, in her fiftieth year, she is a gross, coarse, though not heartless-looking woman, with black eyes, black hair, barely touched with gray, and might play Azucena in the opera with little "making up." Her face is familiar to many, for she drives in the Park nearly every pleasant afternoon, and her turnout is recognized by its vulgar display. She would be mistaken for the proprietress of a bagnio, with her flaring colors, her glittering jewels, her tawdry carriage, for she is the embodiment of the principle of bad taste in all that belongs to her.

Her house, No. 657 Fifth avenue, might well be her abode. The curtains are daubs of color, and every thing about it indicates vulgarity and prosperity. Those who have been inside of it say gilt and gaudiness are visible from cellar to garret. It is not at all the palace it is proclaimed to be in the country papers. On the contrary, it is rather a plain house for the Avenue, and its furniture and appurtenances, probably, cost less than those of hundreds of fashionable dwellings in that quarter.

The Madame has no society—she is a perfect pariah in New-York—but she seems to enjoy herself, and grow as fleshy as if she had the approval of a good conscience, and lived a life of innocence and good deeds. She is fond of making money; her practice is worth $30,000 a year to her; but it is said she gives liberally to those who are poor and in distress, and always without the slightest ostentation. She is reported to have sheltered many a poor girl from the pursuit of libertines, and to have restored not a few to the homes from which, in a moment of weakness and passion, they had strayed.

Let us hope this is so, for it is pleasant to believe that those who are thought the wickedest have redeeming traits.

The Wickedest Woman in the City.

This tall brown-stone dwelling in the Avenue could tell what would make sensation stories for many years, if it had the gift of tongues. Whenever I pass it, it seems to cast a deeper shadow than any other house, and a sense of chilliness, such as comes from opened vaults in the graveyard, to steal from its grim doorways and windows hung with showy curtains, which shut in what few of us dare believe, and none of us care to see.

CHAPTER LXIX.

THE MATRIMONIAL BROKERS.

Matrimonial brokers are of recent origin in New-York. They seem to prosper and decline, to flourish and fail periodically, as if affected by agencies too subtle for detection. Just at present, the season appears unfavorable. They may have an active business; but they do not advertise it as they often have done. Possibly they have become so well established that patronage flows in upon them without publication of their calling. The morning papers now contain few advertisements informing the people where they can obtain excellent wives and husbands, and thus secure their comfort and happiness for life at very small expense. In the Spring, printers' ink will be used more liberally; for then the birds choose their mates, and why shouldn't men and women go to the brokers, pay $5, and be blessed?

The advertisements—we advertise every thing in New-York,—are usually after the following fashion:—

"Marriage.—Young ladies and gentlemen desirous of being wisely and happily married, will consult their interest by applying to the undersigned, who gives all his attention to this branch of business, and who has already been very successful in bringing together persons adapted to each other by similarity of taste, temperament, and sympathy. Terms reasonable. All communications strictly confidential.

"Henry Hymen, No.—— Broadway."

"WEDDED HAPPINESS DESIRED.—It is well known that nothing conduces so much to happiness in life as a proper marriage. To avoid all mistakes in selecting partners, persons of either sex, who contemplate matrimony, should call at once on GEORGE JACOBS,
Matrimonial Broker, No.——Bleecker street.

"N. B.—Mr. Jacobs has the best of opportunities and the amplest facilities for accommodating his patrons. He has had large experience, and can say without vanity, that he has made matches for which hundreds of ladies and gentlemen are eternally grateful to him. They have acknowledged their gratitude in autograph letters, which will be shown to his patrons if desired."

"MATRIMONIAL BROKERS.—John Johnson & Co., No. ——, Bowery, offer their services to ladies wishing agreeable and wealthy husbands, or to gentlemen desiring beautiful, rich, and accomplished wives. They arrange interviews or correspondence between parties, and leave nothing undone to insure a marriage that will result to the satisfaction of all. The success that has heretofore crowned their efforts, induces them to believe they have a firm hold upon the public confidence. They respectfully solicit a continuance of patronage."

One would hardly think such advertisements could attract customers. The idea of seeking marriage before one has experienced the affection that leads to it, seems unnatural to persons who regard the relation of the sexes sentimentally. But the majority of mortals—I mean men—are matter-of-fact, and look upon every thing in a purely practical way. They marry as they buy a house or sell a horse, invest in real estate or go abroad. The reason they remain unwedded is because they don't find time to look for a wife. If any one finds her for them, and throw her in their way, they take her as they would any piece of property that seems desirable.

Matrimonial brokerage is merely match-making systematized. The brokers do for money what amateurs do for excitement and from a passion for managing. They have an uncertain trade, but yet more business than would be supposed. They don't expect much custom from home, or from cities generally; but look for it from the country people, to whom they send circulars soliciting patronage. The marriages arranged by brokers rarely turn out well; but that happens so frequently under all circumstances that it may be unjust to the profession to make them responsible for it. There have been instances of what are known as happy marriages brought about by these gents, whose mode of procedure is interesting.

Peter Pindar lives in Chenango or Cataraugus county, and comes to town. He has often read Jacobs's or Johnson & Co.'s circulars and advertisements, and they have put the notion of a wife into his head. He has a small farm; is 35 or 36 years of age; is in ordinarily comfortable circumstances; likes women; but is shy,—afraid of them, indeed; and consequently, he has never gotten along with them. It has often occurred to Peter that it would be convenient to have a wife; but the trouble and difficulty, as he imagines, of procuring one, have always stood in his way. "If I could get some fellow to do the courting," Peter has said to himself,—never recalling, because he has never read, the sad story of Paolo and Francesca,—"I'd been a husband long ago. But this popping the question I'm not equal to.

It requires a chap of more courage than I can muster." He reads over the advertisements until he has them all by heart. They impress him deeply. The opportunity he has sought seems to be at hand. He goes to the broker's, and announces the object of his visit. The broker is always distrustful of strangers, fearing they are not sincere. But, after a few minutes' talk he sees that Peter is too unsophisticated to be guilty of a ruse. The broker soon puts his customer at ease; says he knows a number of elegant and accomplished ladies who will suit him exactly."

"Perhaps I don't know what an elegant and accomplished lady is," observes Peter, "but I'm afraid it is not exactly the sort I want. I'd like a kind o' nice, good wife, that wouldn't put on too much style, and look down on a fellow because he wasn't quite as good as her."

"Certainly; you need a good, domestic woman who loves her own fireside and is bound up in her children."

"Well, if I had it my way," hesitatingly remarks Pindar, "I'd rather she wouldn't have any children that wasn't mine."

"Precisely. I mean yours, my dear sir. I wish to say, when she had made you the happy father of a beautiful offspring, that she would devote herself to the family; be an angel in her home; a presence of love and peace, filling it with sunshine, and all that sort of thing."

"Oh, yes, that is it," responds Pindar, caught by the cheap rhetoric of the broker; "that's what I want, and will pay for."

"I have a lady in my mind, now—I saw her this

morning—who will be all you desire. I shall charge you $10 for this interview. If we consummate the marriage, you will of course pay more. Our regular price is——."

"I'll do' the handsome thing. I'll give $100 cash down."

"Come day after to-morrow, Mr. Pindar, and I'll tell you the result of my negotiation. Be here at 11 o'clock."

Soon as Pindar has gone, the broker takes a letter from a drawer, and reads :—

"Dear Sir—I should be willing to accept a husband who could come well recommended; who could provide for me handsomely; who had good habits; was well educated; and was of a domestic turn. I have some reputation for beauty and accomplishment; am young, although no longer a silly girl, and would, I think, be an ornament to a well-regulated household.

"Sincerely,   Bessie Baker."

The broker drops a line to Miss Baker, soliciting an interview. She comes, and is not what might be anticipated from her note. She is probably four or five-and-thirty; has a thin face, faded blue eyes, high cheekbones; is freckled, and any thing but handsome or elegant. She talks rapidly; and is intelligent, though not very delicate or sensitive. She has been a teacher and a seamstress; has had a hard struggle with life; and, seeing the broker's advertisement one day, was tempted to write him by way of experiment.

An interview is arranged for her and Pindar in the private office. They meet, and are both disappointed.

"I would never have him," she thinks. "I would not marry her for any thing," he says to himself.

After half an hour's conversation, they find themselves mistaken. They rather like each other. He proves to be candid, upright, independent, good-hearted; she, amiable, affectionate, loyal, truthful. When they have been acquainted three days, they believe they can get along together. Pindar pays his $100 to the broker most willingly; takes Bessie Baker to Chenango as his wife; and they have lived comfortably, rearing pumpkins and babies ever since.

Not seldom, men who have mistresses they wish to get rid of apply to the matrimonial broker, and pay handsomely for the procurement of husbands. This branch of the business, it is claimed, requires unusual exertion and adroitness, and $500 is asked for the service. The man who is a candidate for marriage has no suspicion of the woman. She tells an ingenious story; proclaims herself a widow—the broker indorsing all her stories—and, by her tact and shrewdness, completely deceives him. The marriage is consummated, and strange to say, is sometimes happy; the wife resolving upon, and adhering to, a change for the better, after being invested with the dignity and bearing the responsibility of wedlock.

The brokers are not men of very high principle. They are willing to make money in almost any way. When they have an application for a wife, they are certain to supply the demand. They usually enjoy the acquaintance of a number of adventuresses—women of doubtful reputation and uncertain character. The broker makes an appointment for them; and, as they have city manners, style in dress, and much self-assertion, they are likely to make an impression upon some honest countryman's heart. He marries one of them, perhaps; or, if he does not, he forms a relation that he afterwards regrets. He is threatened with exposure and punishment, and is compelled to compromise by liberal payments. Sometimes he is surprised by a fictitious husband, who demands blood, but is finally persuaded to take money instead. The broker makes sure of his commission, and, after that, he does not concern himself about the future or the status of the couple he has introduced to each other.

The unions made by the brokers are, as I have said, unfortunate for the most part. The parties enter into them without understanding each other's character or antecedents. They quarrel and go apart, denouncing the means used to bring them together. In a number of divorce cases in the courts, it has been shown that the couple seeking separation became acquainted through the matrimonial brokers.

The broker is always a pretender and a trickster; tells more falsehoods than is needful for his trade; describes fine women he never saw; boasts of his correspondence with the members of the best society; contradicts and condemns himself—or would in dealing with a man of the world—fifty times an hour. He is perpetually tempted to become a maker of assignations; to dupe honest rustics; to palm off demireps and wantons for ladies; to swindle all who trust him; and, I am sorry to say, he almost invariably yields to the temptation without a struggle.

Recently, in New-York, matrimonial brokerage has largely passed into the hands of women, who advertise themselves as fortune-tellers and clairvoyant physicians.

The brokers are growing less matrimonial, and more and more mercenary agents for assignation. Therefore they do not advertise as they did in the public prints; but depend upon circulars and anonymous communications. They may change their tactics any time; become less dishonest and unprincipled; but, just now, the time does not presage improvement in a calling that can never have any legitimate success in the United States.

CHAPTER LXX.

HERALDRY ON THE HUDSON.

Many of our Republican Americans show such a silly passion for titles and titled persons, both at home and abroad, that it is not singular they have a secret longing for lineage of their own. Pretension having always been a characteristic, indeed a part, of vulgarity, it is very natural that ignorant men who have suddenly grown rich should wish others to believe they have distinguished ancestors and patrician blood in their plebeian veins. Still, it would not seem probable that such persons would reveal their weakness; though they might pay liberally for a coat of arms when they remember they began life in a coat without arms.

New-York furnishes facilities for the good people that have been so busy in making a fortune that they have forgotten who their ancestors were. It has, drolly enough, an office of Heraldry in Broadway, where the socially ambitious and the pecuniarily prosperous are informed, for a certain consideration, of the past glories of the family. You would imagine that any person who felt an interest in descent, and was anxious to have a noble lineage, would know more of his ancestors than entire strangers; but it is not so.

The managers of the Heraldry office are learned and ingenious gentlemen, who are generous enough to discover his forefathers. They have the history of all the nobility fresh in their memory. They can tell you all about the Norman line for five centuries; about the Saxon kings; about the very complicated Welsh nobility, and even the still more mysterious Milesian royalty. If you have any doubt of their erudition, question them respecting escutcheons, tinctures, charges, the dexter, middle and sinister chiefs, the honor, fess and nombril points, pales, bends, chevrons, crosses, saltires, lines engrailed, invected, nebuly, raguly, and dancette, and you will be amazed at their bewildering acquirements. Gules, azure, sable, vert, purpure, and tenny, color their fluent talk.

They can convince any man of ordinary vanity that he has the blood of the Plantagenets and Nevils in his veins, and that Vandyke and Lely portraits of his progenitors are looking out of costly galleries across the sea. I have said any man; but any woman would have been apter, for women are by nature aristocratic, and care far more for lineage than do the sterner sex.

The longing to be thought distinguished, it is generally observed, is in proportion to the conviction that distinction is impossible. People talk most of their "family" who have none. John Jenkins, who started as a huckster, and grew rich in spite of stupidity, is persuaded by Mrs. Jenkins to set up for a gentleman with generations of culture and luxury behind him.

Mrs. Jerusha Murphy served a long and honorable apprenticeship as a servant girl, but when she married Murphy she changed her name to Juliette, and discovered that her husband was a direct descendant of one of the countless kings of Ulster. Murphy, it must be confessed, had degenerated somewhat, for he made his appearance in New-York as a genius who long hesitated in a choice of callings between prize-fighting and bartending, but selected the latter, as it was more soothing to his sensibilities.

The Heraldry office has been established here for many years, and is a success. It is supported by the class of absurd people who are aspiring to a recognized position, who have more money than ancestors, and wish to exchange a little of the former for a good deal of the latter. The capital invested in the office is trifling. It requires only two or three men who can look serious over a farce; a collection of old volumes full of shields, devices, and mottoes; a lot of genealogical trees hung up on the walls in antique-looking frames, and an uncertain number of histories and chronicles, including Froissart, Burke's Peerage, and kindred works.

The business of the establishment is managed in this wise :—

An applicant for a "family" enters and makes known his errand. A bland and smiling person asks the applicant's name.

"Smithers," is the answer.

"Smithers, Smithers! The Smithers are an old family, Gaelic originally, but the line has nearly died out. It's so with all the very old families. I'm glad to see one of their lineal descendants. What was your mother's name, Mr. Smithers?"

"Flurry."

"Flurry? Ah, yes. Are you of the Scotch or English Flurrys?"

"Hang me if I know! It was what I came here to find out. I don't know nothin' about my ancestors;

but my wife says she's got 'em, and that I must have 'em too."

"Your wife is correct. The Flurrys are a very noble family of full Norman descent, De Fleury was the name before the Conquest, and for nearly a century after. I shall soon be able to trace your lineage from the battle of Hastings to the present time."

"Gad, I'm glad of that. Mrs. Smithers'll give me a little peace now that she can git a crist on her carriage. She's bullragged me about the darned thing for a hull year."

"The fee for insuring investigation is $20, Mr. Smithers. When do you want your tree?"

"What kind o' tree? There's no use o' plantin' trees 'afore our house. The worms allers kills 'em."

"I mean your genealogical tree."

"I never heard of that sort o' tree. Is it any thing like hick'ry?"

"My dear sir, I mean the line of your ancestors; who they were; what they did; what reigns they flourished in."

"Oh yes, I understand now. But I shouldn't never think of callin' that a tree."

"When would you like to have your lineage, your ancestors made out?"

"Oh, any time will suit me. I've got the job off my hands, and the old woman can look after the rest of the rubbish."

"But it is well to fix a date. Do you care to have the papers made out before the end of next week?"

"No; take your time, and do it well."

"Be sure we shall. The price of the work will be $100."

"Go ahead; I'm willin'. Make us out a good first-class tree, and I'll pay you well. If you can find any pious old duck that only hurried or banged about generally, put him in; for my wife's mighty fond of havin' some of that kind in the family. She calls it sufferin' for opinion's sake; though I can't see why the devil they didn't change their opinion if they got into any row about it."

"No doubt the De Fleury's could boast of haughty prelates after the Reformation, who were earnest in their creed, even at the stake. I think I shall have no difficulty in showing you several illustrious martyrs.".

"Well, do so. And if you can get hold of any chaps that died in war, spot 'em. We want a few of that sort too. At least Sarah Jane says so; and she knows what's wanted much better than me."

"Come on the 14th, Mr. De Fleury, and you'll know all about your honorable ancestors."

"Smithers's my name."

"Yes, now; but the old family name was different. Call on the day named, and you'll find every thing prepared."

Mr. and Mrs. Smithers call on the 14th, and she learns to her delight, but not to her surprise apparently, that one of her ancestors lost his life in defending the Black Prince at Crécy.

Smithers objects to that. He says he don't want any "niggers" in his family, and won't have them.

The man of escutcheons informs him the Prince was the eldest son of Edward III., and called black from the color of his armor, not of his complexion, which composes Smithers, who pays his $100, and goes off in excellent spirits, having heard there were no darkies among his ancestors, and because he believes this to be a white man's government.

Mrs. Nancy Maginnis pays a visit to the office, and states to the manager that her family's genealogical tree had been destroyed by fire one month before (she is from Southern Illinois, and never knew who her grandmother was), and she is anxious to have it made out again.

"Maginnis! That is a pure Norman name, running back to the ninth and tenth centuries. The Maginnises were of the Latin race, and were called Maginniensis as late as the battle of Temsford," is the declaration of one of the clerks after tumbling over half a dozen large and dusty tomes.

"Yes, that is correct," she responds. "Maginniesenses is the family name. My dear old grandmother told me of the title of some of our family in the time of the—I forget the king's name."

"Ethelbert, I presume," is the ready reply. "He was one of the Anglo-Saxons and gave your line much trouble."

"Yes, he did. He was a very wicked man, that Ethelbert, and I hate him even now."

"I see you have the true Norman spirit, Madam, that never forgives an enemy of your house. I detect your Norman lineage in the peculiar curve of your nose (her nose is a confirmed pug), and the sparkle of your eye."

"How skilled you gentlemen are in tracing gentle blood. Few persons could have told at first glance that I was of Norman extraction, and yet I am thoroughly such."

"Oh, yes, Madam, we have so much to do with noble families we recognize them at a glance."

Mrs. Maginnis pays her $100 with exceeding satisfaction, and shows her bill to all her common-place friends, for the next twelve months, when they visit her expensive but tawdry new stone-front in the Avenue.

Such are the foolish persons who visit the Heraldry office. They pay $20 to $25 usually before the work is begun, and $100 after it is completed. The managers' labor is little more than a make-believe. They twist the name of any of their patrons into some form that figures in history, or is known in the peerage, and give lineage therefrom. Muggins is made De Mogyns; Jones is made John or Jean, and derived from King John of France or England; Thompson is made Temps fils, the son of Temps, a powerful baron, and so on to the last limit of absurdity.

Who would believe people claiming to be sensible could be so cajoled by their vanity? They learn nothing of those who have gone before them; but they may be certain there have been and are still fools in the family.

CHAPTER LXXI.

THE CHILD-ADOPTING SYSTEM.

It seems as a rule that persons who don't want children have many, and that those who want them very much, have none.

Nature is kind in most things; but like fortune, she often gives to those who have, and withholds from those who need. "A poor man for children," is a proverb constantly verified. There is Hardtoil, who watches with anxiety and regret his steadily increasing family; wishes he had fewer mouths to feed, and more to fill them.

His neighbor Crabtree is wealthy, but childless. He sees the numerous progeny of Hardtoil, and envies him their possession. He would give half his property for one of the rosy-cheeked prattlers, and Hardtoil would have been happy if his last three babes had been born to the rich man over the way.

If we could only exchange what we have and don't want for what we want and don't have, the sum of content in the World would be largely increased.

Where poverty and licentiousness are so common as in New-York, there will always be many parents who are unable to provide for their offspring, or unwilling to acknowledge them. Hence the baby-market is apt to be over-supplied, though at times the demand is fully equal to the supply. As we have no foundling hospitals here, as they have in Paris, Moscow, and other European cities, where infants can be left without any one even knowing who leaves them, parents get rid of them the best way they can.

Desertion of children is very rare among Americans, but quite common among foreigners, who, first landing in New-York, make the City responsible for their sins, as if they were its own. Ignorant, indolent, reckless, and vicious often, they are indifferent to their children, and will abandon them without hesitation, when poverty presses or self-interest demands. It is they who leave babies at other people's doors; who expose them in the street; who abandon them to neglect, or even murder them, to avoid the expense or trouble of taking care of them.

When American women abandon their children it is usually from the shame of their begetting, though the feeling of maternity not seldom proves stronger than the sense of dishonor. Poor girls, without protection or restraining influences, are always being led astray in a great city like this, and to their weakness is added the responsibility of their betrayer's sins.

Every year increases the number of child-murders in New-York. Public attention has been called to it again and again. Foundling hospitals have been urged as a remedy for the evil; but many of the timid-good have holy fears that the establishment will encourage the vice it is proposed to abate. From this apparently abnormal condition of things the system of child-adoption, or adopting-out, which is designed to regulate the supply and demand, has arisen, and is carried on with considerable activity and profit.

The morning papers contain advertisments every day

of children wanted for adoption and to be adopted. The little unknowns are highly favored, if you believe the advertisements; such adjectives as "handsome," "bright," "intelligent," "interesting," "healthy," being applied to them. They are all represented as ideal babies, quite the kind that new mothers bear every day in the year, and which are, without exception, wonderful.

When examined, they frequently contradict what has been said of them. The little beauties become flabby, blinking, ill-shaped, idiotic-looking creatures, that seem so self-disgusted that perhaps they would go back to where they came from, if they were not afraid they would find there more infants like themselves.

Often, however, there are exceptions. The tiny strangers are evidently of fine lineage. You see the culture and superiority that preceded them, and in the delicate features trace the character of their parents. Very small children can rarely be accused of comeliness; but there is a certain conventional standard of the quality which serves the purpose. The baby's fate is determined by that. If it is less homely than the average of children, it is ten times as apt to be adopted as if it fell below that average.

The advertisements read something like this:—

"*Wanted*—for adoption a male child of respectable parentage, not less than six months, nor more than two years old. It must be healthy, intelligent, and good-looking. Address X Y Z, station C, with reference, address, and particulars."

"*To be Adopted Out.*—A beautiful, bright female child, healthy, quiet and interesting, eight months old, and every way desirable. Any gentleman and lady wishing to adopt such a child must address in good faith, box No. 2,968, General Post-office with name, address, and circumstances."

" *To be Adopted Out.*—A fine healthy male child, six weeks old, of respectable parentage. It can be seen at No.—— Bowery, between the hours of 2 and 5 P. M. Any gentleman or lady wishing to adopt such a child would do well to apply early, as the beauty and winning qualities of the babe necessarily insure its immediate adoption."

" *Children for Adoption.*—Madame Pumpernickel, No. ——, Sixth street, has a number of handsome, healthy, and promising children for adoption. Persons anxious to add to their families will consult their interests by calling on Tuesdays, Thursdays, and Saturdays. Any lady or gentleman having children for adoption can find board and accommodations for them at Madame P's., and can make satisfactory arrangements to that end. All business communications strictly confidential."

Sometimes an advertisement appears, that sounds like burlesque, but which is, no doubt, serious. This, for instance :—

" A lady and gentleman of education and position, but in straitened circumstances, from a sudden reverse of fortune, would be willing to part with a beautiful and fascinating female child, of two months old, to respectable people, who will agree to educate it carefully, and rear it in accordance with its birth. Its parents would not be deprived of their dearly-beloved babe, even in the midst of their painful poverty, were they not on the point of leaving the City for the far West, where the advantages of education and proper accomplishments can not be enjoyed."

Or this :—

" *To be Adopted Out.*—A lovely female babe, aged six weeks and nine days, of highly aristocratic parentage. It suddenly became an orphan, and was intrusted to a friend of the family, who has not the means of supporting the child in the manner it has been accustomed to. Address Fashion, No.—, Oliver street. N. B. None but persons of unquestionable respectability need apply. The best and strongest of references required."

The infants of whom the most is said are usually the least attractive. Those whose parents are highly lauded are apt to prove of Milesian extraction, and to be in the market on account of the low price of babies and the high price of whisky.

I have heard of several women who, having gone in quest of " beautiful children," returned in a state of dissatisfaction bordering on disgust, and who afterward declared that all the claim the infants had to beauty consisted in bleared eyes, coarse features, and scrofulous affections.

Madame Pumpernickel, whose genuine name I refrain from giving, is a professional adopter. There are a number of her calling in town, and the number is increasing. She keeps a baby's boarding-house and something else. She knows illegitimate children are very numerous here ; that not infrequently their parents are persons of position, and that she can make something by aiding them to get rid of the evidence of their intimacy. She is aware that after leaving the child they will not inquire for it further. When they or their agent comes she consents to take the little thing for a certain consideration, which she regulates according to the means or position of the parties concerned. She sometimes has a dozen or twenty children on hand at a time; but she keeps the number down as much as possible.

When any one wants to lease a baby with the madame, she either charges a fixed sum, or so much, with its board for a certain number of days added. The customary rate is $100 to $200 for taking the child, and $50 to $100 for disposing of it. When she can she advances her rate two or three hundred per cent., and so drives a good trade. Her interest is to get rid of the babies as soon as possible, and she consults her interest, regardless of humanity.

Children seldom stay more than a week at Madame Pumpernickel's. If they are not sold they are almost invariably attacked with some violent illness that carries them off in a few days. The very disagreeable infants, whom no one wants, are most exposed to fatal maladies. The madame says they die of some inherited ailment; but it is very well known she either starves them, or permits them to perish through neglect. The fact is so notorious that complaint has been made to the police, who have arrested the professional adopters, and brought them before the so-called courts of justice, with which New-York is favored. Nothing could be proved against them. There were no witnesses, none procurable at least, and the child-murderers were released to continue their traffic in infant life and death.

The homes of the adopters are generally in some wretched quarter of the town, and in some building where fresh air and healthful living are impossible. The rooms rented are meagerly, not to say meanly furnished; and in them are six, eight, or twelve infants, —little specters who look as if they would die at once and save trouble if they only knew how. Their keeper teaches them with such success that they soon wheeze out of their wretched little lives, and are thrust into a pauper's coffin. They lie in little beds and are tied in chairs; cry day and night until they are too weak and hungry to cry any longer, when they fall to sucking their little soiled fingers, and not finding the dirt very nourishing, they wink and twitch their little pale eyes and slender limbs, and then stop winking and twitching forevermore.

The adopters are ready to act as agents for the getting of babies if those they leave don't suit. They go to the private lying-in hospitals, whose patients are women that have not been married, and bargain for the babes that have been born, or advertise for the kind that is wanted. As the supply is greatly in excess of the demand, the children are found without difficulty. The adopters, as I have stated, are opposed to keeping on hand a supply that is not marketable, and as they receive none, and part with none, except for what they think a good price, their business can hardly be a losing one.

The baby market has its fluctuations, like any other. In the Winter babies sell higher, because it costs more to take care of them; they are more liable to die, and the demand is greater. During the hot months they decline; for few citizens are in town, and strangers are not good customers. Usually the price of an infant is very variable; for there is hardly any thing that the rightful owner would be so disinclined to sell, and any other person would care so little to buy.

But in New-York, quotations can be depended on to a large extent. A really good, well-conditioned, first-class babe will bring $100, when the market is not overstocked; and a rather inferior but healthy and promising article, about $50. The infant trade, strange as it may seem, is growing to be regular here, and extending every year. It is not impossible, before the century is over, that we shall have children quoted on 'Change, and prime, first, second, and third-rate ones as fixed in value as molasses, wheat, or flour.

CHAPTER LXXII.

BANKERS AND WALL STREET OPERATORS.

AFTER Vanderbilt, whose portrait has been given elsewhere, Daniel Drew is the most prominent figure in the banking quarter, and perhaps the most reckless. Though now in his seventy-second year, he is as energetic, persevering, shrewd (and unscrupulous, his enemies would add), as he was in the prime of life. He gives no sign of physical or mental failure, notwithstanding his constant activity and the perpetual strain upon his brain and nerves.

Drew was born on a small farm in Carmel, Putnam county, and received a very limited education. He learned to read, write, and cypher while working on the sterile land his father owned; but beyond that cared very little for books. At fifteen he lost his father, and at once determined to set up in life for himself—a step he was qualified for by his force of will, strength of character, and natural astuteness, very remarkable in one so young. He began by driving cattle to market and selling them, first in a small way, but gradually increasing his trade until it grew to be of considerable value. For sixteen or seventeen years he was a cattle-drover; but, after he had reached thirty-two, he moved to this City, and established a depot for their sale, sending agents to the country to purchase stock. He gained money rapidly, and, in 1834, made an investment, with others, in a steamboat, which resulted in a great interest in the transportation of passengers on the Hudson River.

Drew's line was so ably managed that it became popular, though it entered into competition with the lines owned by Vanderbilt and others. The rivalry was very sharp for a long while, the steamers, at one time, carrying passengers from here to Albany at a shilling apiece. Drew was a large stockholder in the company formed by Isaac Newton, in 1840, which was the origin of the People's Line. He refused to dispose of his vessels when the Hudson River Railway was completed, though his friends advised him to, declaring he would be ruined if he did not. The road increased the patronage of the boats, as he had foreseen, and to this day, they are most desirable property. The Drew, finished year before last, is the finest steamboat that floats on any interior waters. She is more elaborate and gorgeous even than the famed Bristol and Providence, running between New-York and Boston.

For ten or twelve years Drew was a banker and stock broker, having formed a partnership with Nelson Taylor and his son-in-law. He has been a daring and active operator in Wall street ever since, and is the most formidable opponent Vanderbilt has had. He lost $500,000 in the famous Harlem corner some years ago; but he is not likely to be caught so again. He has long been a heavy stockholder in Erie and other prominent roads, and he plays bull and bear, and sells short and long, as his interest demands, quite confounding those who don't understand his multifarious shifts.

Drew's foes accuse him of numerous "irregular"

transactions; but he claims that he does nothing that the Stock Exchange and Wall street morals do not sanction. He has a wide reputation for charity, having founded the Drew Theological Seminary at Morris, N. J., by giving it half a million of dollars, and having contributed to various religious and educational institutions.

Drew is in no way noticeable in face or figure. He is six feet high, slender, with limbs loosely put together, and rather awkward in his movements. He has a rustic appearance, is careless in his dress, and unconventional in his manners.

David Groesbeck, of the firm of David Groesbeck & Co., the well-known bankers in Broad street, is, like Drew, wholly self-made. He was born in Albany county; had a hard struggle with fortune; picked up a slender education, was apprenticed to a shoemaker, went to the capital afterward, and was clerk in a policy office. Failing to be satisfied there, he came to New-York, where he soon evinced such remarkable capacity for business that he attracted the attention of Jacob Little—so long the great bear of Wall street. He went into Little's office, and rose from one position to another, until he became the eminent banker's confidential clerk. He showed such remarkable financial ability that his employer advised him to go into business for himself, and lent him money for the purpose. For years Groesbeck has been a banker, and though he has failed several times, he has always preserved his reputation for honor, and his house is to-day one of the wealthiest in the City. He is not a reckless speculator; but he buys and sells stocks, and lends money on them; some of his operations being immense. Last year he is reputed to have made $2,000,000, and his private fortune is estimated at $10,000,000. He is about fifty-two, tall, dark, and looks like an anxious, overworked man. He is liberal to a fault, and does many generous acts, of which few ever hear.

Jay Cooke is known everywhere as the agent of the Government during the issue of the 7-30 and 5-20 bonds. By that loan he made a vast fortune, and is now one of great bankers of Wall street. He is a native of Ohio, having been born in Portland, now Sandusky, in the Summer of 1821. His father was a member of Congress (this is not mentioned to cast any discredit on the banker, but merely as a fact for which he can not be held responsible), and having the name of Eleutheros, which nobody could pronounce or spell properly, he determined to give his children short names. So the future financier was called Jay.

The elder Cooke having suffered some adversity, and his son finding it out, determined to help himself. So he went to the store of an acquaintance in town, and without the consent or knowledge of his parents got a situation as clerk. He proved himself excellently qualified for business, and after acting as book-keeper and salesman in St. Louis and Philadelphia, he went, in his seventeenth year, into the banking house of E. W. Clark & Co. (in the latter city), of which he was afterward a partner. Remaining in the firm twenty years, he retired, and in the early part of 1861 opened a banking establishment of his own with his brother-in law, Wm. G. Moorhead, under the name of Jay Cooke & Co. The financial ability of the new firm, displayed in negotiating different loans, attracted the attention of the Government. Secretary Chase made Cooke & Co. the agents in Philadelphia for the three series of 7-30, and also special agents of the $500,000,000 5·20 loan. The risk was great, and large capital was required, but when it is remembered that $\frac{5}{8}$ of one per cent. was paid, on the whole amount, the profit will be seen to have been handsome. The firm made several millions, and Cooke himself, now doing business at the corner of Wall and Nassau streets, is supposed to be worth $15,000,000 to $20,000,000. Cooke is very fresh in his feelings, and remarkable for his cheerful and genial disposition. He has the reputation of a very charitable man, having given freely to churches and colleges. He has a fine country seat on one of the islands of Lake Erie, near Sandusky, and dispenses a lavish hospitality. He has a bright, sympathetic face, agreeable manners, and a firm mouth that represents his character.

Another firm that has made a fortune by acting as agents of government loans is Fisk & Hatch. Before the War they were both living on salaries; Hatch being an officer in a Jersey City bank, at $1,200 a year. Soon as they began to negotiate the bonds they found themselves on the high road to fortune. They now do a very large business in Nassau, near Wall street, and have cleared $1,000,000 a year. They are both young and born financiers. They are much esteemed; do a strictly legitimate business; are conscientious members of the church, and liberal in their charities.

August Belmont came here originally as the agent of the Rothschilds, and is, perhaps, better known as a politician than as a banker. His office is at No. 50 Wall street, in a great, dingy granite building, where the largest transactions are made. He does most of his business on foreign account; is very wealthy, and one of the shrewdest of financiers. His wife is the daughter of Commodore Perry, and his home in Fifth avenue, corner of Eighteenth street, is interiorly one of the most elegant and luxurious in town. His picture gallery alone is said to be worth $400,000 or $500,000. He is the President of the Democratic National Committee, and has always taken a very prominent part in politics. He is small, heavy set, with a short, thick nose, not inviting in appearance, nor conciliating in manner. Though a man of brain and character, he is not at all popular, nor does he wish to be—satisfied with his position and his unquestionable power. He is a German by birth, though he has French blood, and is often alluded to by those who like him not, as a "Dutch Jew." He walks lame, having been wounded in a duel while living on the Continent; but in the peculiar understanding of Wall street he is not likely to be crippled. He is too sagacious and far-seeing to become financially halt.

Brown Brothers & Co., 59 Wall street, is one of the most eminent houses in America. Their great marble banking-house is not surpassed by any similar establishment on this or the other side of the Atlantic. It cost over a million, and is an architectural ornament to the monetary quarter. The founder of the house, James Brown, is still in it. He is from the North of Ireland; began life as a linen-draper, and having made a fortune, established the banking-house with his brother, who had been knighted for his services to the British Government. James Brown is regarded as a high type of business honor; is probably worth $12,000,000 or $15,000,000; is a devout Presbyterian, and prominent in numerous charities. He is nearly sixty, but in excellent health, and one of our most useful citizens.

James G. King's Sons have a very quiet, plain establishment at No. 54 William street. James G. King has been dead for some years, and the business is continued by his sons. It is one of the oldest firms in the City, and in the very best standing. It deals largely in foreign exchange and grants letters of credit available in all the principal cities of Europe. The Kings are an old New-York family, and their commercial honor has never been tarnished. They are very rich, but wholly without ostentation.

Leonard W. Jerome is quite a contrast to such men as the Browns and Kings. He belongs to the present-day school of bold, often reckless operators; represents the fast financiers of the street. He was formerly a newspaper publisher in Rochester, but has for years been a prominent operator in stocks. He is shrewd, resolute, full of expedients and resources; makes and loses fortunes every twelve months, but manages to float conspicuous on the financial tide. He is a noted person; a man of the world and fond of pleasure; dresses showily; drives fleet horses; has fast friends; enjoys display; gives expensive entertainments; is extravagant and careless; is called good-looking; lives with a free hand and a liberal heart in the sunshine of the passing hour.

CHAPTER LXXIII.

CHARLES O'CONOR.

CHARLES O'CONOR is very sensitive about the spelling of his name with a single *n;* perhaps because the double *n* is the common method. He is, as every one may know, whether he has one or two *n's* in his patronymic, of Irish descent; his father having, in accordance with the established custom, quitted his native country on account of his connection with the Irish revolution of 1798.

Charles O'Conor was born here, in 1804, and in such narrow circumstances that he with difficulty obtained an education. He did not graduate, though his studious habits and thirst for knowledge more than made up for the absence of a collegiate course. In his early youth he went to Steuben county; but, after living there for several years, he returned to the City to study law, for which he had long had a partiality. He was a messenger-boy at first, and rose step by step to the position of an attorney. While a stripling in the office of a well-known firm of that day, he used to read Coke and Blackstone whenever he had the least leisure; borrowed law books, and pored over them at night. Those who observed his diligence and determination predicted success for him at the bar. Before he began to study regularly he was well-informed on many legal points, and often surprised his elders by his readiness and knowledge. He was only twenty-one when admitted to practice.

Soon after admission he cherished political aspirations, and was anxious to be chosen Alderman for the Sixth Ward. The doubtful honor was refused him at the polls, where he was gloriously defeated. His failure of election troubled him sorely at the time, and impelled him to confine himself in future to his profession. His application was extraordinary. He worked late and early, and for a period of ten years is said to have been in the courts or at his office sixteen hours out of the twenty-four. He had a hard struggle until he was thirty; but his effective speeches, more remarkable for soundness than eloquence, at last brought him into notice. He took all the cases that were offered him, and did his best in every one of them; and to this he ascribes his professional success.

Having been chosen a member of the Constitutional Convention for revising the Constitution of the State, in 1846, he showed great capacity, legal and political, and was much praised by the Democrats for his consistent course. Two years after he was a candidate for Lieutenant-Governor, and would have been appointed Attorney-General by President Pierce, if General Marcy, of this State, had not already been in the Cabinet.

For the past twenty years O'Conor has been employed in some of the most important cases in the country. He set out as a criminal lawyer, but abandoned that practice as soon as he could command one more lucrative and dignified. The Mason Will, in the courts for fifteen years, and the Forrest Divorce, are among the most famous cases in which O'Conor has been engaged. In the former he made what was called his ablest speech, and gained his cause; the decision being given in favor of the heirs. In the latter he was opposed by John Van Buren (on the side of the tragedian), who was more brilliant than his opponent, though O'Conor was certainly more profound.

O'Conor has a very large practice, but in his sixty-fourth year he is inclined to rest from his labors. His income is $70,000 or $80,000 a year, and he lives in elegance at Fort Washington, where his entertainments are numerous and expensive. His wife, who is fond of society, is said to be amiable and accomplished, and to preside with grace over the hospitalities of her husband.

Charles O'Conor's career on the subject of slavery has been consistent if not admirable. He has from the first been opposed to the negro in every way. He has been against his emancipation, against his education, against his right to the franchise, against every effort for his advancement. It is said he deeply deplores the abolition of slavery, which he considered a beneficent and humanizing as well as a peculiar institution. It is singular a man of O'Conor's learning and intellect can hold so narrow and irrational a view; but he has been accustomed for years to looking at the subject from one side, and the indignation his course has excited among the Republicans and Radicals has, it is presumed, only strengthened his convictions.

In person, O'Conor is of medium height, erect, and rather slender. His face is after the Irish pattern, indicating strength and sternness, will, and resolution to a point of dogged obstinacy. His eye is dark and penetrating, and his hair and whiskers are very gray. When speaking in public, he is deliberate and measured at first; but warming up with his subject, he is fluent and rapid, and often severely sarcastic. On the whole, he seems of a cold temperament, though he is very agreeable and entertaining in private. He is an intellectual egotist, and holds his opinions so firmly that, while he is willing to discuss questions, there is no hope of inducing a change in the position he once has taken.

CHAPTER LXXIV.

JAMES T. BRADY.

JAMES T. BRADY, another prominent lawyer of the City, is personally better known than O'Conor, because of his continual appearance before the public of Manhattan. Like O'Conor, he is native here, having been born in the lower part of town; though he is so fond of dwelling on the wrongs of Ireland, and lauding her sons to the stars on the rostrum, that many suppose him a boy of Blarney. He is so dear to the Irish heart of this City for his sympathy with, and the abundant rhetoric addressed to Erin, that he has been chosen President of St. Patrick's Society, and is always invited to any and every festive board at which the Green Isle is to be glorified. Between his life and O'Conor's there are many similarities. They were both poor, both pre-determined to the bar, both engaged for years in criminal cases, both successful, and both the architect of their own fortune. While Brady's professional reputation stands very high, he has gained very few of his cases. It is said he takes too much personal interest in his clients; makes too many appeals of a flattering character to judges and juries; declares too often and too particularly the innocence and miscellaneous virtues of those he is called upon to defend. That habit, as well as his subtle distinctions on points of law, excite suspicion and create confusion, and he therefore fails of success.

Brady's face and fame are most familiar at dinners, and suppers, and public meetings of all sorts. His *forte* lies in after-dinner speeches. The presence of boon companions, the drinking of toasts, and the flow of wine, act upon him rapidly and favorably. Naturally sensitive, fervidly rhetorical and fond of display, he is in his element in the midst of the jingling of glasses and popping of champagne. He needs little provocation to respond to any sentiment, and he always brings applause from his hearers. If he had a melodious instead of a harsh voice, he would be more interesting; but his admirers forget his tones in his glowing periods and flashes of humor. He has the Irish temperament— a passion for verbal floridity and sensational coloring—and never lets a theme suffer for want of representation.

Brady is the most persevering speaker; has the largest gift of continuance of any orator in Manhattan. No public occasion is thought to be complete without him. He figures in all presentations; at all public dinners; at all private suppers; at all public meetings; at all formal receptions. He must, on an average, deliver one hundred addresses a year. A sarcastic journalist says a reward of $10,000 has long been offered for the discovery of any public or private occasion, within a radius of fifty miles of New-York City, taking Union Square as a center, on which James T. Brady did not speak; and that up to the present time the reward has never been claimed.

Brady lays claim to the earliest recognition of "moral sanity" as the cause of crime; Huntington, the famous "genteel" forger, having been the client in whose defense he first made that a plea.

In politics Brady has been a Democrat, though a less consistent one than O'Conor. During the Rebellion he favored the North; supported President Lincoln's policy, and was appointed to an important commission under that administration. He feels a deep interest in the drama; is a regular habitué of the theaters, and has contributed several minor pieces to the stage that had a certain local popularity. He was one of the founders of the Dramatic Fund Association, and is still a prominent and zealous member. He has written for the press, too, at various times, and continues to have an inclination to divert himself as an imp of the ink-bottle.

Brady is eminently social and sociable; has a gregarious and convivial cast; is a member of two or three clubs; relishes amusements of almost every kind, and is a good specimen of a jovial bachelor. He is about five feet eight in height; well built, slight but compact in frame; has a broad and intellectual forehead, a bright eye and very mobile features. He is rather graceful, and, when his face is lighted up, I have known him to be called handsome. He is a fluent talker, and would, as I have said, be a very agreeable one but for the discordant tones of his voice which he has struggled in vain to correct. He is so well liked by all classes that he may be called one of the most popular men in New-York.

CHAPTER LXXV.

FERNANDO WOOD.

FERNANDO WOOD is one of the shrewdest of New-York politicians, and they have always been remarkable for their astuteness. He was born in Philadelphia, in 1812, and is said to have set out in his metropolitan life as the proprietor of a small drinking saloon in Greenwich street, though he was by profession a cigar-maker. He afterward became a clerk in a counting-house, and was for years a ship-owner and merchant. He is a self-made man, owing little to education, but naturally intelligent and having an intuitive knowledge of character. Very early he showed capacity to manage and control his fellows, and he has improved upon this with his increasing years. During the time he was engaged in mercantile business, his enemies say he did not deal fairly with his partner; but his admirers, of whom he has many, proclaim that he has been slandered. The firm of which he was a member ultimately failed, and Wood entered into political life.

For years he was very active among the Democrats, and became a power in the municipal government. His record was not enviable. He was charged with all manner of corruptions, and when he was nominated for Mayor, in 1857, a howl of indignation went up from the Opposition. That did not prevent his election, however, and, when elected, he disappointed his enemies and disgusted his friends. Instead of being the corrupt official that was expected; instead of being a mere tool in the hands of the party that placed him in office, he acted independently and honestly; established various reforms, and proved himself one of the best and most popular Mayors the City had ever known. For some months he continued his excellent course. He had gained the warmest admirers among his bitterest foes. The journals that had abused him exhausted eulogy upon him. Prayers were even offered up for him in fashionable churches. But he was bent upon disappointing the City in another way.

All of a sudden the improvements he had made were overridden by the worst corruptions. All that had been anticipated of his bad government was more than realized. The City Hall fell into the hands of the worst men in New-York, and the indignant public clamored in vain for reform. The Municipal Police, as they were called, became so insupportable that the State determined to supplant them with police of its own appointment, and did so. There was serious trouble; fighting and riots ensued before the Metropolitan Police were firmly installed, and on Mayor Wood was thrown the entire responsibility of the public disturbances. He was compelled to submit; but during the remainder of his term of office, he did all he could to make himself obnoxious to the Opposition, which, indeed, he had no cause to love. He went out of the Mayoralty amid the execrations of those who at first were loudest in his praise. It was thought that he could never be elected to the office again; but he has been three times Mayor, and without redeeming his reputation. He was defeated the last time he ran for the place; but he still boasts that he can get it when he likes. He has been thrice in Congress, and has just been elected a fourth time.

He is resolute, energetic, and believes the end justifies the means in politics, and that the end is success. His influence with the people, particularly with the Irish, is very great. They seem to have a kind of blind worship for him, and they cleave to him through good and evil report. Even when they are incensed against him, as they are sometimes, he has but to go among them and talk with them to bring them over to his side.

Whatever his defects, Wood is an extraordinary man; has abundant faith in himself, and cares nothing for the abuse that is heaped upon him. Coolness is superabundantly his. In Congress, when torrents of invective have been poured upon his head, he has sat in his chair stroking his moustache and looking more indifferent than any of his fellow-members. From the class of men he controls many fancy him a rude, coarse fellow of the Sixth Ward politician type. They are greatly mistaken. Fernando Wood, with his gray hair and mustache, sober suit of black, tall, erect, lithe figure, quiet, almost solemn manner, would be mistaken for a clergyman. He is perfectly self-possessed under all circumstances; speaks softly and deliberately; dresses neatly, and would be prepossessing were it not for a suggestion of coldness and selfishness that no ease or polish of manner can remove.

Wood lives in good style up town; has a liberal income—having laid the basis of his wealth while he was Mayor in 1857 by buying at advantageous rates real estate sold for taxes. He is fifty-six, of vigorous constitution; seems to grow more cunning with age, and deserves the sobriquet of the Fox, which has been fixed upon him. He was long distinguished as the head and front of Mozart Hall, which he originated in opposition to Tammany. But Tammany was too strong for Mozart, which is now little more than a name. It fears Wood, however, and has consented to his going to Congress, where perhaps he may expiate some of his many political sins.

CHAPTER LXXVI.

GEORGE FRANCIS TRAIN.

GEORGE FRANCIS TRAIN is as difficult to locate as to analyze. He claims a residence in St. Petersburg, London, Paris, San Francisco, Omaha, Chicago, New-York, and Boston; but, as those cities are not conveniently contiguous to each other, it is questionable, should he declare he had a residence in each and all of them, if he would be permitted to vote, even on Manhattan Island. Public opinion is much divided respecting Train. Some persons think him a madman; others a fool. He is neither. He knows what he is about better than most men; but his passion for notoriety is such that he is constantly misunderstood. He believes in notoriety, in self-representation, in self-assertion, in self-appreciation, to the fullest. With him, egotism is, if not the highest of virtues, the first of domestic charities. He holds there is no success without egotism, and that success in some form is what all are struggling for. Self-conscious and self-loving as he is, he does not desire to encroach upon the right of others to be and appear as vain as they choose. He is convinced that modesty "does not pay," as he would express it, and that it is in most cases a sham. He is violently opposed to shams, and prefers Nature, however disagreeable, to the most pleasant make-believe. Not long ago, he spoke to a writer of reputation about a literary work he had completed. "It does not amount to any thing," said the author; "I did it for lack of something better."

"You don't really think so," replied Train. "If you had had that belief, you wouldn't have undertaken the work. Never decry your own performance anyhow. Let other people do that. People take you at your own estimate; and it's good policy to put a high value upon yourself if you want to sell well in the market."

Train is an American in excess; an American raised to a higher power, to put it mathematically; an American run mad. He is a highly exaggerated type of our people and country; and has all the energy, boldness, independence, irrepressibleness, that are popularly supposed to belong to the Anglo-Saxon race. For nearly twenty years he has been before the public in protean shape, and no doubt for twenty, aye, thirty years more, he will insist upon not being forgotten while voice and lungs, pen and ink, type and paper, are to be used or had in the World.

Train was born in Massachusetts, in or near Boston, and an erratic fellow from childhood. He was thought very visionary and fantastic in his youth, and, though unmistakably clever, seemed to have no concentration, no continuity of purpose. Before he was of age he was famous in the City of Notions. He had unusual power of expression, orally and graphically; was constantly talking, speaking in public, or writing. He rambled abroad; returned, and published several volumes, among which were "Young America in Europe," and "Wall Street Abroad." In all of his volumes he glorified Young America, which he claimed to represent; criticised and censured the old monarchies, and predicted the universal-diffusion of republican principles. His books were read; sometimes admired; oftener laughed at. They had cleverness, but were flighty, incoherent, disconnected, and induced many persons of a different temperament to believe their author a little cracked. Then he went abroad again; made extraordinary and ridiculously extravagant speeches that confirmed the impression his books had given.

He set to building street railways in London; but after great boasts of teaching John Bull how to travel, John Bull got out injunctions, stopping the work; and to this day there is not a foot of street-railway in the British metropolis.

Train has been in every European capital, and wherever he is, he is bound to be heard from. He never keeps quiet; but fluctuates between the Baltic Sea and the Pacific coast. His superlative nervous force and activity of brain impel him from one country to another, from ocean to ocean, like the driving-wheels of a locomotive.

He has tried almost every thing, and not long ago became interested, with Thomas C. Durant, the Vice-President, in the Union Pacific Railway. He has had many advantages there in buying property and locating towns, and is reputed to have made a great deal of money. He confesses to have done so, and frequently says: "I have taken a turn at many things. I wrote for the newspapers, and people called me a fool. I made speeches, and they called me a fool. I became author, and they did the same. I built street-railways, and they still called me a fool. Then I went to making money, and since then nobody has called me a fool."

I am afraid Train is mistaken. It is so much easier

to style any one a simpleton than to understand a wise man, that a great many persons have not changed their opinion of the erratic New-Englander. Train claims to have originated the *Credit Foncier* in this country, which is a source of great profit to him in the building of the Pacific Road. No one can imagine all the enterprises and public movements he assumes to be the parent of, and with justice, perhaps; for he is more likely than any man living to project a macadamized road to the moon or a pleasure excursion to the Bottomless Pit, for the notoriety of the thing, if for no other reason.

Train is an amiable, good-hearted, and good-looking fellow, who would be very interesting if he would confine himself to one subject more than ten seconds at a time. He overwhelms you with talk on all themes, and conversation with him is little else than a rambling monologue, in which you are an entirely superfluous figure. He is of medium height, erect, graceful, has brown, curly hair, gray eyes; affects blue, brass-buttoned coats; has an interest in all existences under the stars, but most in George Francis Train; and is one of the most remarkable men of the time, with more good and capacity in him than he will ever get credit for.

CHAPTER LXXVII.

FANNY FERN.

ALMOST every one has heard of Fanny Fern, though very few know who Mrs. Eldridge or Mrs. Parton is; and many will be surprised to learn they are all three one and the same person.

"Fanny Fern" Eldridge-Parton was born in Portland, Maine, July 11, 1811—a fact I have no hesitation in stating, because she is one of the not numerous women who have no objection to telling her age. Her father, Nathaniel Willis, editor for many years of the Boston *Recorder*, removed to that city when she was six years old. She was educated at Hartford, Conn., being a pupil of Catherine E. and Harriet Beecher, now the famous Mrs. Stowe. Sara Payson Willis—her maiden name—was a very rollicking, even hoidenish girl; gave her teachers no little trouble, and teased her school-fellows most unmercifully. She was very popular, however, from her fine sense of justice and her generosity of heart. Not a few of her companions seemed to be really in love with her, particularly the younger and weaker of the class, who went to her for protection and championship, as if she were a man.

Numerous stories are told of her mad freaks and mischievous tricks, which earned for her the well-deserved title of a tomboy. The Beechers have many reminiscences of Sallie Willis as a school-girl. Among other things, she used to be wishing constantly that she was a boy; and those who knew her then were often of the opinion that she nearly had her wish.

Soon after leaving school she was married to Charles Eldridge, cashier of the Merchants' Bank of Boston. She lived in comfort and content with him, and twice bore him children—daughters; but at his death his affairs were found to be involved, and she was soon thrown upon her own resources. She tried to obtain a situation as teacher or saleswoman; offered to do any thing to put bread into her own and her children's mouths, but she was unsuccessful, and finally, as a last resort, concluded to write.

This was in 1851, and Boston was not then a very good literary market. Having shown cleverness with her pen while a girl, she composed a number of sketches, stories, poems and essays. She offered them to all the Boston journals, daily and weekly. The editors acknowledged that they had merit, but they would not pay for them. She wanted money more than fame, and declined to have them printed for glory. After severe struggles with poverty, and when she was on the eve of abandoning the literary field, she found an editor who gave her fifty cents for a sketch. It attracted attention; was copied in other journals, and induced the editor to give her a dollar for the next effusion. She continued to write over the signature of Fanny Fern, and at the end of a few months she had gained a decided reputation.

As soon as she became known, she removed to the City, began writing for the weeklies, and made Fanny Fern a familiar name all over the country. Robert Bonner about that time purchased the *Ledger*, formerly a commercial weekly, and immediately engaged Fanny to write regularly, at $100 a column. Thenceforward her reputation and independence were assured. Her writings were copied everywhere. Drinking saloons and steamboats were named after her, which is indubitable evidence in America of enduring fame. She made a collection of her sketches, and published them in a volume, with the title of "Fern Leaves." The book had a sale of 70,000, and realized to her $8,000 or $10,000. She afterwards published another series of her contributions to the *Ledger*, followed by a novel —"Ruth Hall"—which was really, though not ostensibly, an autobiography. In it she severely censured and ridiculed her brother, N. P. Willis, then the well-known editor of the *Home Journal*, under the name of Hyacinth; showing him to be a vulgar pretender and a selfish snob. Of the taste of such a performance, whatever her provocation, there can hardly be two opinions. But the novel sold, and she had no compunctious visitings.

In 1856 she was a second time married to James Parton, the distinguished biographer. She is still a contributor to the *Ledger*, and in consideration of her writing for no other publication, Bonner gives her $5,000 a year. She lives very comfortably in Eighteenth street, and in her fifty-eighth year is as pleasant and vivacious as a girl of eighteen. She is round and plump; has light hair, laughing, blue eyes and a mobile face. She is a rapid and interesting talker, a strong, self-poised, large-hearted woman; and though her writings are often lacking in delicacy, they are free from sham, earnest for the truth, often eloquent, always pointed, and have done much good by their strong appeals to women and their brave defense of right.

CHAPTER LXXVIII.

TWO STRONG-MINDED WOMEN.

Susan B. Anthony, especially since the establishment of the *Revolution,* has become one of the feminine notabilities of the country. She is a native of South Adams, Mass., though her parents removed to Monroe county, near Rochester, while she was a child. She is of Quaker descent, and the Quakers love peace; but she has departed from the faith of her fathers, and grown enamored of all forms of spiritual warfare. She was a teacher for many years; afterward a lecturer on temperance and anti-slavery. Since her girlhood she has been radical in every thing. She early burst the trammels of old forms; became an uncompromising Abolitionist and an enemy of common and ancient creeds. She was one of the first advocates of woman's rights in their fullness. For twenty years she has talked, written, and spoken in favor of feminine suffrage, and will have little to desire when that becomes the law of the land. She is the publisher of the *Revolution,* and in each of its weekly issues has several vigorous articles on her favorite theme. She is a thorough come-outer, in the strictest sense of come-outerism; but she is sincere, liberal, sympathetic, and, if strong-minded, is tender-hearted.

She has chosen her course from no love of notoriety or sensation, but from principle and conscientious determination to do right. Her life is full of practical charities. No one of her sex, however humble, degraded, or outcast, ever failed to find in her a comforter, helper, and friend. She is tall and slender; has a good, though not handsome face; is very energetic; talks a great deal, but very well. She is unmarried, a vigorous and logical speaker and writer, and, though she has been much misrepresented and ridiculed, as all women are who have courage to step out of what is called their "sphere," she is gentle, courageous, and true; has a high purpose in life, and has done a good work. The World might be better off if it had a thousand Susan Anthonys; this City certainly would.

Elizabeth Cady Stanton is even better known than her co-laborer on the *Revolution*. She has stumped the West; lectured and made speeches throughout the Northern States for woman's rights and woman's suffrage, of which, since Lucy Stone's marriage and retirement to New-Jersey domesticity, she is, perhaps, the most distinguished advocate in the Union. Her name is printed in the London *Times*, the Paris *Moniteur*, and the *Indépendance Belge*. She has sufficient celebrity—notoriety, if you will—to gratify the vanity of any of her sex; and were it not for the heart she has in her work, no doubt she would long ago have retired from a field many have thought uncongenial to her.

Mrs. Stanton (*née* Elizabeth Cady) is a native of Johnstown, N. Y., the daughter of Judge Cady, a gentleman of position and ability. She was married to Henry B. Stanton, a young and rising lawyer, in her twentieth year; and not long after went to Seneca Falls, in this State, where she resided for thirteen or fourteen years. It was there she first felt an interest in the cause of woman's rights. She made her earliest speech there, I think, and was an intimate of Mrs. Bloomer, a resident of the same town, after whom the short skirt that has been so much laughed at was christened. Mrs. Stanton soon became acquainted with Lucy Stone, Abby Kelly Foster, Ernestine L. Rose, Antoinette L. Brown, Frances D. Gage, Elizabeth Oakes Smith, and the whole tribe of feminine agitationists. They received her with open arms and encouraging tongues. She was taken into their innermost circle; made their counselor and confidante; was launched upon a "career," and discovered she had a "mission." Her friends were alarmed, some of them shocked, that a lady so accomplished and highly-bred should ally herself with women who violated all the conventionalities and departed from all the customs of "good society."

Mrs. Stanton had made up her mind, however. Though naturally very sensitive and shrinkingly modest, she resolved to brave public opinion, and do what she had convinced herself was her duty. She plunged into the Rubicon; she crossed, and Rome was—freer than ever. From that time to this she has been untiring in her exertions for the cause. She firmly believes every thing will come right when women vote; that when they go to the polls, and take part in the elections, the country will approach near to Plato's ideal republic, and More's Utopia.

For some years she has lived in New-York; was the founder, and is the guiding and ruling spirit of the *Revolution*. She is the opposite of the popular notion of a strong-minded woman. Instead of being angular, cadaverous, awkward, shrill-voiced, vinegar-faced, she is buxom, blithe, pleasant. Her hair, which is prematurely white, clusters about her well-shaped head in silvery curls. Her eyes are large, blue, and bright; her features regular, and her complexion fresh. She is a very agreeable—many call her a fascinating—woman, and is so full of life and humor that it is difficult to be in her society without feeling the charm of her presence. She has several children, is a most exemplary wife and mother, and is widely and deeply loved by all who know her. She has a fine mind; is logical and trenchant in argument; and one of the most persevering and able advocates her cause has ever had on this side of the Atlantic.

CHAPTER LXXIX.

PETER COOPER.

Peter Cooper's name is familiar all over the country on account of his persevering efforts to educate and elevate the poor and laboring classes, and from the erection of the Cooper Institute for the instruction of the workingmen of the country. Cooper was born in this City in the winter of 1791, and is of Revolutionary stock, his father and grandfather having served as officers during the struggle. His father was a hatter at the close of the struggle, and Peter assisted him in the shop, and had a hard experience, as his parent was in straitened circumstances, and had a large family to support. The boy was very anxious to learn, but he was unable to attend school more than half of each day during a single year, which was all the regular education he ever received. When seventeen he was apprenticed to a coachmaker, and he followed the trade for some years. He afterwards engaged in the manufacture of patent machines for shearing cloth; then of cabinet ware, and at last he entered into the grocery business in Burling Slip. He conducted the last trade for some years with profit; but retired from it to embark in the manufacture of glue and isinglass, which he has carried on ever since—a period of more than thirty years. He has been interested for a long while in iron manufactures, and in his works near Baltimore he built, after, his own designs, the first locomotive ever constructed in the United States. He has shown much interest in the extension of the telegraph, and is a stockholder and an officer in the Atlantic Cable Companies. He has served in both branches of our Common Council, and what is extraordinary, he proved himself a most honest and honorable member—an example that few have been tempted to imitate since his time. The difficulty he had in obtaining an education made him solicitous of securing advantages for others, when he had become rich, and Cooper Institute is the fine result of a self-promise made forty years before its erection. The Institute embraces a school of design for women, evening courses of instruction for mechanics and apprentices, especially as respects the application of science to the practical affairs of life, a free reading-room, galleries of art, collections of models of inventions and a polytechnic school. The building cost $500,000, which is not far from half of Peter Cooper's fortune. He is still healthy and vigorous and no one would believe he was near his eightieth year. He is a peculiar-looking and noticeable person, under the medium size, with a sharp, thin visage, a profusion of brown hair, very little gray eyes, always wears gold spectacles, and seems as amiable, kind, and generous as he really is. No one ever doubted Peter Cooper's honesty. He is popular with all classes, and is never seen in public without eliciting applause. He has lived a true life; is a genuine democrat; an earnest friend of the people.

CHAPTER LXXX.

GEORGE LAW.

A VERY different man from Peter Cooper is George Law. Once a famous personage, he has so sunk out of sight, of late years, that the great public has almost entirely forgotten him. He was born in Washington county in this State, and his parents being poor, he came to the Metropolis to seek a livelihood. It is said he worked for his passage and arrived here penniless. He was in his first teens then; but being very stout and hardy he worked on the docks, and in warehouses for several months. At the end of that time he had saved a hundred dollars. With that sum he began to barter and trade, and soon increased it to $1,000—the hardest amount to get, millionaires tell us, though the statement is not always true. He had a talent for making money out of other people; but he remained in obscurity till he was fully thirty. The first known of him by the public was his appearance as contractor for building High Bridge for the Croton Aqueduct. He made the job profitable, and soon obtained other contracts from the City that rendered him prosperous. He purchased an interest in different ferry and street railway companies, and became an operator in Wall street, where his shrewdness served him to advantage. He was not a bold speculator, but had the sagacity to buy and sell at the right time, and rarely lost.

At one time the *Herald*—in the campaign of 1852, I think—nominated Law for the Presidency, and gave him the sobriquet of " Live-Oak George," which long adhered to him. No one except Law imagined for a moment the journalistic weathercock in earnest; but he was greatly flattered by the nomination, and really cherished aspirations for the White House.

During the Lopez expedition in Cuba he bought a lot of muskets, and placed them on board the Grapeshot. The vessel was seized while lying in port, on the charge that the muskets were intended for the filibusters, which no doubt was true. Law made a fierce protest against the seizure, and appealed to the courts. While the case was pending the attempted revolution failed, and Lopez was garroted. The fire-arms afterward proved of very little value, and if they had been used in Cuba would have been more destructive to their bearers than to the enemy. A great deal was said and written at the time about the George Law muskets, and their worthlessness grew to be a proverb. That venture was one of the very few in which he was not successful. He has the reputation of having made money out of whatever he has touched, and he ought to make it, for he is totally regardless of the feelings or comfort of others. He is still a large owner in ferries and railways, conducts them to please himself, and whistles at the public.

George Law is for himself first, last, and always, and he is, therefore, one of the most unpopular men in the Metropolis—a fact he cares nothing about so long as his coffers are full, and his digestion is perfect. His conscience is easy, for it lies in his bank account. The good he does must be in secret since it rarely becomes known.

Law has a handsome house in Fifth avenue, and is probably worth $5,000,000, though it would not be imagined from his appearance and manner that he would be admitted to his own house, or that his income was $1,000 a year. He must be about five and sixty now; has a strong constitution and muscular frame, and promises to be active and interest-calculating for thirty years yet. He is very large vertically and horizontally; dresses shabbily; has coarse features; resembles a car-man more than a millionaire, and is personally known to few. He is frequently to be seen walking and driving about on his private business; occasionally appears at Fulton Market in quest of oysters, which he swallows voraciously as if he were more savage than hungry; and now and then figures as a vice-president of some public meeting, which he never attends. Such is Live-Oak George, who, as has-been said, is a self-made man, and worships his creator.

CHAPTER LXXXI.

PETER B. SWEENEY.

PETER B. SWEENEY has recently risen into prominence as the Great Mogul of Tammany Hall. He is considered one of the shrewdest of Democratic politicians; makes politics his trade, and thrives by them. He is of Irish extraction, though native here, and seems to be a man of force more than fineness. He is a lawyer by profession; but he has quitted law for more lucrative, if not more disinterested pursuits, within the magic circle of the City Hall. He is the present City Chamberlain, and has made himself famous by paying over to the municipal government certain monthly sums of interest that have heretofore been kept by the incumbent of the office. The proceeding is so unprecedented that few New-Yorkers are willing to believe that any man capable of such conduct is acting from disinterested motives. Until recently, a bank President has usually been made the Chamberlain, and the bank has received the deposits of the City without interest. The balance to the credit of New-York is often $20,000,000, and it is estimated that the interest on the account is not infrequently $200,000 per annum. It is alleged that Sweeney does not give more than one-third of the interest to the Treasury; but that he pays any proportion of it voluntarily, and when there is no law to compel him, should certainly be interpreted to his credit.

As a wire-puller, caucus-controller, and manager of men, he is said to eclipse his astutest predecessors. He is the power behind the throne in the City Hall, and the avowed champion of the Ring. No Democratic body in this region can get along without Sweeney; and no Democratic caucus is complete without him. He is steadily increasing his influence, and in this stronghold of the party will find it to his advantage to stay. He is wealthy—probably $1,000,000 would not cover his fortune—in the prime of life; large, dark-haired, dark-eyed, swarthy-complexioned; feels proud of his political importance, and may long to have engraven on his marble monument in Greenwood, "Here lies the late leader of Tammany Hall."

CHAPTER LXXXII.

DISTINGUISHED CLERGYMEN.

NEARLY all of our well-known members of the clerical profession are doctors of divinity, except two of the very ablest,—Henry Ward Beecher and Octavius B. Frothingham, who have peremptorily declined to accept the degree.

After Beecher, Edwin H. Chapin, the Universalist, is the most popular and famous. Born in Union village, Washington county, in this State, Dec. 29, 1814, and receiving his education in a seminary at Burlington, Vt., he began preaching, in his twenty-third year, to a congregation of Universalists and Unitarians in Richmond, Va. Remaining there three years, he went to Massachusetts; filled a pulpit in Charlestown for six years, and in Boston for two; when he was called to the Fourth Universalist church in this City. He soon took high rank as a ministerial orator, and ever since—a period of twenty years—his reputation has been increasing.

His church, called the Divine Unity, was for many years in Broadway, but is now torn down, and a new and handsome edifice has been built in Fifth avenue. His congregation is very large, and his reputation attracts many strangers; so that, long before the hour of service, it is next to impossible to get a place. His style of eloquence is fervid and impassioned, abounding in ornament and metaphor. He seems to lay himself out, with pen and voice on particular passages; and he is often so theatrical that his audience is prompted to applaud. He is in great demand as a lecturer, and can easily earn $8,000 to $10,000 a season by appearing before lyceums. His salary is $10,000 a year, which, with such perquisites and presents as all popular clergymen receive, gives him a large and comfortable income.

Chapin is quite portly, very genial and amiable, but not at all clerical in appearance. He is very liberal in creed, and one of the best of our pulpit elocutionists and rhetoricians. He has published several volumes of sermons and lectures, and is fond of displaying his scholarship. He is very agreeable personally, and numbers his friends by hundreds.

The Rev. Henry W. Bellows, Unitarian, resembles Chapin somewhat, and is near him in reputation. He is a native of Boston, and now in his fifty-fifth year. He graduated at Harvard before he was nineteen, and completed his theological studies at Cambridge.

During the late Unitarian national convention, he delivered the opening sermon, which was an elaborate expression of his beliefs and desires. He severely, even bitterly, censured many of his brethren; denounced speculation as dangerous and pernicious; declared his faith in Jesus Christ, our Saviour, the only firm rock on which to stand; and, for two hours, spoke as if he had been a rigid Baptist or Presbyterian. In the convention he attacked the Rev. O. B. Frothingham, without mentioning his name, and entered upon issues that would have rent the church asunder, had not oil been ingeniously poured upon the troubled theologic waters.

He became pastor of the First Congregational church

here in 1838, and now presides over All Souls, irreverently called the Holy Zebra, Fourth avenue and Twentieth street. He was for many years the principal writer of the *Christian Inquirer*, which he was largely instrumental in founding, and now contributes to the *Christian Examiner*. He is a popular lecturer, and an eloquent, though rather monotonous, speaker, with many mannerisms. Rhetoric is his forte, as it is Chapin's, and he makes the most of it. He represents the orthodox class of Unitarians, and has for a long while been tending to the usual forms of theologic worship. He has several times threatened to withdraw from the Unitarians; nor is it strange,—for between himself and those who claim to be the most liberal, there is almost as much difference as between Universalists and Calvinists.

Ten or twelve years ago he created a sensation by advocating theaters and theatrical amusements. The broad church applauded, and the orthodox were indignant, and all over the country the theme was earnestly discussed by religious and secular journals. He was here regarded as the exponent of the broad church; but since then he has grown very conservative, and it has been rumored again and again that he was about to disown all connection with the Unitarians.

Bellows is tall, dark-complexioned, bald, rather patriarchal in appearance, and, if not opposed, gracious and gentle. His salary is $10,000, and his circumstances all that can be reasonably desired. He has written a great deal, though most of his writings are pamphlets on current topics, on which he took a decided stand for or against the question at issue.

The Rev. William Adams is the best known of the

Presbyterian clergymen in the City. He is the pastor of Madison Square church, one of the most fashionable in the Metropolis, and his congregation has the reputation of the wealthiest in the country. Bankers, politicians, merchants, and professional men of note, are members of his church; and it is stated that more prominent citizens can be found there than in any other place of worship in Manhattan. He has many enthusiastic admirers, who consider him exceedingly eloquent. It is a pity his eloquence can not induce his hearers who operate in Wall street, and pull political wires, to be more honest and upright in their dealings.

Adams is a native of Connecticut; but while a child, his father—a teacher of distinction—removed to Massachusetts. William was always of a religious turn, and exhibited an interest in the Bible and theological works at so tender an age as to awaken surprise and delight among his father's friends. He was regarded as a pious prodigy, and frequently entered upon discussions with ministers of reputation, and confounded them with his questions and his arguments.

He came to New-York thirty years ago for the benefit of his health; and, while spending the winter here, was induced to accept the pulpit of the Broome Street church. For the last fourteen years, he has been in Madison square, and he attracts every Sunday a very large and highly cultivated congregation.

He is very unlike Beecher, Bellows, or Chapin, in the style of his sermons and delivery. He has a horror of what is known as sensationalism, and consequently his sermons are simple and severe, but forcible and convincing. He is a man of large and varied reading, but like a man of true culture, he shows it in his thought instead of in display of needless learning. He has the usual $10,000 salary, and could have thrice this sum if he would accept it He has written several volumes, which breathe a spirit of eloquent devotion, and have large sales.

He is considered a model of what a clergyman should be in appearance, bearing, and even in costume. He is said to exercise a very wholesome influence on young men, who are much attached to him. He has, from his early years, been interested in foreign missions and in bible societies and has been intimately acquainted with eminent men zealous and energetic in the cause of Christianity. Though not far from sixty, he is still in the vigor of health, and has years of earnest and valuable work before him.

The Rev. H. B. Ridgaway presides over St. Paul's, in Fourth avenue,—the most fashionable and the wealthiest of the Methodist churches in the United States. The Methodists pay smaller salaries than the other denominations, and Ridgaway receives but $5,000, which is the maximum rate. According to the rule of the church, no minister preaches more than three years to the same congregation, which prevents it from forming a strong attachment to its pastor, as it might otherwise do. Ridgaway is young,—not yet forty. He is small in stature; dark and pale; yet looks as if he had studied hard, and led a very abstemious, if not ascetic life. He is neither showy nor brilliant, but is a close reasoner, and gives entire satisfaction to his flock. He formerly had charge of a congregation in Baltimore, and is a new, though by no means unwelcome, citizen and clergyman in this paradise of preachers.

The Rev. Henry C. Potter is the new pastor of Grace

church. He is the son of the eminent bishop, and has already obtained a strong hold upon the fashionable worshipers at that most fashionable temple. He is about forty, and well qualified to please his fastidious and critical congregation. He is called handsome by his feminine parishioners. He has an intellectual, student-like face; clear, expressive eyes; and fine brown whiskers, worn after the English style. He has a rich, well modulated voice, and reads the litany in an impressive and artistic manner, that delights his hearers. After the death of the Rev. Dr. Taylor, Grace found much difficulty in supplying his place. It offered $15,000 as salary, but no one came that was deemed suitable. It then reduced the sum to the regular rate, and Potter, having been put upon trial, was pronounced the man after whom the church had been seeking. The parsonage is exceedingly pleasant, and it and all the surroundings of Grace are so desirable that the bishop's son may well regard himself as fortunate.

The Rev. Thomas Armitage, among the Baptist clergy, is, perhaps, the most conspicuous. He holds divine service in the Fifth avenue Baptist church—a handsome and imposing edifice, that is always well attended. He is a prime favorite. His style of composition is more picturesque than that of most ministers of his creed, and his elocution graceful and winning. He has been called theatric; but that adjective is rarely applied to men who are not open to the suspicion of eloquence. He is about forty-five has a heavy frame and a large face, which looks larger from the entire absence of whiskers or mustache; wears his hair long; and reminds you somewhat of Beecher in his personal appearance. He has a very nervous manner, that shows intensity and earnestness, but does not add to the effect of his oratory.

Rev. Octavius B. Frothingham is one of the three Unitarian clergymen, and the most radical, in the City. He represents the most liberal wing of his church, as Dr. Bellows does the most orthodox. He is a come-outer, and the most eminent of the kind. Creed and dogmas are of no importance to him. What a man does, rather than what he believes, is the essence of his Christianity. He has faith in culture, in just deeds, in humanity, in self-sacrifice, in devotion. Where one's work is honest, earnest, noble, the worker can not be seriously wrong, whatever his form of belief or disbelief.

Frothingham is a native of Massachusetts, a graduate of Harvard; studied theology in the divinity school at Cambridge, and has been regarded as a disciple of Theodore Parker, many of whose opinions, and all of whose sympathies, he shares. Still he can not be justly called a Parkerite; for he accepts no man's views until his mental process makes them his own.

He is eminently an individual; does not claim to-day that he knows what he will think or do to-morrow. He believes in progress, development, purity, charity, and unselfishness: these are the sum of all religion. He is entirely democratic in his opinions, and sternly opposed to forms. For a long while he was unwilling to have a church, preferring to preach in public halls, on account of what he conceived to be the greater freedom of such places. But he was overruled by his congregation, who built a neat and elegant edifice in Fortieth street, known as the Third Congregational Church, where service is regularly held. His hearers are not many; but they are among the most intellectual and cultivated in New-York.

A number of journalists and artists, authors and professional men go there, and they listen to his discourses sympathetically but critically. No one who hears Frothingham can doubt he is a thinker, however much he may fail to take the view of the hearer. The minister is rather a small man, about forty-six, with a nervous, eager, fine face, excellent manners, and thoroughly well bred because reposeful air. He has long, wavy hair, sprinkled with gray; dresses neatly, even elegantly, and gives the impression of fastidiousness and daintiness in every thing.

He often speaks extemporaneously, and very well. His written sermons are vigorous, eloquent and polished. He is very quiet, rarely gesticulating, but reads from his manuscript in a soft, sweet voice the convictions of his heart, the freshest ideas of his brain, gracefully and classically expressed. He is thought by many affected, but he is not, though it is probable that what were mannerisms at first are natural now. He is a clever writer; contributes to the *Radical*, the *Nation*, and other periodicals. He has been accused of coldness, but his life is earnest, generous, and beautiful; and he has warm friendships, that have continued through years.

Rev. Samuel Osgood is the pastor of the new Church of the Messiah, one of the most costly in town, in Park avenue, but not in the best taste. Osgood seems to stand midway between his two Unitarian brothers, Bellows and Frothingham, neither so conservative as the one, nor so radical as the other. He is not very individual in his views, and inclines to form and ceremony almost as much as an Episcopalian; wearing a black silk gown during service, and surrounding himself with all that can add to his ministerial dignity.

He is from Massachusetts also. He is the successor of Dr. Orville Dewey, and has been in the pulpit here for nearly twenty years. He has read a great deal,— more than he has digested perhaps; is receptive rather than creative, and is thought to have modeled himself somewhat, though unconsciously, upon Dr. Bellows.

His sermons are committed to memory, after being written with great care, and abound in quotations, learned allusions, studied alliteration, and all the tempting vices of ornamental rhetoric. He is thoroughly self-appreciative, and would be more effective and interesting if less self-conscious and apparently affected. He is very popular with his congregation, and has decided talent, though no genius. He has written a number of books, and contributes freely to the magazines. Among his writings is an autobiography under the title of "Mile Stones on Life's Journey," which attracted much attention, and sold largely.

He is very fond of writing and speaking, and has delivered numerous orations before colleges, societies, and on public occasions. He is of the $10,000 salary number, and has a very handsome property. He owns a pleasant house in town and a fine country seat at Plainfield, Conn., where he spends the Summer in picturesque and luxurious retirement. A lucky man is Samuel Osgood. He enjoys the material things of life as well as the spiritual things; is fond of society, and is the companion of artists and littérateurs as often as his clerical duties, which are numerous, will permit.

Rev. Morgan Dix, of Trinity, is the apostle of High Churchism; has chants, surpliced singers, and all the pomp of ritualism, and would have still more forms if he had his own way. He is the son of General Dix, a man of good ability, an agreeable preacher, and dear to the heart of his congregation.

Rev. Stephen H. Tyng, Jr., is the antipodes of Dix. Not many months since he drew upon himself the condemnation of a portion of the Episcopal Church for entering the pulpit of a Methodist clergyman in New Brunswick, N. J., and his trial elicited the comments of the press far and wide. That trial was an excellent thing for Tyng's reputation; for ever since he has been among the most talked-of clergymen in the City. His congregation believed that he was persecuted; regarded him as a martyr, and formed a new and deeper affection for him than they had ever experienced before.

The younger Tyng is an earnest and eloquent advocate of Low Churchism; as thoroughly democratic in his feelings and sympathies as Dix is aristocratic. He has of late been preaching to the people in the street, as a protest no doubt against chants, and choristers, and the intoned service of Trinity.

His open-air sermons have been largely attended, and his popularity has greatly increased. He is the rector of the Church of the Holy Trinity, Madison avenue and Forty-second street. He is slight, pale, rather emaciated, intense and eager in temperament, speaking with force and animation, and compelling the attention of his hearers.

The Episcopalians have various grades and degrees of creed and ceremony. Rev. C. W. Morrill, of St. Albans, in Lexington avenue, is the extremist in his ritualism. At that chapel, incense, miters, croziers, banners, and all the elaborate forms of Catholicism, are to be seen. Morrill has the title of Father. He has established auricular confession, and there is little difference between his and the Roman service, save that his is in English. Many of his fair parishioners are devoted to him, and never weary in performing any tasks or sacrifices he may intimate as desirable. He is a large, strong man, the opposite of an ascetic in appearance, positive, imperious at times, and yet full of soft persuasion, and very winning in his manners.

Rev. F. C. Ewer, of Christ's Church, Fifth avenue and Thirty-fifth street, has distinguished himself by declaring Protestantism a failure. He is trying to do what Pusey did; and yet he does not go half so far in ceremony as "Father" Morrill. He is a large, dark man, broad forehead, deep-chested; has a vigorous mind, and seems to hold his congregation by the strings of their hearts.

Rev. Chauncey Giles, of the New Jerusalem Church, Thirty-fifth street, between Fourth and Lexington avenues, is a very able man and an effective reasoner. He is a native of Massachusetts; went West and taught school; was stationed in Cincinnati for some years, and is now firmly established here. His congregation, less than five hundred in number, is enthusiastic about him, and would not part with him on any terms. He is of massive mold, conveying the impression of both physical and mental strength; has profound and varied culture, and deserves his reputation of a scholar and thinker.

Archbishop McCloskey is much loved by an immense population of Catholics. He is an earnest but quiet prelate, appearing particularly so in contrast with his predecessor, Archbishop Hughes, to whom controversy was as the bread of life. He is a pleasant, urbane, and learned gentleman, and has many warm friends among all sects. He is a fluent and an interesting talker, and universally esteemed.

Samuel Adler is the Rabbi of the Jewish Temple, No. 112 East Twelfth street, the handsomest and costliest synagogue in the country. The Hebrews who worship there are of the most liberal sort, and he is held in high repute for his learning. He has all the marked features of his race, and is a man of fine mind and great force of character.

LOW GROGGERY.

LXXXIII.

JOHN ALLEN, THE WICKEDEST MAN.

John Allen, the notorious wickedest man, of No. 304 Water street, having had his day, has fallen almost entirely out of the public eye. It is singular what effect a superlative will have upon the community. John Allen's dance-house had been visited and described again and again by correspondents and magazine-writers; but they did not give his name or address, nor have the audacity to apply the superlative to him. When an unknown writer told Allen's story in plain language in a sensational monthly, Allen became notorious, and the biographer shared his subject's notoriety. Of course, every one wanted to know about the wickedest man in New-York, where there are thousands of such, each one of whom thinks he deserves the distinction. Consequently everybody read the sketch, and a crowd of people, both residents and strangers, hurried to Water street, to see and talk to the moral monster.

Allen, a singular compound of conceit and coarseness, was delighted to find himself a hero, and wishing to continue the character, declared to the wistful clergymen who crowded about him begging him to reform, that he had experienced a change of heart, and was determined to lead a new life. Allen had always been inclined to theological discussion; and considered himself a sort of preacher because he had brothers in the pulpit. He was quite familiar with the Bible; and to repeat its passages, interlarding them with obscene stories, to mix religion with his rum, and quote Genesis over his gin, were his favorite recreations. Allen should have been a Methodist exhorter—his mind and temperament impelled him in that direction; but the influence of early associations and something of the unregenerate evil of his nature drove him upon bar-rooms and dance-houses for a livelihood. He was in his element with the clergymen about him, and when they proposed prayer-meetings in his establishment he leaped at the chance of continuing the sensation.

For weeks No. 304 was the scene of fervid religious exercises. Curiosity filled the place, where there was abundant opportunity to point a moral and adorn a tale. Allen was alluded to as a monument of God's mercy, and as a brand snatched from the burning. Several of the unfortunate women he had employed became affected through their unstrung nerves with the spirit of the hour, and from tippling wantons became weeping Magdalens. The wickedest man enjoyed all that excessively. It appealed to his love of excitement, and he was heard to say privately that the dance-house was a d—d fool to the prayer-meeting.

After awhile religion began to cloy upon Allen. He craved a new sensation, and concluded to lecture. He went to Stamford, Conn., with an essay he had paid some New-York reporter to write for him, and had a select and sympathetic audience of six. Then he visited Bridgeport, and was about to make confession of his past errors and present repentance, when he had a first-class attack of delirium tremens.

After that Allen retired from the lecture field; returned to this City; proclaiming his intention to resume his original business. The police notified him if he did, that they would arrest him and his girls every night. He defied them, and opened his dance-house again. The police kept their word. They arrested Allen and all his supernumeraries, though he was no more guilty than dozens of other dance-house keepers in that neighborhood, who are never molested. But that is the way the Metropolitan police have of doing things; and as it is much less mischievous than many other of their ways, perhaps it is unwise to complain. They had formed a prejudice against Allen, who, they professed, had shocked their moral sense by his duplicity, and they would have locked him up every time he gave his fandangoes. That he did not like. So he offered his notorious den for sale, and went to Connecticut, where he could enjoy his delirium tremens without the interference of the police.

The last has been heard of John Allen. He is an exploded sensation. Water street is not likely to see again his broad forehead and rather intelligent face, his keen blue eye, light hair, thin jaw, and spare sidewhiskers, above a well-knit, compact frame. He may turn up as a preacher or as a prize fighter,—it is about an even thing,—but his career as a rum-seller and dance-house keeper is over. He can repose upon his laurels; for he has made $100,000 by his shameful calling, and declares he doesn't want to make any more.

What is termed the religious awakening, however, continues in Water street. No. 304 is shut up; but at No. 316 daily prayer-meetings are held under the auspices of the Howard Mission, and are productive of much good. Many of the papers and people ridiculed the attempt at a great revival, and referred to John Allen's backsliding as an evidence of its hollowness; but the effort, in addition to its praiseworthiness, has borne excellent fruit. No one will say that prayer-meetings, even if their success be limited, are not better than common prostitution, constant intemperance, and riots of sensuality. Let the prayer-meetings continue! They may help to purify the atmosphere of Water street, and fill its darkest places with rays of hopeful light.

CHAPTER LXXXIV.

MARK M. POMEROY.

MARK M. POMEROY has recently become a citizen of the Metropolis. The extraordinary success he had with the La Crosse (Wis.) *Democrat* convinced him that he needed a larger field and a more appreciative audience than a Western town could give him; and therefore he is here. On this propitious Island he has set up his new daily, the *Democrat,* and will soon issue his weekly from the same office. He says he has prospered beyond his most sanguine expectations, and that the *Democrat* is already firmly established. His non-admirers affirm that he is losing money rapidly, and that he must fail; that the notoriety of his paper made it sell for a few weeks, but that it attracts no attention now. Pomeroy is a notability. A violent and reckless course, that would have ruined most men, seems to have helped him to fortune. His perpetual and violent abuse of President Lincoln, of the Army, of the War, of the Union cause, was quite enough to kill his paper, which has, however, flourished greatly. If it had not, he would not have had the boldness to come to New-York and issue a daily, where there are journals in excess.

Pomeroy was born in Lawrenceville, Penn., on Christmas Day, in 1833; his father being a New-York merchant, still living, and in California. His mother died when he was an infant, and an uncle adopted him. He lived on a farm and worked hard till he was seventeen, being reared according to the severe and somewhat somber teachings of the Presbyterian church, which his mature writings seem to have reflected. In his eighteenth year he went into a printing office in Corning, in this State, and there mastered the art preservative. He afterward went to Waverly, and then to Canada West, where he remained for several years. In 1857 he removed his local habitation to Wisconsin. He there embarked in several newspaper enterprises, and was at one time local reporter of the Milwaukee *News*. When he undertook the *Democrat*, at La Crosse, he found his place. There, and with that, he became known far and wide; all his political opponents quoting his opinions and sentiments to injure his party, and most of his allies consigning him to perdition for his audacity.

Pomeroy is better known as "Brick" than Mark, the sobriquet having been given him, it is said, by the Louisville (Ky.) *Journal*, because of his clever execution of a local sketch copied into its columns. He is an energetic and persevering fellow, vindictive and bitter to the last degree. One of the most earnest and persistent efforts of his late life has been to prove that Abraham Lincoln, whom the whole Nation believes to have been both a great and a good man, and who was one of the foremost characters of the Republic, is irrevocably damned, or, as the *Democrat* tersely expresses it, has gone to hell. Pomeroy's opinion may be entitled to weight, for he speaks like an accredited representative of the place, and as if he felt sure of finding the noble martyr there. Another purpose of Pomeroy's existence is to abuse General Butler, to whom he gave the title of the Beast, and whose name he has associated with the plunder of spoons He has always declared Butler's father was hanged for piracy, though Butler himself has no knowledge of the fact. Pomeroy, in his private life, is said to be amiable, and strongly attached to his friends, which is probable, as he is certainly attached to his foes. He is a mild-looking man, bald above the forehead, blue-eyed, of the medium height, rather heavy and not very prepossessing features.

He is reported to have many of the physical virtues; to abstain from liquor, profanity, and tobacco; though I can't help believing that a man who has so much abuse to heap upon the dead Lincoln and living Butler can hardly find time to indulge in the smaller vices I have named. Pomeroy is self-made, a perpetual clamorer for Democracy and the rights of the People, and on the best of terms with his maker.

CHAPTER LXXXV.

EMINENT BUSINESS MEN.

Few business men in New-York who have shown judgment, energy, and prudence have failed of success. Nearly all of them have accumulated fortunes in a few years; for in this great center the path of good management soon strikes the road to prosperity. Once to get a foothold here is to grow rich, because the moment a house is fairly established trade flows in upon it from every part of the country. The merchants of the Metropolis are truly merchant princes in wealth and their luxurious style of living. Hundreds who are never heard of off the Island, and who are little known on it, reckon their property at $500,000, $600,000, $800,000, and often by more than $1,000,000; nor is it strange, for Broadway, Church, White street, and West Broadway, supply the markets of the United States.

One of the oldest and best known firms is Grinnell, Minturn & Co. This shipping house is located at No. 78 South street, and though the old name is retained, the business is conducted by the sons of the original partners. The business of the house is small compared to what it used to be, for the War gave a blow to our shipping interests, from which they have not yet recovered. Robert B. Minturn, who was universally esteemed in social and commercial circles died two years ago, and Moses H. Grinnell, a most creditable type of the old school merchant, takes no active part in the business. He is the President of the Sun Insurance Company, at $10,000 a year, and his name is mentioned in connection with a lucrative office during the incoming administration. The name of Grinnell became widely known by the expedition Henry, Moses' brother, and one of the original members of the firm, fitted out ten or twelve years ago, for the search of Sir John Franklin, and in which laudable undertaking he spent a large sum of money. Moses was born in New Bedford, Mass., was bred a merchant, and was a representative in Congress from New York from 1839 to 1841. He is sixty-five; has white hair and whiskers, florid complexion, and is quite English-looking. He is very affable and courteous; has been in times past a profuse entertainer, and is still a very pleasant companion. He was to South street what Jacob Little was to Wall street. He formerly resided in the house occupied by Delmonico, in Fourteenth street, but now lives at Irvington, on the Hudson.

Howland, Aspinwall & Co., another famous shipping house, are at No. 54 South street. It is conducted by Gardiner G. Howland and Samuel and Wm. H. Aspinwall, and though still doing a large business, it is much less extended than it has been. The firm formerly owned numerous vessels in the California and trans-Atlantic trade; but the War so prostrated our commerce as to interfere largely with their interests. Gardiner G. Howland lives in affluence; dispenses elegant hospitalities; drives fast horses; stands high on 'Change and in fashionable circles.

Horace B. Claflin & Co., after Stewart, do the heaviest business in dry-goods in the Union. Indeed, Claflin's wholesale trade is larger than that of Stewart, who, by adding his retail department, swells his aggregate sales beyond those of his energetic rival. Claflin's immense house occupies half of the whole block on Church, Worth, and West Broadway; is, Stewart's up-town bazaar excepted, the finest and most conspicuous in the whole City. Claflin employs 600 or 700 persons in his establishment, and pays liberal salaries to all of them, giving his confidential clerk $25,000 a year. He is a native of New-England; has a "down-East" appearance; being thin, angular, smooth-shaven, energetic, prompt, and direct in his dealings. He is much more popular than Stewart; has the reputation of being liberal in his relations, both mercantile and private, and is highly esteemed by his employés. He is probably worth $12,000,000 to $15,000,000, and his trade extends to all the States, the Territories, Canada, and South America. During the busy season his store looks like a human bee-hive. The sidewalks on the three sides of the vast building are covered with boxes, bales, and cases, directed to every town and village in the United States. Every ship that comes to the port, and touches at our piers, brings merchandise for him; and his name is written in the ledgers of all the great firms of Manchester, Glasgow, and London, Paris, Hamburg, and Berlin. His business increases every season, and his is the one controlling, directing mind that computes millions as easily as some men's does pennies.

Abiel A. Low has been twice elected President of the Chamber of Commerce, and his house, A. A. Low & Brothers, stands at the head of the China trade. Low is a native of Salem, Mass., the son of Seth Low, himself an eminent merchant, and in his early manhood removed to this City. His father having been in the China trade, the young man wished to visit that country to acquire a knowledge of the business. He did so, and soon after his arrival became a partner in the well-known house of Russell & Co., of Canton. He remained in the firm for eight years, until he had become its head, withdrawing from it in 1841, and returning to the United States. The same year he established, with his two brothers, the present house, which is at No. 31 Burling slip, retaining his correspondents in China. Messrs. Low are very large ship-owners. Their vessels arrive with teas, silks, crapes, nankeens, and return with what the Celestials desire in exchange. They have recently established a house at Yokahama, and have large interests in the Japan trade. Low's loyalty to the Government during the War was unswerving even in the darkest hours. He gave his money freely to the cause, and has always been a generous encourager of literature, education, and art. He lives in Brooklyn, and in the midst of his family is said to find his purest enjoyment.

E. S. Jaffray & Co., the well known importers, No. 350 Broadway, do a very heavy and profitable business, and stand very high in mercantile circles. Their large brown-stone store is said to be one of the pleasantest in town to be employed in. Every clerk, and salesman, and carman, and porter in the establishment is attached to the firm, and speaks of "our house" with a natural and praiseworthy pride. Jaffray is of Scotch extraction, a sandy-haired, sandy-complexioned man, with many of the qualities of his nationality. His word is literally as good as his bond. He is frequently chosen umpire and referee by his fellow-merchants, and his decision is always acquiesced in.

He has never been known to take any unfair advantage in trade, or in any dealing with his fellows. When his store was injured by the burning of Chittenden's establishment, Winter before last, the underwriters supposed his loss was large, and would gladly have paid him $150,000 to $200,000 for damages. He said it was trifling, however, and made a return of only a few thousands. He is reported to be worth $5,000,000 or $6,000,000, and to give away a large part of his income in charity.

Jaffray, judging from his reputation, is a model merchant, after whom dozens that are better known and much richer might take pattern with advantage to themselves and the community at large.

Jackson S. Schultz is one of our largest leather dealers, at No. 96 Cliff street. He has been very successful in business, having begun life as a practical tanner, and is probably worth $1,500,000 to $2,000,000. He owes his fortune entirely to his own exertions. He attends personally to all the details of his business; but finds ample leisure to devote to charities and humanities of every kind. He was for a long while President of the Board of Health, which owes to him its usefulness if not its origin. He is an officer and director in many of the charitable institutions, and on an average spends five or six hours a day in looking after the good and happiness of others.

Few men are busier than he, or have more to attend to; but his energy, perseverance, and zeal carry him through all he undertakes. He is extremely generous, and hundreds of persons whom he has forgotten, speak with enthusiastic gratitude of the favors they have received at his hands.

Shultz is a muscular, shaggy-haired, strong, large-limbed, large-hearted man, who might have made a prize-fighter, if nature had not put into his bosom the soul of a gentleman, and filled his blood with currents of tenderness that run quickly to the call of every creature in sorrow and distress.

Among the numerous publishing houses in the City the Appletons and Harpers stand at the head on account of their age, their excellence, and their great wealth.

D. Appleton & Co. is still the style of the firm, though Daniel Appleton, the founder of the house, has long since been dead. The business is conducted by his four sons, the eldest of whom is over fifty, and the youngest two or three and thirty. The story current that Daniel Appleton was a practical printer, came early to the Metropolis, and nearly half a century ago had a small printing office in or near Pearl street, is wholly without foundation. He was born in Haverhill, Mass.; was a general storekeeper there; afterward removed to a larger field in Boston, and subsequently to this City. Here he began the importation of English books, and from the small beginning grew up a very considerable business. He changed his quarters to more commodious ones, and soon had more than he could do. From that time till the day of his death his business rapidly and regularly increased, and at present it is still increasing.

Appleton & Co. have recently removed from their handsome marble store in Broadway to the new building corner of Grand and Greene streets, and have their vast printing and book-binding establishment in Williamsburg instead of Franklin street. They have done less and less of late in miscellaneous books and in the retail trade, having turned their attention to the publication of school and Spanish works. In the latter they do an immense business with South America, shipping boxes upon boxes of Don Quixote, Calderon, and Da Vega, and other classics, by almost every vessel that leaves here for Montevideo, Buenos Ayres, and Rio Janeiro. On various books they have made large sums. On the New American Cyclopedia, for instance, they have cleared, up to the present time, not less than $700,000, and the sale is still steady. No one knows how much they are worth; perhaps they do not know themselves. The firm must count its wealth by millions, and their regular business must bring an income of fully $100,000 to each of the members. They are still close calculators and shrewd managers, and look after the dollars as if they had but a slender salary to depend on, which is the way of prosperous human nature, and particularly the way of the Appletons.

Harper & Brothers is the oldest publishing house in the country. The firm is composed of James, aged seventy-three; John, seventy-one; Joseph W., sixty-seven; and Fletcher, sixty-two. They have seven of their sons in the establishment, so it may well be called a family concern. The four brothers are sons of a Long Island farmer, having been born in Newtown. He was very industrious and frugal, and his boys have been like him. James and John were apprenticed by their father to the printing business in this City. They afterward set up as printers for booksellers, though they set type and worked at the press themselves. Wesley and Fletcher were subsequently apprenticed to their elder brothers, and when they had served their time obtained an interest in the business. Fletcher, though the youngest, is the real manager and director of the house. He it was who originated the idea of the Magazine, to which, it is said, the other brothers were opposed, fearful that it would prove an unprofitable enterprise. He persuaded them at last to accept his view, and the result proved the soundness of his judgment. The Magazine succeeded at once, and it now has a circulation of more than 125,000. In 1853, three years after the issuing of the Monthly, the establishment was burned to the ground, causing a loss of $1,500,000. The Harpers were still in comfortable circumstances; but they had no idea of being driven out of business by a fire. They took counsel with each other the night after the occurrence, and determined to go on without delay. In two weeks they had a plan for a new building, which they resolved should be fire-proof, to prevent a repetition of the disaster. The result was the immense structure in Franklin square, which has another entrance on Cliff street. The building is of iron, painted white, seven stories high. The two main buildings are connected by iron bridges, as are the different stories by a circular iron staircase running outside the building. The structure is the largest and completest in the world. It employs seven or eight hundred persons, over a hundred of them women, who read MS., print, electrotype, bind, draw, and engrave. The Harpers have every facility for making a perfect book, and turn out excellent work. Their facilities are so great and their connections so numerous that they can sell enough copies of almost any book they accept to avoid loss. They are practical men; having no idea of publishing a volume they think won't pay. Of course, they make mistakes sometimes; but not half so often as would be supposed. Their issues include every thing, from sentimental novels to purely scientific works, from European guide-books to reprints of the ancient classics. They publish *Harpers' Weekly* and the *Bazar*, both of which have had enormous success.

James was once Mayor of the City, having been elected when the municipal government was so outrageously administered that the people determined upon a change. He is very quiet and undemonstrative; adheres so closely to his duties that if you were to see him at his desk you would imagine him an old and faithful book-keeper, to whom method and application had become second nature. He is very young-looking for his years, and is much taller than John, who is also a reticent, hard worker. Joseph, a thin and diffident-seeming man, bears slight resemblance to his brothers; thinks much and says little. He has more culture and literary taste than any of the others, and is said to write with force and elegance. Fletcher is the talker and humorist of the firm. He is tall, light-haired, blue-eyed, has a well-shaped head, and is very pleasant and companionable withal. He looks after new books, the Weeklies, and the Monthly, and receives authors and writers who have dealings with the firm. John Harper supervises the general business, Joseph attends to the literary correspondence, and James directs the different departments. The four brothers can be found almost any day in the counting-room, which is separated by an iron railing from the general salesroom, on the second floor. They go to their desks regularly, and have no patience with men who fail to do their duty. They enjoy work. They have been actively engaged so long that they could not stop if they would. They are a peculiar old quartette, and though anxious always to drive a good bargain, are among the most liberal publishers in the City.

Among the well-known landlords of New-York, Col. Charles A. Stetson is the most conspicuous. Though he no longer takes an active part in the management of the Astor, he is to be seen daily in its corridors, and is as full of interesting reminiscence, pleasant anecdote, and dramatic illustration as ever. Though over sixty he would pass for forty, and his smooth, rosy face, mild eyes, and genial expression, bring back New-York as it was more than thirty years ago. He is a pattern Boniface; is thoroughly well bred, easy, graceful, elegant, a delightful talker, and a general favorite. A native of Massachusetts, he reveres New-England, and yet loves New-York. Unlike many of his class, he was decided in his political views from the beginning of the War; aided the Northern cause and soldiers with voice and money. His hotel was always open to loyal soldiers whether they had or had not the means of payment. His reply to a dispatch, "The Astor House has no price for Massachusetts soldiers," was a patriotic poem, and will long be remembered.

The Lelands are famed among hotel proprietors. They now have seven or eight houses; the Metropolitan here, the Union and Columbian at Saratoga, the Delavan at Albany, the Occidental at San Francisco, and several others. They seem born to the business; for they have always succeeded where others have failed. Simeon Leland is the principal man here, albeit no one seems to understand where one Leland fades off and another rises into light. They are all energetic, sharp, tactful, good judges of human nature, and understand the peculiar line of their calling.

R. L. & A. Stuart are the famous sugar-refiners. They began life in the most humble way. Their mother, an industrious Irish woman, was so poor that she made molasses candy, and sent her little boys out to sell it. From that homely trade she set up a small candy store in Chambers street, out of which grew the large establishment and the well-known sugar-refinery that have made for the firm a vast fortune. Alexander Stuart still lives a bachelor in Chambers street, but Robert L. has one of the handsomest houses in Fifth avenue, at the corner of Twentieth street. The Stuarts are devout Presbyterians, and are fine examples of what honesty and industry will accomplish for friendless boys.

CHAPTER LXXXVI.

YOUNG MEN'S CHRISTIAN ASSOCIATION.

The Young Men's Christian Association, designed for the mental and more especially the moral improvement of young men, is about sixteen years old. The society was organized here, and held its first meeting at Stuyvesant Institute in Broadway. Since then every large city and town in the country has formed associations of the same name, with the same object. Its present quarters are at the corner of Broadway and Twenty-second street, where they have pleasant rooms.

They expect to remove the coming year to the corner of Twenty-third street and Fourth avenue, where their new building, a six-story brick, which, with the ground, will cost $400,000 or $500,000, is now in process of erection. The stores on the first floor will be rented with other parts of the building, so that the income from the property will be handsome. The Association is to have a large library, lecture and reading rooms, parlors, and a gymnasium, where young men will be invited to pass their evenings instead of exposing themselves to the temptations, or indulging in the vices of the City.

Branches have been established down town—one of them in Wooster street for colored young men—and more will be.

The Association has done much good in furnishing the

means of instruction and rational enjoyment to young men in town, particularly to strangers. Its rooms are always open to such, and a warm welcome is always extended. The members give a standing invitation to the public to attend their prayer-meetings and devotional exercises, and if the greater part of the public fail to seek religion as a source of consolation and happiness, preferring theaters, concert saloons, billiards and bar-rooms to theological discussions and the teachings of Christ, it must be attributed to the wicked perversity that marks fallen humanity. The young Christians do their part energetically and conscientiously, and the sins of the unregenerate multitude are not upon their unsullied souls.

The Association claims the credit of originating the Fulton street prayer-meeting, which has held a protracted session for the past twelve or thirteen years. Any body of men, young or old, who could create a spirit of prayer that would last through such a period can not be too highly commended. The Fulton street prayer-meeting is as actively and enthusiastically conducted as it was before the War; and from all past and present indications is likely to be perpetual. It must be a great relief to the merchants and clerks in the vicinity to sink their trials and cares in noonday devotions, and open their surcharged bosoms to the confidence of Heaven. The merchants thereabout often speak, I am told, of the happy effect of snatching a few minutes from the busiest hours of the day, and giving them freely to the Lord.

At the breaking out of the War, the Association interested itself profoundly in the spiritual needs of the soldiers who had volunteered. The members visited the camps about the City; distributed hymn-books, and bibles, and tracts of a most elevating character, representing the danger of the wicked and the advantage of being on the right side, whether the battle was waged against the South or the devil. After the opening of hostilities the young Christians visited the hospitals of the wounded in and about New-York, and were ready to act as watchers and nurses whenever their services were needed. They rendered invaluable aid in that way, and toward the close of 1861 founded the Christian Commission, whose members visited the armies, and during and after the battles rendered all possible aid to the wounded, whether friend or foe. Those who were in the field can recall, as I do, countless instances of their generous devotion and Christian charity.

The Association now has about seventeen or eighteen hundred members, and when they are in their new building, will have increased facilities for doing good. They now perform much religious mission work, and, by example, counsel, and solicitation, seek to turn the attention and thoughts of all they can influence to the beauty of a purely Christian life. They propose to give a regular course of free lectures each season, and to offer such inducements to young men as will make their rooms attractive and instructive. The religious community has much interest in the Association, and will, no doubt, co-operate with it in all it undertakes. Money has been freely subscribed for the society, and will be again. It works with so much zeal, and has such perfect faith in its future and its benefit to humanity, that it appeals to the generosity and admiration even of many who hold very different views, but who reverence the earnest desire to do good wherever shown.

CHAPTER LXXXVII.

THE PUBLIC SCHOOLS.

Our Public Schools are among the few public things in the City that are creditable; though this is truer of the system than of its application. The schools are under the direction of the Board of Education, composed of Trustees elected from the districts, and of Commissioners from the wards. When the Trustees and Commissioners happen to be educated men of character, the schools they have charge of are well managed; but when, as very often happens, they are ignorant and unprincipled, the schools suffer thereby. There is, therefore, a marked difference in the schools. Some of them are excellent, and others the opposite.

It is not uncommon for the Trustees to be keepers of groggeries, who can hardly write their own name, and who would be last in the lowest spelling-class, if they were submitted to the mysterious test of orthography.

The pupils are as different as they conveniently can be, and vary with the district. In the lower wards, and on the east side of the town, they are mostly of foreign parentage, and very inferior to those of the schools in Twelfth, Thirteenth, and Twenty-eighth streets. Nor are all the pupils, as is often supposed, the children of poor people, though the majority are. In some of the districts the scholars belong to the best families in the City, their parents sending them to prove their democratic principles.

The school-houses are nearly all handsome buildings of brick, well arranged, well ventilated, and well furnished. They number ninety-four in all. Of these, thirty-five contain three separate departments—masculine, feminine, and primary; eight, two departments—masculine and primary; five, feminine and primary; one, masculine and feminine; two, two feminine departments and primaries; two, with one department only for both sexes, and thirty-six separate primary schools, making in all one hundred and eighty-seven separate and distinct departments or schools, viz.: forty-four grammar schools for boys (including colored schools); forty-five grammar schools for girls (including colored schools); seven grammar schools for both sexes (including colored schools) fifty-five primary departments (including colored schools); thirty-six primary schools (including colored schools).

The attendance at the schools steadily increases. Last year it was about four thousand more than during the year previous. The latest report gives the following:—

Schools.	Average Attendance.	Whole No. Taught.
Grammar Schools and Primary Departments	65,139	146,986
Primary Schools	16,459	43,068
Colored Schools	737	2,056
Evening Schools	7,479	16,510
Normal Schools	406	1,000
Corporate Schools	6,074	16,567
Total	96,294	226,187

The whole number of teachers employed in the several schools and departments during last year was 2,206, of whom 176 were men and 2,030 women. Of this number, 241 held certificates of qualification from the State Superintendent of Public Instruction, twenty-six were graduates of the State Normal School at Albany, and the remainder held certificates from this Department. Upward of 1,900 of these teachers have been engaged in teaching six months and over during the year.

Children can begin with the alphabet in the primary schools, and end with graduation, if girls, at the grammar schools ; or, if boys, with graduation, at the Free Academy, now called the College of the City of New-York. The girls have no high school coresponding to the Academy, where Latin, Greek, mathematics, and all the branches of a regular college are taught ; but this want will probably soon be supplied. Those who intend to become teachers study for a year or two in the supplemental classes, in which particular attention is paid to algebra, geometry and trigonometry, physics, chemistry, history, and general literature.

The evening schools, twenty-six in number, with twelve feminine and fourteen masculine departments, are in most flourishing condition. Girls under ten, and boys under twelve years of age are not admitted, and satisfactory evidence as to character deportment, and earnest purpose are always required. The total number of scholars registered during last year was 15,279, and those attending the full term 6,165, only about 40 per cent. of the number registered. Many of the pupils are regular in attendance and very studious ; but more are so irregular as to defeat the object of the teachers. Not a few of the scholars are men and women. Germans over twenty-one are numerous in the Tenth and Seventeenth wards, their object being to learn English.

The evening High School in Thirteenth street is one of the most valuable of the schools. It is intended for young men in situations who wish to fit themselves for advanced positions. The school pays particular attention to book-keeping, the natural sciences, mathematics, and modern languages, especially French, German, and Spanish. All of the pupils are young men, the majority of them over eighteen, and earnest in their effort to improve. They number 900 or 1,000, and are among the most diligent and exemplary of the attendants at the Public Schools. Desire for knowledge with them is a hunger and a thirst, not a mere routine of study as it is with many who are educated at the expense of the City.

The pupils of the schools have no outlay whatever, the City furnishing the necessary books, which are not the same in all the schools. The Board of Education selects such books as it thinks best for the pupils in the different schools, so that the geographies, arithmetics and grammars, even in the same classes, vary very much.

Corporal punishment has been practically abolished, and with excellent effect, and other reforms are in progress.

The teachers' salaries are from $550 to $2,500, and even $3,000; the first for women in the primary schools and the last for men as principals. It is a just ground for complaint that the men receive nearly one-half more than the women for performing exactly the same duties, which may be explained, though it can not be excused, by the fact that the feminine teachers, in proportion to the masculine, are as twelve to one.

The annual expense of the schools, in round numbers, is $3,000,000, which, considering the average attendance at 100,000, makes the cost of educating each pupil about $300 a year.

CHAPTER LXXXVIII.

DISTINGUISHED WOMEN.

ALICE and PHŒBE CARY are so intimately associated in the public mind, and so well known as the poet sisters, that one can hardly speak of them apart. Alice is five years older than Phœbe, and, having written much more, is far better known. But they have always been together from early childhood, and their similarity of taste, and entire sympathy, prove that they are sisters in spirit as well as in blood.

The Carys were born at Mount Pleasant, near Cincinnati, Ohio, and remained in that vicinity until they were young women. They lived in the country most of the time, and from the woods and streams, the hills and valleys that abound in the picturesque region about Cincinnati, acquired the fondness for, and familiarity with, Nature, which have since shown themselves in their writings, particularly in Alice's Clovernook stories.

They were accustomed to commit their thoughts and feelings to paper from their girlhood, contributing verses and stories, as they grew older, to the newspapers and magazines that were within their reach. For years they wrote without pay, because it was a pleasure to them, and so gained much facility and grace of composition, particularly in verse. Alice was always very industrious, but Phœbe had comparatively little inclination to verse or to prose, and had a remarkable fondness for turning the tenderest poems into ridicule. She wrote and printed a number of burlesques; while her elder sister composed sweet and melancholy poems and interesting stories for the Western publications.

About eighteen years ago the Carys concluded to leave the West, come East, and make New-York their place of permanent residence. It was quite a bold movement for young women who, whatever their reputation at home, were hardly known here at all. But they had courage and hope, and struggled so bravely and perseveringly that they won recognition as poets of excellence.

Alice has published seven or eight books, several of them novels, and Phœbe but two, both poems. The latter has shown marked improvement recently. She has far more power and depth, and seems to have developed new capacities for the gentle art. Some of her poems are very fine; "The Dead Love" being pronounced by foreign critics one of the best America has produced. Alice is indefatigable. She writes for all the magazines and principal weeklies, and yet it is doubtful if she averages more than $2,500 a year. Considering her reputation, not to speak of her ability, this is not very encouraging to literary workers.

The Carys, though they have remained unwedded (they deserve credit for having courage enough to bear the reputation of "old maids" without shrinking), are decidedly domestic in their tastes and habits. They have no desire to travel; have never wanted to go abroad; and, excepting a few weeks spent at the White Mountains during the Summer, seldom leave the City. They have a pleasant and comfortable house, which they own, in Twentieth street, near Fourth avenue. It is full of books and pictures, and their friends and all cultivated strangers are always sure of a warm welcome there.

Phœbe is full, round, and very vivacious, with none of the pensiveness or dreaminess popularly associated with bards of either sex. She has dark eyes, black hair, and has such a Spanish look that if you were to meet her in Havana or Seville you would make oath she was a full-blooded Señora. She has a nimble tongue, and fully sustains the reputation of her sex for liberality in its use. She talks very well, and but for an irrepressible passion for puns would be a capital entertainer. She is very popular, and has many enthusiastic friends of both sex.

Alice is very unlike her sister in personal appearance, habit, and temperament. She has long been delicate, while Phœbe is the picture of robust health; but still she is always cheerful, and shows extraordinary patience and power of work under the circumstances. She has a few threads of gray in her abundant hair, and her dark, deep, tender eyes and swarthy complexion make one think of a sentimental gipsy. She is an interesting woman, and though no longer handsome, she has a poetic and decidedly attractive face. An air of calm resignation and gentle sadness hangs over her that adds to her agreeableness with persons of quick sympathy and fine sensibility. She is much esteemed and greatly loved.

The Carys have been for years in the habit of giving Sunday evening receptions, where many of the literary men, journalists, and artists of the City meet. It is one of the few places in New-York where the artistic class meet on common and agreeable ground. I know of no other house, except Mrs. Anne Lynch Botta's, where such réunions are regularly held. A number of our literary women visit the Carys on Sunday, where the tea-table is always set for about twenty persons. No ceremony is used or is necessary. Any one who wishes to come is welcome. The gatherings are so entirely free and unconventional that often persons are not even introduced.

Among the well-known feminine writers to be seen at the Carys is Mrs. Sara Willis Parton, whom every one knows as the redoubtable Fanny Fern.

Mrs. Mary Clemmer Ames, the Washington correspondent of the *Independent,* and a very clever writer, is a visitor there when in the City—she has recently made this her home—and adds to the interest of the assemblies. She is a tall, large, blue-eyed, brown-haired woman, very quiet and retiring in manner, whom it is difficult to draw out. When interested, she speaks earnestly and eloquently, though a natural shyness prevents her from revealing on ordinary occasions her gifts of mind.

Kate Field, daughter of James M. Field, the actor, now deceased, and a bright writer for the *Atlantic* and other magazines, is rather small in stature, a pleasant blonde; seems to be in excellent spirits always, and delights in epigrammatic conversation. She was a friend of that cultivated and peculiar brute, Walter Savage Landor, whom she knew in Italy. She gained considerable fame here by her elaborate *Tribune* critiques, or, rather, eulogies, upon Ristori, when she first appeared in this country. She is frequently at the receptions.

Mrs. Lucia Gilbert Calhoun, of the *Tribune* staff,

declared by Horace Greeley to be the most brilliant writer on the paper, makes periodical calls at the Carys. She is tall, lithe, graceful, and particularly elegant, almost the opposite of what many people fancy a literary woman to be. She is not handsome, though I have heard many call her so when her face is animated. She has abundant chestnut hair, rather a tawny complexion, hazel eyes that look green often, and are really beautiful. She dresses in exquisite taste, and seems thoroughly a woman of society. She is called charming by all her friends and by many who have hardly seen her. She is a fine conversationalist and a most agreeable entertainer.

Madame Octavia Walton Levert, the well-known Southern authoress, whose home was in Mobile, Ala., until she came here to live, is an *habitué* of Twentieth street. She does not personally give the impression you might get from her writings. She is large, and not at all distinguished; but she is highly cultivated, very agreeable in conversation, and winning in manners. Wealthy before the War, she has lost her fortune, but is cheerful and even happy under the shadow of adversity.

Jenny June (Mrs. Jennie C. Croly), the popular fashion writer for most of the leading papers, and the editor of Madame Demorest's magazine, is a very pleasant woman. She is of medium size; has blue eyes and brown hair, is full of amiability and kindness, and is much liked for her freedom from pretense or affectation of any kind. She makes an hour pleasant on Sunday evening at the Carys, and is an accession to their superior company.

Mrs. Mary E. Dodge, author of the "Irvington Stories,"

and many other popular books, is a bundle of sunshine; abounds in lively repartee and pleasant wit. She is small, has very dark hair, and gray eyes; is always busy about something; full of feeling and generous sentiments, and makes friends of her slightest acquaintances. Though long a widow, and the mother of boys taller than herself, she seems like a school-girl in her fresh-hearted humor that never tires.

Mrs. Sarah F. Ames, the renowned sculptor, is also a frequenter of the Carys. She is very foreign in appearance. Her eyes and hair are black as night; her mouth is well shaped and rosy; and she talks with an intensity and eloquence that prove the ardor of her temperament. She is a very independent, strong, efficient woman, entirely in sympathy with every liberal movement and generous purpose. She has no fear of Mrs. Grundy when convinced of the justice or worthiness of her intent, and is worth a thousand of the merely common-place fashionable women who dawdle life away in worse than empty frivolity.

There are other and clever women who visit the Carys; but those I have named are the most regular attendants at the weekly receptions, and types of the cultivated class, who find there sympathy and expression without narrowness, conventionality, or dread of the frowns of a society that is free from brains and innocent of heart.

CHAPTER LXXXIX.

CITY CHARITIES.

IF it be true that Charity covers a multitude of sins, New-York's many and grievous ones should always be veiled. Our charities are, probably, larger and more liberal than those of any city in the World. How loud vice is, and how quiet virtue! The country echoes to the iteration of our corruption, extravagance, and licentiousness; but our great heart, our generous alms-giving, our beautiful sacrifice, go voiceless through the land.

The hospitals of the Metropolis number thirteen, and the asylums thirty-nine.

St. Luke's (Episcopal), Fifth avenue, between Fifty-fourth and Fifty-fifth streets, was incorporated in 1850, and owes its origin to the Rev. Wm. A. Muhlenberg. In addition to furnishing medical and surgical aid, it aims to give instruction in the art of nursing. The principal front is on Fifty-fourth street, and 280 feet long. It is an oblong parallelogram, with wings at each end, and a central chapel flanked with towers. The wards on either side of the central building in the second and third stories are 109 feet long, 26 wide, and 14 high.

The hospital, well ventilated and excellently arranged, is under the direction of the Superintendent and Sisters, a body of Protestant Christian women, bound by no vow, who, after a trial of six months, engage to serve for three years, renewing their services if they like. The spirit of the Sisterhood is very like that of the Lutheran Deaconesses of Kaiserwerth, who have done such efficient work in Germany. Their services are wholly gratuitous, daily food being all they receive from the institution. Many of the prettiest and most fashionable young women of the City have from time to time been Sisters, and the romantic causes that led thereto, if told, would be very interesting. Such charming nurses have been rarely seen, and not a few of the patients have been unwilling to get well when so delightfully administered to. When patients are able to, they pay $7 a week, but the great majority have been supported by charity. They are admitted regardless of creed, though the form of worship is always Episcopal.

The New-York Society for the Relief of the Ruptured and Crippled, at No. 97 Second avenue, is but five years old. Much good has been done by the society, who will soon erect a larger and better building in Lexington avenue. There are about one hundred and seventy applicants a month, few of whom have the means of payment.

The New-York State Woman's Hospital, twelve years old, is the offspring of a remarkable discovery in science made by an American, Dr. J. Marion Sims, of Alabama, who was its founder. Previous to his discovery, surgery was unable to do any thing for the class of affections the Hospital was designed to care for. Its treatment has been very successful, thousands of suffering women having been not only relieved, but permanently cured. Each county in the State is entitled to one free bed. Patients of all denominations are admitted, but only those afflicted with some disease peculiar to women.

The corner-stone of a new and handsome edifice has been laid at Fourth avenue and Fiftieth street, and the building will before long be completed. Mrs. William B. Astor, Mrs. Peter Cooper, Mrs. Robert B. Minturn, Mrs. Moses H. Grinnell, and other prominent ladies are among the managers. This invaluable institution has actually saved the lives of four hundred women during the past year.

St. Vincent's Hospital, under the direction of the Sisters of Charity, is at No. 195 West Eleventh street. It was opened in 1849, and for sixteen years the celebrated Dr. Valentine Mott was its consulting surgeon and physician. It will accommodate one hundred and fifty patients, and is mainly supported by what patients pay for treatment. During the past year it had one hundred and thirty-five free patients.

The German Hospital and Dispensary is what its name indicates, and is on the block between Seventy-sixth and Seventy-seventh streets, and Fourth and Lexington avenues. C. Godfrey Gunther is the President, and prominent German citizens are its other officers and managers.

The New-York Eye and Ear Infirmary, Second avenue, corner of Thirteenth street, was founded in 1820, and has met with marked success in treating cases believed before its establishment to be incurable.

The Mount Sinai Hospital, in West Twenty-eighth street, was founded in 1852, by Sampson Levison, a wealthy Hebrew, and is devoted to the Jews, though all denominations are admitted. During the War many soldiers were treated there.

The Infirmary for Women and Children, No. 126 Second avenue, was organized fifteen years ago, to afford poor women the opportunity of consulting physicians of their own sex; to assist educated women in the practical study of medicine, and to form a school for instruction in nursing and the laws of health. The institution is entirely under the direction of feminine physicians—Dr. Elizabeth Blackwell being the regular attendant.

The Homeopathic Infirmary for Women, No. 57 West Forty-eighth street, has for its object the treatment of diseases peculiar to women.

The Home for Incurables is at West Farms, Westchester county; was organized three years ago, to provide some place other than the almshouse, where persons suffering from incurable diseases could be properly cared for.

Bellevue, east of First avenue, between Twenty-sixth and Twenty-eighth streets, is the great pauper hospital of the City, and one of its noblest charities. It occupies four and a half acres, and the main building is 350 feet long, four stories high, and is excellently adapted for its purpose. It was originally the Bellevue Almshouse; but in 1848 the paupers were removed to Blackwell's Island. It is probably the best adapted for hospital purposes of any in the World, and can accommodate 1,200 patients. The amount paid for salaries and wages is nearly $14,000 per annum. The medical organization consists of twenty consulting physicians and surgeons, and twenty attending physicians and surgeons.

The New-York Hospital, in Broadway, opposite Worth street, was chartered in 1771, and is an old landmark of the town. It is under the direction of twenty-six governors; is of gray granite, and in simple Doric style; will accommodate 250 patients, has six physicians and six surgeons, and is considered the best school of medicine and surgery in the country. Those admitted are supposed to be only temporary patients, and they are persons without means of payment, seamen paid for from the hospital money, collected under the laws of the United States, at the rate of seven dollars a week, and regular pay patients. The grounds are large and well laid out, and worth $3,000,000.

The Nursery and Child's Hospital, corner of Fifty-first street and Lexington avenue, has been established fourteen years, and is intended for children whose mothers have become insane or invalids, or are orphans. Women obliged to go out to service, who have heretofore been compelled to leave their children in the almshouse, can have them cared for at the Nursery by paying a small price, always in proportion to the wages they receive. There are lying-in wards at the hospital, where unfortunate mothers can give birth to their babes, and hide their shame from the public. If this department were generally known it is believed many infant-murders would be prevented. Usually there are about two hundred children and one hundred adults in the Nursery.

The Bloomingdale, the largest and best known of the asylums, is in 117th street, between Tenth and Eleventh, avenues, about a quarter of a mile from the Hudson, on what is known as the Harlem Heights, commanding a fine prospect. The farm has about forty-five acres, most of which are under high cultivation. It was opened in 1821, and its fine brown stone buildings are admirably adapted to the object they have in view. The patients are morally and scientifically treated, and with very happy effect. The asylum is under the care of a special committee, consisting of six governors elected annually. It has never been open for the gratuitous reception of insane persons, as none but pay patients are admitted unless by express direction of the governors. Indigent patients from any part of the State are, however, received at the lowest rate, and all others upon such terms as are agreed upon.

The Deaf and Dumb Asylum at Washington Heights was founded in 1816, and was the first in the country. The grounds comprise thirty-seven acres, and with the buildings, which are of brick, with granite basements and copings, cost $500,000. In 1831 the pupils numbered eighty-five; now they reach four hundred and thirty-three. Since its establishment eighteen hundred have been under instruction. At first it was supported by private benevolence, but was soon taken under the patronage of the State. The regular term of instruction is eight years, and three additional for pupils selected for good conduct and capacity to pursue higher studies. The system of instruction is based on the fact that gestures are the natural language of the deaf and dumb.

The Institution for the Blind, in Ninth avenue, between Thirty-third and Thirty-fourth streets, is thirty-seven years old, and is a school of instruction, which is threefold, mechanical, musical, and intellectual. The pupils advance year by year from one class to another until the whole course is completed. Many who have been educated there now occupy useful and responsible positions; are merchants, manufacturers, teachers, and clergymen.

Leake and Watt's Orphan House, designed as the home of entire orphans, is between Ninth and Tenth avenues and 110th and 113th streets, and owes its origin to a liberal bequest of Leake, who died without heirs.

St. Luke's Home for Indigent Christian Women was organized in 1851; is at No. 481 Hudson street, and what its title indicates. It is Episcopalian, but not sectarian.

The Home for the Friendless, No. 29 East Twenty-ninth street, was established in 1834, and has done much good. It receives all destitute women of good moral character, of whom good conduct and proper discipline are expected.

Among the other asylums are the House of Mercy, Eighty-sixth street, west of Broadway, which offers a home for fallen women; the Colored Orphan Asylum, 151st street, near North River, containing two hundred and sixty inmates, and well managed; the Magdalen Society, Eighty-eighth street, which has done much to restore erring women to a virtuous life; Union Home, Fifty-seventh and Fifty-eighth streets, near Eighth avenue, for the maintenance of children of our soldiers and sailors; Asylum for Lying-in Women, No. 85 Marion street; Women's Prison Association, No. 191 Tenth avenue, for the support and encouragement of prisoners after their discharge; House of the Good Shepherd, foot of Ninetieth street; Protective Union, for aiding women in obtaining situations and money due from unjust employers; also, Catholic orphan asylums and other valuable institutions.

Not less than $10,000,000 or $12,000,000 are probably invested in the city charities, which must be supported at the rate of $1,000,000 per annum.

THE FIRST SNOW.

CHAPTER XC.

THE GREAT METROPOLIS.

As has been so often said, New-York is a City of contrasts. It has no virtue without its corresponding sin; no light without its shadow; no beauty without deformity; for it is a little world in itself, and must necessarily be made up of all the elements of good and evil. Its citizens are as sensible of its grievous defects as strangers can be; but they know of its redeeming qualities as others do not. It is the stock-in-trade of the country press to abuse the Metropolis; to grow eloquent over its corruption, its licentiousness, its crime. The City has sins enough to answer for, Heaven knows; but it is painted blacker than it deserves, and the bright hues that belong to it are hidden under the veil of censure. New-York is worse than other American cities because it is larger; because it is a point all foreigners touch, and many of them linger in, bringing their bad habits, their vices, their pauperism with them. Here all adventurers, and sharpers, and vile characters tend, because this is the great center, and gives support and encouragement to all manner of men.

New-York, like the World it represents, is steadily though slowly growing better. It bears no comparison for wickedness with what it was fifteen or even ten years ago. Rowdyism has no such immunity, lawless ness no such power. Even the municipal government has improved, and will improve. Every thing advances: it is the eternal law; and the time is coming when a corrupt judge and a dishonest councilman will be driven from office on this very Island. New Homers may not sing in the street; nor new Dantes write divine comedies; nor new Shakspeares set the soul of the Universe to music. But there will be braver men and truer women, and the spirit of pure Nature will so enter into them that they will be transformed outwardly and inwardly.

The City, containing a million within its proper limits, and a million and a half within a radius of ten miles, is destined, doubtless before another century has ended, to be the Metropolis of the World as well as of this Continent. Among the centers of civilization, it is now the third in point of population. In 1790 the City had less than 30,000 souls. In 1807, Robert Fulton navigated the Hudson to Albany with the first steamboat. In eighty or ninety years more what may we not look for?

I see the day, though I may not with my mortal eye, when the wretched slums, the vile dens, the loathsome tenements, will be banished from the town; when all the streets will be clean, and the houses wholesome; when the parks and squares will be filled with happy people, and New-York be called the City of the Beautiful. Commerce, and wealth, and intelligence will increase, and ours will become the first of nations as this will be the first of cities. We shall eclipse London in population, and Paris in picturesqueness and elegance. We shall have whole streets of marble, immense libraries and galleries of art. Our people will have so advanced in culture, self-discipline, and above all, in humanity, that what we not only tolerate but advocate now, we shall regard as barbarous then.

Judging by the past, what may not, what will not New-York be in a hundred years? If those now living were to see it after a century, they would not recognize it any more than Hendrick Hudson or Wouter Von Twiller would the Great City of the present day. The future will be as a magnificent dream, but a dream that will be realized. New-York is the City of the time to come. The sea that washes its shores is murmuring of its greatness; the breezes that fan it are whispering of its beauty; the stars that shine over it are silently predicting its excellence. It is now, I repeat, the Great Metropolis of the Continent, and in the next century will be the Great Metropolis of the World. Nothing can resist its progress. Its course is onward and upward. Its destiny must be fulfilled in development, in improvement, in the true democracy that is the basis and builder of all permanent greatness.

Let those who will, despair of the Republic, of the principle of self-government, of the intelligence and integrity of the people. Would that such might live for another century, and behold on our shores, and on this Island, the fruits of our industry, our perseverance, our independence, our perfect faith in ourselves. I see the great and glorious future as with a prophetic eye. New territories will be developed; new States will be added; new resources will be at our command. The vast commerce of China and Japan will be at our doors. Cities now sleeping in untilled prairies, and upon the shores of the far-off Pacific, will awake to power and pleasantness. New-York will be the center and sphere of all the mighty trade, the store-house of the Nation's wealth, the dépôt of its commerce, stretching over every river, lake, and ocean. The wonders of fable will be outdone; the vision of the poet will be eclipsed. This City will be a country of itself, a nation in its strength, its resources, its incalculable riches. Broadway will be the great thoroughfare of the World; Fifth avenue the street of luxury and splendor beyond what history has shown. Our rivers will be spanned with noble bridges, and Babylon, Palmyra, Rome, and Athens, in their palmiest days will be re-created here. Our grandsons and granddaughters will turn to the musty records of the present, and tell their children, and their children's children of the time when New-York had but a million souls. And we, slumbering quietly in our graves, will be glad we lived a century before, that our descendants might dwell amid fairer and happier days in that other century which will round to rosy restfulness all our present pains and carking cares.

THE LEISURE CLASS IN AMERICA

An Arno Press Collection

Bradley, Hugh. **Such was Saratoga.** 1940

Browne, Junius Henri. **The Great Metropolis:** A Mirror of New York. 1869

Burt, Nathaniel. **The Perennial Philadelphians.** 1963

Canby, Henry Seidel. **Alma Mater:** The Gothic Age of the American College. 1936

Crockett, Albert Stevens. **Peacocks on Parade.** 1931

Croffut, W[illiam] A. **The Vanderbilts.** 1886

Crowninshield, Francis W. **Manners for the Metropolis.** 1909

de Wolfe, Elsie. **The House in Good Taste.** 1913

Ellet, E[lizabeth] F[ries Lummis]. **The Court Circles of the Republic,** or The Beauties and Celebrities of the Nation. 1869

Elliott, Maud Howe. **This Was My Newport.** 1944

Elliott, Maud Howe. **Uncle Sam Ward and His Circle.** 1938

Fairfield, Francis Gerry. **The Clubs of New York** and Croly, [Jane C.] **Sorosis.** 1873/1886. Two vols. in one

[Fawcett, Edgar]. **The Buntling Ball:** A Graeco-American Play. 1885

Fawcett, Edgar. **Social Silhouettes.** 1885

Fiske, Stephen. **Off-Hand Portraits of Prominent New Yorkers.** 1884

Foraker, Julia B. **I Would Live It Again:** Memories of a Vivid Life. 1932

Goodwin, Maud Wilder. **The Colonial Cavalier.** 1895

Hartt, Rollin Lynde. **The People at Play.** 1909

Lehr, Elizabeth Drexel. **"King Lehr" and the Gilded Age.** 1935

Lodge, Henry Cabot. **Early Memories.** 1913

[Longchamp, Ferdinand]. **Asmodeus in New-York.** 1868

McAllister, [Samuel] Ward. **Society as I Have Found It.** 1890

McLean, Evalyn, with Boyden Sparkes. **Father Struck It Rich.** 1936

[Mann, William d'Alton]. **Fads and Fancies of Representative Americans at the Beginning of the Twentieth Century.** 1905

Martin, Frederick Townsend. **The Passing of the Idle Rich.** 1911

Martin, Frederick Townsend. **Things I Remember.** 1913

Maurice, Arthur Bartlett. **Fifth Avenue.** 1918

[Mordecai, Samuel]. **Richmond in By-Gone Days.** 1856

Morris, Lloyd. **Incredible New York.** 1951

Neville, Amelia Ransome. **The Fantastic City:** Memoirs of the Social and Romantic Life of Old San Francisco. 1932

Nichols, Charles Wilbur de Lyon. **The Ultra-Fashionable Peerage of America.** 1904

Pound, Arthur. **The Golden Earth:** The Story of Manhattan's Landed Wealth. 1935

Pulitzer, Ralph. **New York Society on Parade.** 1910

Ripley, Eliza. **Social Life in Old New Orleans.** 1912

Ross, Ishbel. **Silhouette in Diamonds:** The Life of Mrs. Potter Palmer. 1960

Sherwood, M[ary] E[lizabeth W.]. **Manners and Social Usages.** 1897

The Sporting Set. 1975

Van Rensselaer, [May] King. **Newport: Our Social Capital.** 1905

Van Rensselaer, [May] King. **The Social Ladder.** 1924

Wharton, Edith and Ogden Codman, Jr. **The Decoration of Houses.** 1914

Williamson, Jefferson. **The American Hotel.** 1930